p 61

p 137

# JOURNAL FOR THE STUDY OF THE NEW TESTAMENT
## SUPPLEMENT SERIES
# 127

*Executive Editor*
Stanley E. Porter

Sheffield Academic Press

# Unveiling the Apocalyptic Paul

## Paul's Interpreters
## and the Rhetoric of Criticism

**R. Barry Matlock**

Journal for the Study of the New Testament
Supplement Series 127

Copyright © 1996 Sheffield Academic Press

Published by Sheffield Academic Press Ltd
Mansion House
19 Kingfield Road
Sheffield, S11 9AS
England

Printed on acid-free paper in Great Britain
by Bookcraft Ltd
Midsomer Norton, Bath

British Library Cataloguing in Publication Data

A catalogue record for this book is available
from the British Library

ISBN 1-85075-590-6

## CONTENTS

## ACKNOWLEDGMENTS

The present study is a revision of my 1993 University of Sheffield doctoral thesis, the acknowledgments to which are retained below. Revision throughout has been limited and largely stylistic, with some trimming here and there and a handful of additional items of bibliography. Much more could surely be done, or redone, but I wish simply to pass the study along to others, timely as I hope it is, and, as is the way with such things, ready as I am to move on. It remains to me to thank the examining readers of the thesis, Loveday Alexander and Anthony Thiselton, for their careful and constructive attention to the work. Also, my indebtedness to Sheffield doubly increases, as I now, from 1994, join the department as a lecturer and as my study joins the Sheffield press's JSNT Supplement Series. And after a year with Andrew as colleague, I have had to wish him and Carol all the best as they move on to Toronto, Andrew to assume his chair at Wycliffe College, University of Toronto. I am saddened to record the passing of my father, Thomas Ray Matlock, while this monograph was in press; he would have been proud to see it appear. Finally, I will also record that, as its predecessor came forth in the early months of our firstborn's young life, we send out the published version expecting our second, both to appear around the same time early '96.

Sheffield; December, 1995

A thesis is meant to be the process by which one 'learns to be a scholar'. At the same time, it is to be a 'contribution to scholarship'. Theoretically, then, one is not able to produce one until having done so. To survive such an anomalous position is to draw on the support of many.

To the Academic Cabinet of the Faculty of Westminster Theological Seminary for the granting of an Edwin L. Jones Graduate Fellowship for the year 1990-91, and to the British Committee of Vice-Chancellors and Principals for the granting of an ORS Award for the year 1991-92, I offer again my sincerest gratitude for the timely assistance given. I have taken with great seriousness the confidence hereby placed in me, and the responsibility that this entails, and I have done simply the best that I could, knowing nothing more was asked of me—indeed, not by any of those here thanked.

To my supervisor, Andrew Lincoln, special thanks are due. I have always been given by him complete freedom to go and do as I will, always knowing that, when it came to assessing critically what I had (and had not) done, he would take such expert care and consideration as only to confirm my implicit trust in his oversight. It is hard to put a price on that, making my debt inestimable.

To my parents and parents-in-law I offer my loving gratitude for, by their unquestioning support, making this possible for me.

Finally, and most dearly, I must speak of my wife, Mitzi, and of our son, Hayden Thompson Matlock, born in the final stages of the more protracted labour of this thesis. Together they put everything into perspective for me. To have this without them would be for me a hollow thing. But to have them without this would leave me still blessed beyond measure. Which leads me, in the end, to offer a higher thanksgiving.

Sheffield, England; September, 1993

# ABBREVIATIONS

| | |
|---|---|
| AGJU | Arbeiten zur Geschichte des antiken Judentums und des Urchristentums |
| *ANRW* | *Aufstieg und Niedergang der römischen Welt* |
| *ATR* | *Anglican Theological Review* |
| *BASOR* | *Bulletin of the American Schools of Oriental Research* |
| BEATAJ | Beiträge zur Erforschung des Alten Testaments und das Antiken Judentums |
| BHT | Beiträge zur historischen Theologie |
| *BJRL* | *Bulletin of the John Rylands University Library of Manchester* |
| BZNW | Beihefte zur *ZNW* |
| *CBQ* | *Catholic Biblical Quarterly* |
| CRINT | Compendia rerum iudaicarum ad Novum Testamentum |
| *ETL* | *Ephemerides theologicae lovanienses* |
| *EvT* | *Evangelische Theologie* |
| *ExpTim* | *Expository Times* |
| FRLANT | Forschungen zur Religion und Literatur des Alten und Neuen Testaments |
| GTA | Göttinger theologische Arbeiten |
| *HBT* | *Horizons in Biblical Theology* |
| *HR* | *History of Religions* |
| *IDB* | G.A. Buttrick (ed.), *Interpreter's Dictionary of the Bible* |
| *IDBSup* | *IDB*, Supplementary Volume |
| *Int* | *Interpretation* |
| *JBL* | *Journal of Biblical Literature* |
| *JNES* | *Journal of Near Eastern Studies* |
| *JR* | *Journal of Religion* |
| *JSJ* | *Journal for the Study of Judaism* |
| *JSNT* | *Journal for the Study of the New Testament* |
| JSNTSup | *Journal for the Study of the New Testament*, Supplement Series |
| *JSOT* | *Journal for the Study of the Old Testament* |
| JSOTSup | *Journal for the Study of the Old Testament*, Supplement Series |
| *JSP* | *Journal for the Study of the Pseudepigrapha* |
| JSPSup | *Journal for the Study of the Pseudepigrapha*, Supplement Series |
| *JTC* | *Journal for Theology and the Church* |
| *JTS* | *Journal of Theological Studies* |
| *LR* | *Lutherische Rundschau* |
| MNTC | Moffat New Testament Commentary |
| NovTSup | *Novum Testamentum* Supplements |

| | |
|---|---|
| *NTS* | *New Testament Studies* |
| *RB* | *Revue biblique* |
| *RelSRev* | Religious Studies Review |
| SBLDS | SBL Dissertation Series |
| *ScEs* | *Science et esprit* |
| *SJT* | *Scottish Journal of Theology* |
| SNTSMS | Society for New Testament Studies Monograph Series |
| SVTP | Studia in Veteris Testamenti pseudepigrapha |
| *TRu* | *Theologische Rundschan* |
| *USQR* | Union Seminary Quarterly Review |
| WMANT | Wissenschaftliche Monographien zum Alten und Neuen Testament |
| *ZNW* | *Zeitschrift für die neutestamentliche Wissenschaft* |
| *ZTK* | *Zeitschrift für Theologie und Kirche* |

# Introduction

## TWO AGES, TWO STAGES

[O]nly a consistent apocalyptic interpretation of Paul's thought is able to demonstrate its fundamental coherence (J.C. Beker, *Paul the Apostle*, p. 143).

'Apocalypticism' is characterized by a recent scholar in terms of the following features: the acute expectation of the fulfillment of divine promises; cosmic catastrophe; a relationship between the time of the end and preceding human and cosmic history; angelology and demonology; salvation beyond catastrophe; salvation proceeding from God; a future saviour figure with royal characteristics; a future state characterized by the catchword 'glory'. All these features bear upon eschatology.

The problem arising from this definition is that many works which belong to the genre 'apocalypse' contain much that is not covered or rendered comprehensible by the above description, while many works not formally apocalypses are imbued with this apocalypticism (M.E. Stone, 'Apocalyptic Literature', p. 393).

'Apocalyptic' interpretation of Paul is, if not a consensus, then certainly a commonplace. Some of this century's towering figures in Pauline studies—such as Albert Schweitzer and Ernst Käsemann—are associated with this approach. One of the latest synthetic accounts of Paul's thought, that of J. Christiaan Beker, presents the apostle as an 'apocalyptic' theologian (and in fact holds synthesis ransom to such an 'apocalyptic' interpretation, as witnessed above).[1] Accounts of 'apocalyptic Paul' have reached the popular level.[2]

However, the apocalyptic literature has not always found itself within

1.    J.C. Beker, *Paul the Apostle: The Triumph of God in Life and Thought* (Philadelphia: Fortress Press, 1984 [1980]); see pp. 15-19, 135-81.

2.    Cf. M.L. Soards, *The Apostle Paul: An Introduction to His Writings and Teachings* (New York: Paulist, 1987), pp. 37-41; C.J. Roetzel, *The Letters of Paul: Conversations in Context* (Louisville: Westminster/John Knox Press, 3rd edn, 1991), pp. 53-55, 183-84 n. 68.

the good graces of biblical critics. It has suffered no end of abuse and neglect on that account. Yet here, to all appearances, we have a prominent interpreter of Paul as much as admitting outright that we just cannot get on without it. So one would think that when a compliment like Beker's comes their way the proprietors of this literature would know how to appreciate it. But instead, one prominent such proprietor (whose connection with Beker is that the 'recent scholar' with whom he takes issue is the chief source of Beker's 'apocalyptic') is ungrateful enough to cloud the issue with the fact of potentially unapocalyptic apocalypses and apocalyptic non-apocalypses.[3] This no doubt leaves many spectators confused. But at least one bystander thinks he knows a thesis when he smells one.

It has probably already been guessed that this 'unveiling' of 'the apocalyptic Paul' is not to be a purely flattering or celebratory one. As to what it *will* be, I should not wish to delay too long in letting that begin to emerge for itself. But a preface to this unveiling is desired, for which I briefly indulge in an autobiographical account of the genesis of the conception of the present study, along with a few words to ease us into what lies ahead.

I first had occasion to make any real use of the notion 'apocalyptic' at an earlier stage of study for a required research paper. Turning, in that portion of the paper in which some discussion of 'apocalyptic' seemed called for, to a standard and widely-used dictionary article, I took over the information provided there eagerly and in implicit trust, hardly thinking to question any aspect of it. It seemed to prove so useful at that particular moment, so amenable to the sort of biblical-theological paper I was required to produce. My confidence was not to last.

For in the later course of pursuing an individual interest in a particular Pauline theme, I returned to the subject of 'apocalyptic', or, rather, it kept returning to me. This other theme was to have provided the subject for my proposed thesis, but the sub-theme became the main one, and 'apocalyptic interpretation of Paul' was now the thing. Two chance 'discoveries' fuelled and formed this interest. For one thing, I had come to see how much was being made of 'apocalyptic' in interpreting Paul—I have in mind the interpretation of Beker here. At the same time I came to see that something was afoot as to the whole question of

---

3.    M.E. Stone, 'Apocalyptic Literature', in M.E. Stone (ed.), *Jewish Writings of the Second Temple Period* (CRINT, 2.2; Assen: Van Gorcum/Philadelphia: Fortress Press, 1984), pp. 392-94.

'apocalyptic'—here I mean the interpretation of Christopher Rowland (which led to others, such as that of Michael Stone, cited above). This interpretation, persuasively taking as its point of departure a few fairly simple observations as to the accountability to the apocalyptic literature of such notions of 'apocalyptic' as are typically encountered, had the effect of putting a radical question mark over against much of what had been—what was and is still being—done in the name of 'apocalyptic'. It was obvious that Rowland's synthesis had completely reoriented interpretation of 'apocalyptic', away from a preoccupation with a presumed distinctive eschatology and toward mystical and speculative knowledge and experience, while others, taking little or no notice of the interpretive issues under contest, were continuing, as according to the now questioned convention, to use the term in its former unreflective way. On the assumption that any finding in a specialist area of New Testament studies takes several years to filter down to such general areas as Pauline theology, I figured that the time was about ripe for a thesis which would take the unaccounted for sea-change from the specialist discussion over into the area of application to Paul, to see how that would alter things. (Or rather, I should hurry and not be beaten to an obvious opportunity.)

At the time this was enough for me. With a well-worn idea of a tripartite thesis plan as (part one) history of interpretation, (part two) sketch of the *new* and *better* way of conceiving 'apocalyptic' (at this point I had simply adopted mentally Rowland's conception), and (part three, in that order) application to key Pauline texts, I was off. But this seemed to make poor business of the history of interpretation; for everybody was, after all, simply following convention on this matter of 'apocalyptic', and so to confront them with my interests and my strictures really amounted only to a constant repetition of the fact that they were none of them doing what I would have them do—that is, to question in a fundamental and methodological way their use of the term and the very notion of 'apocalyptic'. It seemed a shabby way to treat the likes of the interpreters I was dealing with—any interpreter, for that matter. (I am reminded of Hans-Georg Gadamer's comment on a critic's inability to see anything but 'equivocations and conceptual confusions' in Gadamer's hermeneutics: 'This generally means that the critic is relating the author to a question that he does not intend'.[4]) I was not long in

---

4. Hans-Georg Gadamer, 'Hermeneutics and Historicism', 'Supplement I' in *Truth and Method*, (rev. and trans. J. Weinsheimer and D.G. Marshall; New York: Crossroad, 2nd edn, 1989), p. 512.

seeing that what *was* being done with 'apocalyptic' was an interesting story in its own right, and one that would never get told without a broadening of my conception of my task. It was about that time that I realized (to precede myself somewhat) that, on this matter of an 'apocalyptic' Paul, I really had no positive alternative definition of my own to promote at all. It was the other story, the story of modern 'apocalyptic' interpretation of Paul, that interested me, along with what I had dimly seen all along as the hermeneutical story occasionally coming into view.

I should say something more about 'apocalyptic' itself, because in the following it will be seen that I am working with an idea of what is typical of talk of such. Stone's summary of an influential recent approach has already been cited. I also offer a characterization of the standard view given by Rowland:

> [T]he word 'apocalyptic' has been used to describe the beliefs concerning the arrival of a new age. It is seen merely as a form of eschatology which is to be distinguished from the national, this-worldly eschatology of the rabbis. It possesses the following characteristic features: a contrast between the present age, which is perishable and temporary, and a new age, which is imperishable and eternal; a belief that the new age is of a transcendent kind, which breaks in from beyond through divine intervention and without human activity; an interest in the totality of world history; predestinarian elements, and an imminent expectation of the coming of the new age.[5]

Rowland's characterization, though it is of the approach that he opposes, will find ample confirmation in the work ahead. But for now I further offer Beker's definition, followed by the impressions of the two popular studies cited above. '[A]pocalyptic revolves around three basic ideas: (1) historical dualism; (2) universal cosmic expectation; and (3) the imminent end of the world'.[6] '*Apocalyptic* is a special expression of Jewish *eschatology* that was characterized by the *dualistic* doctrine of two ages'.[7] '[T]he similarity between Paul and Jewish apocalypticism goes far beyond the colorful terminology they share. Both are dominated by an eager longing for and an earnest expectation of the messianic kingdom.

---

5. C. Rowland, 'Apocalyptic', in R.J. Coggins and J.L. Houlden (eds.), *Dictionary of Biblical Interpretation* (London: SCM/Philadelphia: Trinity, 1990), p. 34. The definition summarized by Stone and taken over by Beker is that of K. Koch.

6. Beker, *Paul*, p. 136.

7. Soards, *Paul*, p. 38.

In both burns the intensity that comes from living on the boundary between two worlds—one dying and the other being born'.[8]

Ernst Käsemann, when called to account on the matter of his rather free use of the term 'apocalyptic', had this to say: 'It is not in dispute that "apocalyptic" is ambiguous. But of what term is that not true?'[9] Quite right. But I would claim both that 'apocalyptic' is special, in that there is *more* wrong with it than with the average term, and that, at the same time, it is exemplary, in that it points to some widespread tendencies in biblical criticism.

There is little point in anticipating here the critique I have taken such length to offer below of the matter of 'apocalyptic'. The point highlighted at the very outset above, the roughness of fit between talk of 'apocalyptic' and the apocalyptic literature, is both historically what set me onto the question and the starting point for a picking apart of the whole notion, which I, naturally, think is long overdue. But this awaits my fourth chapter. Up until that point, I allow our interpreters to do as they will with the notion, because here that is what I am after. From Schweitzer up to Käsemann (and far beyond for many), the understanding of what 'apocalyptic' is about is constant and unquestioned—it is the eschatological picture noted above, focused on the 'two ages'. There is thought to be no point in re-addressing the literary-historical question of what 'apocalyptic' is, since this is a matter long since settled, resulting in the convention which has so long ruled. But on what we might call the biblical-theological level of what 'apocalyptic' is taken to mean, what our interpreters do with the notion, there is much more of interest.

It is here that our hermeneutical story comes in. One simple reason for the hermeneutical concern is that recognition of the place of 'apocalyptic' is celebrated as a triumph of objective criticism over theological embarrassment at such a foreign and threatening conceptuality. This self-congratulatory claim will not need much help from me in coming

---

8. Roetzel, *Letters*, p. 53; Roetzel continues, noting that 'both hope for the *imminent* fruition of God's promises' and that 'the two share a conviction that their generation is to be the last'. Cf. p. 183 n. 68: 'At the risk of oversimplification, we could say that all apocalyptic literature is eschatological (dealing with the end), not all eschatological materials are apocalyptic. The term eschatology, therefore, is the more general term'.

9. E. Käsemann, 'On the Subject of Primitive Christian Apocalyptic', in *New Testament Questions of Today* (trans. W.J. Montague; London: SCM Press, 1969), pp. 108-37 (109 n. 1).

to appear questionable. But beyond this, I will suggest that objectivist hermeneutical ideals (which I shall often address through their typical expression in a 'two-stage' method) do not ring true to our experience of the interpretative debate over 'apocalyptic' before us, and that, rather, directions suggested by philosophical hermeneutics give a more satisfying account of our experience and a more promising channel for our discontent with objectivism.

In pursuing this interest in philosophical questions of hermeneutical theory, I range somewhat outside my area, to say the least. If I were allowed to stipulate the level on which I would wish my efforts here to be judged, I would hope that the close reading offered of the major interpretative figures and the essentially methodological critique of our past way of dealing with 'apocalyptic' would be seen to be primary. It will then further be seen that, in attempting to make sense of *that* picture and to place *that* interpretative story in its broadest setting, historically and ideologically, I have tried along the way to raise fundamental suspicions against objectivist accounts of the interpretative task and to place a few suggestive pointers in another more adequate direction.[10]

My reading of the discourse of 'apocalyptic' and the hermeneutical discourse it implicitly carries is impressionistic, and not above criticism on that score—not as to the necessity of operating in this way, but

10. Since completing the thesis on which this study is based, in which I had come to use rather unself-consciously terms like 'rhetoric' and in which I had made a number of more or less consistent hermeneutical points, I have introduced to myself 'the rhetoric of inquiry', as a disciplined way of doing part of what I attempt here, and the hermeneutics of S. Fish (and 'neopragmatism', generally), as a sustained effort to work through something like the hermeneutical perspective assumed here. On the former, see J.S. Nelson, A. Megill, and D.N. McCloskey (ed.), *The Rhetoric of the Human Sciences: Language and Argument in Scholarship and Public Affairs* (Madison: University of Wisconsin Press, 1987); H.W. Simons (ed.), *The Rhetorical Turn: Invention and Persuasion in the Conduct of Inquiry* (Chicago: University of Chicago Press, 1990); and A. Megill (ed.), *Rethinking Objectivity* (Durham: Duke University Press, 1994). On the latter, see S. Fish, *Is There a Text in This Class? The Authority of Interpretive Communities* (Cambridge, MA: Harvard University Press, 1980); *idem*, *Doing What Comes Naturally: Change, Rhetoric, and the Practice of Theory in Literary and Legal Studies* (Oxford: Oxford University Press, 1989); *idem*, *There's No Such Thing as Free Speech, And It's a Good Thing, Too* (Oxford: Oxford University Press, 1994). The two, in fact, are not unrelated: cf. S. Mailloux (ed.), *Rhetoric, Sophistry, and Pragmatism* (Literature, Culture, Theory, 15; Cambridge: Cambridge University Press, 1995), and note the extensive literature cited there, particularly on the 'new pragmatism' (pp. 242-47).

rather as to the actual impression drawn. But I have tried to cite at key points enough to defend my impressions. I am trying to tell a story, a narrative from and of the history of interpretation, and such an effort is bound to be highly interpretative in itself. As will emerge, my narrative would restore something of those ideological dimensions which criticism would prefer to remove from the story it likes to tell about itself.

'Paul and apocalyptic' is, by convention, a debate over Paul's eschatology, and on that account I find myself involved in this debate incidentally. But all I have wanted to do is to sort through the question of what is going on with 'apocalyptic', and I do not wish to be drawn into the attempt to resolve the eschatological debate in any particular way. I have no special interest in the question of how we should construe Paul's eschatology, and so I have no solution of my own to promote. These questions will, for many, then, be disappointingly left dangling.

Another matter which might cause concern is that in this account of the 'apocalyptic Paul' I will not be offering any exegesis of Pauline texts, for the simple reason that I will not end up (to precede myself again somewhat) promoting an 'apocalyptic' Paul of any sort (obviating the need to treat those texts where, in this case, something that I have dissolved does not appear). The fact that I am pursuing an interest in what key modern interpreters have been doing I would like to leave just at that. But if forced, I will make a moral point of it. Käsemann, in the place cited above, takes a swipe at the enthusiasm of his day for hermeneutics by suggesting that somebody has got to get down to the real work, history, that is, of course.[11] I would reverse the judgment and say that, with everyone running around after 'the historical Paul', someone has got to mind Paul's historians. But again, I would prefer to say that I just happen to find the sort of questions—basically metacritical or metacommentary questions,[12] asking everywhere what is being done here—that I am pursuing highly interesting. A related matter is the absence of exegetical treatment of apocalyptic texts. My understanding is that our concern with this literature is of the simplest and most general sort, practically reducing to the bare observation of the irreducible diversity of this literature. From this many points will follow, the cumulative effect of which will be to suggest that talk of 'apocalyptic' is

11. Käsemann, *New Testament Questions*, pp. 108-109 n. *.
12. These terms as used in the present study indicate criticism of criticism, commentary on commentary, that is, a move to a higher level of abstraction, a different order of discourse.

clearly meant to do something other than account for this literature. What that 'something' is is my concern. For my sort of project, the texts of our modern interpreters are the 'primary literature'.

A word about my chosen starting point is in order. Though Albert Schweitzer is an obvious choice, other choices could be argued. In the end, the decision is a pragmatic one. Schweitzer does not mark the absolute beginning point of interest in 'apocalyptic' as applied to the New Testament. But I am not seeking the prehistory of that discourse on 'apocalyptic' which was already standard parlance by Schweitzer's day. Schweitzer himself, followed by others, has covered earlier interpretation of Paul in a classic survey, and with a keener eye for attention to eschatology and taking greater care to acknowledge his forebears than I could probably manage for the same now dusty earlier period. The present century marks the time in which early Judaism and particularly eschatology (and thus 'apocalyptic' as this is usually meant) have come into their own in New Testament criticism, and it is here that Schweitzer, as a synthesizer and popularizer and as one making an original contribution in his own right, holds a singular position. And it is this century in the history of interpretation of Paul that concerns us. Interest in the present state of the question of 'apocalyptic' interpretation of Paul, reaching back to those central figures whose influence is still felt, bids us start with Schweitzer.

My choice of other figures for extended treatment should provoke little controversy, but a word or two on the manner of treatment is in order. I have chosen to offer close readings of major figures, bringing others into the picture mostly in footnotes gathered around these. For the more recent interpreters, a briefer survey is given (weighting the history toward the opposite end from what is customary). Those interpreters I do cover in detail—Albert Schweitzer, C.H. Dodd, Rudolf Bultmann, Oscar Cullmann, and Ernst Käsemann—mark a well-worked field. But my experience of each has surprised me in countless ways, leading me to suspect that they have virtually become mere names loosely attached to various views, names invoked by convention and often perhaps as a substitute for actually reading them. As usual in such cases, the reality is much richer than the caricature. I have taken these figures as classic expressions of a spectrum of interpretative possibilities. In treating each, I offer something other than a full introduction—these are available in each case, and selections have been noted, with which I do not attempt to vie. But coming at these interpreters from my angle of entry, with my questions, 'apocalyptic' and hermeneutical, opens, I would claim, a window to something of the heart of each. I am not primarily concerned to index these figures to various exegetical positions; rather, I attempt to give a sense of each *at work* in their own interpretative endeavour, which involves me at times in following them at some length. The reward of this must await its own confirmation. These figures occupy us in the first three chapters.

As for more recent interpreters, the central figure here is J. Christiaan Beker, with many others responding to his approach and to earlier efforts. But this more recent work is highly repetitive and derivative of the classics where the matter of 'apocalyptic' itself is concerned.[13] After Käsemann, questions about 'apocalyptic' finally begin to be raised in earnest, not least in response to his efforts. And so, instead of continuing from Käsemann to the present with a similarly detailed review, I pause to pick up this general questioning and work through my critique of the notion of 'apocalyptic', returning to the recent interpreters in the light of this critique. This fourth chapter completes the treatment of 'apocalyptic' and Paul. A fifth and final chapter takes up briefly a few of the hermeneutical points raised along the way.

The ungainly spectacle of one struggling against so many currents at once, as I shall no doubt come to be seen to be doing, is a pitiful sight indeed. And what cannot be marked down as institutional pathology— for a certain amount of this is expected of one in my position—must be accepted as personal. But I do not really want to leave the impression of standing in isolated opposition to everything and everybody. My objections to typical practice reduce more or less to two: the general confusion engendered over 'apocalyptic' and the hermeneutical triumphalism made to rest comically on its basis. Indeed, the critique I offer of 'apocalyptic' draws on many sources, as do my hermeneutical misgivings. But so far as I know, the matter of 'apocalyptic' generally has not received the sort of sustained critique given here (I refer particularly to my fourth chapter). Nor have the theological and hermeneutical motives of 'apocalyptic' interpretation of Paul been sought after in quite my own way. In all this, I am content to be no more than the child who remarks on the emperor's general state of undress.

In all my commerce with 'apocalyptic', the thought has stolen into my mind a number of times that there might be a simpler explanation

13. Beker has offered his approach in summaries large and small, technical and popular, making an extended treatment here unnecessary.

for my finding myself in opposition to so much—that is, that I am just wrong. But I have always managed to banish the thought, and not out of mere hubris, I think. The way I have come to look at this question of 'apocalyptic' has so worked itself into my head that I can no longer look at 'apocalyptic' interpretation of Paul in the same light. I should like to produce a similar effect on my reader, not necessarily seeking to achieve complete capitulation in the war of attrition I seem to be waging at points over 'apocalyptic', but just to plant a nagging suspicion over the matter, a doubt that will not go away.

That the treatment of the question of 'apocalyptic' and *Paul* might have wider relevance is obvious, though I have not tried to point this out in detail. Clearly, if something like my critique is accepted, the point is easily applied to other areas of 'apocalyptic interpretation of the New Testament'. I have, as already indicated, ranged into very general critique of biblical criticism in two related areas. One concerns the hermeneutical discourse of biblical criticism implicit in this interpretative question of 'apocalyptic'. The other is a very broad methodological critique of the way scholarship has tended to use categories like 'apocalyptic' in terms of what this tells us about the manner of approach (typically very theological) to the period and its literature and history.

In a delightful reminiscence of childhood from well advanced years, Mark Twain recalls an episode of 'Hunting the Deceitful Turkey'.[14] After explaining how a mother turkey, when her young are threatened, will, like many birds, feign injury to lure away a threatening intruder, Twain recounts: 'When a person is ignorant and confiding, this immoral device can have tiresome results. I followed an ostensible lame turkey over a considerable part of the United States one morning, because I believed in her and could not think she would deceive a mere boy, and one who was trusting her and considering her honest'.[15] Though I cannot claim the wisdom of distant reflection back on the matter, something about the twists and turns of my still youthful chasing after 'apocalyptic', and the considerable and exhausting ground covered,

14. *The Signet Classic Book of Mark Twain's Stories*, edited and with an introduction by J. Kaplan (New York: New American Library, 1985), pp. 626-28; this brief sketch is dated 1906 (S.L. Clemens [M. Twain] was born in 1835, and died in 1910), and delightful it is, though even here the dark fatalism of those later years intrudes.

15. Twain, 'Hunting the Deceitful Turkey', in Kaplan (ed.), *Mark Twain's Stories*, p. 627.

recalled this sketch to my mind. And I am not sure how far to carry the analogy. For Twain goes on to tell how, after a very long day's beguilement, he came away empty-handed. Worse still, he was lost. As if to end on a somewhat brighter note, though, he remembers that 'it was while wandering the woods hunting for myself that I found a deserted log cabin and had one of the best meals there that in my life-days I have eaten. The weed-grown garden was full of ripe tomatoes, and I ate them ravenously, though I had never liked them before'.[16] But lest I indulge in ending on such a note of failure in the quest as set out upon but success in finding treasures unexpected, Twain finally notes that, such was the 'surfeit' of that meal, he could not touch another tomato until his middle years. As for what this bodes for me—and I do appear at points to have made a meal of it—I am not sure I care to think.

16. Twain, 'Hunting the Deceitful Turkey', in Kaplan (ed.), *Mark Twain's Stories*, p. 628.

# Chapter 1

## THE BEGINNINGS:
## ALBERT SCHWEITZER AND THE ESCHATOLOGICAL PAUL

[Paul's Mysticism of the presence of redemption 'in Christ'] is the prime enigma of the Pauline teaching: once grasped it gives the clue to the whole... [T]he eschatological explanation is able to show that the Pauline Mysticism is something which necessarily arose out of the problems raised by the conception of redemption. Here... the principle is really exemplified that that which is shown to be necessary is really explained... Understood on the basis of eschatology, Paul becomes a thinker of elemental power who was alone in recognizing the special character of the period which interposed itself between the Resurrection and Return of Jesus... (A. Schweitzer, *The Mysticism of Paul the Apostle*, pp. 3, 139-40.)

Our age is, in especial degree, the age of criticism, and to criticism everything must submit. (Kant, Preface to *The Critique of Pure Reason*[1])

In the context of our age the Christian religion is certainly a piece of antiquity intruding out of distant ages past... A god who begets children on a mortal woman; a sage who calls upon us no longer to work, no longer to sit in judgment, but to heed the signs of the imminent end of the world; a justice which accepts an innocent man as a substitute sacrifice; someone who bids his disciples drink his blood; prayers for miraculous interventions; sins perpetrated against a god atoned for by a god; fear of a Beyond to which death is the gateway: the figure of the Cross as a symbol in an age which no longer knows the meaning and shame of the Cross— how gruesomely all this is wafted to us, as if out of the grave of a primeval past! (Nietzsche, *Human, All Too Human*, §113[2].)

Among the many accomplishments in many fields of the one figure of whom biblical scholarship may incontrovertibly boast as belonging not

---

1.  I. Kant, *The Critique of Pure Reason* (trans. N.K. Smith; London: Macmillan, 2nd edn, 1933), p. 9 n.

2.  R.J. Hollingdale (ed.), *A Nietzsche Reader* (Harmondsworth: Penguin, 1977), pp. 168-69. Nietzsche continues: 'Can one believe that things of this sort are still believed in'?

merely to its own discipline but to 'our age' is the unleashing of the 'eschatological Paul'. This Paul would captivate a century of interpretation, a century now easily seen as, whatever else it is, the age of Schweitzer—that is, the age of eschatology (or, the eschatological age?)—for New Testament criticism.

The labours in theology of the one whose name has become inseparably associated with an 'apocalyptic' approach to Paul are, if anything, a coherent programme consistently carried through. In the preface to his belated *The Mysticism of Paul the Apostle*,[3] a work which brought this programme and with it his efforts in theology to a kind of conclusion, Albert Schweitzer explains this plan, which he conceived in his student days,

> of explaining the evolution of thought in the first generation of Christianity on the basis of the axiom...that the Preaching of the Kingdom of God by Jesus was in itself eschatological, and that it was so understood by those who heard it. My studies on the problem of the historic origins of the Eucharist, on the 'mystery' of Jesus' Messiahship and suffering, on the course of modern investigations of the Life of Jesus and that of the teaching of Paul, all turn about the two questions—whether besides the eschatological interpretation of the Preaching of Jesus there was any room for another, and how the original completely eschatological faith of Christians fared in the course of the substitution of the Hellenistic for the eschatological way of thinking (p. viii).

Schweitzer reacts against a theological climate which had long indulged, as Schweitzer reads it, in the relatively easier solution to the problem of the Hellenization of Christianity (for Schweitzer the central problem of the history of dogma) of assuming in Jesus and especially Paul a mixture of the eschatological and the non-eschatological which well prepared the way for this movement toward ultimate total Hellenization in the Asia Minor theology of the early second century. 'But in reality the need was to explain how the purely eschatological belief had developed into the Hellenistic one' (p. viii). Paul now stands in the middle of a movement from purely eschatological to purely non-eschatological, and so the question turns on him, and Schweitzer's short answer is that, as in the case of the preaching of Jesus, one is again confronted with an either/or, so that a purely eschatological or a purely Hellenistic explanation, as against 'the untenable notion that Paul had combined eschatological and

3. A. Schweitzer, *The Mysticism of Paul the Apostle* (trans. W. Montgomery; London: A. & C. Black, 2nd edn, 1953).

Hellenistic ways of thinking', must be given, and Schweitzer takes the first alternative, leaving Paul on the side of Jesus and the primitive church and seeing the Hellenization of Christianity as a process wholly subsequent to Paul (p. viii).[4] The Hellenized theology of the second century did not—because it could not—make the primitive teaching its own. The 'fading of the eschatological Hope' brought a reinterpretation of their faith in Hellenistic terms, a process aided by Paul's 'mystical doctrine of Being-in-Christ', which could be appropriated by 'substituting a Hellenistic rationale for the eschatological rationale [of Paul]', which latter could no longer be understood (pp. viii-ix).

> So in a most natural way the evolution from Jesus by way of Paul to Ignatius is explained. Paul was not the Hellenizer of Christianity. But in his eschatological mysticism of the Being-in-Christ he gave it a form in which it could be Hellenized.
>
> In this way I believe I have shown that the recognition of the eschatological character of the Preaching of Jesus and of the Teaching of Paul, though it may pose the question of the Hellenization of Christianity in a more abrupt way than formerly, yet at the same time leads to a much simpler solution of the difficulties (p. ix).

Schweitzer's reader, then, is hardly left in doubt as to what Schweitzer has been about and what he hopes to have accomplished.

Schweitzer subsumes under his ambitious plan, as witnessed in his words cited above on this plan and its central questions, his entire combined work on Jesus, Paul, and Christian origins.[5] One wishing to

---

4. Here Schweitzer assumes the results of his own earlier research on the preaching of Jesus. Following particularly the insights of J. Weiss, Schweitzer pronounced his famous 'either/or' of '*either* eschatological *or* non-eschatological' in *The Quest of the Historical Jesus: A Critical Study of its Progress from Reimarus to Wrede* (trans. W. Montgomery; New York: Macmillan, 1968), p. 238. As for those who would seek to combine what Schweitzer has set in antithesis, he remarks, in dry condescension: 'Progress always consists in taking one or other of two alternatives, in abandoning the attempt to combine them. The pioneers of progress have therefore always to reckon with the law of mental inertia which manifests itself in the majority—who always go on believing that it is possible to combine that which can no longer be combined, and in fact claim it as a special merit that they, in contrast with the "one-sided" writers, can do justice to the other side of the question. One must just let them be, till their time is over, and resign oneself not to see the end of it, since it is found by experience that the complete victory of one of two historical alternatives is a matter of two full theological generations' (pp. 238-39).

5. This includes Schweitzer's earliest Jesus research, his two-part study of the Lord's Supper and the Life of Jesus, and his more familiar *Quest*. Schweitzer's two

understand Schweitzer as an interpreter of Paul does well to observe this
unity of conception and execution—to fail to do so would be to settle
for an 'unhistorical Schweitzer'. Indeed, Schweitzer seems today to be
much more cited than read. Although he gave the question of Paul and
eschatology its first and classic complete formulation, he is often now
little more than a name attached to the notion of an 'apocalyptic'
approach to Paul. Considerable space is therefore given to his interpretation of Paul, beginning with Schweitzer's survey of research, continuing with an account of his own exposition, and finally sketching his
influence.[6] But although this story of interpretation will be in the

---

major works on Paul are: *Paul and His Interpreters: A Critical History* (trans.
W. Montgomery; London: A. & C. Black, 1912), and *Mysticism*, the work from
whose preface this statement of programme comes. Schweitzer discusses his earlier
Jesus research in *Quest*, pp. 330-50; pp. 350-97 treat his fuller reflection. Details of
the genesis of these several works are found in Schweitzer's *My Life and Thought:
An Autobiography* (trans. C.T. Campion; London: Allen & Unwin, 1933), pp. 12-21,
25-26, 45-54; 55-62; 141-50; 247-51. G. Seaver, *Albert Schweitzer: The Man and
His Mind* (London: A. & C. Black, 6th edn, 1969), pp. 230-31, states that Schweitzer's
two works on Paul were to form the second volume (with the *Quest* as the first) of a
three-volume history tracing 'the Hellenization of Christian thought through the
Johannine literature and the sub-apostolic age to the Fathers of the Church'. This
final study was not to appear, however, though its main contours are present in the
final chapters of *Mysticism*.
    6.  On Schweitzer, see the standard surveys of W.G. Kümmel, *The New
Testament: The History of the Investigation of its Problems* (trans. S.M. Gilmour
and H.C. Kee; London: SCM Press, 1973), pp. 235-44, and S. Neill and N.T. Wright,
*The Interpretation of the New Testament 1861-1986* (Oxford: Oxford University
Press, 2nd edn, 1988), pp. 205-15, which emphasize Schweitzer's study of the
Gospels; A.C. Thiselton, 'Biblical Classics VI: Schweitzer's Interpretation of Paul',
*ExpTim* 90 (1979-1980), pp. 132-37, provides a corrective emphasis on Schweitzer as
an interpreter of Paul; Kümmel supplements his own earlier account in his *History*
in 'Albert Schweitzer als Paulusforscher', in J. Friedrich, W. Pöhlmann, and
P. Stuhlmacher (eds.), *Rechtfertigung: Festschrift für Ernst Käsemann zum 70.
Geburtstag* (Tübingen: Mohr [Paul Siebeck]/Göttingen: Vandenhoeck & Ruprecht,
1976), pp. 269-89, and T. Wright supplements Neill with respect to Schweitzer's
Paul research in the 2nd edn of Neill's *Interpretation*, pp. 403-10. See also
J.M. Robinson's Introduction to Schweitzer's *Quest*, 1968, pp. xi-xxxiii; H. Groos,
*Albert Schweitzer: Größe und Grenzen* (München: E. Reinhardt Verlag, 1974),
pp. 313-72 on Schweitzer's *Pauline Studies*; C.K. Barrett, 'Albert Schweitzer and the
New Testament', *ExpTim* 87 (1975), pp. 4-10; D.E. Nineham, 'Schweitzer Revisited',
in *Explorations in Theology* 1 (London: SCM Press, 1977), pp. 112-33; 'Schweitzer,
A.', in Coggins and Houlden (eds.), *Dictionary of Biblical Interpretation*, pp. 613-16;

Gospel is capable of being Hellenised may also be considered capable of being modernised' (p. x).

Standing out in the history of critical study of Paul is the figure of F.C. Baur, whose edifice, though fallen, still presents theology with an unfulfilled challenge to think historically about Paul, a challenge which runs like a thread through Schweitzer's review.[10] For although Baur's formulation is unacceptable, his grasp of the need to address the history of dogma and to relate Paul to the primitive church is not matched in the critics who follow him, who are equal to the task of demolishing Baur's impressive structure, but helpless in terms of replacing it.[11]

At about the time of Baur's rise to prominence critics are beginning to notice an important strand of thought in Paul, formerly kept from view by Reformation readings of the apostle. H.E.G. Paulus (1831), reacting against preoccupation with the atoning death of Jesus and legal conceptions, takes as his point of departure Paul's 'new creature' conceptions and traces out an ethical system of sanctification which displaces this juridical system of justification (pp. 10-11). Within twenty years, R.A. Lipsius is able to recognize these two strands of thought, in their character as juridical and ethical systems, as existing side by side in the apostle (pp. 19-20). In another twenty years, H. Lüdemann (1872) traces two conceptions of 'flesh' in Paul, and thus two conceptions of human nature and two notions of redemption, one Jewish, juridical, subjective, the other Greek, ethico-physical, objective, the latter characterizing the 'real' or 'essential' Paul (pp. 28-31). In a further twenty years, R. Kabisch and W. Wrede indicate the eschatological character of this 'physical' redemption in Paul, Wrede further noting that the juridical system of justification by faith and freedom from the Law are 'controversial teachings' arising out of Paul's Gentile mission (pp. 58-63

10. Little space is given to Baur's actual presentation—he is important for Schweitzer in more of a symbolic sense for his commitment to a historical approach to Paul; on Baur within the history of biblical interpretation, see Kümmel, *History*, pp. 126-43; R. Morgan with J. Barton, *Biblical Interpretation* (Oxford: Oxford University Press, 1988), pp. 62-76 and *passim* (in the present study, this work will be cited under Morgan's name, since the discrete sections on Old Testament studies contributed by Barton are not of concern here); and on Baur and Paul see Morgan's 'Biblical Classics II: F.C. Baur', *ExpTim* 88 (1979), pp. 4-10.

11. Schweitzer, *Interpreters*, pp. vi-ix, 12-15, 15-21, 25-116. For Baur, Paul stands over against the primitive church, while the early catholic church synthesizes the two; for excerpts from Baur in relation to Pauline studies, see W.A. Meeks (ed.), *The Writings of Saint Paul* (New York: Norton, 1972), pp. 277-88.

and 166-72). This notion of a 'physical'[12] element in Paul's thought is a momentous discovery in Schweitzer's view, and to recognize the eschatological, 'mystical' redemption of Paul, the conception of dying and rising with Christ to a new creation in the Spirit (Paul's own contribution to primitive Christian thought [p. 215]) is to approach the heart of Paul's theology.

But Lüdemann's insight was lost on his generation, for although the two strands of thought in Paul are henceforth generally recognized (one, the other, or both equally emphasized), the notion of a 'physical' redemption in Paul was firmly resisted, being much less palatable to modern liberal theological tastes than an 'ethical' system (pp. 31-32). Several things seem to conspire to bar the post-Baur critics access to this fundamental insight into Paul's thought. From Lüdemann on, and going back to Baur himself, a Hellenized Paul is pursued, based especially on the assumption that 'flesh and spirit' in Paul is Greek and that Paul's 'mysticism', so unknown in Judaism, must be traced to Greek philosophy/spirituality (pp. 28-99, 100-16). 'Late Jewish theology' (Schweitzer's term) is little understood, and even when gains are made here, only such as modern theology finds distasteful in Paul is given over as 'Jewish'. It is in the eyes of these critics to Paul's credit that he transcends such Judaism, whether of the 'fantastic apocalyptic' or the 'soulless rabbinism' type (pp. 44-63). Even when such scholars as O. Everling and R. Kabisch compare Paul's angelology, demonology, and eschatology with contemporary Jewish eschatological thought, showing this material to be both preceded and systematic, the further clear implication that this eschatological thought in Paul is integrally related to his theology, to his concept of redemption, is simply not allowed (pp. 53-63). Reformation and modern loci succeed in keeping theology safe from any contact with eschatology, which is quarantined to its own appendix-like chapter, if treated at all.[13] Paul as Jew reaches back to the pure Judaism of the Law and Prophets,[14] essentially passing over the dry, stony ground of intervening Jewish thought to the fertile

---

12. 'Physical' (*naturhaft*—see p. 162, n. 3) as opposed to a purely spiritual, ethical, individual redemption; this 'physical' redemption has reference to the whole person and the whole creation, and Paul's mysticism language is intended to be objective and realistic. On Lüdemann, see Kümmel, *History*, pp. 188-91; on Kabisch and Wrede, see further below.

13. Schweitzer, *Interpreters*, pp. vi-vii, 33-36, 53-54, 57-58, 102, 109.

14. Schweitzer, *Interpreters*, pp. 40-41, 44-46, 67-68.

soil of Greek spirituality, and thus theology keeps for itself a Paul after its own heart, a blend of the best of (biblical) Jew and Greek whose unique character is explained by appealing to his personal creativity,[15] psychologizing over his pre-Christian experience and mental state and the Damascus road vision,[16] spiritualizing and modernizing,[17] preferring the subjective to the objective, religion to theology,[18] positing contradictions and antinomies, real or imagined, as evidence of Paul's composite (Jew/Greek) character,[19] or suggesting practical considerations as the source of his distinctiveness.[20] And by such schemes of evasion the Greek Paul is preserved and pursued to the very end—even the eschatology is held by such critics as O. Pfleiderer and E. Teichmann to develop and vanish into Greek spirituality (pp. 70-77). The post-Baur critics to H.J. Holtzmann utterly failed to think historically about Paul, refusing, 'by the scientific instinct of self-preservation' (p. 99), to offer concrete proofs in the place of vague generality concerning Paul's debt to Greek thought.[21]

> The most natural course to follow in the investigation would have been to begin with the eschatology as the most general and 'primitive-Christian' element, and then to have tried to find a path leading from here to the central doctrine of the new life in union with the dying and resurrection of Christ. This course is nowhere followed (p. 54).[22]

15. Schweitzer, *Interpreters*, pp. 38-40, 52, 67, 113, 157, 220, 227, 247-48

16. Schweitzer, *Interpreters*, pp. 38-40, 66-67, 105-106, 115, 220, 247.

17. Schweitzer, *Interpreters*, pp. vi-vii, 39-40, 77, 85, 108-109, 154-59, 161, 162-66.

18. Schweitzer, *Interpreters*, pp. 106-107, 154-59, 161, 162-66, 172, 247.

19. Schweitzer, *Interpreters*, pp. 28-31, 67-74, 85, 112, 239-40, 247.

20. Schweitzer, *Interpreters*, pp. 83, 168, 246-47.

21. Bultmann regards Schweitzer's 'critical account of research from Baur to Holtzmann' as 'the most valuable part' of Schweitzer's review, clearly grasping the dead ends and open questions for research (R. Bultmann, 'Zur Geschichte der Paulus-Forschung', *TRu* 1 [1929], pp. 26-59, repr. in K.H. Rengstorf [ed.], *Das Paulusbild in der neueren deutschen Forschung* [Darmstadt: Wissenschaftliche Buchgesellschaft, 2nd edn, 1969], pp. 304-37 [307]).

22. This early on Schweitzer is revealing where in his view the solution to the puzzle of Paulinism lies, and his preference for explanations which follow Paul's *logic*, rather than attempting to account for his thought in these various other ways, is already clear; see Schweitzer, *Interpreters*, pp. 21, 25, 32-33, 35-42, 52-55, 104-106, 166, 173-78, 217-21, 240-49. This task is taken up in *Mysticism*.

How could this Greek Paul be understood within the primitive community, and how could later Greek theology fail to see the friend it had in such a Paul?

From the turn of the century these schemes of evasion begin to be put aside, as Paul's connection with Jesus and the primitive community begins to be more fully explored. Greek elements are played down and Jewish elements emphasized, including increasing recognition of the importance of eschatology in Paul, and the notion of a 'physical' element, up to now lightly, if at all, affirmed as something on the periphery of his thought, moves closer to centre—'the only question now was how much had to be conceded to this alien system of thought which was endeavoring to draw Paul within its borders, and how much could be saved from it' (pp. 162-63).

> The courage of theological thinkers was put to a severe test. When Baur and his followers made their profession of an unbiased free investigation they could have had no inkling that it would become so difficult for a later generation to remain true to this principle... [T]o follow a purely historical method meant, as things stood at the beginning of the twentieth century, to be left with an entirely temporally conditioned Paulinism, of which modern ways of thought could make nothing, and to trace out a system which for our religion is dead (p. 166).

At this juncture William Wrede gives Paul's 'physical', objective, Jewish system of redemption a classic presentation which, if leaving a few points obscure, moves Pauline criticism into its next phase and marks the point from which it must proceed (pp. 166-72).[23]

23. Bultmann, in his review of Schweitzer's *Mystik* (*Deutsche Literaturzeiting* 52 [1931], cols. 1153-58), remarks on the influence of Wrede (1155). Schweitzer clearly admires W. Wrede's *Paulus*, though he notes the degree to which Wrede has been preceded in Kabisch (p. 168; for excerpts from Kabisch, see Kümmel, *History*, pp. 232-35). In particular, Wrede's presentation of Paul's Christian thinking as preceded by a system of Messianic beliefs into which the facts of the Christ event are fitted (pp. 168, 171-72) was to prove in principle quite important for Schweitzer. See W. Wrede, *Paulus* (Halle: Religionsgeschichtliche Volksbücher, 1904), repr. in Rengstorf (ed.), *Das Paulusbild*, pp. 1-97; ET *Paul* (trans. E. Lummis; London: Philip Green, 1907). Schweitzer makes it clear that for him Wrede's interpretation is a watershed, and the several points of contact between the two make clear why. Kümmel says that 'Wrede was the first to draw the consequences of a radically historical representation of the apostle' and that his 'acute historical perception' allowed him, 'in a way hitherto unknown, to recognize so clearly the reality of the redemption and the basic eschatologico-historical element in Pauline theology...'

However, a further difficulty lay in the path, deferring the full effect of this 'new phase'.

> The fact is that the 'physical' element which is to be recognized in Paul's doctrine is neither all of one piece nor wholly to be explained from Late Judaism. Strictly speaking, it takes three different forms, of which one is peculiar to the eschatology, another to the mystical doctrine of redemption, and the third to the sacraments.
>
> The 'materialism' of the conception of redemption which is directed towards the future has to do with super-earthly powers, with judgment, bodily resurrection and transformation.
>
> Somewhat different is the 'realism' of the mystical doctrine of the new creation, which asserts that believers here and now experience death and resurrection in fellowship with Christ, and so put on, beneath the earthly exterior which conceals it, a nature essentially immune from corruption.
>
> Different from this conception again is the sacramental, inasmuch as it represents in some inexplicable fashion an externalisation of it. What, according to the mystical doctrine, seemed to take place by itself without being connected with an external act, is here to be thought of as the effect of eating and drinking, and cleansing with water. The sacramental conception is a magical conception (pp. 173-74).

(*History*, p. 295). According to Wrede, Paul 'believed with all his might in the speedy coming of Christ and the approaching end of the world. Accordingly in his view the redemptive act of Christ, which lay in the past, and the dawn of the future glory lay close together'. 'It has been maintained that Paul altered the view of salvation held by the earliest community by shifting the stress from the future to the past, stressing the blessedness of the Christian as already attained and emphasizing faith instead of hope. It is easy to see that this is absurdly but a half truth. All references to the redemption as a completed transaction change at once into utterances about the future.' For Paul, salvation is 'something objective, a change in the very nature and conditions of existence', a redemption from the 'powers', 'a change in the nature of humanity'; 'he is not thinking of the individual at all, but always of the race, of humanity as a whole', and 'his mode of thinking is purely historical'. The participatory and anticipatory themes so important for Schweitzer are perceived by Wrede. Wrede makes a keynote of the *distance* of Paul from his modern reader. (See the excerpts from Wrede's *Paul* in Kümmel, *History*, pp. 295-99, from which he is cited here; see also Westerholm, *Israel's Law*, pp. 15-22. The importance of Schweitzer and Wrede in crystallizing the issues that would set the agenda for twentieth-century interpretation of Paul is inestimable. Wrede's interpretation marks the beginning of the 'new phase' (my term, but clearly expressing Schweitzer's intent) from which Schweitzer proceeds, pressing through its insights and obscurities to a new synthesis. (Schweitzer's account of what is lacking in Wrede's presentation offers a good indication of Schweitzer's own agenda; see pp. 169-78; 240-49.)

Only the eschatology 'can be immediately explained from Late Judaism', which knew 'nothing of either mysticism or sacrament' (p. 174). 'The most obvious procedure would have been to attempt to derive the mystical and sacramental conceptions from the eschatological, as being the root-conception' (p. 174). But first 'Comparative Religion'[24] had to try, and fail, to explain Paul's sacraments and redemption conceptions on the basis of the magical rites and redemption ideas of the mysteries, not appreciating that Paul's sacraments and redemption, though out-wardly similar to theirs, are thoroughly eschatological in character and thus of a wholly different order (pp. 175-228). This second 'Paul and Hellenism' phase, the mystery religion approach, which, Schweitzer notes, implicitly denies the older Hellenistic philosophy approach ('a case of Satan's being driven out by Beelzebub' [p. 239]), likewise fails to demonstrate more than general similarity. In both cases a radical wing forces the approach to its logical—and untenable—conclusions (pp. 117-50, 233-36). Once again the history of dogma is not addressed—the *a priori* difficulties of a homeless Greek Paul in the primitive church and a later catholic church which equally has no place for him are not grasped (pp. 228-31).

Schweitzer understands the allure felt by the 'Comparative Religion' (history of religions) school of an explanation from Hellenistic syncretism for Paul's 'mysticism', effecting as it did such respected figures as Wrede. But a true history of religions approach must proceed differently:

> To apply the comparative method to Paul would, therefore, generally speaking, mean nothing more or less than to explain him on the basis of Late Judaism. Those who give due weight to the eschatological character of his doctrine and to the problems and ideas which connect it with works like the Apocalypse of Ezra are the true exponents of 'Comparative Religion', even though they may make no claim to this title (p. 177).

'Paul belongs to Late Judaism' (p. 176)—and Schweitzer belongs broadly to the effort to give a history of religions account of Paul's thought.

In concluding his survey, Schweitzer states categorically his central history of religions agenda, and in doing so he points the way forward to his own projected treatment, isolating the two central obscurities he finds in Wrede which blunt the edge of the 'new phase' in interpreting Paul. Merely to acknowledge the eschatological character and the

---

24. This is Montgomery's translation of the '*religionsgeschichtliche*' school (cf. Schweitzer, *Interpreters*, p. 175 n. 1).

'physical' nature of Paul's thought is not enough. Both these mysteries must be penetrated. This Schweitzer intends to do.

> The solution must, therefore, consist in leaving out of the question Greek influence in every form and in every combination, and venturing on the 'one-sidedness' of endeavoring to understand the doctrine of the Apostle of the Gentiles entirely on the basis of Jewish primitive Christianity. That implies, in the first place, that the Pauline eschatology must be maintained in its full compass, as required by the utterances of the letters. But merely to emphasize it is not everything. The next point is to explain it. What was the scheme of the events of the End, and what answer was given by eschatological expectation to the fundamental questions which could not be avoided (p. 240)?[25]

In pursuing such questions, Schweitzer is after the 'inner logic' (p. 240) of Paul's eschatology, on the basis of which, Schweitzer insists, the eschatological derivation of Paul's 'mysticism' and sacramental conceptions becomes clear.

> That Paul's mystical doctrine of redemption and his doctrine of the sacraments belong to eschatology is plain to be seen. The only question is in what way, exactly, they have arisen out of it. The future-hope, raised to the highest degree of intensity, must somehow or other have possessed the power of producing them. If the impulse, the pressing need to which they were the response, is once recognised, then Paulinism is understood, since in its essence it can be nothing else than an eschatological mysticism, expressing itself by the aid of the Greek religious terminology.
> 
> Theoretically, too, it is possible to form an approximate idea how the intensified expectation of the future might take a mystical form. In apocalyptic thought sensuous and supersensuous converge, in such a manner that the former is thought of as passing away into the latter. Thus there is present in it the most general presupposition of all mysticism, since it is the object of the latter to abolish the earthly in the super-earthly. The peculiarity of the mysticism which arises out of Apocalyptic is that it does not bring the two worlds into contact in the mind of the individual man, as Greek and medieval mysticism did, but dovetails one into the other, and thus creates for the moment at which the one passes over into the other an objective, temporally conditioned mysticism (pp. 241-42).

So, too, Paul's 'intensified eschatological expectation' accounts for his 'sacramental conceptions': 'Those who stood on the threshold of the

---

25. Note the detailed questions Schweitzer goes on to raise here concerning the scheme of events of the end. The 'fundamental questions which could not be avoided' are those turning on the reconfiguration imposed on traditional schemes by the death and resurrection of Christ.

coming glory must have been eagerly anxious to gain an assurance that
they themselves would be partakers therein and to obtain tangible
guarantees of "deliverance" from the coming judgment' (p. 243).[26]

> The Apostle's most general views must be taken as the starting point from
> which to explain how he arrives at the paradox that the believer is united
> with Christ, experiences along with Him death and resurrection, and
> becomes a new creature, emancipated from fleshly corporeity. The assertion
> that these statements are meant in a 'physical' sense does not carry us
> very far. The reason which explains their 'reality' must be shown...
>
> The mistake in the attempts at explanation hitherto made consists in the
> fact that they seek to argue from the facts of the death and resurrection of
> Jesus, simply as such, directly to that which takes place in the believer. In
> reality, it can only be a question of a general event, which in the time
> immediately preceding the End brings about this dying and rising again in
> Jesus and believers as together forming a single category of mankind, and
> thus antedates the future into the present...
>
> The general fact which comes into question must result from the condi-
> tion of the world between the death of Jesus and His parousia. The
> Apostle asserts an overlapping of the still natural, and the already super-
> natural, condition of the world, which becomes real in the case of Christ
> and believers in the form of an open or hidden working of the forces of
> death and resurrection—and becomes real in them only. The doctrine of
> the death and resurrection of Jesus and the mystical doctrine of
> redemption are alike cosmically conditioned (pp. 244-45).

This stated, there is little in Schweitzer's own promised exposition not
preceded in his review of scholarship.

Schweitzer's own approach is clear, both in what he affirms and in
what he keeps to the fore in his review of scholarship. A truly historical
approach to Paulinism[27] must address the history of dogma. Paul's
eschatology, its background in 'late Jewish' theology and its setting in
the primitive community, must be exposed and explained in its intimate

26.  Schweitzer is much more preoccupied with questions about Paul's sacramental thought than the present treatment is able to indicate; another pervasive theme
which has been largely passed over here is Schweitzer's emphasis on predestinarian
thought in Paul. Both of these play a prominent role in Schweitzer's attempt to tease
out the logic of Paul's 'mysticism'.

27.  'Paulinism', the distinctive voice of Paul, is the common goal of Schweitzer
and his fellow critics. On 'Paulinism' as a point of convergence of history and
theology, see Robert Morgan, 'The Significance of "Paulinism"', in M.D. Hooker
and S.G. Wilson (eds.), *Paul and Paulinism: Essays in Honour of C.K. Barrett*
(London: SPCK, 1982), pp. 320-38.

relation to his theology of redemption. The realistic, cosmic, 'mystical' doctrine of redemption, the dying and rising again with Christ and the new creation, is central, and it is to be derived from the eschatological intensity of Paul's Christian thinking, specifically, from his perception of the peculiar eschatological conditions which prevailed at his point in time. The path from this to Paul's relation to Jesus,[28] his view of the Law and the Gentile mission,[29] and the early catholic conception of Paul is opened.[30]

And so this is Schweitzer's relentless call to a historical approach to Paul—his review of modern criticism might well be called 'the Quest of the Historical Paul'. Theology must be made to face the fact that every forced gain in modern utility is a loss of historical integrity. The result may be a Paul with whom one can live, but at what cost?

Schweitzer presents his programme as in the true spirit of Baur, a new 'positive criticism' which tests early Christian literature on the basis of primitive eschatology:[31]

> It may no doubt prove to be the case that this 'positive' criticism will appear distressingly negative to those who look for results which can be immediately coined into dogmatic and homiletic currency.
>
> Their opinion, however, is of little importance.
>
> It is the fate of the 'Little-faiths' of truth that they, true followers of Peter, whether they be of the Roman or the Protestant observance, cry out and sink in the sea of ideas, where the followers of Paul, believing in the Spirit, walk secure and undismayed (p. 249).

The way is well prepared for Schweitzer's own full exposition, to which attention now turns.

## The Mysticism of Paul the Apostle

Schweitzer has given his indictment of German interpretaters of Paul for failing to recognize the centrality of Paul's 'mystical' doctrine of dying and rising with Christ and its relation to his eschatology, and for wishfully

28. Schweitzer, *Interpreters*, pp. vi-viii, 42-44, 158-60, 168, 170, 245-46.

29. Schweitzer, *Interpreters*, pp. 31, 37, 44, 83-84, 104-105, 107-108, 160, 168-70, 245-47.

30. Schweitzer, *Interpreters*, pp. 240-48.

31. By 'positive criticism' Schweitzer points to the utility of his reconstruction of the early eschatological development, onto which developmental scheme one may plot the early Christian literature.

pursuing instead their liberal Paul down dead-end paths. He also chides the instinctive tendency to eschew detailed proof in preference to generality. It is now Schweitzer's turn to follow up his own generalities with detailed proof, and he is, in characteristic style, bold and resolute in taking this up.

What does he mean in speaking of Paul's 'mysticism'? 'We are always in the presence of mysticism when we find a human being looking upon the division between earthly and super-earthly, temporal and eternal, as transcended, and feeling himself, while still externally amid the earthly and temporal, to belong to the super-earthly and eternal' (1). Paul's is not a primitive, magical notion of union with the divine through ritual, nor a developed, intellectual notion of the oneness of all in God; indeed, his is no God-mysticism at all, but Christ-mysticism, through which one comes into relationship with God.

> The fundamental thought of Pauline mysticism runs thus: I am in Christ; in Him I know myself as a being who is raised above the sensuous, sinful, and transient world and already belongs to the transcendent; in Him I am assured of resurrection; in Him I am a Child of God.
>
> Another distinctive characteristic of his mysticism is that being in Christ is conceived as a having died and risen again with Him, in consequence of which the participant has been freed from sin and from the Law, possesses the Spirit of Christ, and is assured of resurrection.
>
> This 'being-in-Christ' is the prime enigma of the Pauline teaching: once grasped it gives the clue to the whole (p. 3).[32]

Attempts to explain Paul's 'mysticism' on the basis of Greek spirituality or primitive or Hellenistic mystery religions (pp. 4-25) fail to recognize the utterly different character of Paul's 'mysticism', as his is thoroughly eschatological, realistic, cosmic, and collective in character.

But Paul is not 'wholly and solely a mystic' (p. 24), as there is room in his thought for other, non-mystical, views of redemption—'there are in fact three different doctrines of redemption which for Paul go side by side: an eschatological, a juridical, and a mystical' (p. 25).[33] The eschato-

32. Schweitzer here announces the central problem (as he sees it) of grasping Paul: as will be seen in the following, the riddle is this construct of realization against the background of Paul's inheritance of futuristic eschatology, hence the attempts of many at a Hellenistic explanation.

33. This marks a further elaboration over *Interpreters*, where Schweitzer is simply concerned to assert the connection of eschatology and redemption; of these three, the eschatological and the 'mystical' are closely related as virtually the outside and inside of the same conception (cf. *Mysticism*, p. 74, and see below), while the juridical is

logical conception concerns the end of the natural world and the defeat of the angelic powers in Jesus' death and resurrection and the expectation that he will soon return to share the messianic glory with the elect; the juridical notion of 'righteousness through faith' rests on the atoning significance of Jesus' death; but the 'mysticism' of the being-in-Christ is the fundamental conception of Paul's own religious thought.

But even as the fundamental character of Paul's thought begins to be properly grasped, attempts to root it in Hellenistic religion go on (pp. 26-36).

> Why has the task not yet been undertaken of explaining the Pauline Mysticism from Eschatology, seeing that it is clearly apparent from the actual substance of his teaching that his 'mysticism' of the Dying and Rising again with Christ is centered in an ardent eschatological expectation? Kabisch and Wrede took the first steps in this direction. How is it that they have had no successors (p. 36)?

Clearly, the seemingly obvious parallels with Hellenistic 'mysticism' are considered to hold more promise than the unlikely Jewish-eschatological approach—how does Paul's assertion of the presence of redemption derive from purely futuristic expectation? But Paul's 'mysticism' is indeed eschatological—the presence of the future which it embraces is an eschatological coincidence of the natural and supernatural worlds, a reading of the cosmic events of the end-time in the light of Jesus' death and resurrection (p. 37).[34]

This strand of Paul's thought, the dawning recognition of which Schweitzer has traced through his earlier review of scholarship, styled as Paul's 'mysticism' of dying and rising with Christ and held to be central to his thought, is basically what is to become known as 'participation' in Christ, and the eschatological tension which Schweitzer is highlighting is to become Paul's 'anticipation' or as his 'already and not yet' motif.[35]

---

extracted by Paul for practical purposes from the eschatological/'mystical' system and developed independently (cf. *Mysticism*, pp. 205-26). The eschatological and juridical are based on tradition, while the overarching 'mystical' system is Paul's own development.

34. That Paul's 'mysticism', with its realized/anticipatory nature, is Paul's own innovation is noted in *Interpreters* (for example, pp. 54-55, 215) and repeatedly stressed in *Mysticism*. Indeed, this 'mysticism' is *Paulinism*, and discovering how this present/future configuration is to be explained is for Schweitzer, once again, the central problem.

35. Cf. Sanders, *Paul*, pp. 434-42; Thiselton, 'Schweitzer', pp. 135-36.

The distinctive voice of Paul is heard in this eschatological participation or participatory eschatology. In this form Schweitzer asks his persistent question of Paul's place in the history of dogma: how else is Paul's uniqueness yet intelligibility in the first Christian generation to be explained except by his drawing the natural inferences from the eschatological presuppositions which he shared with primitive Christianity, and how else is Paul's strangeness to the immediately following generations to be explained but by recognizing that he 'built his system upon a conviction which ruled only in the first generation' (p. 39), namely the expectation of the imminent dawning of the messianic kingdom of Jesus (pp. 37-39)? 'The only practical procedure is to begin with the simple material which Paul shares completely with the Early Church, and then to see how his doctrine develops out of these...This simple material is the eschatological expectation' (p. 40).

Noting the consistent emphasis in Paul on an expectation of the immediate return of Jesus (pp. 52-54), Schweitzer proceeds to unpack further the notion of an eschatological conception of redemption and thus to outline this shared eschatological expectation.[36] 'The conception of Redemption which stands behind this eschatological expectation is, to put it quite generally, that Jesus Christ has made an end of the natural world and is bringing in the Messianic Kingdom. It is thus cosmologically conceived' (p. 54). As it involves a transfer of the world from one state to another, this redemption is not an individual transaction but a world-event in which the individual shares.

The background of such a conception is to be sought in Jewish eschatology, as expressed in the Prophets (including Daniel) and developed through *1 Enoch*, the *Psalms of Solomon*, *2 Baruch*, and *4 Ezra* (and to a lesser extent *Jubilees*, the *Testaments of the Twelve Patriarchs*, and *Ascension of Moses*). 'In general, the view of Jewish eschatology is that the evil of the world comes from the demons, and that angelic beings have, with God's permission, established themselves between Him and mankind. In its simplest form the conception of redemption is that the Messianic Kingdom puts an end to this condition' (p. 55). This world of powers in dominion is the world of Jesus and Paul.

The elements of this conception of redemption are found in Jesus' own teaching (pp. 57-62), and he came to connect his own messianic

36. Here and later, Schweitzer reconstructs in great detail the eschatological schema which, in concluding his *Interpreters*, he had suggested as holding the key to Paul's thought.

and atoning death with the bringing in of the kingdom. The early church expects, in its circumstances, the kingdom at Jesus' return, connecting his resurrection with his instalment as messiah and his atoning death with assurance in judgment when he shortly returns (pp. 62-63). Jesus and the early community are entirely future-oriented in their expectations.

Paul reasserts the direct connection between Jesus' death and resurrection and the coming of the kingdom, as Jesus has struck the death blow to the powers (p. 73). Even now Jesus' power limits their dominion over the elect (pp. 63-65). At his coming their destruction will be completed. When he comes, the messianic elect arise or experience transformation to resurrection life and enter, through the messianic judgment, the earthly messianic kingdom, a continued struggle of limited but unspecified duration with the angel-powers, at the end of which death, the final power, is destroyed. Then is the final resurrection to judgment of all who have ever lived, along with the angels. The messianic elect have already been granted their resurrection existence, joined now by the elect of the former generations, while the unrighteous people and angels are consigned to fire. The elect enter the eternal kingdom of God, the messiah rendering up his authority, and history is consummated, with God 'all in all'.

The Law, itself a means of angelic dominion, is ended in Jesus' death and resurrection, by which he invalidates its curse. Thereby Paul can further assert the presence of redemption in this release from bondage (pp. 68-71). The Law was generally held to be valid until the messianic kingdom, and its end in Jesus' death and resurrection exemplifies the connection of the Christ event with the coming of the kingdom. (Paul also receives the tradition of Jesus' atoning death and develops it into the juridical doctrine of justification by faith alone [p. 63].[37])

However, Paul only occasionally makes use of this 'eschatological Gnosis' (p. 74), as there are other, more complete ways of expressing the presence of redemption. For Paul's eschatological 'mysticism' 'has the power of showing that redemption is already present, while it is superior to the eschatological Gnosis in that it replaces the external interpretation of the death and resurrection of Jesus by an internal interpretation'. Thus the eschatological doctrine of redemption remains

---

37. See Schweitzer, *Mysticism*, pp. 205-26, where Schweitzer offers his infamous metaphor of righteousness by faith as a 'subsidiary crater' (p. 225) within the main rim of the mystical doctrine of Being-in-Christ.

occasional, 'whereas the mystical is the centre of Paul's thought'.[38]

What compels Paul beyond the future redemption of the early church to a 'mysticism' which asserts that redemption is realizing itself in the present? The clue must lie in Paul's eschatological thought, which, far from what is often assumed, actually proceeds in a logical, systematic progression (p. 75).

> The problems of Pauline eschatology all go back to the two circumstances that it is, in the first place, like the Apocalypses of Baruch and Ezra, a synthesis of the eschatology of the Prophets and of the 'Son-of-man' eschatology of Daniel; and, in the second place, that it has to reckon with the facts, wholly unforeseen to Jewish eschatology, that the Messiah has already appeared as man, has died, and is risen again (p. 76).

And so Schweitzer proceeds to show how Paul (by a somewhat ruthless logical process) comes to reinterpret his eschatological heritage in the light of the Christ event, resulting in his notion of *eschatological participation* (pp. 76-79).

The prophets present an earthly, nationalistic future hope, involving a Davidic messiah. The messiah, though, gradually fades from view, and the idea of the kingdom of God replaces the idea of a messianic kingdom. Daniel expects an eternal kingdom of God as the consummation of the ages, in which, preceded by the resurrection and judgment, all the righteous of the ages take part. The Son of Man is God's special agent. The kingdom is transcendent and other-worldly, born through cosmic catastrophe, ruled by this exalted, angelic figure, a process of development continued in *1 Enoch*. The *Psalms of Solomon*, however, mark a return to the prophetic messianic eschatology. There are, then, two distinct future expectations in the time of Jesus and Paul (p. 79), a this-worldly, messianic hope and a transcendent, other-worldly hope.

Jesus (pp. 79-84) clearly follows the Daniel/Enoch tradition, effecting a

---

38. In thus marginalizing the eschatological and asserting the centrality of the 'mystical' conception of redemption, no departure in Paul from this eschatological scheme is meant by Schweitzer. The contrast is between the two as adequate expressions of the presence of redemption. The eschatological doctrine of redemption conceives of redemption as the defeat of the angel powers in Jesus' death and resurrection. (This conception is called a 'Gnosis' in reference to Paul's idiosyncratic and esoteric connection of the powers with the Law, pp. 68-74.) The 'mystical' doctrine assumes the same eschatology but understands the believer as participating in the death and resurrection of Jesus, effecting an invisible but real presence of redemption.

synthesis with the prophetic eschatology only in identifying, in himself, the Son of Man and the Davidic messiah. In this capacity he will come with his angels, and the dead of all ages will rise to judgment, along with the survivors of the last generation, the unrighteous to destruction, the elect to life in the eternal kingdom, final, irreplaceable, the consummation of history.

'Completely different from the eschatology of Jesus is that of the Apocalypses of Baruch and Ezra' (p. 84), for these try to harmonize the prophetic and Danielic traditions. 'They do so by the simple method of regarding the Messianic Kingdom of the Prophets as something temporary, which is to give place to the eternal Kingdom of God, which latter is to be the consummation of history'. On their view (pp. 84-90), the messiah/Son of Man comes at the end of a pre-messianic tribulation, through which those of the final generation who are elect to the messianic kingdom survive; a judgment of the messiah determines entrance to the kingdom, a temporally limited (four hundred years in *4 Ezra*) earthly/superearthly state of blessedness, at the end of which the messiah returns to heaven. There follows the resurrection of all generations to judgment, to eternal life or death. This eternal kingdom is purely a theocracy, in which neither Son of Man nor messiah have a part, and stands at the consummation of history. Thus, unlike Jesus' eschatology of one blessedness, one judgment, and one kingdom, in this scheme there are two of each (p. 88). For Jesus stands in the line of Daniel with the resurrection at the beginning of the messianic kingdom, while in *Baruch* and *Ezra* the resurrection takes place at the end. This latter is the eschatology of the Scribes, who, resisting other speculations, attempt to harmonize the biblical Prophets, including Daniel. And this scheme, though seen here in writings later than the 70 CE destruction of Jerusalem, must characterize the eschatology of the Scribes of an earlier period as well, as Paul himself shows, for 'the eschatology which he presupposes is, as regards its scheme and the events of the end, the same as that of the Apocalypses of Baruch and Ezra. This therefore must have been the accepted view of the Scribes among whom he was brought up' (p. 90).

That Paul (pp. 90-100) shares this two-stage eschatology is evident in that, for him, death is not defeated until the end of the messianic kingdom, at which time the general resurrection and judgment occur. As in the Scribes, the messianic kingdom is for the elect of the last generation, while the elect of all generations take part in the eternal kingdom. But significantly Paul asserts the resurrection life of the elect in Christ in the messianic kingdom—those who survive to the coming of the kingdom are transformed to a resurrection mode of existence, while those who have died in Christ (a point of concern in Paul's churches) are raised to this form of existence. Thus Paul, in asserting the notion of the resurrection life in the temporary, messianic kingdom, creates the idea of two resurrections (pp. 93-94). But how can the dead in Christ arise if Death survives to the end of the messianic kingdom? And how can those who survive to the parousia assume a resurrection life without first experiencing death? Because of this problem Paul 'is obliged, with a view to its solution, to assert the mystical doctrine of the dying and rising again with Christ' (p. 97). This 'mysticism' remains unintelligible apart from the eschatology, which itself remains unintelligible on the common assumption that Paul shares the eschatology of Jesus.

'But it is not only the problem of the mode of existence of the Elect in the Messianic Kingdom which leads Paul as a thinker to his Mysticism, but also direct reflection upon the import of the death and resurrection of Jesus' (p. 97).[39] For Paul the merely futuristic, expectant stance of the primitive community cannot stand undeveloped, for, as resurrection itself belongs to the supernatural age, Jesus' death and resurrection must mean the end of the old age and the dawning of the new. 'If Jesus has risen, that means, for those who dare to think consistently, that it is now already the supernatural age. And this is Paul's point of view. He cannot regard the resurrection of Jesus as an isolated event, but must regard it as the initial event of the rising of the dead in general' (p. 98). Unforeseen in traditional expectations, the present must be the beginning of the resurrection age.

As a result, the period in which Paul stands, between Jesus' resurrection and parousia, is a peculiar one in which, despite outward appearances, supernatural forces are inwardly at work. This time is an intermingling of the ages. 'Thereby the conditions for a peculiar Mysticism are created. In consequence of the actual condition of the world, not merely by a pure act of thought as in other mystical systems, he who has the true knowledge can be conscious of himself as at one and the same time in the transient world and the eternal world'. (p. 99) Paul's 'mysticism' is

---

39. Schweitzer does not label either of the routes taken by Paul to his 'mysticism' as decisive, but Schweitzer's preference for an explanation from logical, rather than practical (that is, the problem of those who have died 'in Christ'), necessity seems to cause him to prefer the explanation of direct reflection on Jesus' death and resurrection.

the result of reflection on the nature of the times and on the character of Jesus' death and resurrection as cosmic events and as the beginning of the general resurrection.

> Thus he comes, contrary to the concepts in which he is accustomed to move, to postulate for the Elect in the Messianic Kingdom the resurrection mode of existence, and to maintain, contrary to the existing naïve belief, that with the resurrection of Jesus the Messianic period had actually already begun and that the resurrection of the dead in general was in progress. Thus the direction of his thought was forced from all sides by the problems of eschatology itself to the paradoxical assertion that the powers manifested in the dying and rising of Jesus were already at work in those who are elect to the Messianic Kingdom (p. 100).

Only Paul in his time modified traditional expectations in the direction they must move now that the Christ event lies behind.

Schweitzer goes on to assert that eschatology further provides the background of Paul's 'mysticism' in the eschatological concept of 'the community of the Saints'.[40] Both Jesus and Paul have a concept of the close, preordained union of the messianic elect with the messiah and with one another. This formerly purely future expectation becomes in Paul, in the light of Jesus' death and resurrection, something presently realized in an anticipatory sense.

Jesus himself prepared the way for this in his teaching that fellowship with him is fellowship with the Son of Man in his kingdom—'he thus teaches Christ-Mysticism in ways appropriate for the time in which the coming Messiah was walking unknown, in earthly form, upon earth' (p. 109). It falls to Paul to express this reality in terms appropriate to his own time between the advents. The setting, then, of Paul's 'mysticism' is his insight into the anticipatory realization of the predestined solidarity of Christ and the elect presently working itself out, which is to be the basis of union in the messianic kingdom. In this kingdom the resurrection mode of existence is to be shared *before* the general resurrection. Christ and the elect share a peculiar corporeity influenced by the powers of resurrection life, and so the idea of the 'community of the elect' 'takes on for Paul a quasi-physical character' (p. 110). What has occurred visibly in Christ is presently occurring inwardly in the elect—they are already, though invisibly, supernatural beings. This quasi-physical conception solves Paul's eschatological problems, both of the elect

40. Schweitzer finds this concept chiefly in certain texts in Daniel and *1 Enoch* (*Mysticism*, pp. 101-105).

experiencing resurrection life in the messianic kingdom, either by being transformed without tasting death or by being raised before death's defeat, and of the correlation of Christ's resurrection with the general resurrection, which are only apparently separated, as the elect are now invisibly risen with Christ. This paradoxical 'mystical' union with Christ in which the world and humanity are in process of transformation is the eschatological conception of redemption viewed from within, as at the moment of Jesus' death and resurrection the powers are passing away and the dominion of the messiah is beginning. The powers, including death, have even now no power over the elect. And since Paul's 'mysticism' is simply the expression of this shared eschatological concept of redemption, developed in consequence of what has happened to and is happening in Christ, Paul, though he alone makes this vital adjustment, can expect to be understood in the primitive community, and can even express his 'mysticism' as something obvious to all.

This conception of his explains the difference in perspective between Jesus and himself (pp. 113-15), and this eschatological matrix is necessary to understand Paul's notion of the church as the 'body of Christ' (pp. 116-18), entered in baptism, a state of communion and fellowship with Christ which mystically, physically creates one body, one person. Further expressing this 'mystical' body are the various formulations of 'being in Christ' (pp. 121-27), a collective, objective experience of this shared corporeity—these alike derive from the eschatological conception of the 'community of God'. '[T]he Pauline Mysticism is therefore nothing else than the doctrine of the making manifest, in consequence of the death and resurrection of Jesus, of the pre-existent Church' (p. 116).

Paul does not explain his 'mysticism'. But an appreciation of its eschatological nature—its background in Jewish and primitive Christian eschatology, its setting in the backward view to Jesus' death and resurrection from the standpoint of awaiting his return, and the unswerving logic by which Paul is compelled to it[41]—offers the only hope of bringing this foundational conception, and thus Paulinism itself, into the reach of the modern reader. 'And how totally wrong those are who refuse to admit that Paul was a logical thinker, and proclaim as the

41. As the above sketch makes clear, the two key elements in Paul's eschatological inheritance according to Schweitzer are the general eschatological schema of expectations and the eschatological doctrine of a 'community of the elect'; Jesus' death and resurrection and awaited return forge these materials into Paul's 'eschatological participation' or 'participatory eschatology'.

highest outcome of their wisdom the discovery that he has no system' (p. 139)! For the door of Paul's 'mysticism', unlocked by the key of eschatology, leads outward from within to the many corridors surrounding this central chamber, a maze through which the reader is now prepared to walk with relative ease.[42]

### Paul and 'Apocalyptic' in Schweitzer

What does one find in Schweitzer concerning that stream of modern interpretative tradition to which his name is attached? What does he have to say about 'apocalyptic Paul'? We have come this far with Schweitzer and the term 'apocalyptic' itself has hardly come up.

To begin with, a strictly terminological point may be made. In fact, one finds in Schweitzer's interpretation of Paul almost nothing about 'apocalyptic' as such. He does at times, in his earlier *Interpreters*, speak vaguely of 'apocalyptic' in the sense of a singular, coherent theological tradition.[43] But even in this earlier work Schweitzer's interest is in 'late Jewish eschatology' generally, using apocalypses and other literature as background to Paul. And in *Mysticism* the term 'apocalyptic' vanishes completely—only Jewish eschatology, as reconstructed from various types of literature, including apocalypses, is under consideration.[44]

---

42. What is central is what leads outward from itself to explain everything else, and so Schweitzer proceeds, in the remaining chapters, to trace the path from Paul's eschatological participation in Christ to suffering and the Spirit, Law and righteousness by faith, the sacraments, and ethics, finally sketching the process by which later generations came to substitute a philosophical/metaphysical mysticism for Paul's eschatological 'mysticism'.

43. Schweitzer, *Interpreters*, pp. 241-42, 175-78, 193 n. 2, 194. Cf. Schweitzer's earlier treatment in his *Quest* (pp. 367-68). There, 'apocalyptic' hovers between being a literary and theological-historical term, more or less signifying (transcendent) 'eschatology' and pointing to a general movement of which early Christianity partakes while at the same time constituting a special moment in the process (an entirely conventional manner of speaking of 'apocalyptic').

44. This terminological point should not be pressed too far. Schweitzer's own earlier usage contributes to the confusion. But his possibly more measured manner in his mature work on Paul might indicate a more considered approach, perhaps indicating less confidence in speaking of 'apocalyptic' as such, and suggesting a dissatisfaction with the terminology. *My Life and Thought*, appearing just after *Mysticism*, likewise refrains from using the term 'apocalyptic', even when referring to the earlier works, and Schweitzer notes that for revised editions of his *Quest* he 'was especially concerned to set forth the late-Jewish eschatology more thoroughly and

A more substantial point concerns the difference of context between Schweitzer and later 'apocalyptic' interpretation of Paul. Although more recent scholars such as J.C. Beker, who makes much of the 'apocalyptic' character of Paul's thought, count Schweitzer as an example of an 'apocalyptic' approach, a certain haste to claim Schweitzer for one's own may be detected here.[45] For in this subsequent discussion 'apocalyptic' is

better' than before (p. 150). As to what shaped Schweitzer's own understanding of 'late Jewish eschatology'/'apocalyptic', he follows the standard studies of Bousset and Schürer (*Interpreters*, pp. 45, 162). Schweitzer's later usage (even if relatively unreflective) has at least the virtue of avoiding the confusion between a literary and a historical/theological category that resides in the term 'apocalyptic'. At any rate, by Schweitzer's time and thereafter, an understanding of 'apocalyptic' (or whatever) as a distinct eschatological construct (radically futuristic, dualism of the ages, acute, imminent expectation, universal, other-worldly hope) is current and uncontroversial.

45. Beker, *Paul*, pp. 16-17, 372 n. 9. Beker also regards W. Morgan, *The Religion and Theology of Paul* (Edinburgh: T. & T. Clark, 1917) as an early 'apocalyptic interpretation'—J.C. Beker, *The Triumph of God: The Essence of Paul's Thought* (trans. L.T. Stuckenbruck; Minneapolis: Augsburg Fortress, 1990), p. 65. Actually, Morgan's interpretation might signal a number of coming trends. He asserts that 'Paul's outlook is at bottom that of Jewish Apocalyptic': 'At the basis of all the Apostle's thinking and constituting its ground-plan there lies the apocalyptic doctrine of the two ages or worlds with its pessimistic and dualistic implications' (pp. 6, 11, suggesting a kinship to Schweitzer). However, he goes on to assert that 'the unconscious movement of [Paul's] thought is away from [Apocalyptic]' (p. 240, suggesting Dodd). He also asserts that, while 'knowledge of its [Paul's thought] precise presuppositions and categories [is] a matter of first-class importance', 'it is inevitable that the original framework, foreign as it has to a large extent become, should be for the most part discounted, and that the Apostle's essential ideas should receive a more modern setting' (pp. 5-6, suggesting Bultmann). Finally, he says that 'History means for Paul but one thing, the story of redemption...In the Cross of Christ he finds the grand centre to which everything is related. All that happens before has for its single purpose to prepare the way for the Cross; all that happens after is but the working out of the redemption there achieved' (p. 241, suggesting Cullmann). Another early work surprisingly overlooked by Beker, seeing that Vos, like Beker, was a Professor of Biblical Theology at Princeton (and likewise of Dutch Reformed tradition), is G. Vos, *The Pauline Eschatology* (Princeton: Princeton University Press, 1930, repr. Phillipsburg, New Jersey: Presbyterian and Reformed, 1986); see particularly the first two chapters on the 'structure' of Paul's eschatology and on the 'interaction between eschatology and soteriology'. Vos's work partakes of the 'new phase', acknowledging a background in Jewish 'apocalyptic' and making eschatology central for Paul's thought, drawing on Schweitzer's heroes Kabisch and Wrede and on Schweitzer himself; he is a forebear of the sort of 'salvation history' approach later found in O. Cullmann and H. Ridderbos.

one type of eschatological interpretation set against rival interpretations of Paul's eschatology: futuristic eschatology versus 'realized eschatology', 'existentialist interpretation', and 'salvation history'.[46] Such a scheme, even if in locating Schweitzer it fairly represents his views and even if the rudiments of these interpretative tendencies precede Schweitzer, is only possible from such a later perspective, and it should not be turned round and read back entire into Schweitzer himself. For the latter, the operative question is not 'What kind of eschatology does Paul represent?' This is evident in his simple point that, with Paul as with Jesus, one is faced with an either/or and one *must* choose between an eschatological and a non-eschatological explanation of his thought. For 'late Jewish eschatology' is, for Schweitzer, the imminent expectation of the end of this world in the beginning of the next (clearly something either about to happen or not). Schweitzer felt that the greatest challenge facing Paul's modern interpreter is what to do with that uncharted region of Paul's thought which speaks of the presence of a new creation in Christ. Interpreters, virtually without exception, had given an ethical, spiritual explanation of this thought complex. Where the influence of Jewish eschatology was recognized, it was kept to the fringes or frontiers of Paul's thought. The reason for this state of affairs was, for Schweitzer, not far to seek: the pill was too hard to swallow. To attempt a consistent application of the categories of 'late Jewish eschatology' to these problem areas of Paul's theology[47] is to discover a Paul who meant just what he seems to have meant by all this. That is to say, he literally believed in the dominion of angel-powers, he literally expected the imminent end of this world and the arrival of the next, he literally preached the actual, (quasi-) physical union of the believer with Christ, participation with whom brought, in the present interim between his

46. So Beker, in *Paul's Apocalyptic Gospel: The Coming Triumph of God* (Philadelphia: Fortress Press, 1982), pp. 64-76. N.Q. Hamilton, *The Holy Spirit and Eschatology in Paul* (Edinburgh: Oliver and Boyd, 1957), writing from the perspective of O. Cullmann's 'salvation history' approach, similarly sets this approach over against Schweitzer, Dodd, and Bultmann as representatives of 'consistent' (or 'futuristic', or 'apocalyptic'), 'realized', and 'reinterpreted' approaches to Paul's eschatology. O. Cullmann, *Salvation in History* (trans. S.G. Sowers, *et al.*; London: SCM Press, 1967), pp. 28-64, and H. Ridderbos, *Paul: An Outline of His Theology* (trans. J.R. de Witt; Grand Rapids: Eerdmans, 1975), pp. 29-43, survey the same period from a 'salvation history' standpoint.

47. This is Schweitzer's programme of 'consistent' or 'thoroughgoing' (*konsequent*) eschatology.

advents, an anticipatory experience of the redemptive power of the new age coming (and now here). According to Schweitzer, this is not Paul being figurative or picturesque, nor less Paul being the occasional speculative mystic, to be ignored in such marginal flights for the sake of the timeless truth of redemption left at the centre. Rather, this is the real Paul, which is to say that Paul is nothing other than a person thinking within the world (as Schweitzer understood it) of first-century Jewish eschatology. The Paul of systematic theology or the Paul of popular piety—either was preferred to such a Paul as this. Theologians were simply not ready for the historical Paul. Thus even when the force of an explanation from eschatology was felt, the unavoidably 'either/or' nature of the case (as Schweitzer presents it) could only be got round by clumsily and desperately (we are still following Schweitzer) attempting to combine the Jewish and Hellenistic explanations, thereby seeing the eschatological world-view as evaporating into Greek philosophy, spirituality, or piety. Hence Schweitzer's burden of demonstrating both the remoteness of Paul's thought from Greek thought and Greek religion and the obvious (to Schweitzer) fit of Paul within Jewish eschatological expectation and speculation. Schweitzer insists that no such evaporation or marginalization of Paul's eschatological 'mysticism' will do—this is the heart of the true Paul, who is not understood at all if he is not understood thus.

Schweitzer, then, clearly was not concerned, as some have since been, to posit 'apocalyptic' (as against other eschatological interpretations) as the foundation of Paul's thought or of New Testament theology generally.[48] The background against which he operates is quite different. His fundamental task is to trace the strand of thought in Paul which he

48. Again, the point at issue here is not whether Schweitzer makes prominent use of apocalypses in his reconstruction of 'late Jewish eschatology', or whether this construct of his is a purely futuristic eschatology—he does, and it is. Rather, the simple point is that Schweitzer must not without further ado be placed with or understood in light of his later 'followers'. H.W. Boers, 'Apocalyptic Eschatology in 1 Corinthians 15: An Essay in Contemporary Interpretation', *Int* 21 (1967), pp. 50-65 (and n. 2), offers a fine example of how Schweitzer can be too easily assimilated into subsequent discussion: Boers has Schweitzer speak of 'apocalyptic eschatology', while pointing out in a footnote that, although Schweitzer wrote simply 'eschatology', by this 'he referred to what we today call distinctively "apocalypticism"'. While Boers may be right in seeing a family resemblance between Schweitzer's interpretation and later, 'apocalyptic' approaches, such an assimilation of Schweitzer into the latter obscures Schweitzer's own interpretative context.

comes to sum up as Paul's 'mysticism' of dying and rising with Christ, to spell out its eschatological structure and 'physical' character, and to demonstrate its centrality to Paul's thought. He attempts, that is, a history of religions account of Paul in terms of contemporary Jewish eschatology. This task he regards as the undischarged duty of historical study of Paul. For the tradition of liberal theological opinion against which he (primarily) operates had, in his view, simply been unable to follow a historical approach when such held in promise only a hopelessly remote Jewish eschatological Paul.

In the drive, still young in Schweitzer's day, for a history of religions approach locating Paul within his contemporary environment, attempts to account for Paul within Hellenism had a much easier time getting off the ground than approaches which sought a background for the apostle within Judaism, for the latter could fare no better than the estimate of Judaism itself, as Schweitzer himself notes, and in a climate which viewed the 'Jewish' negatively as 'particular', to be passed over in favour of the 'Greek' as 'universal', a Paul who transcended his Jewish roots had a distinct edge.[49] And even where Judaism was attended to, it was still often felt to be necessary to reach back to a pure biblical religion or forward to a rabbinic orthodoxy rather than give much space to 'late' eschatological (per-)versions of the Jewish religious traditions.[50] Only against such a background can Schweitzer's championing of 'late Judaism' be understood, which, one-sided though it must now appear, was not motivated by some apologetic reaction to an unholy alliance of Paul with Hellenism, but by the faulty directions theology had manifestly taken—indeed, in Schweitzer's day an alliance with such Judaism as one finds in the apocalypses would be the more fitting candidate for apologetic resistance.

In the interest of accuracy and in fairness to Schweitzer, then, one should ask about his commitment to a 'Jewish' and 'eschatological', not

49. Cf. Schweitzer, *Interpreters*, pp. X, 44-63; Meeks (ed.), *Writings*, pp. 273-76. On this period generally, see Kümmel, *History*, pp. 206-324; R. Morgan, *Biblical Interpretation*, pp. 93-132.

50. K. Koch, *The Rediscovery of Apocalyptic* (trans. M. Kohl; London: SCM Press, 1972), pp. 36-39, 49-50, 59-60, notes that, especially under the influence of such Old Testament scholars as J. Wellhausen and B. Duhm, who sharply differentiated between Israel and (inferior) Judaism, the idea of a 'prophetic connection' of early Christianity directly to the ancient biblical traditions had a long currency, while later scholarship similarly passed over 'apocalyptic' in preference to study of pharisaism and rabbinism (cf. Schweitzer, *Interpreters*, pp. 44-55).

an 'apocalyptic' (as understood in later discussion), interpretation of Paul. From a later perspective one is able to see clearly the character of realized eschatology, existentialist interpretation, and salvation history as (in part) alternative responses to Schweitzer's pioneering attempt at a consistently (and admittedly futuristic) eschatological interpretation of Paul, which interpretation is taken up, modified, and championed against these alternatives in this biblical-theological controversy by 'apocalyptic' interpreters such as Ernst Käsemann and Beker.[51] But, in an important (if only partial) sense, the true intent of Schweitzer's study of Paul is taken up by the history of religions researches of such scholars as W.D. Davies, H.J. Schoeps, and E.P. Sanders,[52] while Käsemann and

51. Cf. E. Käsemann, 'On the Subject of Primitive Christian Apocalyptic', in *New Testament Questions*, p. 109 n. 2; Käsemann sees himself as reviving the challenge of the 'rediscovery of primitive Christian apocalyptic' by, among others, Schweitzer, a challenge which has been 'more or less industriously eliminated or pushed away to the outer fringe of our awareness'.

52. W.D. Davies, *Paul and Rabbinic Judaism: Some Rabbinic Elements in Pauline Theology* (London: SPCK, 2nd edn, 1955); H.J. Schoeps, *Paul: The Theology of the Apostle in the Light of Jewish Religious History* (trans. H. Knight; London: Lutterworth, 1961); Sanders, *Paul*. These three do not form a Schweitzer 'school', but they continue his central aim and interact with his interpretation. The contrast set up here between a history of religions and a biblical-theological agenda should not be pressed too hard, nor is it denied that both might coexist in Schweitzer himself, so that both these sets of scholars (for whom also these two might coexist) may be to some degree continuing his work. But the irony is noted that those who claim (somewhat anachronistically, it is suggested here) to resurrect Schweitzer's appeal do not strike at his centre so much as those who more quietly continue his chief aim. The kinship between Schweitzer, Davies, Schoeps, and Sanders, and the resulting influence of Schweitzer right down to the present moment in Pauline studies, cannot be pursued here, as the present pursuit is not of the fortunes of Schweitzer's interpretation as such, but of 'apocalyptic' interpretation of Paul, under which rubric Käsemann and Beker operate and within which they place Schweitzer. But that these latter figures tell much less than the full story of Schweitzer's interpretation, and that they may in fact be subtly misleading, should not escape attention. A third prominent branch of Pauline interpretation, which combines somewhat these history of religions and biblical-theological strands, revealing in the process another possible configuration of indebtedness to Schweitzer, is the 'salvation history' approach. This approach is represented by, for example, O. Cullmann (preceded in some respects by C.H. Dodd), J. Munck (who, via K. Stendahl, connects with the history of religions tradition of Sanders, issuing in current 'new perspective' interpretation), and H. Ridderbos. As should be becoming clear, it is not at all fanciful to see Schweitzer and the 'new phase' behind a great deal of subsequent Pauline interpretation, traversing various school lines.

Beker, who do indeed offer a fair rendition of Schweitzer's 'biting-the-bullet' rhetoric of bracing oneself for the hard truth about the distant, alien, eschatological Paul, represent a 'subsidiary crater' within the main rim of Schweitzer's history of religions intent. They do not, or not exclusively anyway, bear the mantle of Schweitzer, all talk of championing his cause aside.

But having taken care to note such points of discontinuity, one must then acknowledge the real continuity between Schweitzer's approach and later 'apocalyptic' approaches which appeal to his beginning. For it is his interpretative approach generally which is to be taken up in 'apocalyptic' interpretation, and his tendencies are reflected in later discussion. For Schweitzer, 'late Jewish eschatology', as distinct from earlier prophetic eschatology, is universal, not national, transcendent, not this-worldly, cosmic, not individualistic, and is generally of a heightened intensity; its basic structure and character is summed up in the dualism of the ages. Paul reflects this two-age mentality, this cosmic perspective, and this eschatological intensity. Also, significantly, Paul's eschatological inheritance from this 'late Jewish' theology consists entirely of futuristic expectations—the realized elements in his thought are due to Paul's own Christian reflection on the Christ event and the adjustment this demands of his inherited scheme. For Schweitzer, the interpreter of Paul only succeeds to the degree that he or she successfully reveals the systematic nature of Paul's thought, and Schweitzer's eschatological interpretation manages just this, he contends. Indeed, Beker's assertion that 'only a consistent apocalyptic interpretation of Paul's thought is able to demonstrate its fundamental coherence',[53] granted the warnings here registered against an anachronistic perception of Schweitzer, speaks well for the latter, whose aspirations toward synthesis, like Beker's own, are pursued through an eschatological interpretation, failing which, presumably, interpretative chaos ensues.

## The Legacy of Schweitzer

This is not intended as an apology for Schweitzer. However, if 'Paul and apocalyptic' is to be treated, clarity on the history of the question can only be of benefit. Furthermore, Schweitzer is a window to the world of much twentieth-century interpretation of Paul, an observation which, although it cannot be fully followed through here, justifies the amount of

53. Beker, *Paul*, p. 143.

attention given Schweitzer, including the brief notice of his influence now attempted.

Although it is no part of the present task to evaluate the various works reviewed other than as they relate to the central theme, since such space has been devoted to a 'quest for the historical Schweitzer' it is fitting on balance to note some of his possible shortcomings: his complete dismissal of Hellenistic influences on Paul, even if largely vindicated by later trends, is surely extreme;[54] his talk of 'mysticism' in Paul has been a cause for offence;[55] and few indeed would share his confidence either in his reconstruction of a coherent 'late Jewish eschatology' from *1 Enoch*, the *Psalms of Solomon, 4 Ezra*, and *2 Baruch*[56] or in his

54. For subsequent reactions, see for example H.J. Schoeps, *Paul*, pp. 13-50; H. Koester, 'Paul and Hellenism', in J.P. Hyatt (ed.), *The Bible in Modern Scholarship* (Nashville: Abingdon Press, 1965), pp. 187-95; W.D. Davies, 'Paul and Judaism', in Hyatt (ed.), *The Bible in Modern Scholarship*, pp. 178-86.

55. Often unfairly, for as Sanders notes the term has been rejected 'on the basis of definitions which Schweitzer himself would not have accepted' (*Paul*, pp. 434-35). Schweitzer's 'mysticism' has passed into general acceptance as 'participation' in Christ. Barrett's criticism on this point is hardly recognizable as directed against Schweitzer: 'Paul was a theologian rather than a mystic. He was, as H.J. Schoeps has said, a thinker of the post-messianic situation. Jesus had born the messianic affliction; the risen Jesus was the first-fruits of the dead. But when Paul asserts that we, too, in Christ, have passed these milestones in the story of salvation he is making an objective theological not a subjective mystical proposition' (Barrett, 'Schweitzer', p. 10). One must ask what Schweitzer could possibly have done to make more clear that Paul is a thinker and that his 'dying and rising' points to objective reality (cf. Schweitzer, *Interpreters*, pp. 106-107, 154-59, 161, 162-66, 172, 247, and *passim*, and *idem, Mysticism*, pp. *1-140*). Incidentally, Schoeps (*Paul*, p. 42) describes Schweitzer as presenting Paul as a theologian of the post-messianic situation. Schoeps claims (p. 46) that Schweitzer goes too far in regarding Paul as a logical, systematic thinker—a much more intelligible criticism. Similarly misleading is Barrett's having Schweitzer say that Paul 'transform[ed] eschatology into mysticism' (Barrett, 'Schweitzer', p. 8), as Schweitzer's 'mysticism' is eschatological through and through. No doubt Schweitzer's somewhat unfortunate choice of the term 'mysticism' has been a source of confusion and reveals Schweitzer as a victim of a terminological fashion of his day (see further in Meeks [ed.], *Writings*, pp. 361-64, 374-409).

56. Cf. Thiselton, 'Schweitzer', pp. 133, 136; T.F. Glasson, 'Schweitzer's Influence—Blessing or Bane?', *JTS* 28 (1977), pp. 289-302, forcefully highlights the diversity of this material. Schweitzer's use of the literature generally, for example on the matter of dating, would now be questioned and at many points updated or rejected outright. No judgment is passed here on Schweitzer's knowledge of the literature, other than to say, as already noted, that he (like everyone else) follows the consensus

reconstruction of Paul's eschatology and of the logic by which Paul adapted his system.[57] Nevertheless, Schweitzer's imposing work has inspired confidence, if not always in detail, at least in its general sweep. For subsequent study has largely vindicated some of his major emphases: his general emphasis on the primacy of Paul's Jewish heritage and the eschatological nature of his thought has largely been followed;[58] his highlighting of 'participation' and 'anticipation', of Paul's corporate conceptions and the 'already/not yet' tension in his thought, was a

approach as represented in the handbooks. The judgment of R.H. Charles is no doubt extreme: 'Since Schweitzer's Eschatological studies show no knowledge of original documents and hardly any of first-hand works on the documents, and since further they make no fresh contribution to the subject, no notice is taken of him in this edition' (*A Critical History of the Doctrine of a Future Life in Israel, in Judaism, and in Christianity*, [London: A. & C. Black, 2nd edn, 1913 (1899)], p. viii). Whatever the no doubt inestimable contributions of Charles, it is Schweitzer, even if only as popularizer, whose work forms the watershed insofar as applying 'late Jewish eschatology' to the New Testament is concerned.

57. Cf. Sanders, *Paul*, pp. 452-53: 'We could do no better than guess by what chain of reasoning or under what history-of-religions influence' Paul arrived at his 'participation'; Schweitzer's two-resurrection scheme has not proved persuasive—cf. Sanders, *Paul*, p. 434.

58. W.D. Davies, 'Paul and Judaism', rightly notes that subsequent investigation highlights the variety within the Judaism of Paul's day, the complexity of the relation between Palestinian and diaspora Judaism, and of that between Judaism and Hellenism—'Judaism has emerged as more varied, changing, and complicated than Schweitzer could have appreciated' (p. 183; Davies here anticipates such developments as the conclusions of M. Hengel, *Judaism and Hellenism* [trans. J. Bowden; London: SCM Press, 1974]). No doubt Schweitzer's corrective emphasis on eschatology resulted in an imbalance (p. 186), but Davies's claim (unsupported by reference to Schweitzer's work on Paul) that Schweitzer 'insisted' on 'the old dichotomy between apocalyptic and Pharisaism', seeing 'apocalyptic' as 'utterly divorced from...the Rabbis' and 'opposed to the learning of the Scribes', so that Paul is purely 'apocalyptic', 'divorced from Pharisaism and other first-century currents', is simply mistaken. Schweitzer speaks of 'late Jewish eschatology' as an aspect of the 'Rabbinism' of Paul's day, locating Paul within the eschatology of contemporary 'Scribism' (*Interpreters*, pp. 48-50; *Mysticism*, pp. 89-90). (See also Davies, *Paul*, p. 10, where a reference to Schweitzer's *Interpreters* is taken somewhat out of context, furthermore overlooking the earlier and more provisional character of this presentation as against *Mysticism*.) Davies at times drives an unnecessary and somewhat imaginary wedge between himself and Schweitzer. Understandably, one emphasizes the distance between oneself and one so near; but the degree to which Davies, while going his own distinctive way, is continuing and refining Schweitzer's search for an eschatological Paul should not be overlooked.

foreboding of things to come;[59] and he contributed to and furthered a still current debate over the related questions of the nature and place of justification by faith in Paul, his understanding of the Law, the centre of his thought, and the preferred method of reconstructing his theology.[60]

Pauline theology before Schweitzer, according, at least, to his own history of research, was the handmaid either to a redemption-religion whose inspiration lay in the Protestant Reformation or to the Kingdom-of-God piety of *Kulturprotestantismus*.[61] Both traditional Protestant piety centring on justification by faith and liberal Protestant piety pursuing a social agenda must make way, insofar as a historical reading is concerned (so Schweitzer), for the 'eschatological Paul'. The 'powers', the 'two ages', and 'participation in Christ' typically receive quite a different emphasis and expression in the period since Schweitzer than they did in the heyday of these former interpretative traditions. Ever since Schweitzer, these and associated categories have become commonplace, and in the general eschatological sense on which he insisted. Schweitzer presides over the dawning of the 'new phase' in interpreting Paul, an approach characterized by the dual emphasis on an eschatological matrix and a cosmic redemption.[62] He has altered the landscape of

59. Cf. Sanders, *Paul*, pp. 434-42; Thiselton, 'Schweitzer', pp. 135-36.

60. The latest major instalment of the dialogue (that is, as these topics relate to the matter of an 'apocalyptic' Paul), now with 'apocalyptic' securely in place as the operative term, is the synthesis of Beker, to whom I shall turn in due course. Such questions are also central to the history of religions research indicated above as continuing Schweitzer's main aim. Here a question which organizes many of these smaller ones is the matter of whether Paul's thought runs from plight to solution. For the 'new phase', effected by Wrede and Schweitzer and continued in a sense by Davies, Paul's Christian conceptions are significantly prepared for by prior convictions into which the awaited and now finally achieved reality of the Messiah might be fitted. This is a 'plight-to-solution' interpretation which Sanders attempts to shut down, but which remains a topic of debate.

61. Schweitzer, *Mysticism*, pp. 381; as for Catholic thought, it, like traditional Protestantism, is for Schweitzer a non-eschatological redemption religion focusing on an atoning death for sins; both alike for Schweitzer are determined by Hellenized, not Pauline, Christianity.

62. These two emphases are the eschatological and the 'physical' aspects of Paul's 'mysticism', his participatory eschatology. This 'new phase', as noted above, dates from Wrede and Schweitzer (and, as we saw, Schweitzer presses for elaboration on these two central emphases from Wrede's interpretation). Present 'new perspective' thought makes similarly sweeping claims for its own revolutionizing achievements; but S. Westerholm has shown that Wrede and Schweitzer stand behind these more

Pauline studies. In many ways the clock cannot be turned back on Schweitzer and the eschatological Paul, for Schweitzer has remapped the terrain and redrawn the contours of its central object, namely, Paul himself, such that further progress is forced to take account of Schweitzer. Indeed, for all his idiosyncrasies, Schweitzer's review of former study, passed through the filter of his own exposition, so crystallizes the issues which are to dominate subsequent reflection that he must become both the point of departure and a touchstone constantly to be returned to where 'apocalyptic' interpretation of Paul is concerned.[63] In the end, Schweitzer's legacy, or so it would seem, is an 'eschatological Paul' whom, as such, he takes to be to us a dead figure, 'intruding out of distant ages past'.

In the story which we have largely been following, which narrative is largely Schweitzer's own, Schweitzer holds (need it be said?) a rather congratulatory place. It is not out of any direct desire to subvert this narrative that I, briefly, shift to another, one in which Schweitzer's position is much more ambivalent (but on the whole painted in darker tones). This is not really another story at all, but rather the broader one in which, it is held, the present narrative must be seen—this is a move toward the historicizing of 'the unleashing of the eschatological Paul'. The great demystifiers—and this is exactly what Schweitzer is for theology—seem never to look inward. To turn their critique in on itself and demystify the demystifier, in imitation, while seemingly more deflatory than flattery, is in fact the sincerest form of the latter, and a

recent developments (see *Israel's Law*, pp. 15-32). Wrede and Schweitzer, with their combination of history of religions and theological insight, still hold sway, marking a turning point both for discussion of the Law and justification/righteousness in Paul and for the more encompassing set of issues concerning Paul and eschatology.

63. T. Wright is able to focus fifty years of subsequent Pauline studies through Schweitzer in the form of four sets of concerns: history of religions, theology (of Paul), exegesis, and modern appropriation (Neill and Wright, *Interpretation*, pp. 408-10). That Schweitzer put his finger on much of what, on anyone's view, is important in reading Paul helps explain why what is, from Schweitzer to Bultmann to Käsemann, such a German, and particularly Lutheran, dialogue so captivates Pauline studies as a whole. That the construct 'apocalyptic' (versus other eschatological schemes) came to be attached to and characterize an important strand of the dialogue lies, however, at the door of those to whom Schweitzer left the discussion. But this is not the first time that a 'legitimizing' historical question bears the strain of concerns theological at heart, as Schweitzer himself seems to have had a knack for discerning.

more fitting tribute to Schweitzer than endless congratulation. The question now is: what is it that Schweitzer has really unleashed?

The answer which perhaps first springs to mind (so subtly and thoroughly has Schweitzer's story worked its way into our critical psyche) is that Schweitzer has unleashed the full implications of the historical ideal in New Testament criticism. He has forced a reckoning with eschatology in reading Paul, a hard look at the uncomfortable facts. Schweitzer has dragged New Testament theologians kicking and screaming into a position in which the obvious may no longer be denied. He has kept us honest. But this is to operate entirely within Schweitzer's narrative, a putting of the case in obvious continuity with and dependence on him. But time has done its work, now making Schweitzer's perspective the one operating behind our backs, the one out of which we see, think, value—a potentially corrupting state of affairs for a purely historical reading, if that is what one is after.

We are now operating on the self-consciously hermeneutical level to which Schweitzer's rhetoric of distance, of self-denial, of reverence for the facts provides an entrée (if we choose to see it so). This larger narrative takes us back a step, to the Enlightenment, and back a step further, to the Reformation, before thrusting us back into the present. But first I must consider the bridge which Schweitzer provides to this broader narrative.

Much of the above has been concerned with positioning Schweitzer. But I have not merely been after a cool exposition of Schweitzer's interpretation, even if I have largely operated in that mode. I want also to inquire in a general way as to what Schweitzer is doing, to whom, and why. I attempt, then, to position him not just in terms of ideas, interpretations, critical positions in Pauline theology, but ideologically— Schweitzer's critical work cries out for this.

In various ways, Schweitzer positions himself, and this variously surfacing self-understanding is important for the purposes at hand. Returning to Schweitzer's *Mysticism*, his most distant self-connection is with Paul himself: 'In Paul, the first Christian thinker set himself against the authority of the Church, *and shared the fate of those who have since made the same attempt. And both in this first case and later on* it came about that *the truth of reflection* which had been *opposed to the Church's doctrine* afterwards *became a commonplace of orthodox theology*' (p. 204). The emphasis I have added to Schweitzer's words on Paul highlights what must be a thinly-veiled self-reference. Schweitzer's reflections on 'the permanent elements' in Paul's thought elaborate this self-connection:

> Paul vindicated for all time the rights of thought in Christianity. Above belief which drew its authority from tradition, he set the knowledge which came from the Spirit of Christ. There lives in him an unbounded and undeviating reverence for truth. He will consent only to a limitation of liberty laid on him by the law of love, not to one imposed by doctrinal authority.
>
> Moreover, he is no mere revolutionary. He takes the faith of the Primitive-Christian community as his starting-point: only he will not consent to halt where it comes to an end, but claims the right to think out his thoughts about Christ to their conclusion, without caring whether the truths which he thereby reaches have ever come within the purview of the faith held by the Christian community and been recognised by it.
>
> The result of this first appearance of thought in Christianity is calculated to justify, for all periods, the confidence that faith has nothing to fear from thinking, even when the latter disturbs its peace and raises a debate which appears to promise no good results for the religious life (p. 376).

This very general 'permanent element' of the championing of reason, knowledge, and truth over against authority, belief, and tradition is then made more specific, making more pointed the covert theme of Schweitzer as 'new Paul':

> Christianity can only become the living truth for successive generations *if thinkers constantly arise within it who, in the Spirit of Jesus, make belief in Him capable of intellectual apprehension in the thought-forms of the world-view proper to their time...*If the debate between tradition and thought falls silent, Christian truth suffers, and with it Christian intellectual integrity. This is why it is so deeply significant that Paul undertakes as an entirely obvious duty to think out Christianity in its whole scope and its whole depth by the use of the materials provided by the eschatological world-view of his time (p. 377, emphasis added).

Schweitzer continues, focusing the self-connection still more sharply: 'But it is not merely that Paul was the first to champion the rights of thought in Christianity; he has also shown it, for all time, the way it was to go. His great achievement was to grasp, as the thing essential to being a Christian, the experience of union with Christ' (p. 377).

Moving a bit closer to home, and a bit more down to earth, Schweitzer proceeds to spell out the significance of Paul's 'great achievement'. For Paul's 'mysticism' was able to hold in their intimate connection redemption, presently experienced and completely realized in the future, and the expectation of the Kingdom of God. This sense of balance eludes subsequent Christian thought, for one always seems to recede as the other is grasped, resulting in an 'incomplete Christianity', as when liberal Christianity retains a hope of the Kingdom but finds no place 'for any living concept of redemption through Christ', while traditional Reformation theology prizes such redemption but leaves belief in the Kingdom 'undeveloped' and devoid of 'any living conviction' (pp. 382-83). The loss of Paul's 'mysticism' is an 'impoverishment' from which 'Christianity has hardly recovered to this day' (p. 375). This backdrop of darkness drawn, Schweitzer is ready to emerge as a 'new Luther', ushering in a greater and more far-reaching reformation:

> Great has been the work as a reforming influence which Paul, by his doctrine of justification by faith alone, has accomplished in opposition to the spirit of work-righteousness in Christianity. Still greater will be the work which he will do when his mystical doctrine of being redeemed into the Kingdom of God, through union with Christ, begins to bring quietly to bear upon us the power which lies within it (p. 385).

(Although neither of the connections suggested here, Schweitzer as 'new Paul' and as 'new Luther', is made unequivocally explicit—perhaps leaving some readers shy of affirming this reading—for myself, Schweitzer seems to have stopped, as decorum demands, just short of blurting it out.)

Switching back for a moment to Schweitzer's canonization of Paul as 'the patron-saint of thought in Christianity', Schweitzer asserts 'that thinking Christianity is to have its rights within believing Christianity, and that the Little-faiths will never succeed in suppressing loyalty to truth' (p. 377). Such 'Little-faiths' recall to mind another even nearer self-connection, as a no doubt similar group was met above at the conclusion to Schweitzer's *Interpreters*, sinking in the storm of Schweitzer's 'positive criticism'—here we meet Schweitzer as 'new Baur'. F.C. Baur, cited by one very keen on such things as offering 'the first New Testament theology that can be regarded as essentially historical',[64] is, for Schweitzer, since 'patron-saint' is taken, perhaps 'grand-godfather' of a purely historical ideal in New Testament criticism:

> When Baur and his followers made their profession of an unbiased free investigation they could have had no inkling that it would become so difficult for a later generation to remain true to this principle...[T]o follow

---

64. H. Räisänen, *Beyond New Testament Theology* (London: SCM Press/ Philadelphia: Trinity, 1990), p. 8.

a purely historical method meant, as things stood at the beginning of the
twentieth century, to be left with an entirely temporally conditioned
Paulinism, of which modern ways of thought could make nothing, and to
trace out a system which for our religion is dead.[65]

Baur conceived of New Testament theology as 'the first phase of the
history of doctrine. The task was to present what the biblical writers
believed or considered true, irrespective of the interpreter's own opinion
about it', tracing the history of thought with emphasis on 'the actual
historical relationships between these teachings as they developed'.[66]
Were Schweitzer to be understood within the context of New Testament
theology, as he rarely is but no doubt should be (among other contexts),
his study of Jesus, Paul, and early Christianity (a virtual New Testament
theology), following as it does the logic of his own 'positive criticism' in
conscious imitation of Baur but attempting to find a firmer footing,
suggests a connection which would have to be taken into account.
Another connection with another, nearer theoretician, whom Schweitzer
cites with approval in his *Interpreters* in connection with Holtzmann,[67]
would also call for consideration. This is, of course, Wrede, whose
metacritical programme for New Testament theology (implemented to a
considerable degree by Schweitzer, though this has gone generally
unacknowledged) is discussed below, but whom, for the moment, we
take as a bridge to the final instance of self-positioning expressive of
Schweitzer's self-understanding, namely the 'new phase' in interpreting
Paul, effected decisively by Wrede and Schweitzer.

Enough has been said about the character of this programmatic shift
in Pauline theology—its emphasis on the eschatological matrix and the
cosmic dimensions of Paul's participatory eschatology. What is now of
interest is the rhetoric by which Schweitzer signals this new phase, a
rhetoric everywhere apparent above, but up until now passing largely
unremarked. We could capture this rhetoric well, and offer a fair paraphrase of, or gloss on, Schweitzer's whole agenda, by saying that
Schweitzer calls for theology finally to face the music, to relinquish all
the surrogate Pauls who have served so well and meet the real Paul,
who in the very moment he becomes real becomes really, frightfully

65. Schweitzer, *Interpreters*, p. 166.
66. H.W. Boers, *What is New Testament Theology? The Rise of Criticism and
the Problem of a Theology of the New Testament* (Philadelphia: Fortress Press,
1979), p. 40.
67. Schweitzer, *Interpreters*, p. 100.

*distant*. This real, historical Paul evaporates before the eyes, leaving the barest of trails—as little in fact to grab hold of in the end as the vaporous Pauls he was called forth to dissipate. The only enticement Schweitzer can offer to lead theologians to renounce their fictitious Pauls, even, as it were, for Paul's own sake, is to suggest that here integrity is the price paid for utility, reality the price for familiarity. Thus, Schweitzer's rhetoric, in his history of research and in his own exposition, is everywhere one of truth, of faithfulness and allegiance to a common historical ideal which cannot be gone back upon, a matter requiring courage and resolve, a matter calling for self-denial and appealing to self-evidence. Schweitzer's story is well before us now, peopled with now familiar villains (or rogues, at least), liberal and orthodox alike, who have not been able to bring themselves to embrace this distant, eschatological Paul, but only able to delay the inevitable by writing over, like a palimpsest, the real Paul with the Paul of their hearts and fancies, the Paul of justification by faith or of the social Kingdom of God. Schweitzer can just manage patience, however, as their day is passing, as pass it must, and truth's day is coming, as come it will—time will effect the change that valour fails before. The David of the facts meets the Goliath of self-will. The theme of Schweitzer's story, in classic style, is human folly.

It is a measure of the force of Schweitzer's rhetoric that virtually all must assent. But the upshot of Schweitzer's cautionary tale, with which biblical criticism has kept generations of young scholars on the safe path to grandma's house and out of the clutches of the big bad wolf,[68] may leave us ambivalent. Our doubts may rest not so much with critical results as with this critical ethos. For the dénouement of Schweitzer's narrative, which climaxes in the recovery of the eschatological Paul, is the breaking of the nexus of human folly—the *facts* have won the day, since we finally let down the guard of our preferences. Schweitzer does not impose an agenda on the critical task of Pauline theology—he discovers the language which Pauline theology itself would speak if speak it could (and speak it has through him).

Schweitzer himself, then, has an original and rather self-congratulatory role in his own story (though he modestly gives all the credit to the facts themselves, the five smooth stones in his pouch). But a nagging scepticism, which surely Schweitzer himself taught us if he taught us anything, begs to broaden the narrative. This done, Schweitzer is less the new beginning than the outcome of an inexorable process, less the prophet

---

68. (Symbols I shall leave as ambiguous as does the traditional fairy tale.)

than the (dimly) prophesied. Rather than dwell upon the irresistible force levelled by Schweitzer and the facts against the immovable object of tradition, the force behind them comes in for consideration—Schweitzer rides in now not on a thunderbolt but on the crest of a wave.

The wave on whose crest Schweitzer comes in had broken and surged upward on the rocks of the Reformation—this swell is the rise of historical consciousness.

> Christian theology through the middle ages did not try to think the thoughts of the biblical writers *as distinct from their own*. They thought their own thoughts, which they took for granted as being in continuity with those of the biblical writers. A double continuity was presumed: the material on which Christian thought was based had been provided by the biblical writers, and the tradition of the ongoing life and thought of the church bridged the historical gap separating the Bible from contemporary Christianity.[69]

But this contemporaneity and continuity with the past dissolved 'as a result of the Reformation and the Reformer's insistence on Scripture as the sole basis and norm for all Christian life and thought'.[70]

> The Bible was no longer an integral, contemporary part of the living religion but was separated from it by an intervening history, that very history of the ongoing life of the church which had previously provided continuity with the Bible. A historical consciousness thus arose with the Reformation. This was not immediately recognized, but it was only a question of time before it began to become clear, and historical criticism would emerge.[71]

This move, by which the past became the *past*, was meant to establish more firmly the authority of scripture by placing it as judge over against the church. But, this done, it is not as drastic an inversion as it might at first appear—it is, in fact, inexorable, an unforeseen turn of the same trajectory—for the church to come to stand as judge over against scripture. Furthermore, while formerly allegorical reading reinforced the

---

69. Boers, *What is New Testament Theology?*, p. 16.

70. Boers, *What is New Testament Theology?*, p. 17.

71. Boers, *What is New Testament Theology?*, p. 17. Cf. H.W. Frei, *The Eclipse of Biblical Narrative: A Study in Eighteenth and Nineteenth Century Hermeneutics* (New Haven: Yale, 1974): as a result of this emergence of criticism, 'it is no exaggeration to say that all across the theological spectrum the great reversal had taken place; interpretation was a matter of fitting the biblical story into another world with another story rather than incorporating that world into the biblical story' (p. 130).

contemporaneity of tradition, the Reformers 'tried to provide an immediacy with the Bible despite the historical distance, by an attentive listening to what it said, which meant a binding to the actual words, not a search for hidden meanings behind the words as in an allegorical interpretation'.[72] The singular, clear, literal meaning becomes the interpretative goal. Now, with such former reading strategies denied, the Bible is in an almost adversarial role over against the church (again, a role which may be reversed), which now must earn its bread by the sweat of its brow.

> If it was recognized that the Bible was not an integral, contemporaneous part of the living religion but was separated from it historically, it followed that theology also had to distinguish between contemporary thinking and that of the Bible. That is, Christianity could no longer think its own thoughts as if they were identical with the Bible's thoughts. It could no longer merely draw the material for its thinking from the Bible. It had to think the very thoughts of the biblical writers rather than its own and to interpret the former as they related to the contemporary life of the church...[73]

Thus the pastness of the past begins to settle in, while the rudiments of a rapprochement are already in place in an implicit methodical separation between the 'then' and the 'now'.[75] The logic of this movement is well captured by Hans-Georg Gadamer:

> It seems...to be generally characteristic of the emergence of the 'hermeneutical' problem that something *distant* has to be brought close, a certain strangeness overcome, a bridge built between the once and the now.

72. Boers, *What is New Testament Theology?*, pp. 17-18. See further on allegorical interpretation, Andrew Louth, 'Allegorical Interpretation', in Coggins and Houlder (eds.), *Dictionary of Biblical Interpretation*, pp. 12-15; other relevant articles in this dictionary include G.R. Evans, 'Mediaeval Interpretation', pp. 438-40; A.E. McGrath, 'Reformation', pp. 582-85; F. Watson, 'Enlightenment', pp. 191-94.

73. Boers, *What is New Testament Theology?*, p. 17.

74. A.C. Thiselton, *The Two Horizons: New Testament Hermeneutics and Philosophical Description with Special Reference to Heidegger Bultmann, Gadamer, and Wittgenstein* (Grand Rapids: Eerdmans, 1980), pp. 51-84, focuses on this rise of the 'pastness of the past' with special reference to its more recent implications (see pp. 63-69 on the rise of 'historical consciousness'). On this whole development, see also Kümmel, *History*; E. Krentz, *The Historical-Critical Method* (Philadelphia: Fortress Press, 1975); A.C. Thiselton, *New Horizons in Hermeneutics: The Theory and Practice of Transforming Biblical Reading* (Grand Rapids: Zondervan, 1992), pp. 142-203.

Thus hermeneutics, as a general attitude over against the world, came into its own in modern times, which had become aware of the temporal distance separating us from antiquity and of the relativity of the life-worlds of different cultural traditions. Something of this awareness was contained in the theological claim of Reformation biblical exegesis (in the principle of *sola scriptura*), but its true unfolding only came about when a 'historical consciousness' arose in the Enlightenment...and matured in the romantic period...[75]

It is this story—a story that is still being written—which provides the broader narrative into which the story of Schweitzer and the eschatological Paul must be placed.

The contribution of the Enlightenment to the development of the plot set in play by the Reformation may for the present purposes be glimpsed in Johann Philipp Gabler's 1787 Altdorf inaugural lecture 'On the Proper Distinction between Biblical and Dogmatic Theology and the Specific Objectives of Each'.[76] The backdrop of Gabler's 'proper distinction' is the Babel of interpretive voices heard in the land. On the one hand, a vital agreement obtains:

> All who are devoted to the sacred faith of Christianity, most worthy listeners, profess with one united voice that the sacred books, especially of the New Testament, are the one clear source from which all true knowledge of the Christian religion is drawn. And they profess too that these books are the only secure sanctuary to which we can flee in the face of the ambiguity and vicissitude of human knowledge, if we aspire to a solid understanding of divine matters and if we wish to obtain a firm and certain hope of salvation (p. 134).

75. H.-G. Gadamer, *Philosophical Hermeneutics* (trans. and ed., D.E. Linge; Berkeley: University of California Press, 1976), pp. 22-23; cf. *idem, Truth and Method* (trans. and rev., J. Weinsheimer and D.G. Marshall; New York: Crossroad, 2nd rev. edn, 1989), pp. 174-75, and Gadamer's 'Foreword to the Second [German] Edition', p. xxxiii; *idem, Philosophical Hermeneutics*, pp. 45-47; *idem, Reason in the Age of Science* (trans. F.G. Lawrence; Cambridge, MA: MIT, 1981), pp. 93-95 (pp. 88-101 provide a brief, lucid account of the historical background of contemporary hermeneutics), pp. 123-24, 127-28.

76. Translated from the Latin by John Sandys-Wunsch and Laurance Eldridge in 'J.P. Gabler and the Distinction between Biblical and Dogmatic Theology: Translation, Commentary, and Discussion of His Originality', *SJT* 33 (1980), pp. 133-58 (trans. pp. 134-44). On Gabler see also Boers, *What is New Testament Theology?*, pp. 23-38; R. Morgan, 'Gabler's Bicentenary', *ExpTim* 98 (1987), pp. 164-68; Räisänen, *Beyond New Testament Theology*, pp. 3-5.

Given such presumed agreement on the singular source of the faith and the clarity and constancy of that source (among Protestant listeners, at least, who presumably exhaust the category of those 'devoted to the sacred faith of Christianity', for *sola scriptura* could want no better voice than Gabler gives it), why the confusion of tongues? Through some combination of ignorance and malice, no doubt, many are compelled 'to solidify the frothiness of [their] opinions' by giving 'a divine appearance to their human ideas' (p. 135). At root the problem lies with 'the neglected distinction between religion and theology', a distinction which translates into that between biblical and dogmatic theology—and, ultimately, that between history and theology—which 'must be more sharply distinguished...than has been common practice up to now' (pp. 136-37). 'There is truly a biblical theology, of historical origin, conveying what the holy writers felt about divine matters; on the other hand there is a dogmatic theology of didactic origin, teaching what each theologian philosophises rationally about divine things, according to the measure of his ability or of the times, age, place, sect, school, and other similar factors' (p. 137). Natural inclinations and personal preferences are to be disciplined and kept in check, as when, at the historical level, diversity and contingency are acknowledged and inspiration (which is to be proved, not assumed) is disregarded: 'If we abandon this straight road, even though it is troublesome and of little delight, it can only result in our wandering into some deviation or uncertainty', but if kept to, this road leads to 'the happy appearance of biblical theology, pure and unmixed with foreign things' (pp. 139, 142). Indeed, it is surely this 'straight road' of Reason that sets 'our age' apart from 'the scholastic theology of the Middle Ages, covered with the thick gloom of barbarity', as we proceed 'with reason and not with fear or bias'; 'the nature of our age urgently demands that we...teach accurately the harmony of divine dogmatics and the principles of human reason' (pp. 137, 143, 144). Our moment is portentous, but our tools are equal to the task.

It is a measure of the time that has passed that Gabler could, in part, pitch his appeal for a 'two-stage' approach as a careful separation between the divine (timeless) and the human (timebound) and as a process carried out in service of simple faith.[77] Dating Gabler even more

---

77. Gabler's two stages are actually three, as the first is really two: a historical-critical sifting of the biblical material and then, within Scripture itself, a separation of contingent and particular from necessary and universal, a separation between the human and divine, and of the timebound from the timeless and eternally valid, this

severely is his Enlightenment confidence that biblical scholarship with its critical methods could unite the voices of all right-thinking people of good will into one harmonious strain.[78] If scripture is the 'one clear source' of the faith, the 'only secure sanctuary' in our flight from the uncertainties of human knowledge, affording 'a solid understanding of divine matters' and 'a firm and certain hope of salvation', it is now finally understood that it is such only by the careful observance of something like Gabler's methodological strictures, whereby 'at last a clear sacred Scripture will be selected..., made up of passages which are appropriate to the Christian religion of all times' (p. 143). The interpretative, theological task of each generation ought to 'build only upon these firmly established foundations' of a critically purified scripture (p. 144).

If Gabler may be considered as giving a qualified 'go-ahead' to a 'two-stage' method, a passing century finds William Wrede out of patience and throwing caution to the wind.[79] Wrede's 'The Task and Method of "New Testament Theology"' (1897)[80] cuts right to the point in its opening section, as if to cover the metacritical ground swiftly and sharply.[81] Looking back to Gabler's ideal, he asks whether, after more than a century of lip service and ample chance to get it right, New

core then being passed on for systematic theological reflection (pp. 140-44).

78. See Sandys-Wunsch, 'Commentary and Summary', pp. 144-46. Gabler's contemporary, Immanuel Kant, comments in *Critique of Pure Reason*, p. 9 n. (following on from the citation at the head of the present chapter): 'Religion through its sanctity, and law-giving through its majesty, may seek to exempt themselves from it [criticism]. But they then awaken just suspicion, and cannot claim the sincere respect which reason accords only to that which has been able to sustain the test of free and open examination'.

79. On the period so quickly passed over, and including Wrede, see R. Morgan, 'A Straussian Question to "New Testament Theology"', *NTS* 23 (1977), pp. 243-65; 'F.C. Baur's Lectures on New Testament Theology', *ExpTim* 88 (1977), pp. 202-206; 'Introduction: The Nature of New Testament Theology', in *The Nature of New Testament Theology: The Contribution of William Wrede and Adolf Schlatter* (ed. and trans. R. Morgan; London: SCM Press, 1973); Boers, *What is New Testament Theology?*, pp. 39-60; Räisänen, *Beyond New Testament Theology*, pp. 6-18; for other surveys see Kümmel, *History*; G.F. Hasel, *New Testament Theology: Basic Issues in the Current Debate* (Grand Rapids: Eerdmans, 1978), pp. 13-51; these various works point to much additional bibliography.

80. ET in R. Morgan (ed.), *Nature*, pp. 68-116, 182-93.

81. 'I do not intend to dwell on this question of principle for long, but I must state from the outset that my comments presuppose the strictly historical character of New Testament theology'. (Wrede, in R. Morgan [ed.], *Nature*, p. 69)

Testament theology is 'a purely historical discipline', and although Wrede expects most would answer affirmatively, the ongoing connection of New Testament theology with the 'normative' discipline of dogmatics suggests to Wrede otherwise (pp. 68-69). The relationship of the critical discipline of New Testament theology to its subject matter, properly understood, is such that

> it tries to grasp it as objectively, correctly and sharply as possible. That is all. How the systematic theologian gets on with its results and deals with them—that is his own affair. Like every other real science, New Testament theology has its goal simply in itself, and is totally indifferent to all dogma and systematic theology. What could dogmatics offer it? Could dogmatics teach New Testament theology to see the facts correctly? At most it could colour them. Could it correct the facts that were found? To correct facts is absurd. Could it legitimize them? Facts need no legitimation (pp. 69-70).

The prospective New Testament theologian must prove 'capable of interest in historical research':

> He must be guided by a pure disinterested concern for knowledge, which accepts every really compelling result. He must be able to distinguish between the alien modern ideas of his own thought and those of the past. He must be able to keep his own viewpoint, however precious, quite separate from the object of his research and hold it in suspense. Then he will indeed know only what really was (p. 70).

As for the lament provoked by such a supposed surrendering of the theological task:

> But in what should the specifically theological type of treatment consist? It would always result in a mixture which included the personal theological viewpoint of the scholar, and that could only obscure things. Or can a specifically theological understanding of the discipline guarantee some kind of knowledge that goes beyond the knowledge of the historical fact that such and such was taught and believed by the men of the New Testament (p. 70)?

As for the touching desire of so many 'to serve the church' in fulfilling the historical task:

> On the whole it is not within the historical researcher's power to serve the church through his work. The theologian who obeys the historical object as his master is not in a position to serve the church through his properly scientific-historical work, even if he were personally interested in doing so. One would then have to consider the investigation of historical truth as such as serving the church. That is where the chief difficulty of our whole

theological situation lies, and it is not created by individual wills: the
church rests on history, but historical reality cannot escape investigation,
and this investigation of historical reality has its own laws (p. 73).[82]

Having argued the metacritical point as closely as he considers it needs
to be (it is, after all, a self-evident matter), Wrede proceeds to outline the
discipline of 'the history of early Christian religion and theology' (p. 116).
Where Gabler is eager to help, Wrede could not if he wanted to—faith
will have to take care of itself. Where, for Gabler, history, by an inner
necessity, stands in service of faith, helping it to discern the spirits, for
Wrede, history contains its own goal and its own justification in itself,
and the problems it creates for theology are theology's problems (it is
difficult to be much more unhelpful than that).

Clearly visible, from the Reformation to Gabler to Wrede, is the now
agonizing, now challenging distance which has interposed itself between
the Bible and its earnest reader. The intent focus placed on the Bible
produces not the harmonious voice commensurate with simple faith but
the cacophony of voices of a warring tribe. And faith, for whose sake
this searching look at scripture was commenced, comes to be understood as itself the enemy in the search for truth. The distance, felt by all,
is to be not so much lamented as resigned to and respected, a distance
crossed not by pulling the past forward but by cutting oneself loose
from the present and transporting oneself backward in time, even if only
to return empty-handed. The closing of the hermeneutical gap is to be
accomplished by the methodical, scientific separation of fact from value.
The natural resistance from the side of faith is handled by a combination
of the scientistic rhetoric of purity of method, the ethical rhetoric of
honesty of conviction, and the clinical rhetoric of keeping 'the facts' free
from the infection of value, the contagion of self-will. Hovering over all
is the quasi-religious rhetoric of responsibility to a higher calling, service
to a sterner master, obedience to the laws of history, and reverence for
the sanctity of facts.

There is, then, a profound convergence of the rhetoric of Schweitzer
with that of his respected near contemporary, Wrede. Schweitzer even
manages to implicate Paul directly in this development, portraying Paul,
reason, truth, and knowledge triumphant over church, authority,
tradition, and belief, and making Paul not just a systematic thinker but

82. Wrede's manifesto was delivered at 'a vacation course for clergy'
(R. Morgan [ed.], *Nature*, p. 182); what they—and their parishioners—made of it,
perhaps we shall never know.

an Enlightened thinker. It is our larger story of the rise of the consciousness of acute historical distance bridged only by equally acute methodical rigour that situates Schweitzer. If distance is felt anywhere, it is in
coming face to face with early Jewish and Christian eschatology. If the
movement from the 'descriptive' to the 'normative' moment in 'New
Testament theology' is to encounter difficulty anywhere, it will be here.
Schweitzer is regarded by a latter-day Wrede as a hero of the methodical separation of these moments, courageously drawing, along with
J. Weiss, the inevitable, sorrowful consequences: 'they dared to paint a
Jesus who held a faith different from their own'.[83] Another 'two-stage'
enthusiast similarly lionizes this achievement: 'The recovery of eschatology could well stand as a symbol for the way in which descriptive
biblical theology draws attention to material which has been suppressed
or at least covered over in the process of continuous interpretation'.[84]
What Schweitzer marks, then—and now we speak no longer of an
'unleashing' of some new thing, a grand discovery, but of an arrival at
the end of a long road, an 'unleashing' only in that, perhaps, the harvest
of choices long since made is being reaped—is the ascendancy of a
methodical, 'two-stage' ideal in the discourse of biblical studies. This
situation is not of his invention, nor is it brought self-consciously and
programmatically to the forefront of his narrative. But in him it achieves
the popular appeal, the rhetorical force, and the covert angle of entry
necessary to make it the self-evident and unquestioned simple reality
that it widely remains. The ethos of biblical criticism is thoroughly
Schweitzerian, for good or ill.

The rhetoric of the present rehearsal of these matters has failed if it
has not become obvious that the ascendancy of this critical ethos is here
looked upon with at least a measure of demystifying suspicion. I shall

83. Räisänen, *Beyond New Testament Theology*, p. 112.
84. K. Stendahl, 'Method in the Study of Biblical Theology', in Hyatt (ed.), *The
Bible*, pp. 196-209 (p. 205). For similar sentiments toward Schweitzer and the
'recovery of eschatology', see Stendahl's 'Biblical Theology, Contemporary', *IDB*, I,
pp. 418-32, esp. 418-19, 425; D.E. Nineham, 'Schweitzer Revisited', esp. 129-33;
'Schweitzer, A.', and cf. 'Cultural Relativism', in Coggins and Houlden (eds.),
*Dictionary of Biblical Interpretation*, pp. 155-59; eschatology is, for Räisänen, a
litmus test of credibility—see *Beyond New Testament Theology*, p. xiv and *passim*.
J.A. Ziesler, 'New Testament Theology', in A. Richardson and J. Bowden (eds.), *A
New Dictionary of Christian Theology* (London: SCM Press, 2nd edn, 1983),
pp. 398-403, appeals to Schweitzer in the context of the tortured movement from
'descriptive' to 'normative' as a barrier to easy answers (p. 401).

proceed dialectically, from the very heartland of the fact/value divide, to read this more local tale against itself. Self-will will be seen hidden where it was claimed none lay. But I shall do more than merely relabel some 'facts' as 'values'. I shall, in the final chapter of the present study (and at points along the way), raise the question of the whole hidden metaphysic of fact/value, scheme/content, theory/observation, as well as the hidden anthropology of the Cartesian self on which it relies. But more than this metacritical theme, in which, of course, we are preceded by philosophical hermeneutics, post-analytic philosophy and philosophical anthropology, and post-empiricist philosophy of natural and social science (as well as wider related currents in theory and criticism—social/philosophical, ethical/political, literary/cultural), I shall suggest an *ethical* critique of the 'two-stage' ideal. This critique will highlight in all its naive (or deceitful) absurdity the claim of anyone, by means of methodical, purely descriptive rigour, to lift the veil of illusion and usher us into the presence of reality without concealing normative pretensions. Here an impossibility underwrites a travesty.

The fusion effected earlier in closely following Schweitzer's own story has now perhaps threatened to rupture in the critical distance to which he has been removed—but Schweitzer will not remain entirely under the black cloud I seem to have conjured. Nevertheless, here in connection with Schweitzer it is necessary that such concerns be raised, and then, in part, sharply dropped as my narrative proceeds, only to be taken up again further on. For the moment, simple assertion takes the place of detail. My ethical critique of the 'two-stage' ideal makes two central claims: that this 'purely historical' ideal, in conceiving its goal as an 'arrival' rather than as an open-ended dialogue, tends always to shut things down prematurely, and that, even as it does so, it attempts to occupy a moral and methodological high ground to which it has no right, tending always to subvert its own claims in ways blind to itself. If the story Schweitzer tells is one of human folly, the larger story, in equally classic style, is one of *hubris*.

## Chapter 2

## HISTORY AND ESCHATOLOGY:
## DODD, BULTMANN, AND CULLMANN

'Behold *now* is the accepted time; *now* is the day of salvation'
(2 Cor. vi.2)…Whenever the Gospel is proclaimed, it brings about a crisis,
as in the experience of the individual, so also in the experience of whole
communities and civilizations. Out of the crisis comes a new creation, by
the power of God. Every such occasion is the 'fullness of times' in which
the Kingdom of God comes. Thus history reveals its meaning as an order
of redemption and revelation. Full meaning is not reserved for the last term
in a temporal series, which supersedes and abolishes all previous stages in
the process. Every situation is capable of being lifted up into the order of
'sacred' history. (C.H. Dodd, *History and the Gospel*, pp. 121, 125.)

Paul has histori[ci]zed the Jewish apocalyptic speculation of an intermediate messianic reign preceding the new aeon by conceiving the time of
the Messiah's reign as the time between Christ's resurrection and
parousia—i.e. as the Now in which the proclamation is sounding forth
(1 Cor. 15:23-28). In the 'word', then, the salvation occurrence is
present…[I]t is, by nature, personal address which accosts each individual,
throwing the person himself into question by rendering his self-understanding problematic, and demanding a decision of him…[T]he eschatological occurrence is taking place; the eschatological 'acceptable time', the
'day of salvation'…, is present reality in the Now in which the word
encounters the hearer (2 Cor. 6:2). (R. Bultmann, *Theology of the New
Testament*, p. 307.)

Paul finds himself (2 Cor. 6.2) right at the point where in the execution of
his plan God brought in the 'welcome time' by reconciling the world to
himself through Christ (2 Cor. 5.18). Just at this point in time the apostle
received his precise calling, his 'ministry of reconciliation' (5.18), and
therefore must show himself as a 'servant of God' on this 'day of
salvation'…The apostle is thinking primarily of himself as the one
who . . . stands at a particular point in salvation history…The 'now' is
'now' because there is a 'before' and an 'after' in the divine plan, not
only in relation to the individual person, but also in relation to the whole of

mankind and even the whole of creation...The tension between 'already' and 'not yet'...stands in the foreground in Paul...Paul's whole theology is dominated by this tension...In no way does this tension merely relate to the existence of the individual. It relates to the whole salvation history of the interval which is the basis and presupposition of all existence. (O. Cullmann, *Salvation in History*, p. 255.)

Schweitzer casts a long shadow across the altered landscape of Pauline studies, indeed, across New Testament studies as a whole. The marks of his presence are everywhere apparent, the most obvious effect of his New Testament criticism being to establish eschatology as a matter to be reckoned with—whatever one makes of it—in the study of Jesus, early Christianity, and Paul.

Schweitzer, with his history of religions programme, felt himself to have kicked the final props from beneath what impediments remained to the 'new phase' in reading Paul. The 'new look' Paul thinks creatively and systematically within a Jewish eschatological frame, affirming a present, and very soon to be consummated, redemption cosmic in its scope. But the most immediate response to Schweitzer's Paul comes in three waves on the biblical-theological front, as C.H. Dodd, Rudolf Bultmann, and Oscar Cullmann stake out claims, in the century of Schweitzer, for a decade each of their own, making the 30s, 40s, and 50s respectively—bridging the span from Schweitzer to Käsemann—the decades of their discontent.[1]

But in addition to such casting about for alternatives and carving out of rival domains, there were those wishing to apply more fully Schweitzer's own perspective, more or less as is, to the New Testament, to the early history of doctrine, and to dogmatics generally—that is, a Schweitzer 'school' was formed.[2]

An exemplary work here is Martin Werner's *Die Entstehung des*

---

1. The overlap and longevity of these three careers obviously mar the symmetry of this schematism, but it nevertheless achieves a rough fit. Schweitzer's *Mystik* appears in 1930, and the thirties see the development of Dodd's 'realized eschatology', the forties the articulation of Bultmann's 'demythologizing' and 'existentialist interpretation', and the fifties the maturation of Cullmann's 'salvation history' in dialogue with these three. For the present purposes, Dodd, Bultmann, and Cullmann are approached as *responses* to Schweitzer; but it is acknowledged that this one strand, as important as it is for positioning them, does not exhaust the make-up and significance of these three independent and influential figures.

2. On the Schweitzer 'school', see J.M. Robinson, 'Introduction' to Schweitzer's *Quest*, pp. xx-xxi.

*christlichen Dogmas* (1941),[3] dedicated to Schweitzer and breathing his
influence throughout. Werner shares Schweitzer's assessment of the
process of transformation of primitive Christianity into Hellenized 'early
catholicism' as the central problem of the history of doctrine. Earlier
attempts to account for this process have only been able to observe
it from without, unable to penetrate to 'the *inner* causes of such
Hellenisation, or in other words, the understanding of the transformation
of the Primitive Christian faith into the doctrine of Early Catholicism
under the impulse of tendencies implicit therein' (p. 6). But such an
inner perspective is at last provided by 'consistent-eschatology', enthusi-
astically endorsed by Werner, which interprets 'the essentials of the
teaching of Jesus, of the first Apostles, and of Paul...consistently from
the viewpoint of that sense of eschatological expectancy, current in late-
Jewish apocalyptic, which dominated the whole of Primitive Christianity'.
Paul well illustrates this inner perspective on the history of doctrine, as
the logic by which he modifies his 'apocalyptic' expectations in the light
of Jesus' death and resurrection no longer rules in the following
generation, for whom, beset with the necessity of coping with the delay
of the parousia, everything has been redefined.[4] Werner is thus filling
out the picture of Schweitzer's 'positive criticism', already sketched in
outline, and at points in some detail, by the master's own hand (a sort of
Rembrandt apprenticeship).

It is as obvious to Werner as it is to most of his contemporaries that
'apocalyptic' is the eschatological conception of the two ages, the old
ready to vanish, the new to break in, an intense and entirely futuristic
expectation which controls Jesus' conception of the kingdom:

> Jesus spoke expressly of it as the 'coming Age', connecting it with those
> peculiar supernatural events through which the apocalyptic doctrine of the
> New Age would be realised—the Messianic affliction, the glorious *Parousia*
> of the 'Son of Man' on the clouds of heaven, the General Resurrection of
> the dead, the eschatological World-Judgment, the overthrow of the

3.    Rev. and abr. Werner, trans. S.G.F. Brandon as *The Formation of Christian
Dogma: An Historical Study of its Problem* (London: A. & C. Black, 1957 [Ger. edn,
1941]), cited here. The details of Werner's presentation are not of interest here, but
only his approach to Paul, which so approximates to Schweitzer's that in this respect
at least Käsemann is correct in maintaining that 'he failed to get New Testament
scholars in any respect beyond the theses of Schweitzer' ('On the Subject of
Primitive Christian Apocalyptic', in *New Testament Questions*, p. 109 n. 2).

4.    See Werner, *Formation*, pp. 71-74, 95-106, 283-86; Werner's is a slavish re-
rendering of Schweitzer's Paul.

daemonic powers, the transformation of all things, and the mode of existence of which the companions of the Son of Man were to partake in the Kingdom of God (p. 14).

But what of those who would temper this future expectation by also recognizing in Jesus' proclamation of the kingdom an element of present realization?

> This interpretation would alone be feasible at the cost of the complete removal of every apocalyptic idea from the preaching of Jesus about the Kingdom of God. But the message of Jesus has only to show agreement in one single characteristic element with the apocalyptic conception of the future kingdom of God, and the proposition of a Kingdom of God being already realised in the present is rendered thereby completely problematic (p. 14).[5]

There now comes sharply to the fore (though seemingly unawares to Werner) what has been, as it were, lurking about in Schweitzer: if 'apocalyptic' is so futuristic as to be antithetical to notions of present realization, such that one drives the other from its presence, how does one explain 'apocalyptic Paul', whose 'mysticism' embraces a present/ future tension? As Schweitzer has said, Judaism knows no such 'mysticism'.[6] It is this difficulty which underlies both Schweitzer's and Werner's presentation of 'late Jewish eschatology'/'apocalyptic' as a rigid, well-defined, coherent system or scheme which demands of Paul its own adjustment in the light of his apprehension of Jesus' death and resurrection. Thus Paul, anomaly though he is, is so by being true *both* to 'apocalyptic' *and* to the realities of the Christ event, unable to do other than to combine the two in a manner simply unforeseeable to the former. He is indeed a consistent thinker—consistent to a fault.[7]

5. Werner has in mind particularly C.H. Dodd. See Werner, *Formation*, pp. 13 n. 2, 15 n. 1.

6. Cf. Schweitzer, *Interpreters*, pp. 174-78; *Mysticism*, pp. 36-37 (again, 'mysticism' as in 'participation' and 'anticipation' in Christ). This is why for so long a Greek Paul has been sought rather than attempting a Jewish, eschatological explanation of his thought, and it is Schweitzer's burden to defend the (by appearances) unlikely assertion that Paul's 'mysticism' is so derived.

7. For Schweitzer and Werner at least, this tension in Paul is not meant by him to last for long. Another interpreter of Paul who identifies himself with this Schweitzer/Werner tradition is H.J. Schoeps, *Paul*; see pp. 40-46, 88-110. But it is difficult to know what to make of Schoeps's claims of indebtedness to Schweitzer. Although in a general way Schoeps commends Schweitzer's attention to eschatology as central to Paul and similarly interprets Paul as a 'theologian of the post-messianic

## 1. *C.H. Dodd*

Equally to be regarded as taking his point of departure from Schweitzer, but taking the very line Werner considers impossible, is C.H. Dodd. Dodd, writing in the years just after the appearance of Schweitzer's *Mysticism*,[8] wishes to demonstrate a line of psychological and theological development in Paul, reaching a turning point (a 'second conversion') in the crisis of events reconstructed as lying behind 2 Corinthians, by which Paul moves from being one mindful of power, satisfaction, and vindication, a man of pride, impatience, and self-consciousness, to being a man of humility and tranquillity, whose mind tends toward reconciliation, a selfless person who finds strength in weakness.[9] Interestingly, this movement of mind can for Dodd be expressed in part in terms of a movement away from 'apocalyptic' (which is not to say, as Dodd also seems to suggest, a movement from Jewish to Christian). As

situation', for Schoeps's Paul the Christian present, in which the ages intermingle, is itself the brief, temporary messianic kingdom, with the imminent parousia of Jesus as the next great event on the horizon. He claims to follow Schweitzer's view of Paul's eschatological problem of the resurrection life of believers in the messianic kingdom and the solution of two resurrections. However, he simply does not, for with Schoeps's Paul the general resurrection and consummation occur at Christ's return, and the 'two resurrections' refer to the two categories of believers who, because they have died and risen with Christ, either survive and are transformed or die and are raised at Christ's return. Thus Schoeps quotes (pp. 105-106) in agreement a lengthy excerpt from Schweitzer's *Mysticism* with which he does not in fact agree, at least not on *Schweitzer's* terms. Either Schweitzer has not been fully understood or else Schoeps is only intending to acknowledge a general, reinterpreted indebtedness to him. At any rate, it is not correct to cite (as does Sanders, *Paul*, p. 434 n. 17) Schoeps as following Schweitzer's idiosyncratic 'two resurrections' theory, Schoeps notwithstanding. Neither does Schoeps follow the 'ruthless logic' approach in accounting for Paul's notion of dying and rising with Christ, although for him also, 'apocalyptic', though perhaps understood more fluidly, is purely futuristic; he simply states that this was a solution to the problem of the death of believers before Christ's return. The bewildering result is that Schoeps claims loyalty to a view the inward logic of which he has removed. (Whether in fact this amounts to an improvement on Schweitzer is another matter, as Schoeps, in avoiding Schweitzer's oddities, is in keeping with convention.)

    8.    'The Mind of Paul: I' and 'The Mind of Paul: II', first appearing in *BJRL* in 1933 and 1934, repr. in C.H. Dodd, *New Testament Studies* (Manchester: Manchester University Press, 1953), pp. 67-128.

    9.    Dodd, *New Testament Studies*, pp. 67-84; 108-28.

has been noted, eschatology since Schweitzer becomes a matter to be reckoned with, and so Dodd may frankly admit that 'apocalyptic' forms part of the Jewish background of Paul which exerted its influence on his earlier Christian years. The view of 'apocalyptic' presupposed must be regarded as unexceptional:

> The apocalyptists despaired of the present world-order ('This Age'), as being under the dominion of diabolic powers, and looked for a new order ('The Age to Come'), in which the sovereignty of God would be effectively manifested in a radical renewal of the whole universe. His enemies would be destroyed, the righteous dead would be raised to share in his triumph, and the elect still living would be transfigured into bodies of glory, to inhabit the new heavens and new earth. All this would come about by a catastrophic divine intervention, marked by the appearance of God's vicegerent, the Elect One, sometimes called the Son of Man (or the Man), who would rule the new world in everlasting righteousness.
>
> When Paul became a Christian, his new beliefs were fitted into this framework. The Age to Come, he held, had already begun, with the resurrection of Christ. It must shortly be consummated by His appearance in glory (p. 109).[10]

Thus far, one could still be reading Schweitzer.

What, then, suggests to Dodd that Paul moves away from this framework? The movement Dodd traces through Paul is a movement away from futuristic preoccupations toward present realization: in place of a former emphasis on an imminent parousia, 'we have greater emphasis than ever before upon the idea that the Christian, having died and risen with Christ, is already living the life of the new age. The consummation indeed is still awaited, but awaited without urgency, because the substance of our hope is a present possession' (p. 111). '[T]he eschatological expectation has come to be subordinated to the thought of the heavenly life (the life of the new age) lived here and now' (p. 112).[11] 'This is sometimes described as the transformation of eschatology into mysticism, and the expression will serve. Paul's thought was indeed never wholly eschatological nor did it ever become purely mystical, but there is nevertheless a real development' (p. 112). Whereas 'apocalyptic eschatology' 'implies a radical devaluation of the present world-order in all its aspects', Paul comes to represent life in Christ within the present

10. This retro-fitting of the new into the more familiar on Paul's part is in keeping with 'new phase' observations; as will be seen, though, this is a passing phase for Dodd's Paul.

11. Dodd, *New Testament Studies*, p. 112.

order, taking this order up into itself (p. 113). 'Now Jewish apocalyptic has some very noble elements, but from a psychological point of view it must be described as a form of compensation in fantasy for the sense of futility and defeat' (p. 126). For Dodd it is a solution to the problem of evil, born of the crisis and despair of the Jews, which resolves disparate hopes and realities in a radically transcendent and futuristic expectation of vindication; but there is another solution (that is, the Christian one), implicit in Paul's conversion but only achieved after years of personal struggle, which sees this present world, for all its imperfections and for all the pain and suffering involved in effecting its redemption, as the sphere of God's kingdom and purpose.[12] Paul stops fleeing reality and embraces it. For Dodd it is a self-evident matter that a movement toward present realization is a movement away from—and an implicit renunciation of—'apocalyptic'.

An instructive earlier parallel to Dodd's presentation here is an article by F.C. Porter, which responds in part to Schweitzer's *Interpreters*.[13] Here also is a frank admission of an 'apocalyptic' background to Paul. But again it is the expression in Paul of elements of realization which indicate, not merely a development away from 'apocalyptic', but a fundamental difference at heart. In Porter one sees most clearly that a whole set of issues attaches to the notion of 'apocalyptic', issues which touch the heart of Paul and determine one's approach to him: 'Paul and apocalyptic' is a question of spiritual versus fleshly, inward versus outward, reality versus fantasy, presence versus futurity, ethical versus otherworldly, mystical versus eschatological, security versus anxiety, reconciliation versus vindication, universal versus national, personal versus impersonal. Paul is prophetic, not 'apocalyptic'. And yes (as also hinted by Dodd), Paul is Christian, not Jew. Rather than groping about among the shades, trapped in the blindness of post-biblical Jewish speculation, Paul steps out into the full light of the truth of Christ, reappropriating the pure biblical beliefs and hopes of Paul's more distant Jewish heritage.[14] 'Apocalyptic', one might say, like fasting, in the query

12. Dodd, *New Testament Studies*, pp. 126-28.

13. F.C. Porter, 'The Place of Apocalyptical Conceptions in the Thought of Paul', *JBL* 41 (1922), pp. 183-204. So similar are the two that it is difficult not to see Porter's article behind Dodd's, though it is not cited.

14. For Porter's earlier study of 'apocalyptic', see his *The Messages of the Apocalyptical Writings* (New York: Charles Scribner's Sons, 1905); note pp. 71-72: 'But was it true that the gospel as Jesus preached it was an apocalypse? We have

of John's disciples, is an inappropriate means of response to the presence of the messiah.

To pause and compare Dodd and Porter with Schweitzer up to this point, it is worth noting the different directions from which they come to the question of an 'apocalyptic' Paul. Schweitzer starts (primarily) from a critique of liberal 'kingdom of God' theology which appeals to Jesus and Paul without acknowledging the fundamentally eschatological character of their thought. Schweitzer wishes to elevate to a central place the 'physical' element of Paul's thought, long held to be ethical, and to show that Paul's dying and rising with Christ is an eschatological, cosmic doctrine of redemption. The chief hurdle is accounting for the realized aspects, which is why Schweitzer is so concerned to reconstruct in as great detail as possible Paul's eschatological schema as compared to that of 'late Jewish eschatology'. When this is done, he is able to show (to his own satisfaction at least) that Paul has in fact followed the logic of both his eschatological heritage and his experience of Christ, for Paul's convictions about Jesus' death and resurrection bring him to his 'mysticism'. Far from generating or perceiving in a flash of personal creativity a new religion in Christ, Paul's Christian convictions are preceded by many prior expectations, which are adapted and transferred to Christ at and after Paul's conversion. But the peculiarities of the 'between-the-times' standpoint of Paul were simply not foreseen or foreseeable in the traditional eschatology. '"Christianity" is for Paul no new religion, but simply Judaism with the centre of gravity shifted in

compared prophecy and apocalypse, and have found that closely related though they are, they represent two contrasted conceptions of the nature of revelation, two ideas of the supernatural, two estimates of the present life, two theologies, almost two religions. Christ's own relationship was far closer with prophecy than with the apocalypse. Christianity was a new prophetic movement, pre-announced by a prophet of the older, not the later type, and founded by one in whom the prophetic spirit was present in its fulness. It could not but find its closest point of connection with Judaism in surviving prophecy, degenerate though it was; and it could hardly escape injury from the very degeneracy into which prophecy had fallen. Yet...it can truly be said that there is in the gospels far more of the prophetic than of the apocalyptical type, and that this is still just as true of the letters of Paul'. For Porter's fuller reflection on Paul, filling out the picture sketched in the article cited above, see his *The Mind of Christ in Paul* (New York: Charles Scribner's Sons, 1930). Porter takes brief notice here (pp. 310-12n) of Schweitzer's *Mysticism*, which appeared the same year. In some respects, Porter, again not unlike Dodd, represents shades of the sort of liberal approach Schweitzer had hoped to lay to rest.

consequence of the new era'.[15] This is Paul's distinctiveness. Paul is a perceptive and logical theologian of a reformed eschatological Judaism.

That such a view radically shifts the centre of gravity of traditional readings of Paul—and that Schweitzer himself perceived this—is not to be doubted. But it is clearly with Porter and (to a lesser degree) Dodd that the discussion over Paul and 'apocalyptic' takes on a somewhat worried tone, asking whether Paul exemplifies this or that type of thought and religion. And so it becomes clear that a fair amount may be taken to be at jeopardy over this matter of 'apocalyptic'. What is at stake for some is the greatness of Paul as a Christian theologian and the greatness of his experience of Christ, and these are not to be compromised by elevating to prominence such peripheral elements as 'apocalyptic':

> Paul was of course a man of his time, and we can learn from him much in regard to the thoughts of his time as to heavenly things and beings, and future divine events. We need also the light of all contemporary literature, including the apocalyptic, in order to understand his language and the forms of his thought. But Paul was a great personality and had a great experience; and the new feelings and thoughts which this experience called forth in him are more significant than the forms in which they struggled for expression.[16]

Is Paul a Jew who realigned his messianic expectations in accordance with new facts, or a Christian who left behind his Jewish contemporaries, appealing to the same authoritative texts by the same approved interpretative methods, but offering a Christian interpretation? Jewish esoteric or Christian rabbi?[17]

However, that is not all. For despite the different paths by which they come to the subject, Schweitzer on the one hand and Dodd and Porter on the other all share an important notion: 'apocalyptic' and realized eschatology stand in antithesis. It must be insisted that the understanding of 'apocalyptic' expressed in Porter and Dodd is unexceptional, even if others are inclined to value it less severely and even if Dodd and Porter

---

15. Schweitzer, *Interpreters*, p. 227.

16. Porter, 'Apocalyptical Conceptions', pp. 203-204. The present point applies most fully to Porter; but Dodd's perspective is not far removed from Porter's in tone and import.

17. These impressionistic terms belong to none of the participants in this discussion, but merely attempt to express the drift of the implicit 'continuity versus discontinuity' debate.

have enhanced the picture for rhetorical effect. That which causes Schweitzer to posit a process of irresistible logic is evidence to Dodd that Paul has outgrown, and to Porter that he differs at heart from, 'apocalyptic'—Paul's 'mysticism' bursts the bounds of his 'apocalyptic' heritage. It is significant that both Dodd and Porter play off Schweitzer's 'mysticism' of dying and rising with Christ in Paul against the futuristic, 'apocalyptic' emphasis they see in Schweitzer's overall portrait, yet whereas for Schweitzer this 'mysticism' is a realistic, cosmic, eschatological construction resulting from Paul's reinterpretive process, for Porter and Dodd, who (in Schweitzer's terms) emphasize its ethical character, it is a departure from (futuristic) eschatology. Both sides present a Paul who combines present and future elements in his thought, and for both this sets Paul in tension with his background, inasmuch as realized and futuristic eschatology stand in tension. But the tension is resolved by each in an opposite direction by appeal to the same features of Paul's thought. The curious result is that, because of their shared presuppositions and the way the question has been framed, they can each at times sound much the same note but in fact be playing very different tunes.

But to return to Dodd, as one must in order to avoid a caricature,[18] it is necessary to view his approach to Paul and 'apocalyptic' within Dodd's total interpretive programme, a programme comparable to Schweitzer's in its breadth of perspective and singularity of execution.[19]

18.  That is, although there is clearly a certain antipathy to 'apocalyptic' in Dodd, there is more to the picture than just this. The case of Bultmann is similar a similar picture with Bultmann.

19.  The most important of Dodd's works for the present purposes are three books, each adapted from lecture series and published in the 1930s, which together present Dodd's 'realized eschatology' and outline a 'Christian philosophy of history'. These are C.H. Dodd, *The Parables of the Kingdom* (London: Nisbet, 3rd edn, 1936); *idem, The Apostolic Preaching and its Developments* (London: Hodder & Stoughton, 1936; reset 1944, cited here); and *idem, History and the Gospel* (London: Nisbet, 1938; London: Hodder & Stoughton rev. edn, 1964, cited here). See also Dodd's studies of 'the mind of Paul', cited above; his first published book, *The Meaning of Paul for Today* (London: Swarthmore, 1920; London: Fontana, 2nd edn, 1958, cited here), which contains many early hints and partial formulations of these later developments, and his *The Epistle of Paul to the Romans* (MNTC; London: Hodder & Stoughton, 1932). Dodd's wider theological perspective may be sampled in *The Authority of the Bible* (London: Nisbet, 2nd edn, 1938 [1928]) and *The Bible Today* (Cambridge: Cambridge University Press, 1946), both of which touch on the theme of 'history and eschatology'. C.H. Dodd, *According to the Scriptures: The*

Only in so doing may one see the full scope of Dodd's work as a response to Schweitzer. For Dodd approaches 'apocalyptic' not only as an aspect of Paul's personal development but of the development of early Christian thought as a whole. Paul's heroic breakthrough to reconciliation with the present world and history (we are still following Dodd) is more than a personal triumph: it is a triumph of early Christian thought, and earns for Paul the distinction of being the first to recover the genius of Jesus, a process of recovery which reached its zenith (in New Testament terms) in the theology of John.[20]

The work of Schweitzer forms one clear strand in the background of the development of Dodd's thought.[21]

---

*Substructure of New Testament Theology* (London: Nisbet, 1952), weaves together many of Dodd's distinctive themes. See also his Cambridge inaugural lecture, *The Present Task in New Testament Studies* (Cambridge: Cambridge University Press, 1936) and his Union inaugural lecture 'Thirty Years of New Testament Study', *USQR* 5 (1950), pp. 5-12 (repr. *Religion in Life* 47 [1978], pp. 320-29). On Dodd, see N.Q. Hamilton, *The Holy Spirit and Eschatology in Paul* (Edinburgh: Oliver and Boyd, 1957), pp. 53-70; E.E. Wolfzorn, *Realized Eschatology: An Exposition of Charles H. Dodd's Thesis* (Bruges: Louvain, 1962); J.A.T. Robinson, 'Theologians of Our Time XII: C.H. Dodd', *ExpTim* 75 (1963-64), pp. 100-102; G.B. Caird, 'C.H. Dodd', in D.G. Peerman and M.E. Marty (eds.), *A Handbook of Christian Theologians: Enlarged Edition* (Nashville: Abingdon Press, 1984 [1965]), pp. 320-37; F.W. Dillistone, *C.H. Dodd: Interpreter of the New Testament* (London: Hodder & Stoughton, 1977); S.W. Sykes, 'Theology through History', in D.F. Ford (ed.), *The Modern Theologians* (Oxford: Blackwell, 1989), II.11-14; O.E. Evans, 'Dodd, C.H.', in Coggins and Houlden (eds.), *Dictionary of Biblical Interpretation*, pp. 179-81.

20. Dodd, *Apostolic Preaching*, pp. 65, 73. Dodd is, rightly, remembered more as an interpreter of John than of Paul, as his work on the former is more sustained and systematic. See Dodd's classic studies, *The Interpretation of the Fourth Gospel* (Cambridge: Cambridge University Press, 1953) and *Historical Tradition in the Fourth Gospel* (Cambridge: Cambridge University Press, 1963). Nevertheless, the key place Paul holds within Dodd's thesis of development, the degree to which 'apocalyptic' is a matter of concern, and the importance of Dodd's perspective as a response to Schweitzer in the ongoing discussion of Paul and 'apocalyptic' justifies the attention given to Dodd here.

21. Cf. Caird, 'C.H. Dodd', pp. 321, 323. Caird lists five such strands: 'the radical criticism represented by Wellhausen and Wrede and more recently by Loisy and Goguel; the *Religionsgeschichtliche Schule* of Reitzenstein and Bousset and their modern disciple Bultmann; the thoroughgoing eschatology of Weiss and Schweitzer; the form criticism of Dibelius, Schmidt, and Bultmann; and the revival of biblical theology, heralded by Barth's commentary on Romans. Dodd belongs to all of these

It is indeed clear that the primitive formulation of the Gospel in eschatological terms is as strange as it could well be to our minds. It is no wonder
that it has taken a long time, and stirred up much controversy, to reach the
frank conclusion that the preaching of the early Church, and of Jesus
Himself, had its being in this strange world of thought. For many years we
strove against this conclusion. We tried to believe that criticism could
prune away from the New Testament those elements in it which seemed to
us fantastic, and leave us with an original 'essence of Christianity', to
which the modern man could say, 'This is what I have always thought'.[22]

This is Dodd, not Schweitzer, though one might easily be reading an
abstract of Schweitzer's *Quest of the Historical Jesus*.

Like Schweitzer's work on Paul, Dodd's continues his interpretation
of Jesus' eschatological thought, an interpretation behind which hovers
Schweitzer's already completed work. Schweitzer's *Quest* ends on a
grand either/or represented by the alternative approaches of Wrede and
of Schweitzer himself: either the historicity of the Gospels goes, or else
one accepts their portrait of Jesus as a self-deceived eschatological
prophet.[23] Schweitzer's rhetorically forceful presentation of the
alternatives (as he saw them, of course) demands that one accept the
eschatological Jesus of the Gospels as either a fiction of the evangelists
or the genuine article (simple, elegant, but with an obvious leading slant).
Dodd refuses to be pressed into a choice between these alternatives. He
simply eludes the either/or, preserves (much of) the historicity of the
Gospels by attention to the parables and by a reconstruction of the early
Christian preaching, and restores a more familiar Jesus with his thesis of
'realized eschatology'.[24]

Jesus, taking his point of departure within traditional expectation of
'the "good time coming" as set forth in prophecy and apocalyptic',

schools and to none of them' (p. 321). On Schweitzer and Dodd, Dillistone notes that
'it has been said by one friendly critic that he fought against Schweitzer throughout
his life' (*C.H. Dodd*, p. 57); this 'fight', though, is carried on obliquely, with only
rarely a direct mention of Schweitzer.

22. Dodd, *Apostolic Preaching*, p. 76.

23. Cf. Wolfzorn, *Realized Eschatology*, pp. 45-46; see the final chapter of
Schweitzer's *Quest*, where the choice is 'consistent scepticism' or 'consistent
eschatology'.

24. It might be noted, though, that a measure of the eschatological Jesus is, if not
a fiction, at least a misunderstanding deposited in the Gospels (see below). Dodd's
*Parables* focuses on Jesus' eschatological teaching and raises questions about the
developments on this point in early Christian thought, questions pursued more
systematically in *Apostolic Preaching*.

which hopes might either be 'temporal and political' or else indicate 'the final and absolute state of bliss in a transcendent order', bursts the bounds of these traditional longings in asserting the present fulfilment of past expectations: 'the "eschatological" Kingdom of God is proclaimed as a present fact'.[25] The Kingdom, which 'is itself the *eschaton*, or "ultimate," with which "eschatology" is concerned', has come, such that Jesus' ministry is one of 'realized eschatology'.[26]

> This declaration that the Kingdom of God has already come necessarily dislocates the whole eschatological scheme in which its expected coming closes the long vista of the future. The *eschaton* has moved from the future to the present, from the sphere of expectation into that of realized experience. It is therefore unsafe to assume that the content of the idea, 'The Kingdom of God', as Jesus meant it, may be filled in from the speculations of apocalyptic writers. They were referring to something in the future, which could be conceived only in terms of fantasy. He was speaking of that which, in one aspect at least, was an object of experience.[27]

Thus, though Jesus' thinking is informed by 'apocalyptic', even more decisive is the transformation of the latter in his creative hands. In him 'the time of fulfilment has come: that which the prophets desired to see is now [a] matter of present experience',[28] such that nothing remains outstanding, every expectation is fulfilled, even if in unforeseen (and unforseeable) ways. 'There is no coming of the Son of Man "after" His coming in Galilee and Jerusalem, whether soon or late...'[29] Jesus' creativity in transforming the traditions, in fact, exceeded the grasp of his early followers, for whom such as could not be conceived as being fulfilled in Jesus' death, resurrection, and exaltation was deferred to a second advent.[30] As with Schweitzer, then, there is for Dodd a process

25. Dodd, *Parables*, pp. 36, 37, 44.
26. Dodd, *Parables*, pp. 36, 51.
27. Dodd, *Parables*, p. 50.
28. Dodd, *Parables*, p. 47.
29. Dodd, *Parables*, p. 108.
30. Dodd's presentation of Jesus' own views, and discussion of the genesis and development of eschatological expectation in the early communities, can be found in *Parables*—see the chapters on 'The Kingdom of God' (pp. 34-80) and 'The Day of the Son of Man' (pp. 81-110), and, e.g., pp. 132-35, 154-55, 170-71, 174, 175-76, 193-94; *Apostolic Preaching* continues the reconstruction of the development. For a summary exposition of Dodd's thesis, see Wolfzorn, *Realized Eschatology*; Wolfzorn notes, pp. 44-45, that although Dodd is sometimes said to have moved toward the terminology of such suggested emendations as 'inaugurated' or 'self-realizing'

of eschatological development to be accounted for, and once again Paul plays a pivotal role.

For within perhaps as little as three or four years of Jesus' death (that brief period between Jesus' crucifixion and Paul's conversion), attention shifted to an expectation of a second advent as 'a second crisis yet in the future'.[31] 'The consequent demand for readjustment was a principal cause of the development of early Christian thought'[32]—a 'Schweitzerish' turn of phrase, but signifying something quite different. Instead of a later abandonment of the earlier purely 'apocalyptic' expectations under the force of a different set of prevailing conditions, Dodd depicts a very early flirtation with 'apocalyptic', followed by a renewed appreciation of Jesus' overcoming of the limitations of this tradition, which occurs among those struggling to match the fulfilment experienced with the expectations handed down from the religious past, while drawing on 'the traditional scheme of Jewish eschatology' found in 'the apocalyptic literature'.[33] Paul was among those early Christians who succumbed to the false charms of 'apocalyptic' expectations, as his Thessalonian letters reveal.[34] But this infatuation, thankfully, was a short-lived one:

> this excessive emphasis on the future has the effect of relegating to a secondary place just those elements in the original Gospel which are most distinctive of Christianity—the faith that in the finished work of Christ God had already acted for the salvation of man, and the blessed sense of living in the divine presence here and now...The exposure of the illusion which fixed an early date for the Lord's advent, while it threw some minds back into the unwholesome ferment of apocalyptic speculation, gave to finer minds the occasion for grasping more firmly the substantive truths of the Gospel, and finding for them a more adequate expression.
>
> [According to the primitive *kerygma*] the expectation of the Lord's return was held in close association with a definite valuation of His ministry, death, and resurrection as constituting in themselves an eschatological process, as a decisive manifestation of the mighty acts of God for the salvation of man. Eschatology is not itself the substance of the Gospel, but a form under which the absolute value of the Gospel facts is asserted. The second advent is not the supreme fact, to which all else is preparatory...

eschatology, his own thought actually remains consistent on this point; cf. Dillistone, *C. H. Dodd*, p. 119.

31. Dodd, *Apostolic Preaching*, pp. 31-35 (p. 34).
32. Dodd, *Apostolic Preaching*, p. 35.
33. Dodd, *Apostolic Preaching*, p. 37.
34. Dodd, *Apostolic Preaching*, pp. 31, 37-38.

> Thus the authentic line of development…led to a concentration of attention upon the historical facts of the ministry, death, and resurrection of Jesus, exhibited in an eschatological setting which made clear their absolute and final quality as saving facts.[35]

The first of such 'finer minds' is Paul himself; hence Dodd's outline of Paul's development, sketched above. Paul is the first-order witness to the early Christian *kerygma*, and Dodd sees its distinctive note sounded in him:

> The Pauline *kerygma*…is a proclamation of the facts of the death and resurrection of Christ in an eschatological setting which gives significance to the facts. They mark the transition from 'this evil Age' to the 'Age to Come'. The 'Age to Come' is the age of fulfilment. Hence the importance of the statement that Christ died and rose 'according to the Scriptures'. Whatever events the Old Testament prophets may indicate as impending, these events are for them significant as elements in the coming of 'the Day of the Lord'. Thus the fulfilment of prophecy means that the Day of the Lord has dawned: the Age to Come has begun. The death and resurrection of Christ are the crucial fulfilment of prophecy. By virtue of them believers are already delivered out of this present evil age. The new age is here, of which Christ, again by virtue of His death and resurrection, is Lord. He will come to exercise His Lordship both as Judge and as Saviour at the consummation of the Age.[36]

'It needs only a slight acquaintance with the traditional Jewish eschatology to recognise' that Paul, along with other witnesses to the early preaching, is 'using language which implies that the *eschaton*, the final and decisive act of God, has already entered human experience'.[37]

For Paul, 'the death and resurrection of Christ are interpreted as the divinely ordained crisis in history through which old things passed away and the new order came into being. It is in this light that we must understand all that Paul says about redemption, justification, and the end of the Law'.[38] The revelation of God's righteousness, the judgment of sin, the defeat of principalities and powers, redemption from the present age,

---

35. Dodd, *Apostolic Preaching*, pp. 40, 41-42. The value judgments here, in speaking of that which is 'most distinctive of Christianity', of 'the unwholesome ferment of apocalyptic speculations', of 'the authentic line of development', rest, presumably, on Dodd's reconstruction of Jesus' own interpretation of his ministry and its significance (and, implicitly, on Dodd's appropriation of that interpretation).

36. Dodd, *Apostolic Preaching*, p. 13.

37. Dodd, *Apostolic Preaching*, p. 34.

38. Dodd, *Apostolic Preaching*, p. 43.

union with Christ in dying to the Law and rising to newness of life, thus moving from one age and one humanity to another—indeed, Paul's whole salvation history—these are eschatological categories associated by Paul with the death and resurrection of Christ, events which 'have the actuality which belongs to the historical process as such, and at the same time they possess the absolute significance which belongs to the *eschaton*, the ultimate fulfilment of the divine purpose of history'.[39]

For Paul, the early Christian experience of the Holy Spirit and community 'marked the Church as being the true "Israel of God" in its final, "eschatological," manifestation', against the background of the 'idea of a supernatural Messianic community developed in Jewish prophecy and apocalypse'.[40] 'For Paul, with his strongly eschatological background of thought, the belief that the Church was the "people of the saints of the Most High," now revealed in the last days, carried with it the corollary that all that prophecy and apocalypse had asserted of the supernatural Messianic community was fulfilled in the Church'.[41] And here belongs Paul's 'Christ-mysticism', 'a restatement in more thorough-going terms of the unity existing between the Messiah and the Messianic community'.[42]

The personality of Christ receives, so to speak, an extension in the life of His Body on earth. Those 'saving facts', the death and resurrection of Christ,…are re-enacted in the experience of the Church. If Christ died to this world, so have the members of His body; if He has risen into newness of life, so have they…

This is the basis of Paul's so-called 'Christ-mysticism'. It is noteworthy that as his interest in the speedy advent of Christ declines, as it demonstrably does after the time when he wrote I Corinthians [Dodd here refers in a note to his 'The Mind of Paul', outlined above], the 'futurist eschatology' of his earlier phase is replaced by this 'Christ-mysticism'. The hope of glory yet to come remains as a background of thought, but the foreground is more and more occupied by the contemplation of all the riches of divine grace enjoyed here and now by those who are in Christ Jesus…

This was the true solution of the problem presented to the Church by the disappointment of its naïve expectation that the Lord would immediately

39.   Dodd, *Apostolic Preaching*, pp. 42-44 (pp. 43-44).

40.   Dodd, *Apostolic Preaching*, pp. 59-60. Another of many echoes of Schweitzer, in this case of the eschatological 'community of the elect', put to Dodd's own quite other purpose.

41.   Dodd, *Apostolic Preaching*, p. 62.

42.   Dodd, *Apostolic Preaching*. Again, Schweitzer *déjà vu*.

> appear; not the restless and impatient straining after signs of His coming which turned faith into fantasy and enthusiasm into fanaticism; but a fuller realization of all the depths and heights of the supernatural life here and now...
>
> It is in the epistles of Paul...that full justice is done for the first time to the principle of 'realized eschatology'...That supernatural order of life which the apocalyptists had predicted in terms of pure fantasy is now described as an actual fact of experience...In masterly fashion Paul has claimed the whole territory of the Church's life as the field of the eschatological miracle.[43]

Hence Paul's special place in reappropriating and preserving the genius of Jesus.

The allure of 'apocalyptic' is for Dodd understandable (if lamentable). To grasp the fit of the fulfilment achieved in Jesus' death, resurrection, and exaltation with the long traditions of hope and expectation required a feat of creative insight surpassed only in the creativity of Jesus' own taking up and remoulding of those traditions. Not only was this so, but matters were further complicated for the early believers, struggling to understand all this, by the fact that Jesus continued to use the language of 'futuristic eschatology'. For there remain some sayings of Jesus which speak of futurity, and not, as often, in the sense of a present or impending crisis re-interpreted in the early church as referring to a second advent; here one must 'make full allowance for the symbolic character of the "apocalyptic" sayings', symbolism being 'inherent in apocalyptic'.[44] '[T]hese future tenses are only an accommodation of language'.[45] The more 'deeply spiritual' of the 'apocalyptists' surely knew 'that the ultimate reality lies beyond anything that the mind of man can conceive, and that any form in which he can imagine it must remain strictly symbolic'.[46] Jesus' 'traditional apocalyptic symbolism', centring on the idea of the Kingdom of God, deals in symbols which 'are "eschatological" in character; they are ultimates, and are proper not to this empirical realm of time and space, but to the absolute order'.[47]

---

43. Dodd, *Apostolic Preaching*, pp. 62-63, 65. Again, echoes of Schweitzer resound. Dodd says of John that in his 'Gospel even more fully than in Paul, eschatology is sublimated into a distinctive kind of mysticism' (p. 66). Cf. p. 75.

44. Dodd, *Parables*, pp. 101-10 (p. 105).

45. Dodd, *Parables*, p. 108.

46. Dodd, *Parables*, pp. 105-106.

47. Dodd, *Parables*, pp. 106-107.

> The Kingdom of God in its full reality is not something which will happen after other things have happened. It is that to which men awake when this order of time and space no longer limits their vision...So far as history can contain it, it is embodied in the historic crisis which the coming of Jesus brought about...The eternal significance of history had revealed itself in this crisis. Whether its subsequent span would be long or short, men would henceforth be living in a new age...[48]

Dodd's discussion of the symbolic character of 'apocalyptic', indeed of 'eschatology' generally, shades over into reflection on a Christian philosophy of history (already visible here and there above), and on the very nature of Christianity itself, which provides the broadest context necessary for understanding Dodd's treatment of Paul and 'apocalyptic'.[49]

According to Dodd, 'it belongs to the specific character of Christianity that it is an historical religion'.[50] One sense in which this is so is the importance of the historical facts of its origins, a realization reclaimed by Dodd from the (to Dodd) excessive reaction of dialectical theology to 'historicism' and liberalism. This concern for history animates Dodd's critical work.[51] But more important for a consideration of Paul and 'apocalyptic' in Dodd is 'the most important sense in which Christianity is an historical religion. It depends upon a valuation of historical events as the medium of God's self-revelation in action'.[52]

Embedded in this statement is much of Dodd's philosophy of history

---

48. Dodd, *Parables*, pp. 108-109.

49. On this reflection on history, see Dodd, *Parables*, pp. 206-10; *idem*, *Apostolic Preaching*, 'Appendix: Eschatology and History', pp. 79-96; *idem*, *History*, pp. 9-28; 96-101; 102-25. Cf. Dodd's earlier treatment in *Authority*, part 4 (and see the 1938 preface), *The Bible Today*, chs. 5-7, and *According to the Scriptures*, pp. 128-33. See also Wolfzorn, *Realized Eschatology*, pp. 46-52; Caird, 'C.H. Dodd', pp. 325-29; Dillistone, *C.H. Dodd*, pp. 129-32; 138-39; 223-27. Dodd draws notably on Toynbee in his philosophy of history: cf. *Parables*, p. 209; *Apostolic Preaching*, pp. 90-93; *The Bible Today*, pp. 125-29. Cf. A.J. Toynbee, 'Christianity and Civilization', in *Civilization on Trial* (Oxford: Oxford University Press, 1948), esp. pp. 235-36, 237, 240, 243.

50. Dodd, *History*, p. 11.

51. Caird offers as the 'leitmotif or principle of unity' of all Dodd's work the following: 'the conviction that God is Lord of history, and that the word of God spoken in Scripture is so inextricably interwoven into the fabric of historical events that it can be let loose into the modern world in the fulness of its relevance and power only through historical criticism exercised with the utmost integrity and thoroughness' ('C.H. Dodd', p. 321).

52. Dodd, *History*, p. 15.

(which he claims as Christianity's own). History is not merely a chronicle of facts, events, occurrences; rather, it is events plus meaning, as perceived by a community and relevant to the wider world.[53] History moves, not in some indiscriminate flow, nor by some evolutionary, cyclical, or dialectical process (though all of these might at one point or another have been associated with a Christian view), but by crisis.[54] For Christian faith, this is the crisis of the history of Jesus.

> Once in the course of the ages the spirit of man was confronted, within history, with the eternal God in His kingdom, power, and glory, and that in a final and absolute sense. There was a great encounter, a challenge and response, a death and resurrection; and divine judgment and life eternal came into human experience. By that supreme crisis the meaning of all history is controlled.[55]

God is the God of history, the arena of his 'mighty acts'.[56]

Christianity's ambiguous relation to 'apocalyptic' becomes clear in further considering a Christian philosophy of history, for 'apocalyptic' is itself, in a sense, a philosophy of history (so Dodd), and it furnished Christianity with vital elements for its own perspective not otherwise available, while at the same time tending, where misunderstood, to run against the grain of what is centrally and distinctively Christian.

The prophets developed a distinctive perspective on universal history, focusing on divine providence and purpose working within history, which can only be grasped in foresight of the end, 'the Day of the Lord', 'the consummation of the whole series of events'.[57] 'Apocalyptic' 'works with the prophetic scheme of history', but 'it virtually gives up the attempt to recognize divine meaning in the present...[O]nly in the Day of the Lord will the divine meaning and purpose of history come to light'.[58] Thus, with 'apocalyptic', perspectives on teleology, transcendence, and universality, necessary for an adequate philosophy of history,

53. Dodd, *History*, pp. 19-20.

54. Dodd, *Parables*, pp. 201-208; *Apostolic Preaching*, pp. 94-96; *History*, pp. 15-28, 96-101, 118-25.

55. Dodd, *Apostolic Preaching*, pp. 95-96.

56. See Dodd, *History*, pp. 22-25.

57. Dodd, *Apostolic Preaching*, pp. 79-80. Here and following, what is to be noted is Dodd's interpretative distillation of principles of a philosophy of history from the various 'myths' with which he deals, thus engaging in a form of 'demythologizing'. On 'myth', see further, *The Bible Today*, pp. 112-21.

58. Dodd, *Apostolic Preaching*, p. 80; cf. *History*, pp. 24-25.

begin to be opened up. 'In the *eschaton* is concentrated the whole meaning which, *if* history were to go on, might be diffused throughout a long process...An absolute end to history, whether it be conceived as coming soon or late, is no more than a fiction designed to express the reality of teleology within history'.[59] The 'apocalypticists' portray 'the coming events in forms which do not properly belong to time at all, but to eternity. They thereby imply that the teleology of history is not purely immanent, but is determined by the purpose of a God who transcends the temporal order'.[60] In symbolizing the transcendent perspective from which alone it is possible to speak of a meaning to history in any ultimate sense, 'apocalyptic' prepares the way for Christianity.

> In the New Testament the apocalyptic symbolism of the Old recurs freely, but with a profound difference. The divine event is declared to have happened...[I]t is surely clear that, for the New Testament writers in general, the *eschaton* has entered history; the hidden rule of God has been revealed; the Age to Come has come. The Gospel of primitive Christianity is a Gospel of realized eschatology.
>
> In other words, a particular historical crisis, constituted by the ministry, the death, and the resurrection of Jesus Christ, is interpreted in terms of a mythological concept, which has been made by the prophets into a sublime symbol for the divine meaning and purpose of history in its fullness. The characteristics of the Day of the Lord as described in prophecy and apocalypse are boldly transferred to the historical crisis.[61]

'[H]istory depends for its meaning and reality upon that which is other than history. The real, inward, and eternal meaning, striving for expression in the course of history, is completely expressed in the *eschaton*...'[62] Anyone familiar with 'the language and ideas of Jewish eschatology' can see that, on the New Testament interpretation of the Christ-event, 'all that the prophets meant by the Day of the Lord is realized'.[63] And to assert, as Christianity does, the realization of the *eschaton* is to necessitate various reformulations.

---

59. Dodd, *Apostolic Preaching*, p. 82.
60. Dodd, *Apostolic Preaching*, p. 83; cf. *History*, p. 25: 'Apocalyptic therefore, serves by exaggeration to make clear an aspect of the Hebrew interpretation of history which is implicit in it all through: namely, that the ultimate power in history comes from beyond history'.
61. Dodd, *Apostolic Preaching*, pp. 84-85.
62. Dodd, *Apostolic Preaching*, p. 83.
63. Dodd, *Apostolic Preaching*, p. 87.

Naturally, when a conception hitherto belonging to the realm of mythology is declared to be realized in history, it is itself remoulded by the facts. How far the fantastic imagery of apocalyptic was taken literally by its authors or readers, it will perhaps always remain impossible to say. But when that imagery is applied to actual facts, its symbolic character becomes plain, and some elements in it are tacitly dropped as inappropriate...

One change necessarily follows when the divine event passes from the realm of mythology to the realm of history. While its character of finality remains, in the sense that it is decisive, it can no longer be final in the sense that nothing can happen after it. For it is in the nature of our time experience that it cannot be bounded either before or after... And so the coming of Christ was followed by a further historical period. But the New Testament writers are clear that history is henceforth qualitatively different from what it was before Christ's coming.[64]

There is 'an abrupt break in the relation in which the people of God, and, indeed, the whole human race, stands to the historical order'.[65]

Thus Dodd's philosophy of history is a biblical theology, a Christian salvation history. In Jesus the messiah a new people of God, a new Israel, is constituted, in his dying and rising again.[66] The crisis of events of Christ's advent is 'represented as a "fulfilment" of the law and the prophets, that is to say, of the religious history of Israel'.[67] '[T]he rise of the Church is for the New Testament writers an inseparable element in the eschatological complex. It is the fulfilment of prophetic hopes of a new people of God'.[68] 'Meaning' in any grand or ultimate sense eludes 'secular history', but 'sacred history', 'history as a process of redemption and revelation', provides 'the ultimate meaning of all history', as 'the whole of history is in the last resort sacred history, or *Heilsgeschichte*'.[69]

This principle of the universality of the divine meaning in history is symbolically expressed in Christian theology by placing the history of the Old and New Testaments within a mythological scheme which includes a real beginning and a real end. In the beginning God created heaven and earth and all that is in them. In the end he will unite all mankind, and indeed all orders of being, under His sole sway in a last judgment... Creation and Judgment are symbolic statements of the truth that all history

64. Dodd, *Apostolic Preaching*, pp. 87-88.
65. Dodd, *Apostolic Preaching*, p. 88.
66. Dodd, *History*, pp. 94-96; see pp. 99-100 on Paul's salvation history.
67. Dodd, *History*, p. 96.
68. Dodd, *History*, p. 102.
69. Dodd, *History*, pp. 114-15.

is teleological, working out one universal divine purpose...The story of creation and fall is a symbolic summing-up of everything in secular or empirical history which is preparatory to the process of redemption and revelation. It affirms that in man and his world there is implanted a divine purpose, opposed by a recalcitrant will...[S]acred history supervenes, telling how the victory is won through a dying to the world and a resurrection in power.

[T]he myth of a last Judgment is a symbolic statement of the final reso-lution of the great conflict...But this triumph is something actually attained, not in some coming Day of the Lord, near or distant, but in the concrete historical event of the death and resurrection of Jesus Christ. It is significant that Christianity separated off from the general expectation of Jewish eschatology this concrete, historical element of 'realized eschatology', leaving the residue as a symbolical expression of the relation of *all* history to the purpose of God. For the essential feature of the Last Judgment is its universality...It means that *all* history is comprehended in that achievement of the divine purpose of which the coming of Christ, His death and resurrection, is the intra-historical expression.[70]

The church mediates this narrative whereby the present is taken up into 'sacred history'. 'The task of the Church is to bring all historical move-ments into the context of the death and resurrection of Jesus Christ, in order that they may be judged by the divine meaning revealed in that crucial event'.[71]

Thus history becomes 'sacred' history. Whenever the Gospel is pro-claimed, it brings about a crisis, as in the experience of the individual, so also in the experience of whole communities and civilizations. Out of the crisis comes a new creation, by the power of God. Every such occasion is the 'fullness of time' in which the Kingdom of God comes. Thus history reveals its meaning as an order of redemption and revelation. Full meaning is not reserved for the last term in a temporal series, which supersedes and abolishes all previous stages in the process. Every situation is capable of being lifted up into the order of 'sacred' history.[72]

And so, starting where Schweitzer left off, we have arrived somewhere quite different.

All points converge on Jesus. All the crisscrossing traditions of hope and expectation intersect in fulfilment on his completed work. This fulfilment, *as fulfilment*, requires a highly creative reinterpretation of traditions. The process of 'interpretative imagination' discernible in the

70. Dodd, *History*, pp. 115-17.
71. Dodd, *History*, p. 119.
72. Dodd, *History*, pp. 124-25.

communities behind the New Testament, which includes such a 'fresh understanding of the mysterious imagery of apocalyptic eschatology', is 'a piece of genuinely creative thinking', and Dodd asks who could be responsible for it: 'we found need to postulate a creative mind. The Gospels offer us one. Are we compelled to reject the offer?'[73]

This creative figure is, of course, Jesus himself.[74] One aspect of his creativity, according to Dodd's presentation, is the sovereign mastery of his reweaving of the 'apocalyptic' tradition. All its expectations are most truly realized in him. And this tradition supplies a language, a symbol-system, necessary for expressing the transcendent reality of Jesus' ministry and message. Furthermore, in interpreting history through the lens of the history of Jesus, the early Christians had accessible in 'apocalyptic' the categories of meaning of universal history—teleology, transcendence, ultimacy, universality—necessary for the task. But this appropriation of 'apocalyptic' was not an unmixed blessing. For it was not always possible for the early believers to understand the fulfilment which Jesus provided (unexpected as it was).[75] Thus there was the double danger of both following the future orientation of 'apocalyptic' and thereby lifting one's eyes from the centre given in Jesus' life, death, resurrection, and exaltation, perhaps to some supposed 'second coming', and abandoning present history, the very stage of the revelatory and

73.   Dodd, *According to the Scriptures*, pp. 109-10; Dodd speaks principally here of the creative exegesis of the Old Testament in the New, but these words well express the broader creativity which he projects. In fact, this creative reappropriation of the Old Testament is of a piece with the reinterpretation of 'apocalyptic' traditions we have been following (according to Dodd's presentation).

74.   Caird well expresses Dodd's conception of Jesus' interpretive genius: 'He [Jesus] was a profound and original thinker, capable of reminting the currency of theological speech, of transforming the eschatological hope of his nation into a present experience, and of grasping the Old Testament Scriptures entire, so as to find in them a new conception of God's purpose for his people and his Messiah' (Caird, 'C.H. Dodd', p. 336).

75.   This emphasis in Dodd is a tightrope he must walk with care. The unexpectedness of Jesus' fulfilment of the religious hopes of the Jews must be stressed to account for the recalcitrance of those who continued to think in 'apocalyptic' terms. However, this unexpectedness cannot (for Dodd's case) be so emphasized as to make it appear unlikely that *anyone*, including Jesus himself, could have twisted the traditions to such an apparent breaking point. In other words, that anyone could have seen the connection, clear enough to Dodd, between what Dodd calls the traditional expectations and what he considers their fulfilment (which is to place under suspicion the whole notion of 'realized eschatology').

redemptive work of God, the arena of this meaning-pregnant series of events, the locus of social, ethical responsibility and action. Among the early figures enticed by the (literally) false hopes on offer in 'apocalyptic' was Paul himself. But he led the way back to Jesus. The notion of a second advent never completely leaves the horizon of the New Testament. Those truly future tenses remaining in Jesus' own teaching are an 'accommodation of language'; but they were not, or not fully, perceived as such. So a second coming is kept in view. But, with no small thanks to Paul, the proper emphasis nevertheless faithfully falls on the new creation that now stretches out ahead in Christ. Perhaps only within the experience of the modern church (and here with no small thanks to Dodd, whom we are still following) is it possible to do full justice to Jesus' teaching and significance. But, even in such a time as this, the future coming retains its place and worth as symbol, and thus as what it has, fundamentally, been all along, even if unknowingly: 'The least inadequate myth of the goal of history is that which moulds itself upon the great divine event of the past, known in its concrete actuality, and depicts its final issue in a form which brings time to an end and places man in eternity—the second Coming of the Lord, the Last Judgment'.[76] Dodd follows, then, in the truest spirit of (Dodd's) Paul and John.

Dodd responds to Schweitzer and his eschatological Paul with a sustained reflection on 'history and eschatology'.[77] This reflection ranges widely, resting not merely on the Christ event but on the tradition into which it falls (and from which it arises) and within which it struggles for true recognition. And nothing comes up looking quite the same. Dodd reads 'eschatology' as being about the 'ultimate', about 'absolute' significance, the 'decisive' manifestation of the purpose of God. 'Apocalyptic' is a symbol-system for talking about such things, eschatology a 'form' which carries the 'substance' of the Christian gospel. 'Apocalyptic' deals in transcendentals by means of material symbols, and when that toward which it gropes is actually grasped, actually arrives—when eschatological hopes are realized—readjustment is not so much deliberate as inevitable. This language of 'apocalyptic' is one in which Jesus was fluent, but his creative flair, his touch with metaphor, did, alas, prove too much for his less masterful, too literal followers, who followed instead, with minimal alteration, traditional expectations, some perhaps, like Paul, pausing

76. Dodd, *Apostolic Preaching*, p. 96.
77. Cf. again Dodd's appendix 'Eschatology and History' to *Apostolic Preaching*, an early systematic expression of his philosophy of history.

better to think things through and thus realizing the mistake, others only, if ever, turning back after following such hopes to their inexorably disappointing end. 'Apocalyptic' as a philosophy of history carried not only the symbols but the principles and concepts needed for grasping the significance for history and eschatology of the Christ event, but as such a philosophy it proved misleading for one not first and foremost a perceptive theologian of this event.

Thus, for all this talk of the eclipse of futuristic eschatology, Paul is, for Dodd, through and through an *eschatological* thinker. It is hardly to the point to object that in Dodd 'apocalyptic elements are disposed of by reinterpreting eschatology in terms of the absolute or supernatural rather than the temporal, by replacing teleology with purpose'.[78] For this is precisely the point at issue, with any such accusation of *re*interpretation easily countered by a charge of fundamental *mis*interpretation; for indeed, 'eschatology' is *our* term for a distant reality, and what it is about is for us to find out—the question, that is, is essentially historical, and, in Dodd's terms, a matter of doing a better historical job. True enough, Dodd's reinterpretation of Jesus and Paul follows on from his principle of reinterpretation or depth-reading of 'eschatology' and 'apocalyptic', for which he may appeal back to Jesus and Paul. This may be a circular process, but it is not unlike the circularity masked by the conventionality of the usual understanding of eschatology, whose own principles are now questioned. And even the obvious circularity of the value judgments with which Dodd's exposition is rife (easily indexed by the number of appearances of such terms as 'fantasy' in connection with 'apocalyptic'[79]) is mitigated by noting that Dodd operates with an open commitment to a viewpoint in which such descriptive and evaluative vocabulary coincide. Objections, that is, are forced to move to the level of Dodd's total interpretative framework, and not that of smaller points of detail, begging the larger questions. What must be grasped about Dodd's interpretation is the degree to which it covers itself (surely no accident): it is founded on an interpretation of Jesus, a figure not directly accessible to us, so that any residue of more familiar notions of eschatology and 'apocalyptic' attributed to him in the Gospels may be assigned

---

78.   Hamilton, *Holy Spirit*, p. 58. This charge, as I shall show, is often levelled by Cullmann (whom Hamilton follows). Although I also speak of 'reinterpretation' in Dodd and Bultmann, this is not meant as an accusation.

79.   Another example is the common association of 'apocalyptic' with the setting of the time of the end, an association which Dodd sometimes makes.

instead to the sort of interpretative inertia that Dodd posits among the early followers. Jesus himself relies on an insight into 'apocalyptic', into traditional eschatological conceptions, to which not all were privy, so that any similar residue elsewhere among his followers may be similarly explained.[80] Dodd's response, then, stands over against Schweitzer's interpretation with all the marks of an (incommensurable?) alternative perspective or paradigm.

It was said at the outset that the course of the discussion of Paul and 'apocalyptic' would suggest little interest in fundamental literary-historical questioning on the matter of 'apocalyptic' in its own right and, conversely, urgent questioning at the level of what might be considered the real issues at stake—that is, at the level of biblical-theological inquiry. Dodd indeed raises questions which appear to touch upon the meaning of 'apocalyptic' itself; it is evident, however, that his portrait of 'apocalyptic' is itself conventional. Dodd is opening the question of the language of eschatology, of 'apocalyptic', indeed, of the relation of language and myth, history, and eschatology,[81] and the implications for faith, an ongoing debate,[82] including within its borders in the present

---

80.    Thus Hamilton seems to overestimate the degree to which his pointing out of remaining traces of futuristic eschatology in Paul (which, after all, Dodd admits never leaves Paul's horizon) undermines Dodd's interpretation (Hamilton, *Holy Spirit*, pp. 66-70).

81.    Key terms here are, e.g., 'Kingdom', 'Son of Man', 'Servant', 'Messiah' 'the people of God', and thus salvation history and eschatology are under consideration. On the 'Kingdom', in B. Chilton (ed.), *The Kingdom of God in the Teaching of Jesus* (Philadelphia: Fortress Press/London: SPCK, 1984); W. Willis (ed.), *The Kingdom of God in 20th-Century Interpretation* (Peabody, MA: Hendrikson, 1987), pp. 15-33 on Dodd (and Bultmann); D.C. Duling, 'Kingdom of God, Kingdom of Heaven', in D.N. Freedman *et al.* (eds.), *The Anchor Bible Dictionary* (Garden City, NY: Doubleday, 1992), IV.49-69, pp. 62-65 on the modern debate; on the 'Son of Man', see G.W.E. Nickelsburg, 'Son of Man', Freedman (ed.), *The Anchor Bible Dictionary*, VI.137-50.

82.    Caird builds on Dodd's beginning here: 'He [Dodd] wanted also to underline the mythical nature of all eschatological language; and much work is still to be done on the relation of the literal to the symbolic in the language of the Bible' (Caird, 'C.H. Dodd', p. 329); see G.B. Caird, *The Language and Imagery of the Bible* (London: Duckworth, 1980), chs. 12-14 on language and history, myth, and eschatology. Dodd's influence in this regard is still felt in Pauline studies, via Caird, through N.T. Wright: see S. Neill and N.T. Wright, *Interpretation*, pp. 376-78, and, on Paul, N.T. Wright, 'Putting Paul Together Again: Toward a Synthesis of Pauline Theology', in J.M. Bassler (ed.), *Pauline Theology, Volume 1: Thessalonians,*

context both Bultmann and Cullmann. It is a debate mentioned here not with the design on entering into it, but simply to register notice of it as a vital part of the story presently being told, a pointer to what is at stake, what is truly of concern. Dodd's concern is with the traditional narrative of faith into which Jesus came, with Jesus' own retelling of that story, with the early struggle to come to terms with this reinterpreted narrative, with the expression of this narrative in *kerygma* and scripture interpretation, and with the significance an awareness of this entire interpretative process might have for those who today stand within the same continuous tradition and struggle to make this narrative their own. Nothing less than the very essence of Christianity is on the table. Dodd's interpretation, in a final striking resemblance to Schweitzer's, reveals everywhere a simplicity, elegance, and leading slant of its own.

If theology before Schweitzer was in little mood to consider an 'eschatological' or 'apocalyptic' Paul, it is by no means bound, after finally being forced to strike up the tune, to keep to Schweitzer's score. One might say, with Dodd, that the 'new phase' proves to have been a passing one for Paul, as he indeed fitted the Christ event into existing expectations, but quickly thought better of it. Turning, then, from what he had thought tradition could tell him about the Christ, Paul considers what Jesus means for tradition, thus reversing the interpretative flow. Paul's matrix is one of 'realized eschatology', and his cosmic language is a cipher for life in the Church, the Body of Christ. As a final reference point for Dodd's interpretation of Paul, we turn to his first book, a brief, popular exposition of *The Meaning of Paul for Today*. It is in Paul's corporate conceptions of 'Christ-mysticism' that Dodd hears Paul's keynote sounded:

> Here, then, as Paul saw with a sudden clearness of vision, was in actual being that holy commonwealth of God for which the ages waited. Here was a community created not by geographical accident or by natural heredity, not based on conquest, or wealth, or government, but coming into

*Phillipians, Galatians, Philemon* (Minneapolis: Fortress Press, 1991), pp. 197-201; see also N.T. Wright, *The Climax of the Covenant: Christ and the Law in Pauline Theology* (Edinburgh: T. & T. Clark, 1991), a collection of studies which precedes a promised theology of Paul. The spirit of Dodd's biblical-theological ambitions (and even, in part, intentions) seems to be living still in this growing interpretative project of Wright's (though Dodd is rarely mentioned), as witness N.T. Wright, *The New Testament and the People of God* (London: SPCK, 1992), the first of a projected five-volume New Testament history/theology of which Wright's theology of Paul is to be a part.

existence by the spontaneous outburst of a common life in a multitude of persons. The free, joyous experience of the sons of God had created a family of God, inseparably one in Him: 'one person in Christ Jesus'.[83]

Paul is instrumental in implementing what the ages have awaited—the eschatological community. And thus it seems that Jesus' reinterpretive insight achieves not so much something entirely new as, rather, a purer grasp of something more primordial, obscured by subsequent speculation, a stream of biblical hope now seen more clearly than ever as it is now brought to fruition. Dodd's biblical-theological programme is able to accept, as is, much of the history of religions portrait of the 'new phase', but the signification of this picture is shifted: eschatology does not point in the cosmic and otherworldly direction toward which proponents of the 'new Paul' have strayed, for this is to allow one's interpretation to be ruled by the misunderstandings of those who missed the whole point of it all, failing to see, with Jesus, Paul, and John, that the point of reference of this language is much closer to hand. Schweitzer's eschatological Paul triumphs; and simply learning his language (always of benefit in cross-cultural encounter), the language, that is, of eschatology, allows the modern reader to commune with one who, only the moment before, had seemed so foreign, so distant and remote. (This interpretative twist gives Schweitzer's triumph a hollow ring—and Dodd's implicit celebration of it a cynical tone.) From the standpoint of history, this is a matter of doing a better historical job; from a literary point of view, this is an effort to free interpretation from the constricting grasp of a too-literal approach to the poetic language of eschatology. 'The meaning of Paul for today' is that meaning he has ever struggled to press home. Will he now be heard?

This 'realized' approach has been described as typical of Anglo-American interpretation of the period.[84] Porter's contrast between

---

83. Dodd, *The Meaning of Paul for Today*, p. 154; 'As he [Paul] grew older, the apocalyptic imagery of the earlier days tended to disappear at least from the foreground of his thought, and more and more his mind came to dwell upon the gradual growth and upbuilding of the Divine Commonwealth' (p. 43).

84. E.F. Tupper, 'The Revival of Apocalyptic in Biblical and Theological Studies', *RevExp* 72 (1976), pp. 285-86. Tupper includes under such a 'realized' emphasis 'inaugurated' approaches such as that of J.A.T. Robinson, which 'only preserve a future hope within a framework which otherwise concentrates upon the presence of the rule of God in the Christ event'. Following Dodd's approach to (among other things) Paul (that is, as regards the thesis of a development toward realized eschatology) are T.F. Glasson, *The Second Advent: The Origin of the New*

outward form and inward thought and feeling, echoed in Dodd, provides
a fitting transition to another dominating figure who would preside over
the next wave of response to Schweitzer, expressing with even greater
emphasis the hope that perhaps Paul himself might help us separate
'form' from 'substance'.


## 2. *Rudolf Bultmann*

This is, of course, Rudolf Bultmann, who in the same year as the
appearance of Schweitzer's *Mystik* published, in the second edition of
*Religion in Geschichte und Gegenwart*, a synthetic article on Paul,
sketching in outline the approach given full treatment in Bultmann's
*Theology of the New Testament*.[85]

*Testament Doctrine* (London: Epworth, 3rd edn, 1963 [1945]), and J.A.T. Robinson,
*Jesus and His Coming: The Emergence of a Doctrine* (London: SCM Press, 1957).
Glasson speaks of a movement in Paul whereby 'the teaching of a present spiritual
Kingdom centring in the Cross...gradually comes to the fore while fervid
apocalypticism recedes' (p. 221), and Robinson of 'a shift from an apocalyptic to a
non-apocalyptic form of eschatology' (p. 160 n. 1).

    85.  R. Bultmann, 'Paulus', in *Religion in Geschichte und Gegenwart* (Tübingen:
J. C. B. Mohr, 2nd edn, 1930), IV.1019-45, ET 'Paul', in R. Bultmann, *Existence and
Faith: Shorter Writings of Rudolf Bultmann* (trans. and ed. S.M. Ogden; London:
Hodder and Stoughton, 1961), pp. 111-46; *idem*, *Theology of the New Testament*
(trans. K. Grobel; New York: Charles Scribner's Sons, 1951, 1955 [Ger. orig. 1948-
53]), I, pp. 187-352. Citations in this chapter are from R. Bultmann, *Theology of
the New Testament* (trans. K. Grobel; repr. in one volume; New York: Macmillan,
n.d.). Also important for Bultmann's interpretation of Paul are his surveys of
research: R. Bultmann, 'Zur Geschichte der Paulus-Forschung'; *idem*, 'Neueste
Paulusforschung I'; *TRu* 6 (1934), pp. 229-46, and 'Neueste Paulusforschung II',
*TRu* 8 (1936), pp. 1-22. R. Bultmann, *Primitive Christianity in its Contemporary
Setting* (trans. R.H. Fuller; London: Collins, 1960), is also relevant for present
purposes. See also the collections R. Bultmann, *Faith and Understanding* (trans.
L.P. Smith, edited with an introduction by R.W. Funk; Philadelphia: Fortress Press,
1987 [1969]); *New Testament and Mythology and Other Basic Writings* (ed. and
trans., S.M. Ogden; London: SCM Press, 1985), and R.A. Johnson (ed.), *Rudolf
Bultmann: Interpreting Faith for the Modern Era* (London: Collins, 1987). On
Bultmann, see: W. Schmithals, *An Introduction to the Theology of Rudolf Bultmann*,
(trans. J. Bowden; London: SCM Press, 1968); J. Painter, *Theology as
Hermeneutics: Rudolf Bultmann's Interpretation of the History of Jesus* (Sheffield:
Almond Press, 1987); R. Morgan, 'Rudolf Bultmann', in Ford (ed.), *The Modern
Theologians*, I.109-33; see also R. Morgan, 'Bultmann, R'., in Coggins and Houlden
(eds.), *Dictionary of Biblical Interpretation*, pp. 93-95; N.A. Dahl, 'Rudolf

We begin with Bultmann's exposition of Paul.[86] God, Christ, and humanity are for Paul so intimately connected that to tell the story of human existence is at the same time to tell the story of God and Christ—anthropology *is* theology and Christology. Paul's anthropological terms and conceptions reveal his insight into the unique character of human existence. Human beings as subjects are capable of acting with respect to themselves as objects—this uniquely human reflexivity makes one capable of relationship with oneself and responsible for one's own existence. Human beings, capable of striving, willing, deciding, have ever stretched out before them life, or existence, which confronts them as possibility, and thus as choice, as call to decision, for good or bad, true or false existence, life to God or to oneself. As beings at their own disposal, human beings are capable of coming under the mastery of forces outside themselves in attempting to live by that which is given in creation, the path of self-will and self-reliance, existence 'in the flesh', which is the way of law, sin, and death. This bondage is, in fact, invariably their fate. This is the way of one turned in on oneself, the way of boasting, seen pre-eminently in the Jew's efforts at self-righteousness, and also in the folly of the Gentile's wisdom. This is humanity before faith. But faith comes with the coming of Christ, who brings righteousness as God's gift received in faith, where boasting is excluded and authentic existence is achieved in living toward Creator and not creation, life 'in Christ', 'in the Spirit', a life of freedom from that which formerly robbed one of life. Sin—that is, the past—is removed; the future lies open. In the paradox of the gospel Paul expresses the profundity yet simplicity of losing one's life in seeking to gain it and gaining it back as

Bultmann's Theology of the New Testament', in *The Crucified Messiah and Other Essays* (Minneapolis: Augsburg, 1974), pp. 90-128, 175-77; W.G. Kümmel, 'Rudolf Bultmann als Paulusforscher', in B. Jaspert (ed.), *Rudolf Bultmanns Werk und Wirkung* (Darmstadt: Wissenschaftliche Buchgesellschaft, 1984), pp. 174-93; C.W. Kegley (ed.), *The Theology of Rudolf Bultmann* (London: SCM Press, 1966); (as a general introduction note G. Bornkamm, 'The Theology of Rudolf Bultmann', in Kegley [ed.], *Theology*, pp. 3-20, a reading completely affirmed in Bultmann's reply, pp. 257-58); J. Macquarrie, *An Existentialist Theology* (London: SCM Press, 2nd edn, 1960); R.A. Johnson, *The Origins of Demythologizing: Philosophy and Historiography in the Theology of Rudolf Bultmann* (Leiden: Brill, 1974) and A.C. Thiselton, *The Two Horizons*. For recent interaction with Bultmann in discussion of Paul's theology, note particularly E.P. Sanders, *Paul*, and S. Westerholm, *Israel's Law*.

86. In this paragraph and the following two, Bultmann's interpretation of Paul is sketched, primarily from his *Theology*.

gift in giving it up to the one whose right it is to demand it. Weakness is the way of strength. The greatness of Paul lies 'in the fact that as a *theologian* he gave to the Christian faith an adequate understanding of itself', bringing 'the knowledge inherent in faith itself into the clarity of conscious knowing',[87] expressing in pure form the proclamation of the gospel of grace, God's liberating act in Christ, and perceiving beneath it the true nature and structure of human existence. This insight belongs first and pre-eminently to Paul, the first and great Christian thinker, and this is 'Paulinism', the distinctive voice of Paul. And from here the lines may be drawn to the various elements of his thought.

Paul's anthropology and doctrine of redemption are not, as it were, uninterrupted by mythological intrusions. His consistent holistic interpretation of the human being as one who acts for oneself is invaded at points by mythical dualistic notions.[88] His portrayal of the bondage of inauthentic existence is at times cloaked in language of a mythical slavery to 'powers'.[89] The proclamation of the eschatological 'now' is upset by another mythological intrusion which may serve as an example of Paul's (and Bultmann's, as he is seen through his Paul) handling of such anomalies. Paul 'holds fast to the traditional Jewish-Christian teaching of the resurrection of the dead, and in so doing he also retains the apocalyptic expectation of the last judgment and of the cosmic drama which will end the old world and introduce the new world of salvation...'[90] But alongside such 'apocalyptic' myth stands 'Gnostic' myth, asserting the presence of life, of redemption, showing how little such schemes control his thought.[91] Every such intrusion hardly obscures the focus on existence. This is Paul as a practitioner of Bultmann's celebrated existentialist hermeneutics of 'demythologization'. For myth, by nature, asks to be interpreted in terms of human existence. Furthermore, the New Testament itself asks the modern interpreter to follow its own lead in demythologizing its kerygma, itself showing the relative unimportance of the various mythical schemes used by juxtaposing disparate and even contradictory mythical traditions in the effort to express its kerygma and by making plain, especially in Paul (and

---

87.    Bultmann, 'Paul', p. 120; *Theology*, I, p. 190.

88.    Bultmann, 'Paul', pp. 130-31; *Theology*, I, pp. 201-203.

89.    Bultmann, 'Paul', p. 130; *Theology*, I, pp. 244-45, 257-59.

90.    Bultmann, *Theology*, I, p. 346.

91.    Bultmann, *Theology*, I, pp. 347-52; see also *Primitive Christianity*, pp. 232-46.

John), that the inner kerygmatic concern is existence.[92]

This last point brings into view Paul's focus on kerygma and on proclamation. It is as, and only as, proclamation that the Christ event, God's decisive intervention on humanity's behalf, accosts each individual, rendering his or her self-understanding and self-effort meaningless, offering righteousness by faith, salvation as radically God's gift, and thus holding the only possibility of life, of existence in its only true sense. One may not seek to get back behind the proclamation—it is not pre-evangelization as a gnosis which corrects one's self-understanding or as a history lesson on which to found faith[93]—nor may it be deliberated, for to take issue with it is already to reject it. As a radical, existential confrontation it is the cosmic, eschatological occurrence, the coming of faith in the fullness of time, the 'now' of redemption. Submission to the proclamation places one between the times, between the resurrection and parousia, as the old passes away and the new comes. Human existence in Christ takes on the character of 'already' and 'not yet', as the new creature lives on in the old world, but 'as if not', as believers 'become what they are', leaving behind the old age of sin and living in the age of faith.

As with Schweitzer and Dodd, Bultmann's approach to Paul's eschatology must be indexed back to his account of Jesus' own. Beginning with Jesus and tracing the eschatological development through to Paul, Bultmann's interpretation reveals its indebtedness to and divergence from Schweitzer's (a configuration which readily invites detailed comparison with Dodd, revealing an intriguing array of similarities and differences). According to Bultmann:

> The dominant concept of Jesus' message is the *Reign of God*. Jesus proclaims its immediately impending irruption, now already making itself felt. Reign of God is an eschatological concept. It means the regime of God which will destroy the present course of the world, wipe out all the contra-divine, Satanic power under which the present world groans—and thereby, terminating all pain and sorrow, bring in salvation for the People of God which awaits the fulfilment of the prophet's promises. The coming

92.  On demythologizing, see further below. For Bultmann, New Testament research 'has to work out for the community the formulation of the kerygma that is appropriate today'. 'No sermon may leave its hearers uncertain about what they do and do not have to hold to be true. Above all, it may not leave them uncertain about what the preacher secretly eliminates...' ('Theology as Science' and 'New Testament And Mythology', in Ogden (ed.), *New Testament And Mythology*, pp. 61, 9).

93.  The implicit targets here are Schweitzer's 'mysticism' and Cullmann's 'salvation history'.

of God's Reign is a miraculous event, which will be brought about by God alone without the help of men.

With such a message, Jesus stands *in the historical context of Jewish expectations about the end of the world and God's new future.* And it is clear that his thought is not determined by the *national* hope then still alive in certain circles of the Jewish people...Rather, Jesus' message is connected with the hope of other circles which is primarily documented by the *apocalyptic* literature, a hope which awaits salvation not from a miraculous change in historical (i.e. political and social) conditions, but from a cosmic catastrophe which will do away with all conditions of the present world as it is. The presupposition of this hope is the pessimistic-dualistic view of the Satanic corruption of the total world-complex, which is expressed in the special doctrine of the *two aeons* into which the world's career is divided: The old aeon is approaching its end, and the new aeon will dawn with terror and tribulation. The old world with its periods has an end determined by God, and when the day He has determined is here, the judgment of the world will be held by Him or by His representative, the Son of Man, who will come on the clouds of heaven; the dead will arise, and men's deeds, good or bad, will receive their reward. But the salvation of the faithful will consist not in national prosperity and splendor, but in the glory of paradise.[94]

Yet once more, a textbook definition of 'apocalyptic' is offered. And, with another now familiar turn, Bultmann goes on to assert that Jesus is not ruled by such conceptions: 'What is new and really his own about it all is the certainty with which he says, *"Now the time is come! God's Reign is breaking in! The end is here!"*'[95] This 'does not mean that God's Reign is already here; but it does mean that it is dawning'.[96] 'Man cannot hasten the divinely determined course of events...All that man can do in the face of the Reign of God now breaking in is this: Keep ready or get ready for it. Now is the *time of decision*, and Jesus' call is the *call to decision*'.[97] '[H]e in his own person is the *"sign of the time"*'.[98]

94.  Bultmann, *Theology*, I, pp. 4-5.

95.  Bultmann, *Theology*, I, p. 6. Bultmann's speaking of 'what is new and really his own' calls to mind Dodd's speaking of what is 'distinctively' and 'authentically' Christian.

96.  Bultmann, *Theology*, I, p. 7 (emphasis removed). Here Bultmann, in the last moment, as it were, distances his reading from Dodd's, whose interpretation it is already beginning to resemble.

97.  Bultmann, *Theology*, I, pp. 7-9; this does not indicate a 'messianic consciousness' in Jesus for Bultmann.

98.  Bultmann, *Theology*, I, p. 9. On 'the eschatological preaching of Jesus', see also *Primitive Christianity*, pp. 102-10.

The earliest community regarded itself as the 'eschatological Congregation', as the 'People of God', an eschatological consciousness expressed in baptism and breaking of bread, and visible in the experience of the Spirit, the fulfilment of scripture, and in the early missionary activity.[99] In the Hellenistic community, which forms the immediate backdrop to Paul, this self-understanding remained, through various changes, along with continued 'apocalyptic' expectation of the 'eschatological drama'.[100] For both communities, however, a Paul was needed to correct faulty insights (and a John to perfect Paul's beginning). In particular, Paul's grasp of the Christ event as the decisive eschatological occurrence, of the eschatological 'now' of the proclamation and of the eschatological dialectic of living 'between the times', is sorely missed.[101]

The theology of Bultmann's Paul, then, is anthropological, existentialist, kerygmatic, hermeneutical, and, in Bultmann's sense, eschatological, precisely as is Bultmann's own, exposed in the very act of exposing Paul's thought. These strands are tightly woven together in Bultmann's 'demythologizing'.[102] Up to this point, we have viewed Bultmann focused through (his) Paul; but it is also instructive to view (his) Paul focused through Bultmann, that is, to observe Bultmann's interpretation and use of Paul when Bultmann is speaking more for himself, as he does in many programmatic essays. We turn, then, to consider Bultmann's *Jesus Christ and Mythology*, which presents one of the clearest and most sustained delineations of his demythologizing programme.[103] In so

99. Bultmann, *Theology*, I, pp. 37-43. Bultmann's 'eschatological Congregation' echoes, like Dodd's, Schweitzer's eschatological 'community of the elect'.

100. Bultmann, *Theology*, I, pp. 73-82, 92-108, 117-18, 124, 133, 152, 155.

101. Bultmann, *Theology*, I, pp. 36-37, 42-43, 62, 152, 182.

102. Cf. R.A. Johnson: 'Demythologizing...provide[d] the single theological focus which brought together in one proposal the multiple strands of Bultmann's theology' ('Introduction', in R.A. Johnson [ed.], *Rudolf Bultmann*, p. 42).

103. R. Bultmann, *Jesus Christ and Mythology* (London: SCM Press, 1960). Other relevant essays by Bultmann (consideration of which also goes into the following discussion of 'demythologizing') are collected in Ogden (ed.), *New Testament And Mythology*, which includes the celebrated 'New Testament and Mythology' (pp. 1-43), Bultmann's first programmatic discussion of demythologizing which, expressing though it did only what he had been practising for some years, sparked the whole demythologizing debate, partially chronicled in H.W. Bartsch (ed.), *Kerygma and Myth: A Theological Debate* (trans. R.H. Fuller; 2 vols.; London: SPCK, 1964 [2nd edn], 1962). In speaking of viewing Bultmann through Paul and vice versa, we are observing the hermeneutical nature of Bultmann's theologizing, as he does theology in the very act of interpreting scripture (cf. Painter's title, *Theology as Hermeneutics*).

doing, we gain a fuller insight into the contours of Bultmann's own thought and, in the process, begin to observe his reflections on Paul and 'apocalyptic' in their wider setting and according to their own logic.

Bultmann begins at a point now familiar since Schweitzer.

> The heart of the preaching of Jesus Christ is the Kingdom of God. During the nineteenth century exegesis and theology understood the Kingdom of God as a spiritual community consisting of men joined together by obedience to the will of God which ruled in their wills. By such obedience they sought to enlarge the sphere of his rule in the world. They were building, it was said, the Kingdom of God as a realm which is spiritual but within the world, active and effective in this world, unfolding in the history of this world (p. 11).

But with the work of Johannes Weiss, and later Albert Schweitzer, all this was to change: the kingdom came to be seen as not immanent but eschatological, transcending the historical order, and coming not through human moral endeavour but by the supernatural intervention of God, putting an end to the old world and bringing in the new. Bultmann reminisces: 'When I began to study theology, theologians as well as laymen were excited and frightened' by such theories; but now 'nobody doubts that Jesus' conception of the Kingdom of God is an eschatological one' (p. 13). Jesus' conception was common currency in the earliest community, shared by all, including Paul. In fact, 'Christianity has always retained the hope that the Kingdom of God will come in the immediate future'—and Bultmann continues, pointedly—'although it has waited in vain' (p. 14).

> The course of history has refuted mythology. For the conception 'Kingdom of God' is mythological, as is the conception of the eschatological drama. Just as mythological are the presuppositions of the expectation of the Kingdom of God, namely, the theory that the world, although created by God, is ruled by the devil, Satan, and that his army, the demons, is the cause of all evil, sin and disease. The whole conception of the world which is presupposed in the preaching of Jesus as in the New Testament generally is mythological; i.e., the conception of the world as being structured in three stories, heaven, earth and hell; the conception of the intervention of supernatural powers in the course of events; and the conception of miracles, especially the conception of the intervention of supernatural powers in the inner life of the soul, the conception that men can be tempted and corrupted by the devil and possessed by evil spirits (pp. 14-15).[104]

---

104. Clearly, then, for Bultmann, the 'new phase' Paul is a mythological Paul, a candidate for demythologizing. (It is worth pausing to speculate on how Nietzsche,

Bultmann forcefully presses the contrast between such a conception of reality and that conception implicit in what constitutes the normal state of affairs in which the modern person lives out his or her day to day life. The modern scientific mentality, a closed world-view of cause and effect relations, is far removed from the mythological. 'Then the question inevitably arises: is it possible that Jesus' preaching of the Kingdom of God still has any importance for modern men and the preaching of the New Testament as a whole is still important for modern men' (p. 16)? This preaching, from its earliest, is mythological—one cannot press back to a point at which this is not so. 'This raises in an acute form the question: *what is the importance of the preaching of Jesus and of the preaching of the New Testament as a whole for modern man*' (p. 17)? This very question sets Bultmann's critical agenda.

If an uncritical and, from Bultmann's point of view, dishonest acceptance of the eschatological world-view of the New Testament is not possible, neither is the simple elimination of eschatology in favour of ethics, the liberal solution of 'the so-called social gospel'; and so Bultmann asks whether there is a 'third possibility':

> We must ask whether the eschatological preaching and the mythological sayings as a whole contain a still deeper meaning which is concealed under the cover of mythology. If that is so, let us abandon the mythological conceptions precisely because we want to retain their deeper meaning. This method of interpretation of the New Testament which tries to recover the deeper meaning behind the mythological conceptions I call *de-mythologizing*—an unsatisfactory word, to be sure. Its aim is not to eliminate the mythological statements but to interpret them. It is a method of hermeneutics. The meaning of this method will be best understood when we make clear the meaning of mythology in general (p. 18).

What, then, is the meaning of mythology?

Bultmann has already dealt with mythology in one sense, that of a mythological versus a modern scientific world view or perception of external reality. As Bultmann claims elsewhere, the mythological world-view is not unique to early Christianity, but common currency across the religions of Hellenistic antiquity.[105] And it has been left behind in the

whose similar catalogue of incredulities is quoted above at the head of the chapter on Schweitzer, might have reacted to such a stealing of his thunder, mere decades after he wrote, *from within Christian theology itself.* But time does not stand still. And perhaps theology, like philosophy, buries its own pall bearers.)

105. See Bultmann, *Primitive Christianity*; cf. R.A. Johnson (ed.), *Rudolf Bultmann*, p. 29.

course of (Western) history. But is there some deeper meaning to mythology, now in focus not so much as a conception of external reality but for what it expresses of the human condition, what ancient men and women struggled to express, even if unwittingly, through mythology?[106] 'Myths express the knowledge that man is not master of the world and of his life, that the world in which he lives is full of riddles and mysteries and that human life also is full of riddles and mysteries' (p. 19). 'Mythology expresses a certain understanding of human existence...It may be said that myths give to the transcendent reality an immanent, this-worldly objectivity' (p. 19).[107] For example, mythological conceptions of the spatial distance of God express the still perfectly acceptable notion of God's transcendence; conceptions of demonic powers express the mysterious, superhuman quality of evil still perceived by moderns.

On this basis, then, Bultmann continues: 'Now the question arises: is it possible to de-mythologize the message of Jesus and the preaching of the early Christian community? Since this preaching was shaped by the eschatological belief, the first question is this: *What is the meaning of eschatology in general*' (p. 21)?

> As in the conception of heaven the transcendence of God is imagined by means of the category of space, so in the conception of the end of the world, the idea of the transcendence of God is imagined by means of the category of time. However, it is not simply the idea of transcendence as such, but of the importance of the transcendence of God...Eschatological preaching views the present time in the light of the future and it says to men that this present world, the world of nature and history,...is not the only world; that this world is temporal and transitory, yes, ultimately empty and unreal in the face of eternity (pp. 22-23).

106. Implicit, then, is the notion that mythology is an 'objectification' of such existential concerns; see below. Various nuances have been detected in Bultmann's use of 'myth', and various different meanings are distinguished (see Thiselton, *The Two Horizons*, pp. 252-58); but for the present purposes, and, it seems, according to Bultmann's basic intent, two basic meanings may be distinguished, as here, between 'mythology' as a picture of external, objective reality, now obsolete, and as a world view expressing, as every world view does, some perception of human existence and of transcendence.

107. Here the ease with which Bultmann shifts from 'existence' to 'the transcendent reality' should be noted. Bultmann's retention of the reality of transcendence might constitute for some a point of tension in his thought, a failure to follow through fully his demythologizing programme.

It is the intensity of Jesus' perception of the transcendence of God, that is, the finiteness of humanity and its world, that lies behind and finds expression in an expectation of the 'end' in the immediate future: 'The majesty of God and the inescapability of his judgment, and over against these the emptiness of the world and of men were felt with such an intensity that it seemed that the world was at an end, and that the hour of crisis was present' (p. 25).

> This, then, is the deeper meaning of the mythological preaching of Jesus— to be open to God's future which is really imminent for every one of us; to be prepared for this future which can come as a thief in the night when we do not expect it; to be prepared, because this future will be a judgment on all men who have bound themselves to this world and are not free, not open to God's future (pp. 31-32).

Bultmann's demythologizing of Jesus' preaching is not meant to be taken solely on Bultmann's accuracy of perception of its 'deeper meaning', for Jesus himself may be said to begin the process of reinter-pretation of Jewish 'apocalyptic', continued in the demythologizing of Paul and John, by shifting the emphasis from another world of another time to the 'now' of his ministry.

Paul and John, then, hold a place in Bultmann's scheme analogous to that which they occupy for Dodd:

> The eschatological preaching of Jesus was retained and continued by the early Christian community in its mythological form. But very soon the process of demythologizing began, partially with Paul, and radically with John. The decisive step was taken when Paul declared that the turning point from the old world to the new was not a matter of the future but did take place in the coming of Jesus Christ...To be sure, Paul still expected the end of the world as a cosmic drama, the *parousia* of Christ on the clouds of heaven, the resurrection from the dead, the final judgment, but with the resurrection of Christ the decisive event has already happened... Therefore, Paul can say that the expectations and promises of the ancient prophets are fulfilled *when the gospel is proclaimed*...(p. 32, emphasis added).

Bultmann offers an example of Paul's demythologizing:

> In the Jewish apocalyptic expectations, the expectation of the Messianic kingdom played a role...Paul explains this apocalyptic, mythological idea of the Messianic *interregnum*, at the end of which Christ will deliver the Kingdom to God the Father, as the present time between the resurrection of Christ and his coming *parousia* (1 Cor. 15.24); that means, *the present*

*time of preaching the gospel* is really the formerly expected time of the
Kingdom of the Messiah. Jesus is now the Messiah, the Lord (p. 33,
emphasis added).

For Bultmann, as for Dodd, John radicalizes Paul's insights.

Although Bultmann is forthright about the fact that in his view the
modern scientific world-view is a criterion for interpreting scripture and
the Christian gospel, he regards this as a simple, unavoidable consequence for one for whom there is no turning back to an obsolete,
mythological world-view; but it is the world-view, and not scripture or
gospel, that is critically removed or reinterpreted, with the abiding
relevance of the latter as a controlling principle. 'To de-mythologize is to
deny that the message of Scripture and of the Church is bound to an
ancient world-view which is obsolete' (p. 36). Only in this way may the
true character of Christian preaching be perceived, which 'does not offer
a doctrine which can be accepted either by reason or by a *sacrificium
intellectus*', but comes as '*kerygma*, that is, a proclamation addressed
not to theoretical reason, but to the hearer as a self...De-mythologizing
will make clear this function of preaching as a personal message, and in
doing so it will eliminate a false stumbling-block and bring into sharp
focus the real stumbling-block, the word of the cross' (p. 36).

If the world-view of modernity from one prespective passes judgment
over the mythological world-view as having been rendered no longer
capable of assent by the course of events, and as having been shown by
increased knowledge to be inadequate to reality, from another perspective the flow of critique is reversed, as the mythological world-view has
a crucial point in its favour over against modernity: it retains the perspective of transcendence. 'Certainly', says Bultmann, 'it is a philosophical problem whether the scientific world-view can perceive the whole
reality of the world and of human life' (p. 38). The 'modern man'
forgets the requirement of obedience to God's command and that true
security exceeds the grasp of purely human effort.

> It is the word of God which calls man away from his selfishness and from
> the illusory security which he has built up for himself. It calls him to God,
> who is beyond the world and beyond scientific thinking. At the same time,
> it calls man to his true self. For the self of man, his inner life, his personal
> existence is also beyond the visible world and beyond rational thinking.
> The Word of God addresses man in his personal existence and thereby it
> gives him freedom from the world and from the sorrow and anxiety which
> overwhelm him when he forgets the beyond (p. 40).

Striving for mastery and control of self and world through science and technology, modern humanity loses itself, loses its freedom, and is itself mastered and controlled, imprisoned by its own self-deception in a paradoxically precarious search for security. The story of modern humanity, for Bultmann, is rife with such irony. And Bultmann offers, with Luther and Paul, remedial ironies of his own: security in abandonment to insecurity, freedom in obedience, or, simply, *faith*. It is the sole purpose of the proclamation to awaken this response of faith, and it is the sole purpose of demythologization to unleash the proclamation in its full force, 'asking for the deeper meaning of mythological conceptions and freeing the Word of God from a by-gone world-view' (p. 43). Implicit in every world-view is some conception of existence, of humanity in relation to its world. The kerygma weighs them all alike in the balance, and modernity comes up wanting, even more so than does myth. The only real problem that attaches to myth is that its perception of the reality and import of the transcendent is caught in an 'objectifying' conceptuality which subverts its potentially liberating effect.

Thus the door which myth opens to faith it promptly closes in attaching itself to an 'objectification' of the acting of God. Such an 'objectifying' conceptuality is improper for God, for human beings, and for faith. Yet both myth and modernity, though in different ways, attempt to entrap them in some 'objectifying' frame. But God is not an entity constituted by a Kantian knowing subject, nor does he relate to humanity as an immanent acting subject to a passive object or placating subject. To press God into such structures of claim and control is to move in the realm of work, not faith. To press human existence into these structures is to move in the realm of inauthentic existence, the realm of flesh, not Spirit, of slavery to sin, not freedom in obedience—again, work, not faith.

Modernity fails to perceive the depth of reality. The problematic of modernity strikes at its own very roots, in its celebration of 'objectifying' inquiry, so successful in natural science and daily coping, so impoverished in terms of capturing God's acting and humanity's essence. For God's acting remains hidden, visible only to faith and out of reach of rational investigation and proof. Our own personal existence, equally opaque to 'objectifying' inquiry, is perceived only in the dialectical flow of true 'historicity'.[108] Neither God nor human existence can be frozen, mounted,

108. This term (*Geschichtlichkeit*), a favoured expression for indicating the true historical, temporal character of human existence, will be clarified below from Bultmann's *History and Eschatology*, where it occurs more frequently.

and passed under the microscope of abstract, timeless 'objectification'—they do not survive such an examination intact, since the process is destructive of their very nature.

A mode of inquiry is required that does not violate God's transcendent acting, abandon humanity to inauthenticity, or sell faith out to works. Existentialist analysis provides just this. Existentialist philosophical reflection contrasts existence with merely being 'extant': 'Only men can have existence, because they are historical beings. That is to say, every man has his own history. Always his present comes out of his past and leads into his future. He realizes his existence if he is aware that each "now" is the moment of free decision...' (p. 56). This temporal structure is true historicity, and this 'now' is for Christian theology the moment of the kerygma, the proclamation of God's acting in Christ.

'Man's life is moved, consciously or unconsciously, by the question about his own personal existence. The question of God and the question of myself are identical' (p. 53). For the Christian tradition, the Bible speaks with authority to this question, and furthermore it becomes a Word which offers real existence. The hermeneutical principle by which the modern reader may give these distant texts a clear and contemporary voice is what is wanted.

Demythologizing is conceived as just this hermeneutical principle and process. The distance it is required to span is crossed in its perception of a uniquely human nature, possessed by all, untouched by passing time, affirmed or denied by each in every moment. Hermeneutics, as historical inquiry and understanding, is, purely conceived, existentialist. 'Thus, negatively, demythologizing is criticism of the mythical world picture insofar as it conceals the real intention of myth. Positively, demythologizing is existentialist interpretation, in that it seeks to make clear the intention of myth to talk about human existence'.[109]

---

109. Bultmann, 'On the Problem of Demythologizing', in Ogden (ed.), *New Testament and Mythology*, p. 99. Bultmann's explicit hermeneutical theorizing cannot be given the space it perhaps merits, but the entire discussion here and below of 'demythologizing' and of 'history and eschatology' is a hermeneutical one, and is expressive of Bultmann's hermeneutical programme. The keystone of Bultmann's hermeneutics is the concept of a 'preunderstanding' (*Vorverständnis*) in the form of a 'life-relation' to the 'subject-matter' (*Sache*) of a text which makes the connection achieved in understanding possible, and this life-relation is that of existence, of historicity. See Bultmann, *Jesus Christ and Mythology*, pp. 45-59; 'The Problem of Hermeneutics', 'Science and Existence', and 'Is Exegesis Without Presuppositions Possible?', in Ogden (ed.), *New Testament and Mythology*, pp. 69-93, 131-44, 145-

Only talk of God which is talk of our personal existence avoids 'objectifying' conceptions. The language of myth, inasmuch as it continues to be used, operates as symbol and image, or, better, as analogical speaking: 'When we speak of God as acting, we mean that we are confronted with God, addressed, asked, judged, or blessed by God' (p. 68) '[O]nly such statements about God are legitimate as express the existential relation between God and man. *Statements which speak of God's actions as cosmic events are illegitimate'*—even an affirmation of God as Creator can only properly be a personal affirmation of creatureliness (p. 69, emphasis added).[110]

Bultmann is forging a conceptuality appropriate to God, human beings, and faith. For this it is necessary to part company both with the anthropomorphism of ancient myth and the subject/object division of modern science. The centrality of proclamation and faith is given for Bultmann in the Lutheran tradition, which anchors itself in Paul. With Paul Bultmann seeks to explicate the self-understanding implicit in the faith provoked by the proclamation. A 'fit' is sought between the transcendent acting of God, the historicity of human Being, and the faith by which all this fuses in the kerygma.

> [T]he criticism of the mythological world-view of Biblical and ecclesiastical preaching renders a valuable service to faith, for it recalls faith to radical reflection on its own nature. The task of de-mythologizing has no other purpose than to take up this challenge. The invisibility of God excludes every myth which tries to make God and His action visible; God withholds Himself from view and observation. We can believe in God only in spite of experience, just as we can accept justification only in spite of conscience. Indeed, de-mythologizing is a task parallel to that performed by Paul and Luther in their doctrine of justification by faith alone without the works of law. More precisely, de-mythologizing is the radical application of the doctrine of justification by faith to the sphere of knowledge and thought. Like the doctrine of justification, de-mythologizing destroys every longing for security. There is no difference between security based on good works and security built on objectifying knowledge...Man before God has always empty hands (pp. 83-84).

Bultmann's exercise in Pauline and Lutheran epistemology achieves, in demythologizing, a remarkable fusion of theology, philosophy, and

53; see also R. Bultmann, *History and Eschatology* (Edinburgh: Edinburgh University Press, 1957), pp. 110-22.

110. Thus 'transcendence' may only properly be affirmed, as myth fails to perceive, in an affirmation of human finitude.

hermeneutics turning on the axis of the Lutheran faith/works divide.[111]

Bultmann, in his 1955 Gifford Lectures, 'History and Eschatology', broadens the reading of modernity offered in *Jesus Christ and Mythology* (where he suggests a realm of perception that escapes scientific observation, a realm of knowledge that eludes the exercise of pure reason, a realm of uniquely human Being beyond the reach of the relativism and nihilism of historicism), placing his interpretation of Paul's eschatology in its broadest setting.[112] Here Bultmann's themes of 'historicity' and 'reinterpreted eschatology' become most clear and coherent, as he aspires to a generality of discourse most rare for biblical critics.

The several lectures develop the following points: The 'problem of history' and of the 'historicity of man' is the loss of the ability even to speak of meaning in the wake of 'historicism', whose relativism and nihilism dissolve humanity itself, which *is* simply history, which latter has become simply nature. True history arises not with ancient Greece and Rome, for whom likewise history is nature, but with ancient Israel, with its interest in self-knowledge and responsibility before God. With 'Jewish apocalyptic thought', with its world-historical viewpoint, its individualization and de-nationalization of the old hopes, and its other-worldly, 'two Aeon' perspective, 'history is understood from the point of view of eschatology'. In other words, the meaning of history may now come into view as history becomes a completed whole seen from its final outcome, developments continued in Jesus and early Christianity whereby 'history is swallowed up in eschatology' for a community which 'understands itself not as a historical but as an eschatological phenomenon' (pp. 29, 37). The course of history proved either that such a conception must be abandoned as fiction and fantasy, or else either reinterpreted in the 'new understanding of eschatology' in Paul and John (p. 40) or secularized, as in Hegelian idealism, Marxian materialism, and in the general 'spirit of

111. Judgment is not passed here on the stability of this fusion; but its breadth and ambition is truly striking. On the matter of Bultmann within the Lutheran tradition, as Johnson notes, Bultmann's Lutheranism is mediated through the nineteenth century developments in this tradition: R.A. Johnson, *Origins*, p. 84; cf., following Johnson, Thiselton, *The Two Horizons*, pp. 210-17.

112. Bultmann, *History and Eschatology*; see also Bultmann's 1953 Society for New Testament Study Presidential Address, 'History and Eschatology in the New Testament', *NTS* 1 (1954), pp. 5-16. On this theme, see P.S. Minear, 'Rudolf Bultmann's Interpretation of New Testament Eschatology', and H. Ott, 'Rudolf Bultmann's Philosophy of History', in Kegley (ed.), *Theology*, pp. 65-82 and 51-64, along with Bultmann's replies on pp. 262-68.

the age' of Enlightenment faith in progress. The latter optimism dissolves into the aforementioned historicism, which 'understands history by analogy with nature' as a realm of pure facts, to be approached in pure objectivity, with all subjectivity and value-judgment eliminated, which, combined with a consequent relativistic despair of finding meaning in history, leaves historicism 'swallowed up by naturalism' (pp. 78, 79). Corresponding to this dissolution, the 'historicity' of human being, clearly understood by Paul in his emphasis on imprisonment to sin in self-striving and freedom from this past and for the future by grace through faith, is lost or seriously obscured. 'Objectivity' in historical science cannot be conceived as it is in natural science, for with history truth is perspectival and meaning implicates the existence of the inquirer. Reflection on the philosophy of history reveals the qualitative difference between natural and historical science and elucidates the character of historical knowledge as self-knowledge. Finally, historicism itself points the way beyond itself toward the solution found in true 'historicity'.

History itself falsifies eschatology taken literally; historicism dissolves its secularized versions. This leaves standing only the 'reinterpreted eschatology' of Paul and John. '*How is the Church to understand the relation between history and eschatology? A new understanding of eschatology, which appears for the first time in Paul and is radically developed in John, is the first stage in the solution of the problem*' (p. 40, emphasis added).

'*The Pauline understanding of history* is determined by eschatology' (p. 40). Bultmann proceeds to show how Paul reinterprets the 'apocalyptic' perspective on 'history and eschatology' and how he perceives, beneath gospel and faith, the 'historicity of man'. For Paul, the history of Israel is not a national history but a history of humankind in sin. The end and meaning of history is not perceived immanently, but is God-given, as history is the story of sin preparing the way for God's grace. As a universal view of history with a 'two age' structure, Paul shares 'the apocalyptic view of history' (p. 41).

> The apocalyptic view of history, however, is altered by Paul in a decisive manner in that, according to him, the history of humanity under law and sin has a meaning. In other words: Paul has interpreted the apocalyptic view of history on the basis of his anthropology. The Pauline view of history is the expression of his view of man: man can receive his life only by the grace of God, but he can receive the divine grace only when he knows himself annihilated before God; therefore the sin into which man is plunged is paradoxically the presupposition for the reception of grace.

> Paul has interpreted history in terms of this view of man. The law which
> came in between Adam and Christ must carry sin to its culminating point
> in order that grace can become mighty (Rom. v.20). That this view of
> history is derived from anthropology is indicated by the fact that Paul can
> present the course of history from Adam, by the way of the law, to Christ,
> in the form of an autobiographical 'I' (Rom. vii.7-25a) (p. 41).

Then the fulfilment of divine promises becomes problematic, as for Paul
the national and world-historical dimensions of traditional eschatology
are inadequate and inappropriate, since 'Paul has decisively modified the
current eschatology as well as the apocalyptic view of history'—thus,
'his conception of the eschatological time of bliss is also determined by
his anthropology' (p. 42).

> To be sure, he does not abandon the apocalyptic picture of the future, of
> the parousia of Christ, of the resurrection of the dead, of the Last
> Judgment, of glory for those who believe and are justified. But the real
> bliss is righteousness, and with it freedom. The reign of God, he says, is
> righteousness and peace and joy in the Holy Spirit (Rom. xiv.17). And
> that means: the conception of bliss is thought of with regard to the
> individual: and this state of bliss is already present. The believer who has
> received baptism is 'in Christ'. Therefore it is true that 'If any one is in
> Christ, he is a new creature' (2 Cor. v.17), and that 'The old has passed
> away; behold, the new has come' (*ibid.*). The New Aeon is already reality,
> for 'When the fullness of the time was come, God sent forth his Son'
> (Gal. iv.4). The time of bliss, promised by Isaiah, is present: 'Behold, now
> is the acceptable time; behold, now is the day of salvation' (2 Cor. vi.2).
> The Gift of the Spirit, which the Jews expected to come at the time of the
> end, is now bestowed upon believers; therefore they are now already 'sons
> of God' and free men instead of servants (Gal. iv.6f.) (p. 42).

Whatever elements of futurity and of universal and cosmic perspective
remain are overshadowed in this emphasis on realization and the
individual.[113]

'But although the history of the nation and the world had lost interest
for Paul, he brings to light another phenomenon, the historicity of man,
the true historical life of the human being, the history which every one
experiences for himself and by which he gains his real essence' (p. 43).

---

113. See Bultmann, *History and Eschatology*, p. 43. Bultmann speaks here, much
like Dodd, of 'apocalyptic' both as a philosophy of history and as an eschatological
doctrine, and Paul modifies both these aspects of 'apocalyptic' ('history' and
'eschatology').

This historical life is born in personal encounter through the decisions such encounters precipitate.

> [T]he life of a man is always one which stands before him and acquires its character as forfeited or as real by his decisions. What a man chooses in his decisions is...himself as the man he is to be and intends to be, or as one who has forfeited his real life. For Paul human life is a life before God; the real life then is the life confirmed by God, the forfeited life is the life condemned by God (p. 44).

The problem of the freedom of such decisions arises, and 'Paul is convinced that man is not able to be free from his past, indeed, that he does not wish to be free but prefers to remain as he is. That is the essence of sin' (p. 44).

> Paul's thought becomes still clearer in his description of Christian existence. To exist as Christian means to live in freedom, a freedom into which the believer is brought by the divine grace which appeared in Christ. The one justified by faith is set free from his past, from his sin, from himself. And he is set free for a real historical life in free decision (p. 45).

Furthermore, the 'real historicity of the Christian life becomes apparent also from the fact that this life is a continuous being on the way, between the "no longer" and the "not yet"' (p. 46). 'There is a dialectical relation between the indicative and the imperative'—a dialectic of continuing to become what one already is (p. 46). 'I leave it undecided how far Paul makes explicit thoughts contained in the preaching of Jesus. *At all events the Pauline conception of historicity and his unfolding of the dialectic of Christian existence contains the solution of the problem of history and eschatology as it was raised by the delay of the parousia of Christ*' (p. 47, emphasis added).

This movement of thought in Paul is fortuitous, for his own standing in our eyes and for our own ability to make use of him, for Bultmann concedes the relativist point of historicism that meaning eludes us on the level of universal history. For Jewish/Christian eschatological thought, meaning was perceived in history on the presumption of knowledge of the end—meaning in any ultimate sense requires such an ultimate, 'above-and-beyond-history' perspective. Likewise, secular eschatologies presume knowledge of an ultimate goal. 'Today we cannot claim to know the end and the goal of history. Therefore the question of meaning in history has become meaningless...[But] there remains the question of the importance of single historical events and deeds of our past for our present, a present which is charged with responsibility for our future' (pp. 120-21). Historicism, when its consequences are followed through, historicizes the historian; that is, no neutral, ahistorical standpoint is available for historical inquiry, no 'Archimedean point'. If meaning is to be found, if it is to be had at all, it is not available to any 'objectifying' inquiry—this is to launch forth into a shoreless sea of relativity. But utter despair of meaning only follows on the assumption of the identity of history and nature. To collapse history into nature is to naturalize humanity, to conceive of humanity on the level of inanimate objects and animals—the objects of natural science. If humanity is quite happy on the whole with this debasement, this is only symptomatic of the depth and enslaving power of sin, whose essence is just such a flight from historicity, from true humanity.[114]

> Historicity...[is] responsibility over against the future, which is at the same time the responsibility over against the heritage of the past in face of the future. Historicity is the nature of man who can never possess his genuine life in any present moment, but is always on the way and yet is not at the mercy of a course of history independent of himself. Every moment is the *now* of responsibility, of decision. From this the unity of history is to be understood (p. 143).

114. The distinction between history and nature is basic to Bultmann. It is a distinction between human actions, which are driven by purpose, intention, consciousness, revealing directedness, involving risk, implicating personality, and the pure contingency of events. This is a matter of freedom, will, and decision as opposed to necessity, obligation, and determination, a methodological distinction between understanding and explanation, between *Geistes-* and *Naturwissenschaften*. The latter pole invades the former at the expense of meaning and at the cost of humanity. Historicism delivers one up to this naturalism. This distinction is expressed in some of Bultmann's earliest programmatic discussion, as in 'The Problem of a Theological Exegesis of the New Testament', excerpted in R.A. Johnson (ed.), *Rudolf Bultmann*, pp. 129-37 (from 1925) and the methodological prologue to *Jesus and the Word* (trans. L.P. Smith and E.H. Lantero; New York: Charles Scribner's Sons, 1934 [1926]), pp. 3-15 (repr. in R.A. Johnson [ed.], *Rudolf Bultmann*, pp. 92-98). All the essays collected in Ogden (ed.), *New Testament and Mythology* (between 1941 and 1961), are relevant here: see especially the final three. Bultmann's *Historie* versus *Geschichte* distinction belongs here as well. (On this whole theme see Thiselton, *The Two Horizons*, pp. 245-51.) Bultmann's entire hermeneutical, epistemological programme, viewed here through the 'demythologizing' and 'history and eschatology' themes, is bound up with these metaphysical and metaphilosophical issues. Another important essay for relating this dichotomy to Bultmann's theologizing is 'What Does it Mean to Speak of God?', in *Faith and Understanding*, pp. 53-65 (repr. in R.A. Johnson [ed.], *Rudolf Bultmann*, pp. 80-90).

'Such personal self-understanding usually finds its expression in so-called world-views (*'Weltanschauungen'*) and religions' (p. 147).[115] World-views and religions open a window to a view which allows something of a release from contingency and particularity:

> these 'Weltanschauungen' and religions are permanent possibilities of human self-understanding which once they have found expression in history remain as ever-present possibilities coming to life at different times in different forms. For fundamentally they are not answers to special historical problems in definite historical situations, but are expressions of personal self-understanding, of personality, however they may be stimulated by special historical situations (pp. 147-48).

A complete relativism, then, does not follow: 'On the contrary, the view of the different possibilities raises the question of the legitimate self-understanding' (p. 148). The recovery of an understanding of historicity articulated with the aid of Heidegger's existentialist analytic provides a standpoint for critique: 'A "Weltanschauung", we may say, is the more legitimated the more it expresses the historicity of the human being. Self-understanding is the more astray the more it fails to appreciate historicity and flees from its own history' (p. 149).[116] And 'there can be no doubt that the radical understanding of the historicity of man has appeared in Christianity, the way being prepared in the Old Testament' (p. 149).

> According to the New Testament, *Jesus Christ is the eschatological event*, the action of God by which God has set an end to the old world. In the preaching of the Christian Church the eschatological event will ever again become present and does become present ever and again in faith. The old world has reached its end for the believer, he is 'a new creature in Christ'...
> It is the paradox of the Christian message that the eschatological event, according to Paul and John, is not to be understood as a dramatic cosmic catastrophe but as happening within history, beginning with the appearance of Jesus Christ and in continuity with this occurring again and again in

115. 'So-called' presumably in that they speak less of the 'world' than of the self.

116. For Bultmann, this apparently neutral and ahistorical critical standpoint is made possible by the phenomenological analysis of existence provided in existentialist reflection and the phenomenological analysis of the essentially timeless nature of world views expressing some perception of existence. Is this timeless, neutral standpoint another possible point of tension in Bultmann's thought, a bid for security, a flight from humanity and historicity?

history, but not as the kind of historical development which can be confirmed by any historian. It becomes an event repeatedly in preaching and faith (p. 151).[117]

The decision of faith in response to the preaching is a decision for a new self-understanding of freedom from oneself by the grace of God, for a new self freed for responsible decision and action, motivated by love. 'It is the paradox of Christian being that the believer is taken out of the world and exists, so to speak, as unworldly and that at the same time he remains within the world, within his historicity'—a paradox 'analogous with the Lutheran statement *simul iustus, simul peccator*', a tension expressed in Paul's formulations of the 'between the times' character of Christian eschatological existence (pp. 152, 154).

Bultmann follows through the problematic of historicism, only to emerge and find waiting on the other side (Bultmann's) Paul and Luther.

> *[T]he meaning in history lies always in the present*, and when the present is conceived as the eschatological present by Christian faith the meaning in history is realised. Man who complains: 'I cannot see meaning in history, and therefore my life, interwoven in history, is meaningless', is to be admonished: do not look around yourself into universal history, you must look into your own personal history. Always in your present lies the meaning in history, and you cannot see it as a spectator, but only in your responsible decisions. In every moment slumbers the possibility of being the eschatological moment. You must awaken it (p. 155).

Bultmann wishes to pilot some course between the perils of the hegemony of 'objectifying' thinking in Neo-Kantianism[118] and the dissolution of meaning and truth in the relativizing impact of historicism. Scientism leaves humanity comfortably damned in inauthenticity, historicism delivers it up to nihilism, to utter nothingness. Overcoming this positivism is Bultmann's deepest problematic. If Paul, through Luther, has been able to influence Western history in revolutionary ways, he is now called upon to help fortify the final frontier outpost against the social and cultural benightedness of the nihilistic invasion, the new Dark Ages. 'How can I find a gracious God?' has become 'How can I find true meaning and true humanity?'

---

117. Bultmann, then, uses Paul and John to rule out the possibilities represented by Schweitzer, Dodd, and Cullmann.

118. On Neo-Kantianism and Bultmann, see R.A. Johnson, *Origins*, pp. 38-86; R.A. Johnson (ed.), *Rudolf Bultmann*, p. 25; Thiselton, *The Two Horizons*, pp. 208-17.

In following through these themes of 'demythologizing' and 'history and eschatology' we may seem to have strayed dangerously from the question of the 'apocalyptic Paul'. But when we understand existence as an interpretative key, being both the true focus of Paul and the proper focus of the modern reader, demythologization as an interpretative programme, bringing Paul's language and thought to bear on existence, and proclamation as interpretative goal, confronting modern humanity with the possibility of authentic existence, we may then raise the question of Bultmann's approach to Paul and 'apocalyptic'. Bultmann's understanding of 'apocalyptic' is clearly unexceptional (it is the familiar futuristic eschatological construction of the two ages poised in an imminent, transcendent turn[119]), and, as does everyone who labours in Schweitzer's shadow, Bultmann acknowledges its significance for early Christianity and its presence in Jesus and Paul—Paul as interpreter of the Christ-occurrence is heir, through both his Jewish and primitive Christian antecedents, to two great mythological traditions: the 'Gnostic' and the 'apocalyptic'.[120] But 'apocalyptic' is precisely such—a mythical tradition—which is only a medium of expression of kerygma and existence, and its peripheral status in Paul's own thought is confirmed in the fact that Paul demythologizes it by setting alongside it expressions of the presence of redemption. 'Apocalyptic and Gnostic eschatologies are demythologized insofar as the day of salvation has already dawned for believers and the life of the future has already become present.'[121] 'In Jewish apocalyptic, history is interpreted from the view of eschatology. In Paul, history is swallowed up in eschatology. Thereby eschatology has wholly lost its sense as goal of history and is in fact understood as the goal of the individual human being.'[122] '[T]he beginning of the new aeon is not a cosmic catastrophe, but an event of history. One can say that mythology is historicized, or begins to be historicized.'[123] 'Paul has histori[ci]zed the Jewish apocalyptic speculation' in the 'Now in which

119. On 'apocalyptic', in addition to the literature already cited, see Bultmann, *Primitive Christianity*, pp. 94-102.
120. Bultmann, 'New Testament and Mythology', in *New Testament and Mythology*, pp. 2, 14.
121. Bultmann, 'New Testament and Mythology', in *New Testament and Mythology*, p. 19.
122. Bultmann, 'History and Eschatology in the New Testament', p. 13.
123. Bultmann, 'Man Between the Times According to the New Testament', in *Existence and Faith*, p. 254.

the proclamation is sounding forth'.[124] Thus 'apocalyptic', as purely mythical future expectation, has on the one hand, though still present, been demythologized—and thus eclipsed—in Paul's controlling emphasis on the 'now', while on the other hand it is retained as future expectation but in a demythologized—that is, reinterpreted—sense as to its existential significance within the horizons, not of universal history, but of the 'historicity' of an individual human life.[125]

Once again, an antithesis is assumed between 'apocalyptic' or 'futuristic' eschatology and the presence of redemption, and the tension created by Paul's troublesome and unexpected combination of the two constitutes the chief interpretive crux. Schweitzer overcomes the history of religions obstacle of this tension by reconstructing Paul's logic in realigning his eschatological schema, but Porter and Dodd, in a more biblical-theological vein, picture the Isaac of presence driving out the Ishmael of futurity.[126] Bultmann attempts, on the one hand, to leave in place Paul's futuristic expectations as highlighted by Schweitzer, but *this very tension* in Paul's thought, already highlighted by Schweitzer, is evidence for Bultmann of Paul's demythologizing interpretation. And, on the other hand, inasmuch as Bultmann has Paul's future hope overtaken in importance by the 'now', another means of playing off realization against expectation has been found, this time in the kerygma as existentially conceived.

It is important for Bultmann that Paul himself begins the reinterpretive process of demythologization, continuing, furthermore, a process set in motion by Jesus himself.[127] This is not unlike Dodd. And the significance for Bultmann's own interpretation is that he may present his method as employing *Sachkritik*, a critical appraisal of Paul's thought as to how consistently Paul holds to his own best intentions (and to the intentions

124. Bultmann, *Theology*, I, p. 307.

125. Here, again, the dual 'apocalyptic' dimensions of 'eschatology' and 'history' are visible, as Paul turns futuristic expectations in a 'realized' direction and turns universal history into 'historicity', in each case in the 'now' of proclamation and Christian existence.

126. Admittedly, the matter is more complicated with Dodd, who relies not merely on the hypothesis of a developmental scheme in Paul but on a wide-ranging reinterpretation of eschatology and reflection on the philosophy of history; thus Dodd and Bultmann may not only be contrasted, as here, but also compared, and in considerable detail, as will be seen below.

127. This suggests, perhaps, a residual 'biblicism' which might be a third point of tension in Bultmann's thought.

of the kerygma).[128] *Sachkritik* constitutes an even more encompassing interpretive category than 'demythologizing', as the obscuring inter-position of a mythological or cosmological presentation between the proclamation and the modern reader is one of several cases that call for criticism as to the subject-matter of the kerygma.[129] According to Bultmann, Paul himself takes such a critical stance toward the contem-porary eschatological beliefs in which the kerygma is wrapped, and to the degree that Paul stops short the modern interpreter is obliged to continue the *Sachkritik* of demythologization. Again, the comparison with Dodd is suggestive, for although Dodd does not use any such technical term, he interprets as what is central to Paul that in which Paul faithfully follows Jesus' insight into the realization of former hopes in his own person and ministry, noting that there remains in Paul a residue of futuristic expectation on which Jesus' reinterpretative genius has not been allowed to do its work. The Paul of the moments of insightful genius, of personal triumph, Paul the visionary theologian, as perceived in some respects similarly by both Dodd and Bultmann, is read against his own less perceptive moments. And Dodd, though again using no such term, is not far off from 'demythologizing', wishing, like Bultmann, to interpret (and not remove) myth, turning it, though, in an ecclesiolo-gical and world-historical rather than an anthropological and existential direction. And for Bultmann as well as for Dodd such an interpretation according to Paul's own best intentions provides a ready defence against any incredulity as to whether Paul in fact presents a 'realized' eschato-logy or demythologizes 'apocalyptic', for to the degree that Paul failed to do so there is simply more work left to be done by the modern inter-preter (once more, simplicity, elegance, but with a sharp leading slant). Bultmann, like Dodd, forces objections onto the level of his broad interpretative programme.

It might have seemed, at first glance, that Bultmann takes a less defensive, more receptive stance toward Schweitzer's critical conclusions. Bultmann refers in his introduction to his own *Jesus and the Word* to the brilliance of Schweitzer's *Quest of the Historical Jesus*.[130] He credits

128. On *Sachkritik*, see Schmithals, *Rudolf Bultmann*, pp. 245-46 (which includes several citations from Bultmann); R. Morgan, *Nature*, pp. 42-52; '*Sachkritik*', in Coggins and Houlden (eds.), *Dictionary of Biblical Interpretation*, pp. 604-605.

129. See Bultmann, *Theology*, II, p. 238.

130. Bultmann, *Jesus and the Word*, p. 8; Bultmann refers especially here to Schweitzer's exposure of the illusions of 'life of Jesus' research.

(as does Schweitzer) his teacher Johannes Weiss and Schweitzer himself with bringing the eschatological message of Jesus irrevocably before the attention of all.[131] 'Apocalyptic' stands alongside 'Gnosticism' as one of the two major mythological traditions behind early Christian thought.[132] And Bultmann champions Schweitzer's insights into the importance of Jewish 'apocalypticism' and the 'delay of the parousia' against what he perceives as Oscar Cullmann's effort to 'trivialize' them.[133] If Schweitzer's 'apocalyptic' has been absorbed into the ethos of critical New Testament study, then this is reflected in Bultmann, who fully imbibes and fully embodies this ethos.

Bultmann seems content, then, to leave Schweitzer's interpretation of Paul in place. As we have seen above, he is careful to emphasize repeatedly that the 'cosmic drama' of 'apocalyptic' expectation remains on Paul's near horizon. This, though, hardly differs from Dodd's similar insistence. The criticism of Schweitzer's presentation of the eschatological Paul implicit in Bultmann's programme is now clear: 'demythologization' is a 'deobjectification' or 'decosmologization' of eschatology. The language of eschatology is turned inward to operate within the horizons of 'historicity', and Schweitzer, so successful in rescuing Paul from all those fearful of acknowledging Paul's thoroughly eschatological thought, is shown to have failed himself to the degree that he fails to see what Paul has done with history and eschatology. Once more, again as with Dodd, we find a refusal to allow interpretation to be ruled by the misunderstandings of those who missed the whole point of the traditions of eschatological hope. For Bultmann as well it is necessary to learn Paul's language—but now the language is that of 'historicity'. For Bultmann also the 'new phase' for Paul is, not so much a passing one, but one representing something never embraced with full and unqualified conviction. (What is more, Paul deserves a hand up from the modern interpreter at those points where he found it beyond his power to maintain against the currents of his time his critical insights.)

The results are curious. Both Bultmann and Dodd may affirm virtually

131. Bultmann, *Jesus Christ and Mythology*, pp. 11-13; Bultmann here speaks of Schweitzer taking Weiss's theory 'to extremes', referring especially to the detailed, eschatological, messianic consciousness Schweitzer reads in Jesus.

132. Bultmann, 'New Testament and Mythology', in Ogden (ed.), *New Testament and Mythology*, pp. 2, 14.

133. Bultmann, 'History of Salvation and History', in Ogden (ed.), *Existence and Faith*, pp. 235-38.

as is Schweitzer's 'new Paul'. But each subverts Schweitzer's reading, pushing it to the opposite pole, while at the same time managing to emerge at opposite poles from one another, and that despite the many similarities of their respective aims and methods. In each case the eyes of Schweitzer's Paul are averted from the cosmic, transcendent direction in which Schweitzer has left him longingly gazing, but Dodd turns Paul's intent focus toward the Church and universal history, Bultmann toward the individual and 'historicity'. Again, reflection on 'Paul and apocalyptic' is the occasion of questioning the relation of language and myth, history, and eschatology, and the implications for faith. But a markedly different conception of faith rules in Dodd and Bultmann, insuring that, however much their disaffections with Schweitzer may find in common, they will end up poles apart themselves. For faith's sake Bultmann must also demythologize Dodd (he and Dodd having demythologized Schweitzer and the 'new Paul'), since, for Bultmann, nothing is gained by turning Paul's gaze from another world to the world around: in either case, to supplement the proclamation with a doctrine to which one must assent is to make faith a work.[134] Schweitzer, Dodd, and Bultmann, then, form a triad of possibilities in reading Paul and eschatology, alternative paradigms which set the same 'facts' (no longer the same) in very different configuration.

One prominent post-Bultmannian has presented Schweitzer and Bultmann as the two great alternatives which this century of Pauline

134. This basic difference between Dodd and Bultmann is seen in their different conceptions of the kerygma, a key term for each, but with the focus being, for Dodd, on its content, while for Bultmann the sheer fact of proclamation is in view. Direct interaction between Dodd and Bultmann is minimal, but see Bultmann's '"The Bible Today" und die Eschatologie', in W.D. Davies and D. Daube (eds.), *The Background of the New Testament and Its Eschatology: Essays in Honour of C.H. Dodd* (Cambridge: Cambridge University Press, 1956), pp. 402-8: 'Must not a theological understanding of history take as its point of departure an understanding of historicity (as that which is of the essence of human existence), not, however, from an understanding of history as a connected series of past occurrences' (pp. 407-408)? There is little to say, it seems, beyond a bare acknowledgment of the operation of fundamentally different perspectives or paradigms (cf. below on Bultmann's interaction with Schweitzer). Detailed comparison and contrast between Dodd and Bultmann—born the same year, with long careers (ending in death in 1973 and 1976 respectively) variously overlapping but rarely (directly) intersecting—would be instructive. We hope here only to introduce enough of a comparison to suggest a common, though very differently conceived and executed, moment in the biblical-theological upsurge of our century.

interpretation has called forth.[135] And while we have just spoken of a triad of possibilities, in terms of major moving forces in interpreting *Paul*, and in prospect of locating the interpretation of Käsemann, this schematism may be pursued. Bultmann's individualistic emphasis on the proclamation of justification by God's grace through faith alone reflects his stance within the Lutheran tradition. But Schweitzer's interpretation of Paul poses a serious challenge to this tradition. A detailed comparison and contrast between the two as alternative approaches to Paul is instructive.[136]

Both are interested in and present a grand synthesis of early Christianity from Jesus to the early second-century church. Both have a comprehensive hermeneutical methodology ('consistent' application of eschatology or existence). Both operate against a history of religions background. For both the eschatological world view of early Christianity is an impossibility for the modern reader. Yet for both a core is discernible which the modern reader may make his or her own ('ethical mysticism'[137] or 'existential proclamation'). For both Jesus and Paul stand independently of one another and Paul is the proper focus of the modern reader, yet in such a way that it is not 'Jesus or Paul', but rather that Paul shows the true way to Jesus.[138] For both Paul's distinction lies in his accomplishment as *theologian*. The programme of 'positive criticism' of each makes both claimants to the mantle of Baur.

Differences are just as striking. Schweitzer's interpretative programme demonstrates the *distance* of the historical Jesus and Paul, which distance has a liberating effect, freeing the modern reader to receive their

---

135. H. Conzelmann, 'Current Problems in Pauline Research', *Int* 22 (1968), pp. 171-86 (174-75): 'Up to the present the investigation has been determined by the two monumental presentations of the subject by A. Schweitzer and R. Bultmann. Their formulation of the problem persists—mysticism or justification, being in Christ or faith/grace/righteousness of God. Each, following consistently his own point of departure, has a different focus; Schweitzer is concerned with the reconstruction of the historical form of Paul's thinking, Bultmann with *existential* interpretation through which he presents the theology of Paul as anthropology in order to do justice to its own intention'.

136. Much more detail than is here allowed could be offered. And clearly, Dodd (and Cullmann) could also easily be included in much of this comparison.

137. On which see further below in the return to Schweitzer's hermeneutics at the close of the present chapter.

138. See Schweitzer, *Mysticism*, pp. 389-96; Bultmann, 'Jesus and Paul', in Ogden (ed.), *Existence and Faith*, pp. 183-201.

'spirit' in ethical action, while Bultmann's programme discerns *nearness* in the common concern with existence on the part of both Jesus and Paul and the modern reader.[139] Their history of religions leanings are notably at odds, with Schweitzer emphasizing Judaism and Bultmann Hellenism. Schweitzer's Paul is eschatological in his thought, and his 'mystical' or participatory conceptions are realistic (for Schweitzer this is Paul's centre), while Bultmann's Paul is *existentialist* in his thought, and such realistic (-sounding) language is either rhetoric or myth (and thus peripheral). For Schweitzer, Paul's thought is cosmic and collective in character, while for Bultmann it is inward and individualistic. Schweitzer stresses election, Bultmann decision. For Schweitzer, Paul's critique of the Law stems from his eschatological participation, while for Bultmann this is a result of Paul's existential insight.[140] In a similar way, for Schweitzer, Paul's doctrine of justification by faith cannot be the centre of his thought, as it is neither independent nor central, while Bultmann's existentialist approach is able to present justification by faith as fundamental to Paul.[141]

---

139. Cf. *Mysticism*, pp. 291, 376-96 (but, as noted above, Schweitzer's distance inverts easily into nearness, and there is much of distance in Bultmann as well). Again, on Schweitzer, see the discussion below.

140. On Paul and the Law, see Schweitzer, *Mysticism*, pp. 177-204, and Bultmann, *Theology*, I, pp. 259-69, 340-45.

141. On justification, see Schweitzer, *Mysticism*, pp. 205-26, and Bultmann, *Theology*, I, pp. 270-85. According to Schweitzer, Paul's 'mysticism' could not be derived from 'righteousness by faith', while the latter could be, and in fact was, derived from the former when, in controversy, the need was felt to present freedom from the Law and salvation by faith independently of participatory speculations, as inherent in the nature of humanity and the Law. But freedom from the Law and forgiveness of sins are, in fact, the results of participation in Christ. 'Righteousness by faith' is not independent, as it does not produce of itself freedom from the Law, and it is not central, as no lines proceed from it to an ethic or to the sacraments. There are two conceptions of forgiveness of sins in Paul: eschatological participation, based on the death and resurrection—a realistic cosmic and collectivistic or corporate transaction—and justification by faith, based on the atoning death—a simple non-cosmic and individualistic exchange between God and human beings. Paul preferred the former, but subsequently the church has tended to feel more at home with the latter. It should be noted that Schweitzer's 'subsidiary crater' characterization of justification by faith does *not* make it peripheral, but rather subsumes it within the more encompassing 'main rim' of eschatological participation, so that Paul's 'mysticism' is the necessary and understood context of justification by faith, and not the reverse. Neither Schweitzer nor Bultmann appear interested in making a *single*

In the mythology of modern New Testament interpretative tradition Schweitzer and Bultmann stand as the archetypal proponent and opponent respectively of an 'apocalyptic' interpretation of Paul; but when the tradition is demythologized, or when a quest for the historical Schweitzer and Bultmann is made, such half-truths (at best) can no longer satisfy. They represent indeed two alternative and competing perspectives on Paul.[142] But 'apocalyptic' is probably not the best or most direct means of differentiating them or of crystallizing the issues that separate them.

*doctrine* the centre of Paul's thought—their respective centres are the broader constructs of 'eschatological participation' and 'existential proclamation' (which latter gives central place to 'justification by faith', interpreted existentially).

142. Schweitzer's interpretation of Paul is set long before any interaction with Bultmann became possible. Bultmann seems to hold Schweitzer's interpretation in high esteem, recognizing its stature as a conception rivalling his own. But in the nature of the case, a detailed interaction with Schweitzer, as much as Bultmann desires it, seems to exceed his grasp, since for both the same features of Paul's thought are read in such different configuration that it seems difficult to get much beyond a bare statement of fundamental difference. In his 'Zur Geschichte der Paulus-Forschung', Bultmann complains that neither Kabisch not Schweitzer raise the question of Paul's concepts of existence, and that according to Schweitzer 'for Paul it is the new age and…therefore redemption in Paul is not individualistic, but must be understood as an event concerning the whole world' (p. 320). In an appreciative review of Schweitzer's *Die Mystik des Apostels Paulus* in *Deutsche Literaturzeitung* 52 [1931] cols. 1153-58) (1154-55), Bultmann notes that Schweitzer has correctly seen that the chief problem is explaining the characteristic Zwischenzustand of believing existence in Paul's thought (1156). Bultmann's 'crucial objection' is that Schweitzer has Paul inferring Christian existence from his speculative system building whereby he combines traditional eschatological expectations with the now accomplished Christ event. Rather, human existence as perceived in this eschatological Christ event and as guided by the practical interest in proclamation (and not the theoretical interest in a speculative system) confronts critically the conception of existence underlying Jewish eschatology (1156-57). '[Paul's] theology is not primarily an apocalyptic world view, but an explication of believing existence' (1157). Bultmann is disappointed that Schweitzer does not examine in detail Paul's anthropological expressions, which, though they do indeed make use of an 'eschatological Gnosis', actually subvert the latter, such that 'for him [Paul] the eschatological event essentially loses its cosmic-natural character' (1157-58). Schweitzer's emphasis on the 'physical' character of redemption, then, is 'only a reproduction, not really an interpretation' of Paul's expressions (1158). Bultmann closes with a promise of a more detailed interaction to follow, a promise repeated a few years later ('Neueste Paulusforschung II', p. 10 n. 1) but never fulfilled. One wonders what more beyond this statement of fundamental difference (which amounts to the simple assertion that Schweitzer is not Bultmann) could be said.

For Schweitzer the real Paul is the eschatological Paul, whose cosmic, participatory language is to be taken seriously, at face value (that is, literally), as intending to express something objective, something real. For Bultmann, the real Paul is the existentialist (eschatological) Paul, who uses the richly figurative or symbolic language of myth to express the depth of Christian existence for the individual in the community. The 'new phase' Paul confronts the 'new Lutheran Paul'.

'Apocalyptic' interpretation of Paul does not properly begin until Ernst Käsemann announces his verdict, with Paul as chief witness, that 'apocalyptic' is the beginning of Christian theology. And it is in the light of Käsemann's palace revolt within the Bultmann school that his fellow post-Bultmannian sets up the scheme of the two rival traditions of Schweitzer and Bultmann, the two alternatives between which a choice has to be made. Before I turn to Käsemann, though still another alternative must be briefly explored, in the present byway of 'history and eschatology', before the ground is truly prepared for Käsemann and his 'apocalyptic' Paul. This is Oscar Cullmann, tireless champion of 'salvation history', whom, on the score of an association with either Paul or 'apocalyptic', we might perhaps overlook, but whose programme we must also place before ourselves in order to position, not just Käsemann, but Schweitzer, Dodd, and Bultmann as well. For part of the story I have been struggling to tell reaches its climax just here, where the question which scholarship typically feels compelled to put in some more institutionally respectable form (such as, 'Did Jesus present an interim ethic?') is finally put at its most direct: 'If Christianity was designed to last, say, a few months, or even a few years, can I still, in any respectable sense, be a Christian today?'

### 3. *Oscar Cullmann*

With the responses of Dodd and Bultmann to Schweitzer behind us, I can now bring this strand of my story to something of a point of closure with Oscar Cullmann, behind whom looms the imposing work of these three, now seen side by side as successive attempts to slay the same critical dragon, which itself, however, still looms ever more threateningly in spite of—on account of, even—their efforts.[143]

143. The writings of Cullmann which are of particular relevance here are his three synthetic and programmatic works (especially the first and last; H. Räisänen, *Beyond New Testament Theology*, notes that the three taken together 'come close to a total

Cullmann, in his *Christ and Time*, wishes to outline the history, or story, of salvation fundamental to New Testament theology, a narrative of Christ which is the story of God and humanity. This is accomplished by means of a reflection on the meaning of time and history in New Testament thought.

> We shall establish the fact that Primitive Christianity places both the divine creation 'in the beginning' and the divine goal of all becoming 'at the end of the days' in precisely the same Christocentric perspective of Biblical history, that is, in precisely the same temporal Christ-line which it uses to view the historical events in which figure the people of Israel and the activity of Jesus and the apostles and the Primitive Church. In this cosmic extension of the historical line, that which is so offensive for modern thought in the claim of Christian revelation becomes particularly clear, namely, the fact that *all Christian theology in its innermost essence is Biblical history*...(p. 23).[144]

presentation of New Testament theology' [p. 51]): O. Cullmann, *Christ and Time: The Primitive Christian Conception of Time and History* (trans. F.V. Filson; London: SCM Press, 2nd edn, 1962 [3rd Ger. edn, 1962 (1946)]); *idem*, *The Christology of the New Testament* (trans. S.C. Guthrie and C.A.M. Hall; London: SCM Press, 2nd edn, 1963 [Ger. orig. 1957]); and *Salvation in History* (trans. S.G. Sowers, *et al.*; London: SCM Press, 1967 [Ger. edn, 1965]). On Cullmann's methodological self-understanding, see also his 'The Necessity and Function of Higher Criticism', in A.J.B. Higgins (ed.), *The Early Church* (London: SCM Press, 1956), pp. 3-16. On Cullmann, see: S.C. Guthrie, Jr, 'Oscar Cullmann', in Marty and Peerman (eds.), *Handbook*, pp. 338-54; R. Bultmann, 'History of Salvation and History', in *Existence and Faith*, pp. 226-40 (a 1948 review of *Christ and Time*); C.K. Barrett, 'Important and Influential Foreign Books: Cullmann's "Christ and Time"', *ExpTim* 65 (1954), pp. 369-72; V. Taylor, 'Professor Oscar Cullmann's "Die Christologie des Neuen Testaments"', *ExpTim* 70 (1959), pp. 136-40; J.P. Martin, 'A Hermeneutical Gem', *Int* 20 (1966), pp. 340-46 (an enthusiastic review of *Heils als Geschichte*); G.F. Hasel, *New Testament Theology: Basic Issues in the Current Debate* (Grand Rapids: Eerdmans, 1978), pp. 111-19, 148-53 (see the note on additional discussion of Cullmann's programme, pp. 111-12 n. 235); T.M. Dorman, *The Hermeneutics of Oscar Cullmann* (New York: Edwin Mellen Press, 1991).

144. Thus Cullmann has the 'scandal' of Christianity precisely where Bultmann says it cannot be, and Cullmann announces his own scruples against any such attempt to work things out favourably and comfortably for ourselves, but at the expense of Christianity (revealing already Cullmann's leading slant). This stricture Cullmann tirelessly repeats, always implicitly against Bultmann, though one comes to feel that the 'biblical history' is not nearly so foreign and scandalous in his own eyes, in spite of his hermeneutical and methodological posturing.

This 'biblical history' is a 'revelatory' and 'redemptive history', a history of salvation and revelation which is 'the heart of all New Testament theology', 'a *continuous time process* which embraces past, present and future', with 'all points...related to the *one historical fact* at the midpoint..., decisive for salvation. This fact is the death and resurrection of Jesus Christ' (pp. 26-27, 32-33).[145]

Primitive Christianity follows Judaism in regarding 'all expressions of faith' as having an 'emphatically temporal character', yet Christian thought completes what is only 'intimated' in Judaism: 'the New Testament writings for the first time give to all revelation an essential anchorage in time; here for the first time the time line is consistently carried through in its significance for salvation and faith' (pp. 37-38).[146] The time-line of salvation history is structured by the two ages, this present one and the coming one, and is punctuated and defined by the saving acts of God.[147] Its movement is linear, not cyclical; Hellenistic philosophy and Gnosticism dissolve this temporal-redemptive line.[148] Distinct from Platonic conceptions of the qualitative difference between time and eternity (timeboundedness versus timelessness), primitive Christianity, like Judaism, conceives of eternity as endlessly extended time. Yet God is not bound up in time, but is Lord over time, a lordship expressed pre-eminently in the Christ event, the midpoint of the time line, decisive and determinative for the whole, and making the present a

145. This historical correlation of revelation and redemption or salvation is what is meant by *Heilsgeschichte*, translated here as 'redemptive history', left untranslated in Cullmann's *Christology*, and translated 'salvation history' in his *Salvation in History*. Here and following, we are concerned primarily with the first two parts of *Christ and Time* (which make up the bulk of the work).

146. In the early pages of *Christ and Time*, Cullmann builds his argument for 'biblical history' on word studies of terminology for 'time' which I pass over here.

147. Cullmann also speaks of a common threefold division of time, extending endlessly before creation, from creation to the end, and endlessly forward from the end; the twofold division is superimposed on this threefold scheme (Cullmann, *Christ and Time*, pp. 67-68, 81-82).

148. Cullmann here engages in an indirect, and at times also direct and explicit, polemic against 'reinterpretations' of the temporal, eschatological nature of New Testament thought as in Dodd and Bultmann. Dodd is not specifically addressed in this early work, in which the polemic against notions of 'time and eternity' is directed primarily against Barth; later, though, in Cullmann's *Salvation in History*, Dodd's 'Platonizing' of eschatology comes in for direct criticism [Dodd's 'realized eschatology' thesis not entering continental debate until after the war, 'brought into the debate by Kümmel for the first time' (Cullmann, *Salvation in History*, p. 38)]).

period of tension between the ages, a period in which by the Spirit a
foretaste of the future age and knowledge of the 'mystery' of God's
redemptive plan are to be had.

The dividing point of the ages rests for Judaism with a future coming
of the messiah; but for Christianity the dividing point, the midpoint or
decisive incision into time, has been reached in the now past historical
life and work of Jesus, whereby a 'between the times' period is created.
The division of time as understood by Judaism

> is not abandoned in the thought of primitive Christianity; it is rather
> *intersected* by a new one. For here the mid-point between the present and
> the coming age comes to lie on a definite point which lies at a more or less
> short distance (depending on the individual author) *before* the old dividing
> point. And yet *this old dividing point is still valid* (p. 82).[149]

A present/future tension for early Christian thought results, which
Cullmann illustrates with an analogy for which he has become known:

> *The decisive battle in a war may already have occurred in a relatively
> early stage of the war, and yet the war still continues.* Although the
> decisive effect of that battle is perhaps not recognized by all, it nevertheless
> already means victory. But the war must still be carried on for an
> undefined time, until 'Victory Day'. Precisely this is the situation of which
> the New Testament is conscious, as a result of the recognition of the new
> division of time; the revelation consists precisely in the fact of the
> proclamation that *that event on the cross, together with the resurrection
> which followed, was the already concluded decisive battle* (p. 84).

The shifting of centres which Cullmann observes is, in a manner
recalling Dodd, urged against Schweitzer and Werner as proponents of
'consistent eschatology'.

> They [Schweitzer and Werner] regard as the mid-point of the process the
> future coming of the Messianic Age, whereas the mid-point of time in the
> entire New Testament and *already for Jesus* is rather the historical work of
> Jesus himself. Accordingly, everything is to be explained from the point of
> view, not of the future, but of this event. It simply is not true that Primitive
> Christianity has the same eschatological orientation as does Judaism. To
> be sure, it has *also* an eschatological orientation. The Jewish expectation
> concerning the future retains its validity for Jesus and throughout the
> entire New Testament, but it is no longer the center. That center is the
> victorious event which the historical Jesus sees is being fulfilled in the

---

149. Cullmann presents a diagram of this shifting conception on p. 83 of *Christ
and Time*.

exercise of his calling...For the Primitive Church after the death of Jesus, the crowning act of this work is the mighty fact of the resurrection of Christ...

He who does not see that the radically new thing in the New Testament is the Primitive Christian shifting of the center of time can understand Christianity only as a Jewish sect. In reality, the Christian hope is not the Jewish one. To be sure, hope is also present in Primitive Christianity in its full intensity, indeed in increased intensity, although the event hoped for is no longer the center of time...

With the decisive battle is connected the New Testament 'expectation of the imminent end'. This expectation...really roots in the faith that the redemptive event has already occurred and been completed. It must be strongly emphasized that this faith is the prior ground of the expectation that the end is imminent. Therefore it is not true that this faith in a fulfillment that has already taken place in Jesus Christ is a 'substitute' for the unfulfilled expectation of the immediate coming of the Kingdom of God; on the contrary, this faith produced the expectation (pp. 85-86).[150]

To think of the timing of the imminent end as the decisive thing is to miss the 'theologically important point', which is 'that since the coming of Christ we already stand in a new period of time, and that therefore the end has drawn nearer' (p. 87).

Of course, for Primitive Christianity, this nearness is 'at most a matter of decades and not of centuries or indeed millenniums' (p. 87).

But this error in perspective...does not constitute the theological content of the statement that 'the Kingdom has come near'. This statement has to do primarily, not with the determination or limitation of a date, but with the division of time...*The error is explained on a psychological basis in the same way that we explain the hasty determination of the date of the end of the war when once the conviction is present that the decisive battle has already taken place* (pp. 87-88).

The importance of the point for Cullmann is clear: 'It is emphatically not true that the Primitive Christian hope stands or falls with this expectation of the imminent end, although this would be the case if in fact the limitation of date were the main point' (p. 88). Thus Paul, though he came to view the possibility of his own death before the parousia, was not led to alter 'the entire time scheme of redemption', nor did he suffer a crisis of faith with respect to the intensity or foundation of his future hope, 'because from the outset its starting point had been that *the center, the*

---

150. Note the explicit attention to continuity/discontinuity with Judaism (as in Schweitzer, Dodd, Porter and Bultmann, see above, and Käsemann, see below).

*fixed point of orientation*, lies not in the future but in the past, and accordingly *in an assured fact which cannot be touched by the delay of the Parousia*' (p. 88). And this holds, for Cullmann, for the entire New Testament.

> In the light of this Primitive Christian outlook, the entire complex of questions concerning the expectation of the imminent end and the delay of the Parousia has lost its importance in Primitive Christianity. It does indeed possess importance from a psychological point of view, but not in its theological bearing. This complex of questions can have theological significance only where the center of the time line lies in the future (as it does in Jewish apocalyptic); *and the criterion of the Christian character of an apocalyptic viewpoint is precisely the question whether the center of the line is the crucified and risen Christ or whether it is the returning Christ.* Only where the Christ who died and rose forms the center do we have Christian apocalyptic (pp. 89-90, emphasis added).

Again, for Cullmann, observance of this shifting of centres, recalling Dodd, effectively 'refute[s] the entire New Testament basis of "consistent eschatology"', though, unlike Dodd, Cullmann then insists that this 'does not mean that the returning Christ has no place at all in the gospel' (pp. 86, 90).

Not only does the new mid-point reinterpret the future; the past as well is redrawn from, or to, this centre. The time before creation, creation itself, the history of Israel—all is interpreted in light of the Christ: 'in this interpreting mid-point of time is gathered up all that takes place' (p. 91). The present also partakes of this interpretative connection to the centre, resulting in 'the time tension in which we find ourselves. Thus we stand in a section of time in which we are already redeemed through Christ, in which we already have the Holy Spirit, who is characteristic of the new section of time, but in which also the sin characteristic of the entire period before the Parousia is not done away' (p. 92).

Appropriating this perspective on time is an act of faith, made possible in the revelation of the 'mystery' of the redemptive plan.[151] Thus, the entire redemptive history is prophetic history. 'The Primitive Christian understanding of the history of salvation is correctly understood only when we see that in it history and myth are thoroughly and essentially bound together, and that they are both to be brought together, on the one side by the common denominator of prophecy and on the other by

---

151. This is clearly an un-Bultmannian faith, however.

the common denominator of development in time' (p. 106).[152] This
Cullmann asserts expressly against Bultmann's demythologizing and
existentialist (detemporalizing) interpretation.

The midpoint is the starting point, both logically and historically, for
the Primitive Christian reinterpretation of salvation history, in all directions. But the redemptive line may be laid out in sequence, and when
this is done one sees

> that this is really the line of Christ: Christ the Mediator of the Creation—
> Christ, God's Suffering Servant as the one who fulfills the election of
> Israel—Christ the Lord, ruling in the present—Christ the returning Son of
> Man as the one who completes the entire process and is the Mediator of
> the new creation. The Pre-existent One, the One who yesterday was
> crucified, he who today exercises hidden lordship, he who returns at the
> turn of the ages—they are all one; it is the same Christ, but in the execu-
> tion of his functions in *the successive stages of time in the redemptive
> history* (p. 109).[153]

This reading of the New Testament salvation history, in its character as a
Christ-line with the Christ event as the midpoint, is finally confirmed for
Cullmann by 'the further fact that the movement of this development in
time is determined by a notably theological principle, namely, that of
election and representation' (p. 115). Behind the redemptive line lies
God's initial revelation and humanity's initial revolt, a fall into sin
cursing humanity and all creation. The redemptive process removes the
curse of sin and death, effecting a reconciliation that extends to a new
creation where the curse is not known. 'The principle of this gracious
process is that of the *election of a minority for the redemption of the
whole*. Otherwise expressed, it is the principle of *representation*'.
(p. 115) The resulting picture is of a narrowing of the many to the one,
and then a broadening of the one to the many, from creation to its
representative, humanity, and from sinful humanity to one people, Israel,
then to a remnant, finally to one man, the Suffering Servant, the Son of
Man, the Christ, then to the apostles, to the Church as the new remnant,
the 'new Israel', to a redeemed humanity and a redeemed heaven and
earth, a new creation (pp. 115-18).[154] (In Cullmann's presentation this
brings into view the cosmic horizons of redemption.)

---

152. The relation of history and myth for Cullmann is clarified in *Salvation in
History*, pp. 93-97; 136-50.
153. See the fuller summary, Cullmann, *Christ and Time*, pp. 108-109.
154. This concludes the first part of Cullmann's *Christ and Time*.

Past, present, and future are reconceived as a result of Christ the midpoint. The past, '*the entire redemptive history of the Old Testament*', the creation and the history of Israel, '*tends toward the goal of the incarnation*'; the relation between this past and the midpoint is that relation, 'conceived in a strict time sense, between *preparation* and *fulfillment*' (p. 135).

> The Christ-event at the mid-point...is on its part illuminated by the Old Testament preparation, after this preparation has first received its light from that very mid-point. We have to do here with a circle. The death and resurrection of Christ enable the believer to see in the history of Adam and in the history of Israel the preparation for Jesus, the Crucified and Risen One. But only the thus understood history of Adam and the thus understood history of Israel enable the believer to grasp the work of Jesus Christ, the Crucified and Risen One, in connection with the divine plan of salvation...
>
> It would be the task of a New Testament theology to show in detail how, viewed in the Christian light, it becomes clear from the standpoint of Adam what it must mean when Jesus is called 'the Son of Man'...It would further have to be shown how from the standpoint of Abraham—that is, on the basis of the election of the people of Israel and on the basis of the prophetic designation, conditioned by this election, of a 'remnant' and of a Suffering Servant of God—we are to understand what the vicarious character of Christ's atoning death must signify in connection with God's plan of salvation. These two lines, the Adam–Christ line and the Abraham–Christ line, show how the Old Testament belongs to the Christian revelation. As Son of Man, second Adam, Jesus fulfills the destiny of the man created by God; as Servant of Yahweh he fulfills the history of his people. Both lines permit us to perceive that the entire history in which Christ effects salvation is connected with *human sin* (pp. 137-38).

As for the future, 'eschatology is not put aside, but it is dethroned, and this holds true both chronologically and essentially' (p. 139). '[T]he future is no longer, as in Judaism, the *telos* or "end" which gives meaning to the whole...The "end" as the meaning of redemptive history...is Jesus Christ, who has already appeared...While the "end" was previously only expectation, it is now acknowledged as fulfillment' (p. 140). Yet, though sounding very like Dodd's 'reinterpretation' of eschatology as teleology or the 'ultimate', Cullmann categorically rejects any such reinterpretation:

> In spite of this dethronement, however, eschatology continues to possess, as do the other sections of the redemptive line, its own significance for redemptive history. Indeed, no part of that line can be torn loose from it. Primitive Christianity does indeed think eschatologically; but it now no

longer thinks in a 'consistently', that is, an exclusively, eschatological manner—not if we understand the word 'eschatologically' in the futuristic sense, as we must do, since all other speech concerning eschatology is a reinterpretation of the thing involved (p. 140).[155]

Does the shifting of centres, then, devalue eschatology, leaving it with nothing new to contribute since the decisive event has already arrived?

> [I]t remains true for the Primitive Christian eschatology just as for the Jewish one that it does not occur in a purely otherworldly sphere. Indeed, we must actually say that particularly for Primitive Christianity the eschatological drama must take place in a setting that includes the earth, because here the new thing that the final completion adds to the already reached decision consists in the fact that the Spirit, which in a preliminary way, in baptism, lays hold only of the inner man, now creates anew the whole of matter which has fallen into the state of sinful flesh (141-42).

This expectation rests on the presence of the Spirit on the basis of Christ's resurrection, in which the believer participates.[156]

A particular significance attaches to the present stage of redemptive history in which Primitive Christianity finds itself, a 'consciousness of standing as a Church in redemptive history's quite definite plan, and of being on the way from the resurrection to the Parousia', an awareness of being in a period of 'tension between "this age" and the "coming age"' which tends to recede gradually from the self-understanding of the Church (pp. 144-45).

> The result of this tension is that the particular significance of the post-Easter present lies in a special relation not only to that mid-point, but also to the future...
>
> It is already the time of the end, and yet is not *the* end. This tension finds expression in the entire theology of Primitive Christianity...To anyone who does not take clear account of this tension, the entire New Testament is a book with seven seals...(p. 145).

As distinct from a dialectic between this world and the beyond, or between time and eternity, this is 'the dialectic of present and future', contrasting also with a Kierkegaardian 'contemporaneity' (pp. 147-48).[157]

---

155. As we shall see below, the primary target here in speaking of reinterpretation is Bultmann (although Dodd also comes in for censure).

156. Here Cullmann invokes the 'dying and rising' with Christ, the new creation anticipated in participation with Christ, interpreted in the eschatological, 'new phase' sense; see pp. 142-43, 231-42.

157. This continues the indirect critique of Dodd (Barth) and Bultmann.

The Catholic conception of the period of the Church (to which Protestantism has over-reacted) preserves something of the primitive Christian awareness, if in muted form.

> [T]his conception nowhere comes more clearly to expression than in Rom. 13.11: 'We know concerning the *kairos*, namely, that it is time to wake out of sleep, for our salvation is *now nearer than when we first believed*'. In view of this text, all philosophical reinterpretations of the Biblical redemptive history, with its eschatologically future goal, should be impossible. Every passing minute brings us nearer to the point, and from the viewpoint of redemptive history every passing minute, when seen from the center, is important in the Church (pp. 147-48).[158]

Jesus himself expected such an intermediate period, and he must, then, have envisaged some role for the disciples here. 'For the Primitive Church, at any rate, it is a fixed fact that the present stage of redemptive history is the period of the Church, the earthly Body of Christ.' (p. 150) This redemptive-historical present is not identical with the present as such, but concerns rather 'the line of things that occur in the Church of Christ in connection with Christ's present Lordship' (p. 150). The delimitation and unity of this segment of time is precise, framed 'between Christ's ascension and his Parousia', a departure upon a cloud and a return in kind (pp. 150-51).

> This unity has its factual ground in the particular Christ-event that fills this segment: *Christ rules over all things in heaven and on earth. The spatial center of this Lordship is the Church, which constitutes his Body upon earth*...In chronological respect (although not in the spatial [as Christ 'sits at the right hand of God']) the kingly rule of Christ and this Church completely coincide. Like the Church, this Lordship of Christ began with the ascension. While the Kingdom of *God* will begin only at the end of the revelatory process, when Christ shall have subjected himself to God (1 Cor. 15.28), we already stand in the Kingdom of *Christ* (Col. 1.13). Like the Church, therefore, the Kingdom of Christ has a beginning and an end (p. 157).

This lordship of Christ from the heavenly right hand entails his subjection of the hostile powers—a 'binding' which, though awaiting a final defeat in the end, again reveals the characteristic tension of this period. This tension further finds expression in the Church itself, as the

---

158. Again, an implicit critique of the sort of reinterpretation Cullmann finds in Dodd and Bultmann. This one verse, Cullmann argues, ought to disallow their philosophical tampering with the 'biblical history'.

'firstfruits' of the Spirit are at work in the Body of Christ, even though the flesh still rules. Sin is defeated by the Spirit, yet the Church is composed of sinful humanity.

For the primitive community, these are 'the last days', 'preliminary signs' of the end. There *are* signs in the more limited, 'apocalyptic' sense which belong to the end of the present period, but 'this entire intermediate process is a preliminary sign in the wider sense' (p. 156).[159] 'Above all, however, the one great task that is assigned to the Church to do in its period, namely, the missionary preaching of the gospel, is likewise evaluated as a preliminary sign of the end' (p. 157). '*This missionary proclamation of the Church, its preaching of the gospel, gives to the period between Christ's resurrection and Parousia its meaning for redemptive history; and it has this meaning through its connection with Christ's present Lordship*' (p. 157). This meaning is anchored in the proclaimed Christ event and is connected intimately with the future fulfilment toward which it points. This mission is bound up with the bestowal of the eschatological Spirit. '[T]he end will come only when the gospel shall have been preached to all peoples' (p. 158). This understanding pervades the New Testament, not least Paul, who must be understood in the light of this expectation. Paul, in pursuing with urgency his Gentile mission, a mission pivotal as well for Israel, is 'an instrument of the eschatological plan of salvation' (p. 163).[160] The Primitive Church, then, felt with intensity the decisive eschatological significance of its mission and moment in time.[161]

Having presented this redemptive line and the interconnection of its parts, Cullmann proceeds to draw the lines of connection to world history and the individual person.[162] The lordship of Christ is seen to extend universally and cosmically, encompassing all creation, including the hostile 'powers' and beneath them the state. The lordship of Christ operates at the level of the individual, who is addressed against the entire backdrop of redemptive history, yet in such a way that the goal of redemptive history is the individual. Faith makes this story one's own, and election, Spirit and ethics, and personal resurrection in the final hour bind one personally, past, present, and future, to the redemptive line.

159. 'Apocalyptic' violates the Primitive Christian attitude when it falls into reckoning the time of the end Cullmann, *Christ and Time*, pp. 155-56.

160. See Cullmann, *Christ and Time*, pp. 163-66 on Paul.

161. This concludes Part Two of Cullmann's *Christ and Time*.

162. These correspond to the final two parts of Cullmann's *Christ and Time*.

Both the cosmic and the individual realms are marked by the eschatological tension of 'already' and 'not yet'.

Cullmann's *The Christology of the New Testament* assumes the picture developed in *Christ and Time*.

> We have seen that it is characteristic of New Testament Christology that Christ is connected with the total history of revelation and salvation, beginning with creation. There can be no *Heilsgeschichte* without Christology, no Christology without a *Heilsgeschichte* which unfolds in time. Christology is the doctrine of an 'event', not the doctrine of natures...[F]rom all the variety of individual New Testament books and individual concepts there emerges in the thinking of early Christianity one total picture of the Christ-event from the pre-existence to eschatology (p. 9).

Cullmann clarifies, then, the nature of the Christ-line as *Christ*-line, 'from creation through the reconciliation in the cross and the invisible present lordship of Christ to the still unaccomplished consummation in the new creation' (p. 324). The work of Christ, as viewed according to Jesus' own self-understanding and the understanding of his early followers as to his earthly ministry, his future coming, his present lordship, and his pre-existent creative activity—here Cullmann presents the conclusion 'which has forced itself on us as we collected the material'— is the redemptive process of representation and the revelatory unfolding of God's self-communication (p. 316).[163] In the early effort to express developing Christological conceptions, history of religions connections were made, as the Christological titles witness: 'Syncretistic elements, even myths, were indeed appropriated, but they were subordinated to a Christological structure which received its character not from syncretism, not from Hellenism, not from mythology, but from the *Heilsgeschichte*. It is characteristic of this structure that from the very beginning it centres in a real history' (p. 322). Thus any existing schemes into which the Christ event were fitted are secondary to the controlling line of salvation history. In particular, within that line the coming advent, at times viewed under the threatening influence of existing schemes of expectation, is properly interpreted by the past advent (a realization gained in the light of the present experience of the lordship of Christ).[164]

163. See the summary in Cullmann, *Christology*, pp. 315-28.

164. See the paraphrase of Cullmann in Guthrie, 'Oscar Cullmann', pp. 346-47: 'The Christology of the early church is not an attempt to fit Christ into *any* conceptual scheme, but to adjust all concepts, of whatever origin, to the events connected with

*Christid and Time* is itself a synthesis of many years' work.[165] From the standpoint of *Salvation in History*, a second synthesis of the perspective of 'salvation history' worked out in further years of reflection, *Christ and Time* is an 'outline' of the perspective which may be assumed, nuanced, and refined, a 'prolegomenon', insofar as the question of the 'relation between salvation history and eschatology' is concerned, to the working out of the wider implications of the approach (pp. 14-15).[166] The eschatological tension between the 'already' and the 'not yet', the real '*leitmotiv*' of the earlier study, is elaborated and made unequivocally central (p. 38).[167] 'Salvation history', the narrative of God's saving plan, is more closely defined, especially as regards its genesis as a progressive revelatory dialectic of 'event and interpretation'.[168] Paul's salvation-historical self-understanding is more fully presented in the matrix of this eschatological, salvation-historical tension and as part of this revelatory, reinterpretive dialectic (pp. 248-68).

The most important advance of this second synthesis for the present purposes is the bringing to the fore of the polemical context of Cullmann's interpretation, polemics that are largely kept implicit (but just barely) in the earlier outline but are confidently elaborated in the more mature treatise. Again, the core—and very much of the detail—of

him. Only when we recognize this can we see the radical newness of the theology of the New Testament and its radical difference from a timeless mythology or nonhistorical kerygma...Cullmann emphasizes that all New Testament Christology is founded upon and begins with the life of Jesus himself, not with a ready-made mythology or eschatology, and not even with the experience and theology of the early Christian community after Easter...So profound was [the] cultic experience of the present Lord, Cullmann believes, that it was really from this center that the whole line of redemptive history was given its Christological interpretation'.

165. Cullmann, *Christ and Time*, p. xiii.

166. 'In the earlier work I already characterized salvation and revelation in the New Testament as a history of a special kind. But whereas it was my concern in *Christ and Time* merely to work out the outline of a New Testament salvation history, here every aspect of the content of this history is to be discussed—its origin, its total importance, its relation to eschatology' (Cullmann, *Salvation in History*, p. 14). Thus *Salvation in History* is commentary on, and not a supersession of, *Christ and Time*, which latter was released in a new edition preceding the appearance of the more mature synthesis.

167. See pp. 36-40, 166-85, and cf. the new 'Introductory Chapter to the Third Edition' of Cullmann, *Christ and Time*, pp. xviii-xxv.

168. Cullmann, *Salvation in History*, pp. 84-135. These two elements concern the 'redemptive' and the 'revelatory' aspects of salvation history.

*Christ and Time* is assumed: New Testament thought has an irreducibly temporal and historical character, a temporality marked by linearity, such that there is a 'now' and a 'then', with one event following on another in sequence. The total narrative of salvation and revelation, which stands as the presupposition of all New Testament theological reflection and development, is a Christ-narrative, with each moment interpreted from Christ the centre, as a result of whose incision into time the present stands under his lordship in a state of tension constitutive of this moment in salvation history. This core perspective Cullmann urges against the 'detemporalization' and 'dehistoricization' represented by the 'Platonizing' interpretation of Dodd and the existentialist interpretation of Bultmann. Here Cullmann is able to make common cause with Schweitzer against Dodd and Bultmann, that is, against any effort to 'reinterpret' eschatology, to turn it into something other than a literal, realistic expectation for the salvation-historical future.[169] At the same time Cullmann regards Schweitzer, and Bultmann following him, as dismissing salvation history altogether as an expediency dreamed up in disappointment over the failure of the end to materialize. Thus, Cullmann is able to make common cause with Dodd against Schweitzer and Bultmann in insisting that the decisive interpretative motive for early Christianity is the death and resurrection of Jesus and not some unfulfilled longing for his expected imminent return.[170] But, significantly, at no point does Cullmann's agenda sufficiently overlap with Bultmann that similar common cause may be made. Bultmann is, point by point, Cullmann's interpretive alter-ego, the polemical counter-force against which Cullmann's whole agenda is defined.[171]

---

169. On this polemical theme, see Cullmann, *Christ and Time*, pp. xii-xiii, xvii-xxx, 26-32, 52-56, 61-68, 92-93, 94-106, 125-30, 146, 168, 213; *Salvation in History*, pp. 11-16, 28-47, 64-83, and *passim*. (I argued above concerning Schweitzer that the 'types of eschatology' debates subsequent to him should not be simply read back into his own self-understanding, clearly an anachronistic move. Cullmann points, however, and with some justification, to Schweitzer's critique of liberal interpretation as a critique of the sublimation or reinterpretation of eschatology—an implicit critique, perhaps, of later reinterpretation.)

170. See Cullmann, *Salvation in History*, pp. 28-47.

171. Cullmann's very title, *Christ and Time* (*Christus und die Zeit*), must surely be a polemical statement against Heidegger's *Being and Time* (*Sein und Zeit*), a title so expressive of Bultmann's approach; cf. also the original subtitle to *Salvation in History*: '*Heilsgeschichtliche Existenz im Neuen Testament*'. Cullmann's whole interpretative programme seems designed to confront and shut down at every point

In fact, the first question Cullmann must address to himself in his interpretation of Paul is the viability of *Bultmann's* interpretation: 'the "now of decision"...is very important for Paul. But not only does it not conflict with a salvation-historical attitude—it is subordinate to one. We can even say that Paul's faith in salvation history creates at every moment a basis for the existential decision...' (p. 248). In confronting Bultmann, since it is agreed by all that salvation history is present in Paul, the question comes down to whether it is 'only a remnant from Paul's Jewish past' or whether it in fact 'constitutes the kernel of Pauline theology' (p. 248). Pausing briefly to remark on Bultmann's 'Marcionism', Cullmann proceeds to reveal just how central salvation history is for Paul. Paul's calling, apostolic self-understanding, gospel, and mission are bound up with God's precise saving plan—and all are marked by the urgency of the present eschatological 'interval':

> Paul finds himself (2 Cor. 6.2) right at the point where in the execution of his plan God brought in the 'welcome time' by reconciling the world to himself through Christ (2 Cor. 5.18). Just at this point in time the apostle received his precise calling, his 'ministry of reconciliation' (5.18), and therefore must show himself as a 'servant of God' on this 'day of salvation'...
>
> The apostle is thinking primarily of himself as the one who...stands at a particular point in salvation history. But the 'now' is also a 'now' of decision for his readers...The 'now' is 'now' because there is a 'before' and an 'after' in the divine plan, not only in relation to the individual person, but also in relation to the whole of mankind and even the whole of creation...A 'now' so conceived, leaving ample room for individual decisions, gives a totally different impulse for acting from a disconnected 'now' that can be tantamount to 'always' and 'in every moment'...
>
> The tension between 'already' and 'not yet'...stands in the foreground in Paul...Paul's whole theology is dominated by this tension—his conception of the Holy Spirit, the Church, the sacraments, and his ethics. In no way does this tension merely relate to the existence of the individual. It relates to the whole salvation history of the interval which is the basis and presupposition of all existence (p. 255).

This eschatological, salvation-historical tension supplies the logic of Paul's 'indicative and imperative', his 'dialectic of Christian existence', without a knowledge of which rationale a coherent account could not be given of Paul's thought, which would then appear to lapse into contra-

Bultmann's response to Schweitzer. For Cullmann, believing existence is determined precisely by salvation history, and faith responds to just this history.

diction (pp. 256-58). Further, Paul addresses the whole complex of issues concerning Israel, election, and the Law against a salvation-historical backcloth. Without salvation history, Paul's interpretation of scripture and his cosmic eschatological perspective become obscure. Bultmann's interpretation, then, must be salvation-historically grounded and emended.

Cullmann regards Schweitzer's *The Mysticism of Paul the Apostle* ('theologically...his most significant work'), as showing 'in a particularly clear and truly classical way how for the apostle the significance of the present for redemptive history is bound up with the future'.[172] Further, Cullmann appreciates Schweitzer's interpretation for making the present eschatological 'interval'

> the main characteristic in Paul's thought. In accord with his thesis of Paul's eschatological mysticism, he describes being in this time as 'being in Christ', and thereby he certainly takes account of one side of the Pauline conception. But it corresponds still better with the apostle's intention if we define this, 'being' *functionally*, in relation to the origin of Paul's view, that is, as being determined by the fact that in God's plan the gospel must be preached in this time, and that we must be tested in this way...Paul has [a] tremendously heightened consciousness of standing in this interval as an apostle...(p. 254).

Schweitzer's eschatological interpretation is to be welcomed; but it too needs a more careful nuancing as to its proper relation to *Heilsgeschichte*: 'The future expectation is, of course, important for all early Christian thinking, and consequently in interpreting the New Testament message it is necessary to take eschatology into account *in the form of an expectation of an imminent end*, as Albert Schweitzer does' (p. 147, emphasis added). Schweitzer is a powerful ally against Dodd and Bultmann. But Cullmann continues: 'Still, it must not be forgotten...that eschatology is determined primarily by its connection with historical events and not *vice versa*' (p. 147).

Cullmann also regards Ernst Käsemann's approach as, like Schweitzer's, kindred to his own. Indeed, he seems to greet Käsemann's rehabilitation of 'apocalyptic', coming as it does from within the Bultmann camp, with a certain sense of self-satisfaction (pp. 59-61). 'Apocalyptic', or 'revealed eschatology', is welcome, then, so long as it does not lose its connection with salvation history and degenerate into unwholesome and fantastic speculation (pp. 80-83).[173]

---

172. Cullmann, *Christ and Time*, p. 29 n. 14.
173. Kindred salvation-historical approaches to Paul include: N.Q. Hamilton,

We earlier spoke of Schweitzer, Dodd, and Bultmann as a triad of possibilities in reading Paul. When we add Cullmann as a fourth, we find him variously playing Schweitzer and Dodd off against each other (sharing with the former a literal reading of eschatology and with the latter a *heilsgeschichtliche* perspective[174]) over against Bultmann (making the configuration of similarity and difference earlier observed even more complex). For Bultmann, Cullmann's 'salvation history' is just 'Jewish apocalyptic speculation' (and is thus subject to the strictures of Bultmann's *Sachkritik*).[175] Looking ahead somewhat, Cullmann would seem to represent a classic exhibit for Käsemann's complaint against

*Holy Spirit*; J. Munck, *Paul and the Salvation of Mankind* (trans. F. Clarke; Richmond: John Knox Press, 1959); H. Ridderbos, *Paul* (trans. J.R. de Witt; Grand Rapids: Eerdmans, 1975). Theologies of the New Testament from a related perspective, revealing the context in which Paul and 'apocalyptic' are addressed according to 'salvation history', include (by no means belonging to a single coherent school) E. Stauffer, *New Testament Theology* (trans. J. March; London: SCM Press, 1955); W.G. Kümmel, *The Theology of the New Testament* (trans. J.E. Steely; London: SCM Press, 1974) and L. Goppelt, *Theology of the New Testament* (2 vols.; trans. J.E. Alsup, ed. J. Roloff; Grand Rapids: Eerdmans, 1981-82); see also Goppelt's 'Apocalypticism and Typology in Paul', repr. in his *Typos: The Typological Interpretation of the Old Testament in the New* (trans. D.H. Madvig; Grand Rapids: Eerdmans, 1982).

174. A. Richardson, *The Bible in the Age of Science* (London: SCM Press, 1961), selects Dodd, Cullmann, and G.E. Wright as examples to introduce the *Heilsgeschichte* approach (pp. 122-141).

175. Bultmann, 'History of Salvation and History', in *Existence and Faith*, p. 236. Bultmann's reaction to Cullmann is given in compact and classic form in this review of Cullmann's *Christ and Time*, which is more or less Bultmann's first and last word on the matter (the debate being left to his students). Bultmann, then, is not drawn into the constant engagement with Cullmann that the latter so desires, as he, presumably, sees (as Cullmann apparently does not) that the two inhabit such different perspectives that there is not much to say beyond a clear statement of the basic differences. (We have noted similar situations between Bultmann and Schweitzer and Bultmann and Dodd, above). Bultmann insists, then, that 'the criticism that he directs against my demythologizing exegesis does not even touch me; for on the basis of his presuppositions, everything that he says is completely correct. The problem only arises when one asks what meaning the concept "history" has in the phrase "history of salvation"' (p. 234). Different conceptions of 'theology', 'faith', 'occurrence', and 'history' rule (pp. 231-34). Bultmann complains of Cullmann's 'illicit harmonization' (p. 234), history of religions simplicity, avoidance of the problem posed by the 'delay of the parousia' (p. 237), and failure to raise the question of 'the temporality of Christian existence' (p. 239).

attempting to 'conquer apocalyptic and escape scot-free'. Cullmann further provides another means of playing realization off against expectation.

Cullmann makes clear, with a candour absent from much of the debate, that the legacy of Schweitzer is a crisis for faith. Thus Cullmann opens his *Salvation in History*: 'In the present study, we are striving for nothing less than an answer to the old question "WHAT IS CHRISTIANITY?"' (p. 19).[176] Cullmann's remarks on Schweitzer are telling:

> [F]rom Schweitzer's exegetical premises the conclusion must actually be drawn that Jesus' whole teaching stands or falls with this expectation [of an imminent end] as its central point, and therefore must fall and be given up. We all know that Schweitzer did not draw this conclusion. We know what Jesus and Paul actually meant for Schweitzer. But he based his own philosophy of life neither on Jesus' expectation that the end was imminent, which was proven an illusion and in no case could be reinterpreted, nor upon some kind of de-eschatologizing 'salvation history' understood as a solution to an embarrassment created by the delay of the *parousia* and therefore valueless because it had its beginning in an illusion. Schweitzer founded his own personal attitude on 'reverence for life'. For Schweitzer, this went hand in hand with a practical Christianity. But theoretically it was neither rooted in the eschatology of Jesus, as Schweitzer understood it exegetically, nor in the eschatological mysticism of Paul, which he rejected because it was worked out in an effort to come to grips with an illusion. Since Schweitzer as an exegete is averse to every reinterpretation of the New Testament, an impassable gap opens between his exegetical and his religious-philosophical attitudes. With his extremely consistent, but purely hypothetical, exegetical account of Jesus' teachings and his flagrant inconsistency in his practical conclusions, Schweitzer's imposing theological work left behind burning and unanswered questions and therefore has determined the debate of the present to an extent which the parties in dialogue today hardly recognize (pp. 31-32).[177]

Schweitzer 'has not given any foundation to justify this double point of view' (p. 40). And Cullmann can find no real comfort in Bultmann's

176. Cullmann continues: 'Thus, we see how tremendous is the responsibility of this inquiry about the essence of the Christian message common to all New Testament books' (Cullmann, *Salvation in History*, p. 19).

177. See also especially, Cullmann, *Christ and Time*, pp. 29-30. Compare and contrast Schweitzer's own hermeneutical reflections, below. Implicit in Cullmann's worried complaint here is a definite notion of the properly literal nature of interpretation and of the proper relationship of exegesis and faith, the latter being built directly onto the former.

'solution' to this problem of criticism, myth, history, and faith. For Bultmann, faith is subverted into its opposite in any attempt to find by criticism a 'foundation' in history, and interpretation of history is itself properly a 'non-objectifying' enterprise which turns the 'objectifying' projections of myth in a direction commensurate with faith—the problem thus reduces to a non-problem when each term is understood. For Cullmann, history is of the essence of faith, as faith itself is in large measure an affirmation and appropriation of biblical history, and faith and its founding history can never be compromised by allowing myth to insinuate itself too near to the heart of things. This leaves Cullmann with the necessity of insisting that salvation history, in its interpretative dialectic of event and interpretation, always involves eyewitness testimony of prophets and apostles to *real, historical salvific events*, the interpretation of which (also a part of the revelatory process) might make use of 'myth', 'either by placing the non-historical elements alongside the historical reports or by investing the accounts of historical events with legendary, mythological, and fabulous elements' (p. 93).[178] The challenge which criticism presents may be perceived 'in the particularly difficult question of the Red Sea episode. Even if research comes to the conclusion that in this case the historical core was nothing more than the destruction of a band of chariots, this event is not irrelevant as one of the causes of the *kerygma* which has effects that extend right into the New Testament' (p. 95).[179] But the more radically critical putting of the

178. See pp. 84-126, 136-66; cf. Cullmann, *Christ and Time*, pp. 94-106, 26-32. The biblical theologians 'historicized' myth, says Cullmann, that is, they anchored myth in salvation history—the proper, *biblical* form of 'demythologizing'.

179. Cullmann is here insisting on historical criticism, as against the decision that faith does not rest on such reconstructed history; but the critical sword cuts both ways, not only exposing that to which faith reaches out, but disposing of it as well. In the present context, Cullmann is promoting *as a theological necessity* the search by historical criticism for the historical roots of the kerygma, the 'attempt to distinguish history and interpretation, history and myth at its very origin' (Cullmann, *Salvation in History*, p. 95). 'It would seem that we approach their [the biblical salvation-historians] understanding in faith if we at least *dare to make the attempt*, however uncertain its success may be, to place the events alongside the interpretation in such a way that in the naked events disclosed to us the interpretation of those events is forced upon us as it was upon the biblical witnesses. Do we not comprehend the interpretation even better if we also *allow it to come to us out of the naked events* which for us, of course, lie in the past? When we become acquainted with the naked event as well, does not the *reliving of the event in the present* become more real for us? Since we, in contrast to the biblical witnesses, possess scholarly methods allowing us to make the past present,

case, which Cullmann does not here countenance (and which in fact seems ruled out of court in the very definition of 'salvation history'), asks: Supposing one, at the end of such an inquiry, arrives at the scene of 'salvation' to find nothing at all? Precisely this situation (which, incidentally, holds for many concerning the Red Sea incident, not to mention the resurrection of Jesus) obtains for many—and here no special inquiry is required—when one turns from the past to the future and the non-event of the expected end-time occurrence. Here is the heart of Cullmann's crisis of faith.

I have placed Schweitzer in the context of the rise of historical consciousness and the rise of criticism, a context of the confrontation of faith and criticism, faith and modernity, which (sooner or later) raises the question of a hermeneutical consciousness. It is in this space that debate about an 'apocalyptic' Paul is occurring. I have at various points above hinted that there is a set of related concerns underlying this debate which might be regarded as the 'real issues' at stake (an assertion that already implies a hermeneutical perspective on this history of interpretation). I have expressed this conviction, in the form of the theme 'history and eschatology', as a heading under which to unite Dodd, Bultmann, and Cullmann as responses to Schweitzer. We have seen with Dodd and Bultmann that language and myth, history, and eschatology, and the implications for faith, constitute this core concern. Now the polemics of Cullmann permit even greater clarity about this inner core:[180] What is the motive force of the genesis and development of early Christianity? Is it the expectation of an imminent end and the delay of the parousia? Is, then, Christianity a desperate and pitiful—and thus discredited and contemptible—attempt to propagate a lie or prolong a delusion? Is an escape from this critical impasse provided by a recognition of an emerging conception, amid these failed hopes, of human existence, of 'historicity', in early Christianity? Or does early Christianity centre on the completed work of Christ (perhaps still to be consummated), representing a coming to the surface, amid many admitted false starts, of something utterly new (a newness of, perhaps, long-standing, even primordial, development)? Is

---

we should and must make use of those methods, however unsure they are, and however great the danger may be of creating a source of error if we make a false separation between history and myth, as happened so often in the "quest of the historical Jesus"' (p. 96). See further below on Cullmann's hermeneutics.

180. Here the oppositions expressed are chiefly between Bultmann and Cullmann, with Dodd usually ranging close to Cullmann.

this new reality then the Church on Earth? Or a divine plan of cosmic proportions, still to be brought to its ultimate fruition? Is Christianity merely a product of random syncretistic reshuffling? Does the Christian gospel reduce to myth? Or, again, is there something unique coming to birth? A new self-understanding, an inner-historical perspective expressed in myth? Or does Christianity place a self-conscious and non-negotiable value on its own historical salvific core? Another set of questions concerns tradition and interpretation, the New Testament use of the Old, continuity and discontinuity. Yet another cluster of issues concerns the matter of a centre or essential core to the New Testament and to (say) Paul, which raises the (implicitly) hermeneutical question of a 'kernel' and a 'husk', of inner content, essence, or substance and outer form— something, that is, which reaches the 'now' and is not left behind in the distant 'then' to which time and criticism have removed Scripture. Still another matter concerns literal and non-literal language and, by extension, faith. What, theologically and hermeneutically, does a modern profession of faith, in the light of criticism, require, and can reflection on language help? Criticism has fathered on modernity two great, intricately interconnected problems: the 'historical Jesus' and 'myth and history', of which latter 'history and eschatology' is an aspect. Albert Schweitzer stands at a focal point in the development of each of these problematical points, and the long and winding careers of C.H. Dodd, Rudolf Bultmann, and Oscar Cullmann crisscross the twisting paths of each in intimate detail. There is, it must be repeated, no design here on resolving any facet of this ongoing dialogue. The object is merely to register notice of it. The interconnection of the historical and theological issues—the penetration, that is, of the whole dialogue to the level of the very meaning and possibility of faith—should leave us at least mildly suspicious that something more than cool reason is at work here. Yet, paradoxically, Cullmann, who perhaps more than any other exposes (though usually unwittingly) the implication into the very fabric of the dialogue of the polemics and politics of church and academy, insists on a methodically pure, scientific, two-stage critical approach with a hermeneutical naiveté that might have made Wrede blush.[181]

If, then, the response is anything to go on, the state in which Schweitzer left things seems inherently unstable and intolerable, creating as it does a

181. On Cullmann's hermeneutical ideals, see Cullmann, *Salvation in History*, pp. 13-14, 40-47, 64-74, 187-93, 319-28; *Christ and Time*, pp. xxvii-xxx; 'The Necessity and Function of Higher Criticism'; see further below.

vacuum abhorrent to the nature of New Testament theology—Dodd,
Bultmann, and Cullmann clearly mount a series of biblical-theological
rearguard actions against the assault of Schweitzer. Each represents a
unity movement to repair the fragmentation and dissolution in which
criticism has issued. We have done our criticism, Dodd asserts, and 'the
present task in New Testament studies' is interpretation, a movement
now from diversity to unity, a 'centripetal movement' to balance the
'centrifugal movement' of criticism.[182] Bultmann, after surveying the
syncretistic milieu of early Christianity, asks: 'Is Christianity then really a
syncretistic religion? Or is there a fundamental *unity* behind all this
*diversity*?...Does primitive Christianity contain a single, new and unique
doctrine of human existence?'[183] Cullmann's stated concern is with an
elucidation, amid all the diversity (a devil which has received its due), of
'the *basic presuppositions of all New Testament theology*'.[184] Each
may be regarded as presenting in his own way (to adapt a phrase from
Dodd) 'the narrative substructure of New Testament theology'.[185] Thus,
each pursues his biblical-theological agenda through some version of
*Heilsgeschichte*. Dodd has in view the salvation history of the establishment of the 'Divine Commonwealth', the 'Community of God' on
earth, with the movement of *Unheilsgeschichte* being understood as the
empire building of secular states as well as the immanent kingdom of
liberalism. Bultmann presents the salvation history of the individual's
'historicity' and 'authenticity', the counter-story now being the state of
alienation implicit in 'objectification' and the resulting plunge into the
darkness of inauthenticity. Cullmann, of course, presents a salvation

182. Dodd, *The Present Task in New Testament Studies*, *passim*, esp. pp. 29-41
(p. 35); eschatology is for Dodd an important test case here (see pp. 33-34, 39-40).
Dodd's unity movement is pursued through the thesis of 'realized eschatology',
through reconstruction of the early kerygma, and through investigation of the early
scripture interpretation (which reveals a 'substructure', a salvation-historical narrative).

183. Bultmann, *Primitive Christianity*, p. 213 (emphasis added), a question raised
and answered in outline here and fully in Bultmann's *Theology*.

184. Cullmann, *Christ and Time*, p. 26; cf. the new introduction to the 3rd edn,
p. xix: 'I am especially interested in the question of the assumptions common to all
New Testament writers'. This interest in synthesis is clear throughout Cullmann,
*Christ and Time*, *Christology*, and *Salvation in History*.

185. Consider the quotations cited at the head of the present chapter, all concerning the 'now', but understood as the 'now' of the Church (in its kerygma), the
'now' of decision (in the face of the kerygma), and the 'now' of the precise present
moment in salvation history (which is of the essence of the kerygma).

history as it is, perhaps, more usually understood in the universal-historical and cosmic sense of a divine plan of salvation encompassing all creation, realistically conceived, and opposed by all the forces of evil aligned against the Creator. And each ('new Pauls' one and all) achieves an intimate interpretative connection with Paul and his time. Dodd, British subject and dissenter, against a background of secular empire building and of philosophies and theologies investing utopian hopes in human effort, looks to Paul, Roman citizen and Christian missionary, with his message of a kingdom from God.[186] Bultmann, struggling against the 'objectifying' structures of modernity, finds a comrade-at-arms in Paul's struggle against the 'objectifying' myths of his own contemporary world-view, and the mood of darkness and despair which has beset modernity finds deep echoes in the Hellenistic world of Paul.[187] Cullmann pictures faith's enrapturement in being caught up in the sweep of salvation history, an awareness apparently as overtaking and consuming now as it clearly was for (Cullmann's) Paul.[188] Irrespective of what is claimed for the hermeneutical dialogue, we witness a process of hermeneutical fusion which, implicating as it does the deepest interests and commitments of the inquirers, might signal understanding.

Having followed through this far with Dodd, Bultmann, and Cullmann, and having arrived again at a point of hermeneutical reflection, I return briefly to Schweitzer, picking up again the hermeneutical discussion at the point where, in the closing reflections of his *The Mysticism of Paul the Apostle*, Schweitzer asserts that 'Paul was the first to champion the rights of thought in Christianity; he has shown it, for all time, the way it was to go' (p. 377).

---

186. See Dodd, *The Meaning of Paul for Today*; *The Bible Today*. Dodd was able to maintain a sense of humour about the Empire, however. In *The Bible Today*, when commenting on the stereotypical notions of the 'natural genius' of the Hebrews for religion, the Greeks for philosophy, and the Romans for government, Dodd (a Welshman) quips 'one might no doubt add, "God's Englishman" for empire-building (or is it shop-keeping?), so that we can all feel comfortable about it' (p. 106).

187. See Bultmann, *Primitive Christianity*, pp. 161-205; cf. R.A. Johnson (ed.), *Rudolf Bultmann*, p. 30.

188. Cf. Cullmann, *Salvation in History*, pp. 69-70, 115-22, 319-28. Cullmann, for all his talk of respecting the distance of the New Testament, throughout implies a virtual contemporaneity in faith, an ironic turn in one so zealous of avoiding the dissolution of time.

> By penetrating to the depths of the temporarily conditioned, Paul wins his
> way to a spiritual result of permanent value. Strange as his thoughts are to
> us in the way they arise out of, and have their form moulded by, the escha-
> tological world-view which for us is so completely obsolete, they never-
> theless carry a directly convincing power in virtue of their spiritual truth
> which transcends all time and has a value for all times. So we too should
> claim the right to conceive the idea of union with Jesus on the lines of our
> own world-view, making it our sole concern to reach the depth of the truly
> living and spiritual truth (p. 378).

Schweitzer then goes on to raise the question of the inner essence of
Paul's 'mysticism':

> The fact of being thought out by the aid of the conceptual apparatus of the
> eschatological world-view constitutes only its outward character, not its
> inner. This inner character is determined by the fact that Paul has thought
> out his conception of redemption through Christ within the sphere of
> belief in the Kingdom of God...For him, believers are redeemed by
> entering already, through the union with Christ, by means of a mystical
> dying and rising again with Him during the continuance of the natural
> world-era into a supernatural state of existence...Through Christ we are
> removed out of this world and transferred into the state of existence proper
> to the Kingdom of God, notwithstanding the fact that it has not yet
> appeared. This is the fundamental idea of the concept of redemption, which
> Paul worked out by the aid of the thought-forms of the eschatological
> world-view (pp. 379-80).

There results for Paul a conviction of the presence of redemption, 'to be
completely realised in the future', a redemption associated with the still
expected Kingdom, but intimately connected with the already accomplished Christ event, so that 'belief in redemption and in the Coming of
the Kingdom becomes independent of whether the Kingdom comes
quickly or is delayed. Without giving up eschatology, he already stands
above it' (p. 380).

> Paul takes the belief in Jesus as the coming Messiah, in which these
> beliefs are comprehended, and thinks it out so thoroughly that it becomes
> freed from its temporal limitations and becomes valid for all times. He thus
> solves in a definitive fashion that pressing problem of the Christian faith of
> all times, namely, that although Jesus Christ has come His Kingdom is
> delayed (p. 380).

Paul's solution rests in his perception of 'the inner connection between
the conception of redemption through Christ and a living belief in the
Kingdom of God', a sense of balance which, as we have seen,

Schweitzer regards as having eluded so much of subsequent Christian thought (p. 381).[189] Paul calls us, then, to a rejuvenating reintegration of faith, a return to Paul's expression of the early Christian faith:

> No doubt a reintegration of Primitive-Christian faith as such is impossible, because it was embodied in temporally conditioned conceptions to which it is impossible for us to return. But the spiritual essence of them we can make ours. This we can do in proportion as we toilfully win for ourselves a living faith in the Kingdom of God, and realise ourselves within this as men redeemed by Christ (p. 384).

In this way, the individualistic frame in which Christianity has been trapped is overcome.

But is not the way to such a return to our Christian roots barred by the distance time has put between us and Paul?

> A change has come over our belief in the Kingdom of God. We no longer look for a transformation of the natural circumstances of the world; we take the continuance of evil and suffering, which belong to the nature of things, as something appointed by God for us to bear. Our hope of the Kingdom is directed to the essential and spiritual meaning of it, and we believe in that as a miracle wrought by the Spirit in making men obedient to the will of God (p. 384).

Our circumstances have indeed changed; but no less had Paul's over against his own tradition. His implicit reinterpretative overcoming of eschatology serves our ends as he could not have known. But what, then, of the 'physical' character of Paul's conception of redemption on which Schweitzer has so strenuously insisted?

> Much as it needs to be emphasised, as against all false spiritualising and symbolical interpretations of Paul's mystical doctrine of redemption, that it is thought of on the lines of a natural process, it is equally certain that the quasi-natural process takes on, as it were of itself, [a] spiritual and ethical significance...[which] shine[s] through the naturalistic conception in a marvellous way. This shows that the naturalistic-eschatological constitutes only the outward character of his mysticism, whereas its inner essence is determined by the close connection of the concept of redemption with the belief in the Kingdom of God, which retains its significance even when the concept of the Kingdom of God is transformed from the natural into the spiritual. That is why Paul's teaching about the dying and rising with

189. See Schweitzer, *Mysticism*, pp. 380-85, and also the treatment of 'Jesus and Paul', pp. 389-96.

> Christ, which are to be experienced in the circumstances of our lives and in
> all our thinking and willing, are just as true for our world-view of to-day as
> they were for his (pp. 385-86).

The transcendence of the Kingdom and the finitude of humanity are
brought to expression in Paul's insight into the life-transforming
empowerment to ethical action achieved only 'in Christ'. Paul did not
reckon with a Kingdom working itself out in this natural world.

> No doubt, as men who have left behind them the eschatological world-view,
> we cannot do otherwise than desire the transformation of the conditions of
> human society in the direction of the Kingdom of God, and work to that
> end. The Spirit of God, that speaks to us out of the non-fulfilment of the
> eschatological expectation of the Kingdom of God, demands it of us. But
> our belief in the Kingdom of God must remain Primitive Christian, in the
> sense that we expect its realisation not from deliberate organised measures,
> but from a growing power of the Spirit of God. For we also know that the
> manifestation…of the Spirit of the Kingdom of God, of which we become
> partakers in the dying and rising again with Christ, is the true way of working
> for the Kingdom of God, without which all others are in vain (p. 389).

Paul, always taking 'the faith of the Primitive-Christian community as
his starting point', but never hesitating 'to think out his thoughts about
Christ to their conclusions', found both a powerful voice and the fitting
words to interpret Christ to his own generation, in its changed circumstances, and to generations to come (p. 376).[190] In this Schweitzer implicitly claims Paul as a profound model for his own self-understanding—
and to the good of Schweitzer's own generation.[191]

Nevertheless, Schweitzer's hermeneutical reflections here may cause
us to stop short. Does his solution to the problem of distance, which he
himself made seem so problematic, subvert his critique of former interpretation? Does he himself not sit now in obvious uneasy tension with
his own earlier rhetoric? Has he cleared the field before him only to re-
erect the former idols? We must retrace more closely Schweitzer's
*hermeneutical* quest.

In his autobiography, dating from about the time of his concluding

---

190. The many ways in which we see Schweitzer himself here sounding notes we
have found in the subsequent dialogue should hardly need elaboration.

191. Obviously Cullmann is not satisfied. But we can now see that Cullmann's
characterization of Schweitzer's hermeneutics is defective and misleading. What is
more truly the case is that Schweitzer, in intimate dialogue with Paul, attempts to think
out a non-literal faith, which offends Cullmann's more literal penchants.

meditations to his *Mysticism* on the 'permanent elements' in Paul, Schweitzer reflects on the significance for faith of his conclusions concerning the historical Jesus and on his own relation to the 'spirit of the age' in which he finds himself and must somehow make his way.[192]

Schweitzer's historical research forces in acute form the question of what his distant, eschatological Jesus can be to us. 'The satisfaction which I could not help feeling at having solved so many historical riddles about the existence of Jesus, was accompanied by the painful consciousness that this new knowledge in the realm of history would mean unrest and difficulty for Christian piety' (p. 65). Christian truth has been in irrational flight from historical truth. 'Instead of allowing this truth its rights, she treated it, whenever it caused her embarrassment, in various ways, conscious or unconscious, but always by either evading, or twisting, or suppressing it' (p. 66). 'Because, while I was busied with the history of earlier Christianity, I had so often to deal with the results of its sins against the truth in history, I have become a keen worker for honesty in our Christianity of to-day' (p. 67).

Jesus' message of religious truth did not fall from heaven free of all historical attachment, to be taken up without effort by each generation.

> We have, therefore, to reconcile ourselves to the fact that His religion of love appeared as part of a world-view which expected a speedy end of the world. Clothed in the ideas in which He announced it, we cannot make it our own; we must re-clothe it in those of our modern world-view.
>
> Hitherto we have been doing this ingenuously and covertly. In defiance of what the words of the text said we managed to interpret the teaching of Jesus as if it were in agreement with our own world-view (p. 67).

'So far as its essential spiritual and ethical nature is concerned, Christianity's religious truth remains the same through the centuries... Thus [it is with] the religion of love which Jesus taught...Whether it is worked out in terms of one *Weltanschauung* or another is only a matter or relative importance. What is decisive is the amount of influence over mankind won by the spiritual and ethical truth which it has held from the first' (pp. 67-68).

The preacher, then, who would 'let the historical Jesus Himself be the speaker when the Christian message is delivered to the men and women of our time' need not feel bound to 'the eschatological Messianic world-

---

192. Schweitzer, *My Life and Thought*; on the former, see ch. 6, 'The Historical Jesus and the Christianity of To-day', pp. 65-75, and on the latter, see pp. 231-35, 254-83.

view' (having duly taken note of Jesus' presupposing it); rather, he must 'work his way up through the historical truth to the eternal. During this process he will again and again have opportunity to notice that it is with this new beginning that he first truly realizes all that Jesus has to say to us' (pp. 69-70)!

> Even if the historical Jesus has something strange about Him, yet His personality, *as it really is*, influences us much more strongly and *immediately* than when He approached us in dogma and in the results attained up to the present by research. In dogma His personality becomes less alive; recent research has been modernizing and belittling Him.
>
> Anyone who ventures *to look the historical Jesus straight in the face* and to listen for what He may have to teach him in His powerful sayings, soon ceases to ask what this strange-seeming Jesus can still be to him. He learns to know Him as One who claims authority over him (pp. 70-71, emphasis added).

Arriving at this realization can be a painful process.

> I myself have suffered in this matter, by having had to join in the work of destroying the portrait of Christ on which liberal Christianity based its appeal. At the same time I was convinced that this liberal Christianity was not reduced to living on an historical illusion, but could equally appeal to the Jesus of history, and further that it carried its justification in itself.
>
> For even if that liberal Christianity has to give up identifying its belief with the teachings of Jesus in the way it used to think possible, it still has the spirit of Jesus not against it but on its side (p. 73).

For Jesus, religion is ethics, and ethics is love, and liberalism grasps just this. And, now that the eschatological world-view is gone and done with, Jesus' religion of love can shine forth all the brighter. 'We are now at liberty to let the religion of Jesus become a living force in our thought, as its purely spiritual and ethical nature demands' (p. 74). This is thanks to Schweitzer's historical research (the tables have been subtly turned on those who would see in Schweitzer a departure from Christianity, as Schweitzer actually insinuates that the conditions have at long last been created for true Christianity). 'I find it no light task to follow my vocation, to put pressure on the Christian Faith to reconcile itself in all sincerity with historical truth. But I have devoted myself to it with joy, because I am certain that truthfulness in all things belongs to the spirit of Jesus' (p. 75).

'With the spirit of the age I am in complete disagreement, because it is filled with disdain for thinking' (p. 254).[193] The spectre of scepticism,

193. See Schweitzer, *My Life and Thought*, pp. 231-35, 254-83.

relativism, and nihilism which raps insistently at the door is refused entry. Nineteenth-century thought is a bad dream from which the hour has come to awake, an irresponsible evasion of the weighty task of Enlightenment, whose rationalistic humanism beckons back to the work. True, the way is not as easy as was once thought. Schweitzer, recalling a passage from Bultmann addressing the problem of the disappearance of meaning from history, promotes the way of 'mysticism' (where Bultmann recommended 'existentialism'):

> The world is not patient of any interpretation which gives a definite place to ethical activity on the part of mankind...
> However [the world] is looked at it remains to many a riddle.
> But that does not mean that we need stand before the problem of life at our wits' end because we have to renounce all hope of comprehending the course of world-events as having a meaning. Reverence for Life brings us into a spiritual relation with the world which is independent of all knowledge of the universe. Through the dark valley of resignation it leads us by an inward necessity up to the shining heights of ethical world- and life-affirmation...
> It is not through knowledge, but through experience of the world that we are brought into relation with it. All thinking which penetrates to the depths ends in ethical mysticism. What is rational is continued into what is non-rational. The ethical mysticism of Reverence for Life is rationalism thought to a conclusion (p. 235).

The 'thought' Schweitzer promotes leads inexorably, and by some mystical intuition (and not by 'pure reason'), to the reality he celebrates, that of the 'ethical world- and life-affirmation' of 'Reverence for Life'. In this the spirit of Jesus and of true Christianity is fulfilled.[194]

Returning to Schweitzer's *Quest*, he registers there a few pointers to the hermeneutical drift of his criticism.

> That act of the self-consciousness of Jesus by which he recognized Himself in His earthly existence as the future Messiah is the act in which eschatology supremely affirms itself. At the same time, since it brings, spiritually, that which is to come, into the unaltered present, into the existing era, it is the end of eschatology. For it is its 'spiritualisation', a spiritualisation of which the ultimate consequence was to be that all its 'supersensuous' elements were to be realised only spiritually in the present

194. Schweitzer's rehabilitation of autonomous, individualistic, ahistorical thought as opposed to authority, community, and tradition has its point against the backdrop of the rise of fascism and Stalinism. Whether he provides an ultimately satisfying position is another matter.

> earthly conditions, and all that is affirmed as supersensuous in the
> transcendental sense was to be regarded as only the ruined remains of an
> eschatological world-view (pp. 284-85).

This, 'the de-nationalising and the spiritualisation of Jewish eschatology',
is truly the beginning of Christianity and, wider still, of the 'movement
in the direction of inwardness which brings all religious magnitudes into
the one indivisible spiritual present, and which Christian dogmatics has
not ventured to carry to completion', a 'struggle between the present and
the beyond' and the 'resolute absorption of the beyond by the present,
which in looking back we recognize as the history of Christianity, and of
which we are conscious in ourselves as the essence of religious progress
and experience—a process of which the end is not yet in sight' (p. 285).

Liberal Protestantism as a 'step' along the way by which 'ethics
became world-accepting' is 'in harmony with the spirit of that great
primal act of the consciousness of Jesus'—though out of step with
certain central sayings (p. 285). But just as we earlier saw Schweitzer
acknowledging the Reformation understanding of Paul while promoting
a more comprehensively reforming insight, he continues here in
connection with Jesus:

> But it will be a weightier revolution still when the last remaining ruins of
> the supersensuous other-worldly system of thought are swept away in
> order to clear the site for a new spiritual, purely real and present world. All
> the inconsistent compromises and constructions of modern theology are
> merely an attempt to stave off the final expulsion of eschatology from
> religion, an inevitable but a hopeless attempt. That proleptic Messianic
> consciousness of Jesus, which was in reality the only possible actualisa-
> tion of the Messianic idea, carries these consequences with it inexorably
> and unfailingly. At that last cry upon the cross the whole eschatological
> supersensuous world fell in upon itself in ruins, and there remained as a
> spiritual reality only that present spiritual world...That last cry, with its
> despairing abandonment of the eschatological future, is His real acceptance
> of the world (p. 285).

Schweitzer, then, has anchored the true inception of Christianity in the
failure of Jesus' eschatological hopes, and in Jesus' own self-consciousness but in at most a most subconscious sense—and all by a symbolic
reading of Jesus' cry of abandonment.

Thus 'the whole history of "Christianity" down to the present day,
that is to say, the real inner history of it, is based on the delay of the
Parousia, the non-occurrence of the Parousia, the abandonment of
eschatology, the progress and completion of the "de-eschatologizing" of

religion which has been connected therewith' (p. 360).

Schweitzer's concluding reflections to his *Quest* concern, then, the usefulness and limitations of history for religious faith:

> The study of the Life of Jesus has had a curious history. It set out in quest of the historical Jesus, believing that when it had found Him it could bring Him straight into our time as a Teacher and Saviour. It loosed the bands by which He had been riveted for centuries to the stony rocks of ecclesiastical doctrine, and rejoiced to see life and movement coming into the figure once more, and the historical Jesus advancing, as it seemed, to meet it. But He does not stay; He passes by our time and returns to His own...
>
> The historical foundation of Christianity as built up by rationalistic, by liberal, and by modern theology no longer exists; *but that does not mean that Christianity has lost its historical foundation.* The work which historical theology thought itself bound to carry out, and which fell to pieces just as it was nearing completion, was only the brick facing of the real immovable foundation which is independent of any historical confirmation or justification.
>
> Jesus means something to our world because a mighty spiritual force streams forth from Him and flows through our time also. *This fact can neither be shaken nor confirmed by any historical discovery.* It is the solid foundation of Christianity...History can destroy the present; it can reconcile the present with the past; can even to a certain extent transport the present into the past; *but to contribute to the making of the present is not given to it...* We modern theologians are too proud of our historical method, too proud of our historical Jesus, too confident in our belief in the spiritual gains which our historical theology can bring to the world. The thought that we could build up by the increase of historical knowledge a new and vigorous Christianity and set free new spiritual forces, rules us like a fixed idea, and prevents us from seeing that the task which we have grappled with and in some measure discharged *is only one of the intellectual preliminaries of the great religious task...It is nothing less than a misfortune for modern theology that it mixes history with everything and ends by being proud of the skill with which it finds its own thoughts...in Jesus, and represents Him as expressing them...* It was no small matter, therefore, that...theology *was forced by genuine history to begin to doubt the artificial history* with which it had thought to give new life to our Christianity, and *to yield to the facts,* which, as Wrede strikingly said, are sometimes the most radical critics of all. *History will force it to find a way to transcend history,* and to fight for the lordship and rule of Jesus over this world with weapons tempered in a different forge...[T]he truth is, it is not Jesus as historically known, but Jesus as spiritually arisen within men, who is significant for our time and can help it. Not the historical Jesus, but the spirit which goes forth from Him and in the spirits of men strives for new influence and rule, is that which overcomes the world.

> *It is not given to history to disengage that which is abiding and eternal in the being of Jesus from the historical forms in which it worked itself out, and to introduce it into our world as a living influence.* It has toiled in vain at this undertaking...*The abiding and eternal in Jesus is absolutely independent of historical knowledge*...(pp. 399-401, emphasis added).

Jesus is only truly known mystically.

Paul and early Christianity faced, as does our generations, and as has every generation, the problem of continuity with Jesus in altered circumstances, in which the Christian faith and the preaching of Jesus are not simply identical.

> We, too, have to come to terms with the facts and problems of the period subsequent to the death of Jesus. Our faith, like that of Primitive Christianity, must grasp the appearance and the dying of Jesus as the beginning of the realisation of the Kingdom of God, must become certified of the future redemption as being already present, and must rise superior to the fact that the substitution of the Kingdom of God for the Kingdom of the world is still delayed.[195]

Paul's 'Christ-mysticism', though outwardly obsolete, achieves something spiritually everlasting. Jesus' preaching

> promises in mysterious sayings the attainment of the Kingdom of God, and the redemption which is bound up with it, to those who are in fellowship with Jesus as the future Lord of the Kingdom...In Paul's doctrine of dying and rising again with Christ the sayings live again in which Jesus adjures His followers to suffer and die with Him, to save their lives by losing them with Him.[196]

Paul's 'mysticism', that is, does something very like Schweitzer's, bringing life once more to Jesus' mysterious sayings.[197]

There is, then, an emerging picture of Schweitzer's implicit hermeneutics in which an Enlightenment confidence in the ability by reasoned historical criticism to separate the dead from the living in scripture has

195. Schweitzer, *Mysticism*, p. 394.

196. Schweitzer, *Mysticism*, pp. 395-96. Here Paul becomes a practitioner of 'mystical' exegesis like Schweitzer's own.

197. I noted in setting out Schweitzer's interpretation of Paul that Schweitzer's use of the term 'mysticism' in the case of Paul corresponds more or less to phenomena we continue typically to acknowledge but using other, less objectionable terms. I also noted that Schweitzer uses the term 'mysticism' out of a fashion of his day. We might now also consider how Schweitzer's own mysticism influences his use and intent in bringing Paul under that term.

been undermined by a sharpened historical consciousness. Following through with history itself forces one to a dead end. But this very predicament further forces one to explore other ways of founding theology—in other words, history is only a preliminary to a more constructive theological task. Though theology cannot build on history in the same (direct) way that it once thought, it may still build on the 'real' Jesus and Paul and not on mere illusion or fancy. The mystical intuition in good working order reaches inexorably through to the real Jesus and Paul, breathing life across an interpretative valley of dry bones. Paul becomes a profound guide in this. The interpretative literalism released by the Reformation reaches a point at which the letter is, insofar as faith is concerned, utterly dead (slain on the altar of history); but the Spirit is thereby given flight.

I now return to the hermeneutical movement from the Reformation to Gabler to Wrede. A recent history of (general) hermeneutical theory and practice ancient and modern remarks:

> If one were to look for a symbolic moment of transition between ancient and modern hermeneutics, one might choose the winter semester of 1513-14, when Martin Luther began preparing his first lectures as professor of theology at the University of Wittenberg. He was to lecture on the Psalms and wanted each of his students to have a copy of the scriptural text to consult. Luther therefore instructed Johann Grunenberg, the printer for the university, to produce an edition of the Psalter with wide margins and lots of white space between the lines. Here the students would reproduce Luther's own glosses and commentary, and perhaps (who knows?) they would have room for their own exegetical reflections as well. At all events Luther produced for his students something like a modern, as opposed to medieval, text of the Bible—its modernity consisting precisely in the white space around the text. In a stroke Luther wiped the Sacred Page clean as if to begin the history of interpretation over again, this time to get it right.[198]

This moment—whereby the Bible, formerly 'materially embedded in the history of its interpretation' in that each verse was surrounded by the glosses of the Fathers, is now set before its reader to speak with its own voice, set free from its own, and its reader's, history—seems well chosen as symbolic of the shift to modernity.[199]

Behind Gabler and Wrede lies the rise of interpretative literalism and

---

198. G.L. Bruns, *Hermeneutics Ancient and Modern* (New Haven: Yale, 1992), pp. 139-40.

199. Bruns, *Hermeneutics*, p. 139. Bruns distinguishes as two ways to effect such a release from history, mystical exegesis and literalization (p. 140).

individualism, and they each begin dimly to perceive the trouble this interpretative self-consciousness is creating for itself. Gabler sees Protestant unanimity having trouble getting further than the principle of *sola scriptura* itself, but for him the notion that history stands in service of theology, that by a methodically controlled exercise of reason one may separate the timeless from the timebound, is still an article of faith. The confusion of tongues may be ended in the universal language of Criticism, now to complete the tower and reach the heights of interpretative univocality. Wrede, though revealing no obvious disenchantment with the Enlightenment, quietly changes the subject. He sees the problems pressing in on faith: here 'the chief difficulty of our whole theological situation lies, and it is not created by individual wills: the church rests on history, but historical reality cannot escape investigation, and this investigation of historical reality has its own laws'.[200] History is no longer faith's—or anybody else's—friend, and the historian, whose allegiance is now owed to *another* higher power, does not have it in his or her power to help, like it or not. 'How the systematic theologian gets on with its [history's] results and deals with them—that is his own affair'.[201] It is not the historian's problem, and if reality is hard on theology, so much the worse for theology—a biting sentiment, but one which seems to smuggle something in somehow (something crouching beneath that term 'reality'). In discerning just what it is that has been slipped in, one must (even if only in the sketchy and derivative fashion employed here) retrace some of the historical steps which have brought us to this hermeneutical moment.[202] Wrede's stance makes sense against a quite specific historical backdrop of elements merging with our suggested story of the emergence and ascendancy of interpretative

200. R. Morgan (ed.), *Nature*, p. 73.

201. R. Morgan (ed.), *Nature*, p. 69.

202. D.F. Ford, 'Introduction to Modern Christian Theology', in Ford (ed.), *Modern Theologians*, sketches the nineteenth-century background to twentieth-century theology (I, pp. 8-15); A.D. Galloway, 'Nineteenth and Twentieth Century Theology', in P. Avis (ed.), *The History of Christian Theology, Volume One: The Science of Theology* (Basingstoke: Marshall Pickering/Grand Rapids: Eerdmans, 1986), pp. 231-352, provides a fuller sketch; each offers more sources for even fuller coverage. Some of the items mentioned in the text following are surveyed in these. For some reason, consideration of the sort of philosophical, social, political, and ideological issues routinely surveyed in the case of theology rarely makes its way into surveys of biblical criticism—apparently because it is not seen as relevant. On this see further the final chapter of the present study.

literalism and individualism. Such elements include method-ism Cartesian and scientistic; the rise and success of modern natural and physical science and of a historical consciousness and the historical (or moral/human/ social) sciences and the attendant clash of scientism and historicism in the developing self-understanding of the *Natur-* and *Geisteswissenschaften*; the Kantian fact/value divide, Hegel's attempted but failed bridging of it from an absolute perspective on history, which failure leaves standing only a historicism whose trajectory seems to lead inexorably, along with that it sought to rescue, to relativism and nihilism; religious wars and the social and political processes of secularization and the rise of a class of scholar-professionals who engage in wresting from an entrenched ecclesiastical establishment a realm of prestige and power (and payment) for a 'disinterested' specialist who must, lacking in the traditional sense a church constituency and legitimation, demonstrate a utility to society at large in terms of a contribution to the store of pure historical knowledge (expecting such an appeal to stick). This is a scenario of bewildering complexity but clearly so ideologically fraught as to make the wedding of historical consciousness to an ahistorical ideal of critique (disinterested, neutral, value-free, that is, 'purely' historical and scientific) even more ironic than it is in its own right.

Given the Kantian fact/value divide and the history/theology division which is mapped onto it in the wake of the ascendancy of historical consciousness, and failing Hegel's metaphysical hand, how is the pact made with criticism by liberalism—enshrined in a Ritschlean Jesus and his Kingdom—to appear as anything other than an exercise of arbitrary will? And if the Nietzschean mirror held up to historicism is not of itself enough to make attractive the option of making a virtue of necessity and celebrating such wilfulness, what course is open other than either the continued ever more loud insistence that interpretative reason is in good working order (an insistence ever open to the charge that it simply hides its arbitrariness from itself) or a hermeneutical rethink from the ground up?

'The nineteenth-century critical movement...had its own theological axes to grind. It stood for liberalism in theology'—this holds as true for Wrede, whose liberal Jesus was kept safe from 'apocalyptic', as anyone.[203] That this recent assessment may proceed with little fear of contradiction is above all a result of Schweitzer's own critical interpretative history. If

203. R.M. Grant with D. Tracy, *A Short History of the Interpretation of the Bible* (Philadelphia: Fortress Press, 2nd edn, 1984), pp. 117-18.

liberalism found it a matter of great ease to train its historical consciousness and its critical methods onto the traditional orthodox dogmatic
conception of the Christ, Schweitzer may with the same weapons turn
on liberalism itself, and with equally gay abandon.

But for Schweitzer this historical consciousness does not lead to a
hermeneutical consciousness. His critique of liberalism keeps within the
bounds of a stated shared commitment to 'an unbiased free investigation'
and 'a purely historical method'.[204] His critique is framed as being
against liberalism's failure to remain true to this shared ideal. A more
rigorous application, and not a scepticism, of this ideal is intended. That
liberalism's criticism leads inexorably to itself does not shade over into a
hermeneutical insight. Schweitzer, who gives more momentum to a
search for the theological motives of historical research than any other
single figure, grants himself the usual exemption. He plays the prophet,
standing apart from the (biblical-critical) spirit of the age in a stance of
judgment and righteous indignation. (That every generation seems so
jealous of this prophetic role as against the generation prior to it passes
unremarked.)

Indeed, for Schweitzer, the sort of hermeneutical suspicion I am
suggesting cannot arise—not, that is, without exposing the soft white
underbelly of Schweitzer's own criticism. For his critique of liberalism
happens to coincide with something of a souring of the utopian optimism
of *Kulturprotestantismus*, whose naive pretensions are repudiated.
Schweitzer's history, that is, stands in service of at least this, and of
much more besides. For he takes history right up to the point where, he
thinks, it is clear that history is a dead end for faith, and from there goes
on to extol the virtues of mysticism. He is pushing, that is, toward his
own solution to the problem of history, criticism, and faith. True, he
makes this a matter of squaring oneself with inevitable reality, staying
with a positivistic historicism right up to the limit and having it lead
inexorably to mysticism. In this way he seeks to rescue religion and
salvage some sense of the transcendent—and along quasi-liberal lines, no
less (he never means to be quite as unhelpful as Wrede).[205] If Schweitzer

    204. Schweitzer, *Interpreters*, p. 166.
    205. J.M. Robinson, in his 'Introduction' to the 1968 edition of Schweitzer's
*Quest* cited here, makes some interesting observations on Schweitzer's hermeneutics
(see pp. xvi-xviii, xxi-xxvi). However, his suggestion that Schweitzer transcends his
early positivism in such a way as to precede the 'new hermeneutic' (pp. xxv-xxvi)
seems unlikely, as the support he adduces from the 1913 2nd German edition of this

is a focal point for the ascendancy of a two-stage ideal, as asserted earlier, he is also, from a certain way of looking at it, a focal point for the radical questioning of such a positivist ideal, though this, too—even more so—happens behind his back (as he provides the impetus for such a hermeneutical revolution by making its need seem obvious and urgent).

Schweitzer is not, then, quite the scapegoat for positivism that I might earlier have seemed to make of him. Actually, he is in the same boat as everybody else, and he is rowing for the shore as hard as anyone. The trouble is, there is no agreement as to what direction that should be—some are even beginning to suggest there is no shore—as land has not been sighted for so many days. Conditions are ripe for a mutiny.

Enter Karl Barth. The problem has been variously glimpsed—Wrede gives a succinct statement of 'the chief difficulty of our whole theological situation'. Schweitzer stands at a critical moment for criticism—call in the Nietzschean moment—shared with Franz Overbeck, among others.[206] Faith and history is the question of the hour. It is this hour to which Barth rises, for good or ill (a unanimous verdict has still not been returned). Barth's Romans commentary, arising from the needs of the pastorate, puts hermeneutical issues back on the agenda:

> I know myself what it means year in year out to mount the steps of the pulpit, conscious of the responsibility to understand and to interpret, and longing to fulfil it; and yet, utterly incapable, because at the University I had never been brought beyond that well-known 'Awe in the presence of History' which means in the end no more than that all hope of engaging in the dignity of understanding and interpretation has been surrendered.[207]

work, when read along with the comments from the earlier edition and the *Mysticism* and *Autobiography* cited here (from years later), suggests otherwise. What Schweitzer laments is not 'the shallowness of disinterested research' (as according to Robinson, p. xxvi), but the lack of a sense for Schweitzer's ethical mysticism in our time, its failure to find resonance in a spiritually bankrupt age.

206. On Overbeck, see Kümmel, *History*, pp. 199-205; E. Jüngel, *Karl Barth: A Theological Legacy* (trans. G.E. Paul; Philadelphia: Westminster, 1986), pp. 54-63. It was the critical highlighting of the early Christian eschatology that forced Overbeck's infamous break with Christianity.

207. K. Barth, *The Epistle to the Romans* (trans. E.C. Hoskyns; London: Oxford University Press, 1933), pp. 2-15 (p. 9). On the hermeneutical debate sparked by Barth's 'hermeneutical manifesto' (so Gadamer, *Truth and Method*, p. 509), see Kümmel, *History*, pp. 363-71; J.M. Robinson, 'Hermeneutic Since Barth', in J.M. Robinson and J.B. Cobb, Jr (eds.), *The New Hermeneutic* (New Frontiers in Theology, II; New York: Harper & Row, 1964), pp. 1-77, esp. pp. 22-28; Jüngel, *Karl Barth*, pp. 70-82.

Scripture has been 'torn asunder into a thousand shreds...by unimagi-
native historico-critical omniscience'.[208] 'The critical historian needs to
be more critical'.[209] The biblical-theological movement given rise by
Barth situates Dodd, Bultmann, and Cullmann.

Dodd, further located more near to hand in the Forsythian 'crisis
theology' movement which precedes and, to some degree, merges with
Barth's biblical theology, responds to Barth's beginning.[210] Looking
back, he remembers the dismay in Britain over the apparent surrendering
of the historical task in Germany after the First World War: 'They had
even coined the word *Historismus* as a term of reproach...In some
quarters, what would have seemed to many liberal theologians of the
earlier period an extravangantly [*sic*] skeptical attitude in historical
criticism went with a dogmatic rigidity in theology which to our minds
savored of fundamentalism'. Dodd adds, with apparent pride: 'In Great
Britain the pendulum does not swing with such violence as in Germany;
and we took our Karl Barth in water'.[211]

There is an ambivalence about Dodd's hermeneutics. On the one hand
there is a celebration of the '*critical method*': biblical criticism operates

> not by guess work, and certainly not by indulging personal preference or
> caprice, but by employing scientific methods of observation, analysis,
> hypothesis and verification, which are well tested in other fields of study. It
> is a rational and scientific discipline, and its findings are true or untrue
> according to the evidence in each particular case...As a special branch of
> study it aims at being objective, rational, scientific. Its methods may
> in future be improved, its presuppositions revised, but it stands firm as a
> self-justifying part of the reasonable search for knowledge, and its
> abandonment would be a 'flight from reason'.[212]

208. K. Barth, *Church Dogmatics* IV/2, cited from C.A. Baxter, 'Barth, K.', in
Coggins and Houlden (eds.), *Dictionary of Biblical Interpretation*, pp. 77-79 (p. 78).

209. Barth, *Romans*, p. 8.

210. See S.W. Sykes, 'Theology through History', in Ford (ed.), *Modern
Theologians*, pp. 6-14.

211. 'Thirty Years of New Testament Study', *Religion in Life*, p. 321; see p. 329:
'And so we turn back to the unfinished "quest of the historical Jesus"; for we cannot
escape it, in spite of the flourishes against *Historismus* with which our period opened.
As the great tradition reveals afresh in its wholeness and essential unity, the yawning
gap which earlier criticism left between the Jesus of history and the emergent church
disappears; and we begin to see that to make a separation between the historical and
the theological understanding of the Gospels is to put asunder what God hath joined.
But here a task confronts us which has still to be taken in hand'.

212. Dodd, *The Bible Today*, p. 25.

Nineteenth-century liberalism reflects ('like all of us', Dodd adds) its own climate; it operated in the shadow of evolutionary dogma. 'It is not the result of a purely objective analysis of the documents. It presupposes a particular theory about the nature of history, and the evidence of the documents is interpreted in subordination to that theory. Looking back, we can see that this presupposition has often given a distorting bias to the work of the critics'.[213] What this prejudice caused them, unfortunately, to miss is 'the fact that the Bible has its own doctrine about the nature of history, which deserves to be understood and appreciated in itself'.[214] A more strenuous application of the 'critical method' is called for. Here, then, is the solution to a dilemma posed with the rise of criticism, where we seem faced, on the one hand, with the imposition of a rigid foreign scheme (critical *or* pre-critical) on the Bible and, on the other, with the license of multiplied, private, individual interpretations (of the sort Gabler feared): 'The critical method finds its way between the horns of the dilemma. It rejects restraint from without upon liberty of interpretation, and at the same time excludes an arbitrary or capricious use of liberty by accepting the intrinsic control of the historical movement within the Bible itself'.[215]

On the other hand (and the ambivalence has come into view already) Dodd, in relation to this 'historical movement within the Bible itself' (the 'Bible's own philosophy of history'), can assert that *meaning* eludes 'secular history' and is available only to 'sacred history', as history is not a matter of naked facts but of events plus meaning or significance for a community. The Bible is a narrative of 'revelation in history' within a continuous community from whose perspective access to the meaning of history may be gained.[216] The biblical interpretation of history speaks to our own contemporary 'crisis of history' in judgment and renewal, in the history of Jesus, in whom is comprehended the history of the whole, summing up all that went before in his person and all that comes after in that extension of his person, the Church, the Kingdom, the Body of which each by faith is a member and which ultimately takes in the world of humanity. This universal history is elaborated and interpreted by the use of 'myth', including 'apocalyptic', to which our ears should become attuned.

213. Dodd, *The Bible Today*, p. 26.
214. Dodd, *The Bible Today*, p. 26.
215. Dodd, *The Bible Today*, p. 32; see pp. 15-32.
216. See Dodd, *The Bible Today*, chs. 1, 5-7.

Dodd's combination of a scientistic method-ism and a biblical-theological hermeneutics of 'revelation in history' is a watery Barth indeed—designed perhaps to create some critical space for a less radical, more constructive and unifying approach to scripture while reserving the right to call the results 'scientific'—and makes it difficult to map his approach onto our concern with the matter of a 'two-stage' ideal. Apparently, 'apocalyptic' is a part of the great haul of exegetical facts which now need interpretation; 'apocalyptic', as it stands, may be urged, à la Schweitzer, against a liberal (evolutionary, immanentist, utopian) philosophy of history, and, as interpreted, it may contribute to an appropriation of a biblical perspective on universal history, to the formation of a 'religious *Weltanschauung*'.[217]

Dodd is no more satisfied than Schweitzer with the interpretative task conceived as a separation between the 'timebound' and the 'eternal', offering his own hermeneutical moral to the story of 'the rediscovery of eschatology':

> The problem of interpretation has not been fully comprehended, to my mind, if it be conceived as an attempt to disengage (according to a popular formula) the 'permanent' element in the New Testament from its 'temporary' setting. Whatever is true is permanently true; but there is no such thing, for us, as disembodied truth, nor an expression of truth which is timeless...
>
> I may perhaps make my meaning clearer by an example. It has been felt that the eschatological element in the New Testament might safely be written off as 'temporary'. Certainly it is alien from our modern ways of thought. But closely related to it is the idea of the Kingdom of God, which lies at the heart of the Gospels. This idea, it was supposed, could be separated from the eschatological context in which it has come down to us, and understood in a sense congenial to the humanitarian idealism of the pre-war period, as a Utopian ideal of social progress. The result was to draw a veil between our minds and a great part of the Gospels. Not only so, but the idea of the Kingdom of God, so understood, seemed to have no relation to other New Testament conceptions, such as those of redemption and eternal life. These too come down to us in an eschatological setting; but eschatology having been relegated to a museum of antiquities, the ideas hung in the air. But in the New Testament the ideas of redemption, eternal life, and the Kingdom of God emerge in a total context which includes at every point those eschatological ideas which were rejected as temporary. In this sense the idea of the Kingdom of God is also temporary. Our task is not thus to pick and choose, but to grasp the whole first-century Gospel in

217. Dodd, *The Bible Today*, p. 120.

its temporary, historical, and therefore actual, reality, and then to make the bold and even perilous attempt to translate the whole into contemporary terms.

The ideal interpreter would be one who has entered into that strange first-century world, has felt its whole strangeness, has sojourned in it until he has lived himself into it, thinking and feeling as one of those to whom the Gospel first came; and who will then return into our world, and give to the truth he has discerned a body out of the stuff of our own thought.[218]

Elsewhere, Dodd offers a description of Paul as a 'biblical theologian':

[he] expressly bases his theology upon the *kerygma* as illuminated by the prophecies of the Old Testament; or, in other words, upon the historical facts which he had 'received' ὃ καὶ παρέλαβον from competent witnesses, set in the larger historical framework witnessed, both as fact and as meaning, by the prophetic writers. Upon this fundamental material he sets reason and imagination to work, in the context of an active Christian life of labour, prayer and charity within the *koinonia* of the Church, and so brings forth his massive theology for the enlightenment and guidance of generations of Christian believers.[219]

No doubt Dodd's description of Paul would happily be taken by its author as his own (at least in ideal).

Hermeneutical reflection would appear to be much more Bultmann's forte than Dodd's. Bultmann is quite clear (where Dodd blows hot and cold) that the historical-critical method does not lay hold of the whole of reality—the claim of 'historicism'—and that the ideal of objectivity is ill conceived with respect to history properly understood. Still, there is something of a similarity with Dodd even here, as, presumably on the level of (mere) *Historie*, the critical highlighting of 'apocalyptic' may stand, useful, again, for the critique of liberalism, in which Bultmann joins the chorus; on the level of *Geschichte*, though, 'apocalyptic' must be interpreted and understood. Bultmann's core criticism of Schweitzer's presentation of Paul is that it is 'only a reproduction, not really an interpretation'.[220] Thus a certain ambivalence attaches to Bultmann's

218. Dodd, *The Present Task*, pp. 38-40; Dodd continues (pp. 40-41): 'If there are other qualifications of which it is less fitting to speak in an academic lecture, I may be allowed to hint at them in a phrase familiar to theologians—*testimonium Spiritus Sancti internum*'.

219. Dodd, *According to the Scriptures*, p. 135; see pp. 127-38 on the 'biblical theology' of the New Testament itself.

220. See again Bultmann's review of Schweitzer's *Mystik*; and note once more Conzelmann's setting up of the alternatives of Schweitzer and Bultmann ('Current

hermeneutics as well, whereby every effort is made not to offend against the critical ethos, which is allowed to stand as is; except that it is trumped by Bultmann's superadded existentialist hermeneutics. Criticism is unproblematic as far as it goes; it just does not go far enough (or rather, there are just certain things that it cannot reach).

As to Bultmann's perspective on a now familiar question, the New Testament proclamation 'cannot be saved by reducing the amount of mythology through picking and choosing'.[221] The choice to be made moves to a different discursive level:

> Since the New Testament is a document of history, specifically of the history of religion, the interpretation of it requires the labor of historical investigation. The method of this kind of inquiry has been worked out from the time of the Enlightenment onward and has been made fruitful for the investigation of primitive Christianity and the interpretation of the New Testament. Now such labor may be guided by either one of two interests, that of reconstruction or that of interpretation—that is, reconstruction of past history or interpretation of the New Testament writings. Neither exists, of course, without the other, and they stand constantly in a reciprocal relation to each other. But the question is: which of the two stands in the service of the other? Either the writings of the New Testament can be interrogated as the 'sources' which the historian interprets in order to reconstruct a picture of primitive Christianity as a phenomenon of the historical past, or the reconstruction stands in the service of the interpretation of the New Testament writings under the presupposition that they have something to say to the present.[222]

Bultmann's own interest coincides, of course, with the latter.

For Dodd the sword of criticism, wielded aright, cuts true, and unfailingly in favour of truth—that is, of course, Christianity—faith has nothing to fear from criticism.[223] Bultmann concludes, famously, that the fires of criticism may burn on—nothing needful to faith will be consumed (nor anything fatal uncovered)—for faith stands out of reach of

Problems in Pauline Research', p. 175): 'Each, following consistently his own point of departure, has a different focus; Schweitzer is concerned with the reconstruction of the historical form of Paul's thinking, Bultmann with *existential* interpretation through which he presents the theology of Paul as anthropology in order to do justice to its own intention'.

221. Bultmann, *New Testament and Mythology*, p. 8; see also Bultmann, *Jesus Christ and Mythology*, p. 18; cf. Bultmann, *Theology*, II, pp. 242-51.

222. Bultmann, *Theology*, II, p. 251.

223. On the whole, Dodd is very like Cullmann hermeneutically, on whom see below.

criticism (an ontological point for Bultmann).[224]

The ambivalence which Dodd and Bultmann to some degree share, now letting 'apocalyptic' stand (defending it, even), now 'reinterpreting'/ 'demythologizing' it, is reflected in their shared double-barrel strategy for dealing with 'apocalyptic'. On the one hand, each represents its eclipse, either by positing a developmental move beyond it or a *sachkritische* outflanking of it; on the other hand, each reinterprets 'apocalyptic'/ 'eschatology' itself (at least where Jesus, Paul, and John are concerned).

We may insert at this point a reaction of Schweitzer to all this hermeneutics business, taken from the preface to his *Mysticism*:

> My methods have remained old-fashioned, in that I aim at setting forth the ideas of Paul in their historically conditioned form. I believe that the ming-ling of our ways of regarding religion with those of former historical periods, which is now so much practised, often with dazzling cleverness, is of no use as an aid to historical comprehension, and of not much use in the end for our religious life. The investigation of historical truth in itself I regard as the ideal for which scientific theology has to strive. I still hold fast to the opinion that the permanent spiritual importance that the religious thought of the Past has for ours makes itself most strongly felt when we come into touch with that form of piety as it really existed, not as we make the best of it for ourselves. A Christianity which does not dare to use historical truth for the service of what is spiritual is not sound within, even if it appear to be strong. Reverence for truth, as something that must be a factor in our faith if it is not to degenerate into superstition, includes in itself respect for historical truth.
>
> Just because Paul's mystical doctrine of Christ has more to say to us when it speaks to us in the fire of its primitive-Christian, eschatological, manner of thought than when it is paraphrased into the language of modern orthodoxy or modern unorthodoxy, I believe I am serving in this work the cause not only of sound learning but also of religious needs. It is in this conviction that I have worked.[225]

Without mentioning names, Schweitzer takes clear sides against Barth and Bultmann, and he does so in such a way as to provide a very fitting transition to Cullmann (who would take the greatest of pleasure in such a statement of method).

Cullmann is as jealous as one well could be of securing the accolades— which many appear loathe to grant—'objective' and 'scientific' for his criticism; indeed, in the polemics that pepper his work, it is on this point

224. See Bultmann, *Faith and Understanding*, p. 132.
225. Schweitzer, *Mysticism*, pp. ix-x.

that he becomes most shrill.[226] Cullmann turns the tables. He suspects—with good reason, one might also suspect—that salvation history gets such a rough time among contemporary interpreters because it is foreign and unhelpful, an embarrassment even, for theology. The secret of Cullmann's success is simple: as required by all good science (now Cullmann is the scientific one), he chastens such preferences, difficult though it may be, refusing to squelch a salvation-historical perspective simply because it offends our modern sensibilities: 'I believe that I am on the right track, precisely because I have not withdrawn that which is the apparently strange and scandalous to our modern mind and because I consider this to be the nucleus of the New Testament'.[227] Yet it would require a feat of self-discipline even more strenuous to resist a certain cynicism as to how offensive salvation history is, how truly distant and embarrassing it seems, for Cullmann.

Cullmann also addresses the question of separating the timeless from the timebound in the context of the usefulness of critical method: 'we must...refute an attitude of mind which is dear to the upholders of the liberal view, that we find in the Bible side by side with truths which are valid for all time others which are adapted to the ideas of the period. Now we must emphasize that biblical texts as a whole wear a dress which belongs to the time of their writers'.[228] The historical-critical method provides a means of vision by which 'we may see *with* the writer the truth which he saw and *with him* may attain to the revelation which came to him', such that 'at any moment we may become the actual contemporaries of the writer'.[229] Despite this protestation, and even though he accuses Bultmann of something like the 'liberal attitude' in conceiving of 'myth' as a 'shell' which may be removed from the 'kernel' without loss, it is in fact Cullmann who so emphasizes the notion of a 'kernel', 'core', 'centre', 'nucleus', or 'essence' of the New

226. See the introductory chapter (3rd edn), Cullmann, *Christ and Time*.
227. Cullmann, *Christ and Time*, pp. xxix-xxx; Cullmann makes constant appeal to the notion of salvation history as the 'scandal' or 'offence' of the Gospel, usually against Bultmann: See Cullmann, *Christ and Time*, pp. 23, 26-32, 123-30, 179; *idem*, *Salvation in History*, pp. 22-23, 27-28, 120, 180, 253, 319-28. Cullmann does not seem to find it incongruent to speak in the same breath of a scientific and historical approach and of the 'nucleus' or 'core' or 'kernel' of the New Testament; salvation history as a community practice scientifically and historically uncovered secures such a core.
228. Cullmann, 'Necessity', pp. 12-13.
229. Cullmann, 'Necessity', p. 13.

Testament, the object of his constant and unwearying pursuit.[230]

It is in Cullmann's interests to join the chorus of voices acknowledging Barth's 'theological exegesis' against 'a naive "historicism"' which would pretend to do justice to theological texts like the Bible from an *a priori* elimination of God.[231] Beyond this he sees no reason to go, and thus, having secured this opening, he feels he must pull in the reins on a certain over-reactive obsession with hermeneutics.[232]

Cullmann can only look on with a sense of bemusement and consternation at the fashion for hermeneutics. There is just entirely too much of it about (time was when exegetes just got on with their work). 'A resigned acknowledgement that our exposition can never be completely free from presuppositions is not felt to be enough'.[233] Rather, many seem unhappy with anything short of a complete subversion of hermeneutical common sense.

> Never before has so much been said and written about hermeneutics by New Testament scholars as today. But is exegetical achievement thereby greater or better than in the time when one impartially concentrated upon the object of exegesis separate from the subject, and (perhaps in too naive an optimism which was in danger of self-delusion) thereby strove obediently to 'listen to' the text from a conscious distance?...
>
> It is surely correct that an exegesis without presuppositions is an illusion...Today this has become an obvious point we no longer need to labour. It seems rather that the time has come to warn against an over-emphasis on the impossibility of exegesis without presuppositions. Certainly there is no exegesis without presuppositions. But to make this conclusion (almost hackneyed today) into a principle appears to me far more dangerous than not to observe it at all. The fact that complete absence of presuppositions is impossible must not excuse us from striving for objectivity altogether, going so far as to regard such striving primarily as an outmoded standpoint, and making a necessary fact a virtue...So it seems to me, now as before, far more important than all the philosophical

---

230. See, for example, Cullmann, *Christ and Time*, pp. xix; 23-32; *idem, Salvation in History*, pp. 19-23. Bultmann distinguishes his method and interests precisely from a 'liberal' distinction between 'husk' and 'kernel', timebound and timeless: see Bultmann, *New Testament and Mythology*, p. 12 'Demythologizing', is, again, a process of interpretation, not elimination (at least in its author's view; Bultmann does, though, in this early statement, sometimes speak unguardedly of 'elimination' of myth [p. 9]; he clarifies this in *idem, Jesus Christ and Mythology* [p. 18]).

231. Cullmann, 'Necessity', pp. 3-5 (p. 4).

232. Cullmann, 'Necessity', pp. 7-16.

233. Cullmann, *Salvation in History*, p. 65.

observations about the object-subject relationship, to take to heart the simple necessity that has become a perennial principle of all sound exegesis. This principle is, not to interpret myself into the text, in the exegesis of the text.[234]

Cullmann's nostalgic and common-sense antitheoreticism further takes on directly theological significance for him. As a result of a certain Heideggerian 'conceptuality' (Cullmann has in mind all along, of course, the hermeneutical debate as sparked and shaped by Bultmann), he fears,

> the distinction may not be drawn between 'objective' saving events and their subjective appropriation in faith nor, therefore, between phases of exegesis...What interests us is knowing whether the New Testament distinguishes between God's acting and the believing subject. Is not faith for Paul of such a quality that this distinction *belongs to its essence* independently of any conceptuality? Does not faith for Paul mean believing that someone else has already accomplished the saving work *for me*, precisely because it has been done completely *independently of me and my believing*?...
>
> If this is the concept of faith found in the New Testament, then it has hermeneutical consequences. On the one hand we need a neutral study of events communicated to us by others. On the other hand, for a deeper comprehension of that interpretation of faith, we need a personal act of faith by virtue of which we align ourselves with the saving events in our place and time in the same way as the first witnesses did in theirs. This means that in exegesis two things are warranted and required: the exclusion of the exegete's own person and at the same time its inclusion.[235]

Cullmann insists, then, on the strictest separation of two phases of exegesis along fact/value lines, a descriptive and an evaluative phase. And to the import of their austere observance he adds theological weight, correlating the two exegetical phases with the two evangelical phases of 'hearing' and 'believing'. The basis of Cullmann's distinction between subjective and objective

---

234. Cullmann, *Salvation in History*, pp. 65-67.

235. Cullmann, *Salvation in History*, pp. 69-70; see also pp. 94-97; 115-22; 319-28. Cullmann clearly thinks that appeal to 'the New Testament concept of faith' settles the matter—there is no notion, as in Bultmann, of criticism of the New Testament's own formulations. Cullmann offers here a clear statement of faith (then and now) as a matter of aligning oneself with salvation history (a very unBultmannian faith). Cullmann's point here seems to run together the hermeneutical 'subject/object' concern and the theological one (the classical question of an 'objective' redemption), the latter understood apparently as a matter of philosophical realism versus idealism.

is the plain and simple New Testament concept of faith as it is developed especially clearly in Paul. *The act of faith itself requires this distinction.* Faith means that in humility I turn away from myself and look only to the radiant light of an event in which I am totally uninvolved, so that I can only fall down in worship before him who has brought about this event (Rom. 1.21). As I humbly turn away from myself and look to the event, I appropriate the event in faith. Faith means excluding myself and thus including myself. *So I gain my self-understanding when I am not observing my self-understanding.* Therein lies the paradox of New Testament faith.[236]

The paradox of exegesis corresponds, then, to the paradox of faith.

The *scholarly* requirement to find out first of all by means of the philological, historical method what the text has to say to us that is new and perhaps completely foreign, thus coincides with the *theological* requirement to listen to the Word of Scripture as to a revelation completely new to us and to let ourselves be given *new questions* by that Word.[237]

Bultmann is not the only one who can weld epistemological and evangelical concerns. Now (and in keeping with his being a biblical theologian) Cullmann wishes to retain a sense in which faith amounts to a deepening of understanding and in which the church is the proper setting of such interpretation—but all this belongs strictly, he insists, to 'the second of the exegetical phases which we have distinguished'.[238] As for the first stage, here it is possible to lay out in all pristine purity the 'biblical history' irrespective of faith or unbelief.[239] 'Granted that, without faith, from an historical standpoint we shall find this ["biblical history"] meaningless'.[240] Faith sees its going beyond a purely historical concern as a deepening of understanding—but this, again, is a simple scientific and methodological observation for Cullmann, as each is merely observing the limits of its own realm. Faith stays away from the first stage, being only a nuisance to it, while the historical stage, by definition, must bracket that which faith apprehends, cut off in its own terms from such further possibilities. This is merely the simple separation of fact and value. At the first stage, everyone properly sees the same thing (by the ordinary eye of the mind); at the second, faith's insight

236. Cullmann, *Salvation in History*, p. 321; see also p. 71: Cullmann's distinction 'is in harmony with the distinction made by Paul between hearing and believing'.
237. Cullmann, *Salvation in History*, p. 71.
238. Cullmann, *Salvation in History*, p. 327; see pp. 68, 71, 72, 326-27.
239. Cullmann, *Salvation in History*, pp. 71-72.
240. Cullmann, *Salvation in History*, p. 72.

knows itself as an even clearer, more penetrating vision.

Just how is this division of labour possible? By critical method, of course. 'Now this effort is in no way merely theoretical wishful thinking, for the *philological, historical-critical* method is available to us to help us approximate its realization'.[241] Once hermeneutics has taught historicism (which smuggles theological claims into its contention that the first stage sees all there is to see—a scientific, let alone a theological, breach of objectivity) a lesson and opened up some space for conceiving faith as a deepening, it must leave well enough alone. Critical method, now truly given freedom to operate, can take over from here. It is, in fact, a sort of proxy for the inspiring Spirit and a passable substitute for actually 'being there':

> is there not an element of salvation-historical development in the fact that in the post-biblical period, when there are no longer eyewitnesses to the decisive events, these aids are granted to us which, at least within the confines of human knowledge, place us before these events which have provided the initiative for their own interpretations, which in turn make the claim that these events have occurred for our salvation?[242]

'Revelation in history' requires historical exegesis; and the return to allegorical exegesis and to the 'Marcionism', 'Docetism', and 'Gnosticism' which Cullmann sees embodied in Bultmann would dispense with history.[243] Critical and theological integrity are under severe threat from such an arbitrary imposition of an external standpoint onto scripture, an arbitrariness once instanced in liberalism, wedded as it was to philosophical idealism, and now seen in Bultmann's 'existential exegesis'—the Bultmann school is 'controlled by an arbitrariness influenced by a definite, theological, dogmatic standpoint'.[244] And nowhere is this 'arbitrariness...more blatant' than in interpreting the early eschatology.[245] The proper application of critical method will reveal the Bible's own standpoint, namely (who would have guessed?) salvation history. 'The frame within which the writers of the New Testament worked ought to be the same limits which New Testament scholars accept for their work. This means that we must at least attempt

241. Cullmann, *Salvation in History*, p. 73.

242. Cullmann, *Salvation in History*, p. 328.

243. Cullmann, 'Necessity', pp. 7-10; *Christ and Time*, pp. 55-57; 125-30; *Salvation in History*, pp. 23-28; 49-53; 87, 91, 94; 133 n. 1; 170; 249.

244. Cullmann, *Salvation in History*, p. 188; see pp. 187-93.

245. Cullmann, *Salvation in History*, p. 191.

to avoid philosophical categories'.[246] Biblical scholars need to learn simply to look and listen.

Cullmann is mystified that Schweitzer and his 'school' can rightly recognize the salvation-historical centre of the New Testament (in high-lighting eschatology), then personally 'reject in their theological position that which they have recognized in historical study to be the center of the New Testament faith, and, yet, in what seems to me a very inconsistent manner, they affirm this faith'.[247] Instead of adhering to the centre, they take hold of some other element, also present, and tear it loose from that centre from which its meaning derives. 'This arbitrarily chosen element (such as "reverence for life") they designate as essential only because it appears to be something decisive when viewed from the standpoint of some philosophical judgment concerning our "existence," that is, from a position which in itself has nothing to do with the Christian message'.[248] 'Less arbitrary', at least, is Bultmann's solution of 'demythologizing', which 'strips the Christian proclamation of its time setting in redemptive history', inquiring after 'the meaning—non-temporal and nonhistorical—of the redemptive-historical "myth" itself' in an attempt to locate the proper 'centre'.[249]

> Yet when he thus from the outset regards the temporal and historical element as a mythological covering that can be separated from a kernel, *this* a priori is not derived from a historical investigation of the Primitive Christian attitude; it must then be asked whether in reality the existence philosophy of Heidegger, with which the enduring kernel is found to agree..., is not the starting point of the entire undertaking.[250]

At least, Cullmann allows (in something of a backhanded compliment), 'Bultmann's demand for removing the entire mythology is much more consistent than is the demand for removal of the eschatology'.[251]

As against all this, Cullmann wishes 'simply . . . to show on the basis of the Primitive Christian sources that [salvation] history is not, to use a word of Rudolf Bultmann, a "myth" of which the New Testament revelation can be unclothed...'.[252]

---

246. Cullmann, *Christ and Time*, pp. xxvi-xxvii.
247. Cullmann, *Christ and Time*, p. 30.
248. Cullmann, *Christ and Time*, p. 30.
249. Cullmann, *Christ and Time*, p. 30.
250. Cullmann, *Christ and Time*, pp. 30-31.
251. Cullmann, *Christ and Time*, p. 31.
252. Cullmann, *Christ and Time*, p. 28.

> We here seek to show by pure historical study that the specifically
> '*Christian* kernel', as we derive it from all the Primitive Christian sources,
> really stands or falls with the redemptive history...
>
> He who refuses to be satisfied with the historical proof that the redemp-
> tive history is the heart of the Primitive Christian New Testament
> preaching, and is determined to go on to take his own chosen attitude to it,
> should know that he thereby makes his personal decision for or against the
> Christian message itself.[253]

It is just as simple as that. (This *sounds* like a heresy charge, a species
not too often encountered in biblical criticism any more, and hardly
mitigated by Cullmann's insistence that 'In saying this we do not intend
to support a rigid Biblicism...'[254]) It irritates Cullmann no end that
Schweitzer and Bultmann find it as easy as they appear to do to get out
of the historical corner Cullmann has worked them into. If they would
only listen...

By various 'historical devices' (we might say), Cullmann bids to
make theology 'stick' to history in the most direct, unproblematic, and
simplistic of ways. Thus, in *Christ and Time*, he attaches (in the heyday
of Kittel[255]) theology to word-study, by which 'objective' means—
simple examination of the New Testament 'concepts' of 'time' and
'history'—he attempts to ground his salvation history. He reveals
throughout his critical enterprise a striking primitivism (attaching great
and grave significance to early Christian confessions, controversies, and
so forth), whereby 'early' slides almost imperceptibly into 'correct', and
a thoroughgoing biblicism, by which the interpreter endeavours to
become an empty receptacle before the biblical text, bringing nothing
from without. By the time *Salvation in History* (where word-study is
quietly dropped) is published, 'salvation history' has become, as it were,
something that is self-consciously done by the theologians of the Bible,
according to the strictest of rules, such that the 'purely historical' and
'scientific' simple description of salvation history already vouchsafes by
definition the 'real history' beneath the kerygma; finally, even
Cullmann's hermeneutics are claimed as Pauline. The (properly) literal
nature of interpretation and faith and the proper (non-arbitrary) connection of exegesis and faith (the latter built squarely on the firm foundation

253. Cullmann, *Christ and Time*, p. 29.
254. Cullmann, *Christ and Time*, p. 29.
255. Note Cullmann's celebration of the Kittel dictionary in 'Necessity', p. 15,
and his brief response to J. Barr (who, of course, has been much concerned with the
matters to hand) in *Christ and Time*, pp. xxx-xxxi.

of the former) are entirely self-evident and unproblematic matters.

On taking a closer look at an instance of this, I note the (already mentioned) repeated charge of 'Gnosticism' levelled against Bultmann. Cullmann has enough confidence in this knock-down argument to use it a number of times. The most mature and careful version goes something like this: the early debate between Christianity and Gnosticism (a revealing 'description') is absolutely decisive for the survival of the former, a heart and soul, life or death struggle which Cullmann takes to be basically about salvation history, which Gnosticism would remove by speculative philosophical reinterpretation (there can already be little doubt as to where this 'description' is leading); salvation history inoculated early Christianity against syncretistic absorption and dissolution into a sea of Hellenistic religion—take away the connection with the saving history, and 'Christianity' might just take up with anything...even Heideggerian philosophy. Bultmann represents a new syncretism. 'Christianity emerged victorious from that decisive crisis because it preserved the only thing that kept it from ruin, namely, the idea of salvation in history'.[256]

> Far be it from me to charge with heresy other commentators on the New Testament who honestly try to understand it and come to other conclusions than I do. I dare to ask, however, whether that decisive debate in Church history with Marcion and Gnosticism does not contain a lesson for our times. Certainly things are different today. But the situation is still the same as far as the salvation-historical character of Christian faith is concerned. Although in antiquity there was no radio and no one knew of atomic energy, nevertheless this salvation-historical character of Christian faith was even then a scandal for philosophical and religious-philosophical thought just as it is today. The philosophical systems which were to provide the framework for the acceptance of Christianity into syncretism were certainly not the same as the existentialism prevalent today. On the contrary, they were very different from it. But salvation history simply would not be united with those systems, just as it cannot be blended with existentialism and its understanding of the 'temporality of existence'.[257]

Far be it indeed.[258]

Cullmann's hermeneutical antitheoreticism is hand in glove with his 'historical devices'—it underwrites them, stands in service of them, is an

256. Cullmann, *Salvation in History*, pp. 26-27; see pp. 23-28.

257. Cullmann, *Salvation in History*, p. 27.

258. Cullmann elsewhere uses this 'far be it from me' rhetoric in order not to bring up the (in any case, irrelevant) association of Heidegger with Nazism against Bultmann's collaboration with Heidegger (*Salvation in History*, p. 170).

instance of them. It shields them from view. Cullmann stands back, in wide-eyed innocence, from the interpretative task and wonders aloud 'What's all the fuss?' (The cynic might be forgiven for suspecting that an affirmation of value-free criticism comes much easier for one able so successfully to hide his value judgments from himself.) In this Cullmann is unwittingly the mirror image of the positivistic historicism he affects to despise.

So what do we see when we just 'look and see'? We see what Cullmann saw, of course. That, after all, is the beauty of a truly scientific method—it is ever repeatable transhistorically. But what of those who do *not* see what Cullmann saw? Well, they will just have to look harder (else either their competence or their integrity must begin to be questioned). This is Cullmann's hermeneutics. Whether or not Cullmann's ideal of 'objective interpretation' meaningfully exists will continue to be debated this way and that. But whether anyone is likely to accuse Cullmann of any such 'objectivity' may be given a more definitive answer.

The reader who has remained with me to this point deserves—besides, perhaps, a long holiday—some indication of where, if anywhere, I have arrived and where I hope to go from here. What I persist in regarding as a single, rather epic story, with various sub-plots, divides naturally into two strands: the interpretative quest of the historical, 'apocalyptic' Paul and the hermeneutical discourse implicit in the search, with the latter story remaining largely buried within the narrative of the former, but eager to be exposed. I have tried implicitly to show that the latter story does not intersect the former tangentially, that I have not, that is, brought it in on a pretext merely to indulge an idiosyncratic preoccupation with such matters (though such a preoccupation is not denied), but rather that the hermeneutical concerns are intimately interwoven with the former, interpretative history. The interpretative history itself divides into two smaller strands, one, roughly, the literary-historical, the other the biblical-theological quest. We have found little of interest on the former side, a front on which all seems very quiet, with only the assertion of an 'eschatological' or 'apocalyptic' Paul, an assertion made against an apparently uncontroversial history of religions background. But when considering the debate as to what to make of this 'apocalyptic' Paul, we have caught a glimpse, at least, of a dizzying swarm of activity. This is what we have followed through Schweitzer, Dodd, Bultmann, and Cullmann. In the process we have begun to gain some purchase on the questions thrown upward by the hermeneutical focus. Irrespective, perhaps, of what is claimed for it, the interpretative debate resembles much more an ongoing hermeneutical circle.[259] Thus, some talk of gain might seem warranted. The general attention given to Paul and eschatology, the eschatological tension so many have variously perceived, and the cosmic horizons of Paul's thought which have come into view for many suggest a move forward in understanding.[260] But any attempt to shut down the circle—whether from the 'left' or the 'right'—seems out of place. The largest questions— the sort in which the subject of 'Paul and apocalyptic' is heavily implicated—seem to fight closure the hardest.

In shifting to the next chapter, which focuses on Ernst Käsemann and the debate over an 'apocalyptic' Paul which he sparked, I aim to shift to the literary-historical side of the interpretative history. For with Käsemann there occurs what has been called a 'renaissance' of 'apocalyptic', an interpretative budding and flowering, presumably after a long, dark winter's dormancy. Thus we might hope that, rather than the utter uniformity on this score that we have seen so far, there will be some attention to the sort of historical and methodological issues that might reasonably be thought to attach to speaking of an 'apocalyptic' Paul (who, so far as we know, wrote no apocalypses) but which seem to have been settled before we arrived on the scene. Käsemann might appear to raise these very hopes in us, with an expectation of satisfaction at long last.

I may bring together some summary observations on a few more strands of our story before proceeding to Käsemann. All four of our protagonists above are playing with some notion of substance versus form, essence versus accidents—some central core which survives the ravages of time. A non-arbitrary means of moving from 'now' to 'then' and (even trickier) back again is what is wanted. But the reach of the four seems to exceed their grasp. Schweitzer criticizes a simplistic attempt to mark off the 'timeless' from the 'timebound', and he verges on making the hermeneutical observation that this distinction will always only be made on the arbitrary basis of some or other current preference. He attempts to show that any item isolated and removed from its place

259. For each of our interpreters, Paul's hermeneutics—his manner of interpretation of the Old Testament, of tradition, or of Jesus—bears a remarkable family resemblance to the account by each of his own.

260. For a synthesis of the period of interpretation under review, expressing a consensus which yet remains, see C.K. Barrett, 'New Testament Eschatology', *SJT* 6 (1953), pp. 136-55, 225-43.

in the logic of the first-century eschatological world-view and trans-
planted elsewhere will have undergone a drastic change of meaning. The
whole, then, must be left behind, has been left behind. The distance
between the 'then' and the 'now' is only, if ever, bridged in a mystical
flight which cannot be picked apart by reason. (Few would think the
arbitrariness overcome.) Dodd and Bultmann agree that one cannot set
about arbitrarily picking and choosing that which thrives and is still
fruitful, leaving behind that which is dead and should be pruned away, in
the New Testament. Each, then, sets about a totalizing reinterpretation,
attempting to avoid arbitrariness by working from a philosophy of
history (empirically derived) or of 'historicity' (phenomenologically
derived), each claimed as the Bible's own. Cullmann makes the 'husk
versus kernel' question an acid test of objectivity, he, too, insisting that
one cannot arbitrarily choose—and so he takes *his* version of the
essence of the Gospel from the Bible itself, rather than inserting it there
in the manner of some less careful or less scrupulous critics.

Another emerging strand that has up until now gone unremarked is
an implicit critique of the hagiography typical of 'history of interpretation' in biblical criticism. Biblical critics by now know that, in their
historical-critical probing into, say, Christian origins, they may not proceed as though their object were a mere parade of ideas floating free of
society, politics, and ideology. But when criticism turns on itself, it is all a
matter of the best idea winning the day by the sheer weight of its
method and the sheer force of its argument, an edifying tale of heroes
and villains and of truth triumphing over superstition. Modern criticism
dissects the past with a cold steely eye, but turns to itself and begins
myth-making with a vengeance. (These myths are of an aetiological
type, recounting the story of the triumph of criticism and explaining
thereby the present hegemony of the victors. Criticism's story of itself is
itself a *Heilsgeschichte*—call it Cullmann's revenge.) By the standards of
the usual self-congratulatory hagiography Schweitzer is lionized as a
hero, while Dodd, Bultmann, and Cullmann, and despite the noble
objectivist ideals of the first and last of these three in particular, allow the
needs of the present to intrude into the critical task, despoiling the
results. But then all four seem to stand pretty comfortable and self-
confirmed at the end of their criticism. This should not surprise us. Our
criticism, like our autobiography (itself an endlessly interpretative enterprise, and otherwise an apt comparison here), *never fails us*—wherever
we go...*there we are*. We draw the lines looking backward (or, we

might say, *they have already drawn themselves when we turn around to look*), and they cannot but converge on where we stand (and if in the critical process our ground shifts, that will be, *has been*, taken into account). Though we might like to believe that they relate in a discrete and logical succession, how may we mark off where our criticism ends and where we begin?

When 'apocalyptic' is not needed, it is kept locked securely away. When it becomes useful, it is paraded forth with all fanfare. ('Apocalyptic', alas, must mutely bear this manhandling.) Critical historio-hagio-graphy tells the side of the story about an embarrassing 'apocalyptic' pushed out of sight and mind to great effect. The other side gets strangely lost.

'Apocalyptic' means the same for all four of our interpreters—this is clear enough from the various indications offered incidentally as to what 'it' is 'about'. And none of them, not even Cullmann, cares at all for it as such. We move closer to grasping what 'apocalyptic' *means* in the discussion by considering its use. 'Apocalyptic' is very useful against liberalism (which surely gets killed more often than any dead concern could ever require or deserve). In this context, 'apocalyptic' means simply 'otherworldly' and 'transcendent' and thumbs its nose at liberal immanence. It is also good for telling traditionalists and fundamentalists to get lost—here it means something like 'the game is up'. Further, on a fairly local level 'apocalyptic' is useful in a number of ways: without it, many agree, we must despair of giving a coherent account of Paul's thought, which then, failing this unifying framework, comes apart at the seams, falling in a number of incompatible and irreconcilable pieces; in particular, 'apocalyptic'/'eschatology' helps us solve the perennially vexing problem of the 'eschatological dialectic of Christian existence' in Paul's thought (a very plastic construction, to which 'apocalyptic' obligingly stretches to match). It can also help reconcile Jesus and Paul (again, a most variable undertaking). (Incidentally, things can be made to seem much simpler, and the hermeneutical questions can be better kept from seeping in, if the field is limited to Paul; but Paul is not thus isolated, neither theologically nor historically, and certainly not for any of the interpreters under consideration.) 'Apocalyptic' as reinterpreted or properly qualified or grounded might prove very useful for expressing an ecclesiastical or existentialist or cosmic salvation history. When we move to bigger-picture levels of discourse, however, what gets done with 'apocalyptic' seems to depend more than anything else on the strategies available (and acceptable) for reconciling history and theology, faith and criticism, or, alternatively, the lack of any such need. If we are willing to go this far with meaning-as-use, the question of 'apocalyptic' comes down to how closely one feels it necessary to bind the Faith to the self-consciousness of Jesus: Schweitzer seems content (as it might look from most other perspectives) with the barest whisper of a connection; all our other interpreters need something more than this.

The impatient positivist might wish to interject—in an antitheoretical reflex that precisely mirrors Cullmann—that all this is beside the point, this business of bridging the 'then' and the 'now' and this agonizing over faith and criticism. What has this to do with anything? The point is simply to settle this question of 'apocalyptic'—even if (at this point, it is usually thought to be good form to add a 'regrettably' or something such) it means that Christianity is over and done with. The question is settled, that is, in isolation of all this. (Then one might pause for consideration of the implications.) It is true that Schweitzer, Dodd, Bultmann, and Cullmann all take to their arduous interpretative paths out of a commitment to the idea that Christianity is worth saving (and a logically prior conviction, of course, that it is in trouble)—whether or not one makes this bridging effort depends upon whether or not one needs to. One just would not otherwise. But what my imaginary positivist interlocutor would not wish to accept is that this question of need is settled (even if open to revision) prior to, and on grounds other than (or at least additional to) exegesis—and this is the essence of his or her positivism.

The surest sign of the breadth of the concerns carried by the interpretative dialogue over 'apocalyptic' is the breadth of the interpretative strategies with which our interpreters greet these concerns in confronting the question of Paul and 'apocalyptic', strategies which move on the level of ultimate commitments to what is held to be ultimately real.[261] Yet a certain objectivism is visible in all, an objectivism called

261. That the historical and hermeneutical questions which concern us here intimately intertwine may be confirmed by the 'new hermeneutic' and 'theology as history' debates: see Robinson and Cobb, Jr (eds.), *The New Hermeneutic*, and *idem*, *Theology as History* (New Frontiers in Theology, III; New York: Harper & Row, 1967); C.E. Braaten, *History and Hermeneutics* (London: Lutterworth, 1968). These debates focus prominently on, among others, the work of W. Pannenberg, whose interaction with hermeneutics and with 'history and eschatology' and 'apocalyptic' makes him certainly relevant to the present study. However, his encyclopaedic interests take us too far afield from Paul and 'apocalyptic'; see W. Pannenberg (ed.), *Revelation as History* (trans. D. Granskou; London: Macmillan, 1968) (which

upon in defence of the 'scientific' status of each perspective. The hermeneutical turn intuitively commenced by Barth and systematically pursued in contemporary philosophical hermeneutics[262] is diluted by various half-measures.

Finally, it should be possible now to highlight another strand of this over-wrought tale. This relates to that side of the hermeneutical narrative which does not arise as a result of what criticism has uncovered but as a result of tensions within criticism itself (though not necessarily recognized as such), tensions that result in barely perceptible cracks in the critical enterprise. Criticism seems to rest on a parcelling up of the human subject and the phenomenal world in such a way as to force a choice between something like 'the way things really are' (as we see by 'pure reason') and 'that which matters to us most' (as we judge by 'practical reason'). As long as value floats free of fact in a world of Cartesian selves, will not all (really important) interpretative moves (attempts to make value 'stick' to fact) appear arbitrary? 'Mysticism' and 'existentialism' try to resolve this tension, but in such a way as to capitulate unconfessedly to the prevailing critical paradigm. And yet one more equally ominous strand consists in suggesting that the struggle over Paul and 'apocalyptic' is throwing up the classical hermeneutical question of why things read differently from an 'insider' and an 'outsider' perspective, and (something usually impels us to add) which is right? That is a big question.

includes U. Wilckens on Paul; see also U. Wilckens, 'Die Bekehrung des Paulus als religionsgeschichtliches Problem', *ZTK* 56 [1959], pp. 273-93); see also W. Pannenberg, *Jesus—God and Man* (trans. L.L. Wilkens and D.A. Priebe; Philadelphia: Westminster, 1968); further on the matter of a theological reading of 'eschatology'/'apocalyptic', an interesting comparison of two contrasting approaches would be J. Moltmann, *Theology of Hope* (trans. J.W. Leitch; London: SCM Press, 1967), and J.H. Yoder, *The Politics of Jesus* (Grand Rapids: Eerdmans, 1972); for 'apocalyptic' in this discussion, see H.D. Betz, 'The Concept of Apocalyptic in the Theology of the Pannenberg Group', *JTC* 6 (1969), pp. 192-207; C.E. Braaten, 'The Significance of Apocalypticism for Systematic Theology', *Int* 25 (1971), pp. 480-99; S. Laws, 'Can Apocalyptic Be Relevant?', in M. Hooker and C. Hickling (eds.), *What About the New Testament? Essays in Honour of Christopher Evans* (London: SCM Press, 1975), pp. 89-102; Tupper, 'Revival'. Another important study relevant in a number of ways to our various concerns here is V.A. Harvey, *The Historian and the Believer: The Morality of Historical Knowledge and Christian Belief* (London: SCM Press, 1967).

262. Cf. J.M. Robinson, 'Hermeneutic Since Barth', pp. 26-27.

## Chapter 3

## ENTHUSIASM FOR AN 'APOCALYPTIC' PAUL:
## ERNST KÄSEMANN

[A]pocalyptic is the driving force in Paul's theology and practice.
(E. Käsemann, *Commentary on Romans*, p. 306.)

The heart of primitive Christian apocalyptic...is the accession to the throne
of heaven by God and by his Christ as the eschatological Son of Man—an
event which can also be characterized as proof of the righteousness of
God...But exactly the same thing seems to me to be happening in the
Pauline doctrine of God's righteousness and our justification—which I
therefore derive, so far as the history of religion is concerned, from
apocalyptic. (E. Käsemann, *New Testament Questions*, p. 105.)

[I]t has to be recognized that only apocalyptic could offer the history-of-
religions possibility of extending the doctrine of justification beyond the
individual sphere and dealing with the salvation-historical problem of
Israel under the banner of this doctrine. This is the function of the doctrine
in its characteristic distinctiveness. (E. Käsemann, *Commentary on
Romans*, pp. 317-18.)

Historical criticism will insist that it is the texts themselves that are decisive, not an image of Paul which we find desirable. (E. Käsemann, *New
Testament Questions*, p. 244.)

Scripture is essentially a document of the past before it is anything else
and to this extent is subject to historical criticism as the universally tried
and tested way into documents of the past. (E. Käsemann, *New Testament
Questions*, p. 7.)

'Tell me, what does 'historical' mean? And 'critical'? And what is
the significance of the hyphen between the two words?' (K. Barth to E.
Käsemann[1].)

1. Quoted from E. Busch, *Karl Barth: His Life from Letters and Autobiographical Texts* (trans. J. Bowden; London: SCM Press, 1976), pp. 447-48 (p. 448).
The occasion was a meeting, in 1960, of Barth with Käsemann to discuss, as according
to Barth in a letter inviting Käsemann to visit, 'the problem of the relationship

Whatever its virtues as a précis of the critical issues of its time, the title essay to Ernst Käsemann's collection of *New Testament Questions of Today* serves well as a personal manifesto for its controversial author.[2] It sets the programme for Käsemann's interpretation of Paul, in direct confrontation with Käsemann's esteemed teacher, Rudolf Bultmann, and in the milieu of the hermeneutical mélange we have been intermittently following.

As Käsemann sees it, Bultmann stands in relation to his generation where Baur once stood in relation to his, a classic and monumental putting of the historical and theological questions with which all must come to terms, beginning from within the Bultmann school itself, a process of 'Socratic midwifery which leads to truth and freedom' (p. 11). (Bultmann, so it seems, gives us only questions, not answers.[3]) Beginning with the (no small thanks to Käsemann) once more pressing problem of the 'historical Jesus', Käsemann declares that a way forward

> will depend on defining in a new and better way the relationship of the message of Jesus to the proclamation about the Crucified and Risen One. We shall however be unable to do this without taking due account beforehand of the specific intention of the primitive Christian preaching of the Cross and Resurrection. Indeed, the message of Paul and John certainly proves that it is not just brute facts which are being proclaimed here. It was because Bultmann recognized the full impact of the task which now lies before us that he was able...to introduce a new epoch in the study of Paul and John (pp. 12-13).[4]

Thus (and with a sideways glance at the likes of Cullmann and Dodd[5]) Käsemann reopens the question of the intention of the early Christian proclamation and the interpretation of Paul and John—Bultmann's

between exegetical and "systematic" theology, which evidently concerns us both'. Busch relates that 'Barth disconcerted him [Käsemann] at this first meeting with the "simple" question' cited above.

    2.   E. Käsemann, *New Testament Questions*, pp. 1-22.

    3.   For the allusion to Socrates, see Plato's *Theaetetus*, 150b-c.

    4.   For Käsemann's earlier celebrated contribution to the reopening of the 'historical Jesus' quest, see 'The Problem of the Historical Jesus', in his *Essays on New Testament Themes* (trans. W.J. Montague; London: SCM Press, 1964), pp. 15-47.

    5.   There is a constant polemic through this essay against 'salvation history', whose 'brute facts' are here brought under suspicion (cf. p. 7); Cullmann is not named here (nor Dodd in this connection), though elsewhere he is directly opposed as a major proponent of such an approach.

entire interpretative programme, that is, crystallized in his method of *Sachkritik* and his *magnum opus*, the *Theology of the New Testament*. The entire Bultmannian synthesis is thrown back open for debate.

Bultmann's distinctive emphasis on Paul's anthropology, which places him in further continuity with the tradition of Baur, corrects this tradition, restoring Paul's thought to a systematic unity and removing the anthropological dualism and the soteriological schism which had resulted from earlier reflection on 'flesh and spirit' in Paul. For Bultmann, this antithesis expresses Paul's 'historical dialectic of human existence', before and after the coming of faith, the 'turn of the ages in the life of the individual' (pp. 13-14). Bultmann thereby restores to its rightful centrality, against Wrede and Schweitzer, Paul's doctrine of justification.[6] Bultmann famously concludes, then, that Paul's theology *is* anthropology. But now Käsemann draws back:

> I find it more than doubtful that such a conclusion is actually permissible, and in any event I cannot see that the apostle himself drew it. I should regard the anthropology which incontrovertibly characterizes Paul neither as the sum total nor the central point, but as a specific and, of course, highly important function of his theology: through it the reality and radical nature of Christ's seizure of power as the Cosmocrator comes to expression. This seizure of power applies to the whole world, as both Paul's conception of the Church and his apocalyptic demonstrate (p. 14).

The individualism of Bultmann's interpretation now comes in for direct criticism: 'The fact is that in Paul the depth of redemption as it affects the individual corresponds to its cosmic breadth…But the essential thing is this, that this individual be regarded as the concrete piece of worldly reality that I myself am. Individualism, however well conceived, must in no circumstances be allowed any place here' (p. 14). The corporate dimensions of salvation history are lost to such an individualistic anthropological approach as Bultmann's.

Further probing of this point implicates the doctrine of justification of Bultmann's Paul, which 'is concerned only with the justification of the individual', whereas (the real, that is, Käsemann's) Paul, in Romans 9–11, speaks of the righteousness of God not merely in terms of the faith/works challenge to the individual but as expressing 'the fulfilment of the promise given to the people of God' (p. 15). Furthermore,

---

6.   See *New Testament Questions*, p. 14; the degree to which Schweitzer's crystallization of the interpretative issues in reading Paul still holds sway should be noted.

Bultmann's conception of the eschatological, dialectical tension of Christian existence leaves no room for the fact that Paul's doctrine of justification 'cannot be understood at all without his apocalyptic in which it is not a question of reward or completion but, according to 1 Cor. 15.28, a question of God's becoming all in all', the continued confrontation with sin being, for Paul, not a comfortable state of affairs but rather 'the expression of the fact—established only by groaning and travailing—that in this present God still meets with contradiction and his enemies do not yet lie definitively under his feet. *Paul was unable to allow redemption to end in earthly contradiction*' (p. 15, emphasis added).[7]

> Apocalyptic is therefore not less meaningful in his theology than anthropology. It proclaims that the apostle was very deeply moved by the quest...for the revelation of the godhead of God, and his doctrine of justification revolves around the rightful claim which God will make good on his own created world. If that sounds mythological, the same is true in the last resort of all utterances about the work of redemption and in any event is no good reason for the elimination of this nexus of ideas. The interpretation of it will however play a real part in the determination of the total outlook of Pauline theology (p. 15).

With that the first child born of Bultmann's 'Socratic midwifery' is brought forth with what might well have been taken for a battle cry (a rebel yell, no doubt).

Käsemann's manifesto exposes the several themes which must concern us in sorting out the logic of his interpretation of Paul and 'apocalyptic'. The dialogue—and ultimate disillusionment—with Bultmann is clearly central, decisively affecting the shape and tone of Käsemann's interpretative agenda. Appreciative in principle of the unity to which Bultmann has restored Paul's thought, Käsemann nevertheless regards Bultmann's unity as bought at too great a price. Bultmann's emphasis on Paul's anthropology, on his 'eschatological dialectic of Christian existence', and on the centrality of justification to his thought, is both a triumph in perceiving the proper agenda for the interpreter and a failure in presenting an ultimately satisfying portrait of Paul. Bultmann's treatment of the dialectic of present and future eschatology collapses the latter into the former; he allows Paul's anthropology, individualistically conceived, to swallow Paul's theology; and he rescues justification from the hands

---

7.    This points to the way in which Bultmann has, for Käsemann and his Paul, left things in an intolerable state.

of its enemies only to have it, too, die the death of an individualistic conception. The 'demythologizing' debates still smoulder in the background, fanned by the mythical proportions assumed by Käsemann's 'Cosmocrator'.

The contours of Käsemann's own approach are already coming into view. If Bultmann's interpretation, by Käsemann's estimation, is a narrowing of Paul's anthropology, ecclesiology, 'apocalyptic', and doctrine of justification into a constricting and distorting individualism, Käsemann's interpretation will reverse all this, will open things up and straighten things out and let in some air and light. (One is hardly surprised to find that Käsemann has the cure to the malady he has diagnosed in Bultmann's Paul). Käsemann sets Paul's anthropology within the context of 'Christ's seizure of power as the Cosmocrator', a motif here brought into association with Paul's ecclesiology and 'apocalyptic'. This is a bringing to the fore of the corporate and cosmic—the salvation-historical—horizons within which Paul's anthropology operates. 'Apocalyptic' assumes a large role in Paul's thought, bound up as it is with this cosmocratic Christology and, broader still, with 'the revelation of the godhead of God', which itself holds Paul's doctrine of justification in its orbit. This constellation of 'apocalyptic', the 'Cosmocrator', and God's 'righteousness', and all that goes with each, forms a 'nexus of ideas' vital to a 'determination of the total outlook of Paul's theology'. It creates a triple axis made up of universal history, the lordship of Christ, and the righteousness of God on which turns the whole of Paul's thought. The volume to which this programmatic essay lends its name contains several occasional pieces which together develop this theme of an 'apocalyptic' Paul in providing a survey of the historical development of 'apocalyptic' from Jesus to Paul to 'early catholicism'.[8]

8. In addition to *New Testament Questions of Today* and *Essays on New Testament Themes*, see Käsemann's *Perspectives on Paul* (trans. M. Kohl; London: SCM Press, 1971 [Ger. orig., 1969]) and his *Commentary on Romans* (trans. and ed. G.W. Bromiley; Grand Rapids: Eerdmans, 1980 [4th Ger. edn, 1980]). For present purposes, *New Testament Questions of Today* is important beyond its essays on Paul for situating Käsemann's interpretation in its wider setting. See also his *Jesus Means Freedom: A Polemical Survey of the New Testament* (trans. F. Clarke; London: SCM Press, 1969 [3rd Ger. edn, 1968]) and cf. 'The Problem of a New Testament Theology', *NTS* 19 (1972-73), pp. 235-45. Shorter studies on Käsemann include G.A. Lewandowski, 'An Introduction to E. Kasemann's Theology', *Encounter* 35 (1974), pp. 222-42; F. Kerr, 'The Theology of Ernst Käsemann - I' and 'II', *New Blackfriars* 62 (1981), pp. 100-13, 148-57; R.A. Harrisville, 'Crux Sola Nostra

## 'Apocalyptic' from Jesus to Paul and beyond

An earlier essay offers a first glimpse of the Christian origins and biblical-theological setting of Käsemann's 'apocalyptic' interpretation of Paul. In 'Sentences of Holy Law in the New Testament',[9] Käsemann highlights a 'form' of early Christian proclamation (the 'sentences of holy law') which he sets in the milieu of charisma-endowed primitive Christian prophets. The form, at its purest, is a chiastic expression of the divine *jus talionis*, arising from 'apocalyptic' and from Old Testament prophecy. The logic of these 'sentences' places them within the heightened eschatological sensitivity to the presence of Christ in the Spirit as Lord and ruler of the community and the heightened eschatological

Theologia: A Retrospective Review of the Work of Ernst Käsemann', *RelSRev* 11 (1985), pp. 256-58; R. Scroggs, 'Ernst Käsemann: The Divine *agent provocateur*', *RelSRev* 11 (1985), pp. 260-63. See also the following reviews of Käsemann's *Romans*: G. Strecker, 'Perspektiven der Römerbriefauslegung', *LR* 24 (1974), pp. 285-98; R. Morgan, Review of *Romans*, by E. Käsemann, in *HeyJ* 16 (1975), pp. 68-70; J.K. Riches, Review of *An die Römer*, by E. Käsemann, *SJT* 29 (1976), pp. 557-74; G. Sauter, 'Systematische Gesichtspunkte in Ernst Käsemanns Römerbrief-Kommentar', *Verkündigung und Forschung* 21 (1976), pp. 80-94; K.P. Donfried, Review of *Romans*, by E. Käsemann, in *RelSRev* 7 (1981), pp. 226-28; L.E. Keck, 'Käsemann on Romans', *Int* 36 (1982), pp. 413-19; N.T. Wright, 'A New Tübingen School? Ernst Käsemann and his Commentary on Romans', *Themelios* 7 (1982), pp. 6-16 (see also his review in *Churchman* 96 [1982], pp. 60-62). See also J. Friedrich, W. Pöhlman, and P. Stuhlmacher (eds.), *Rechtfertigung*. Full-scale studies are offered by P. Gisel, *Vérité et histoire. La théologie dans la modernité. Ernst Käsemann* (Théologie historique, 41; Paris: Beauchesne, 1977) and B. Ehler, *Die Herrschaft des Gekreuzigten: Ernst Käsemanns Frage nach der Mitte der Schrift* (BZNW 46; Berlin and New York: Walter de Gruyter, 1986). But, for Käsemann on Paul, see D.V. Way, *The Lordship of Christ: Ernst Käsemann's Interpretation of Pauline Theology* (Oxford Theological Monographs; Oxford: Clarendon Press, 1991). For a succinct placement of Käsemann in his context, along with a sketch of his life and a brief summary of his interpretation of Paul, see Way, pp. 1-52. My own treatment of Käsemann picks up well into his career with what Way reveals as its later phase; for a treatment of the earlier development, with careful attention to continuity and discontinuity with the later work, see pp. 53-118. For recent interaction with Käsemann in discussion of Paul's theology, note particularly E.P. Sanders, *Paul*; L.E. Keck, *Paul and His Letters* (Philadelphia: Fortress Press, 2nd edn, 1988); C.B. Cousar, *A Theology of the Cross: The Death of Jesus in the Pauline Letters* (Minneapolis: Fortress Press, 1990).

9.   Käsemann, *New Testament Questions*, pp. 66-81. Page numbers in the text throughout this section refer to essays in this volume.

expectation of the imminent coming in judgment of this Christ in the Last Day, and the world they open up evinces and requires a thoroughly legal setting, one of blessing and curse, promise and threat, the setting of the tribunal, of the ordeal. Paul as apostle assumes a role analogous to that of these early prophets, such that 'through the co-operation of the apostle and the community the Spirit—and that means the present Lord—himself takes action' (p. 71). These 'sentences' pronounce an anticipation of judgment which functions to vindicate God's righteousness and stands in service of his grace (as it cannot nullify the right of the Lord over one of his own claimed in baptism), averting, if met with repentance, the impending judgment.

Thus the way was prepared for Paul by the nameless, faceless Christian prophets of the earliest Palestinian community, and Käsemann prepares his own way in giving a first run-through of the entire historical sweep he will ultimately develop. The Christian origins and biblical-theological backdrop of his 'apocalyptic' Paul are already visible as Käsemann explores the history of religions setting—early Christian prophecy within the tradition of Jewish 'apocalyptic'—of the theological themes and interests which will be the mainstay of his interpretative agenda: the early proclamation, Paul's anthropology and ecclesiology, the gift and power of God, the lordship of Christ, the vindication of the righteousness and godhead of God, Paul's eschatological dialectic, the 'new obedience', law, freedom, and Spirit, demythologization.[10] In the process, Käsemann edges closer to direct confrontation with his former teacher.

I move, then, to consider the charter of the 'apocalyptic renaissance' in biblical studies, a renaissance whose Florence is the Tübingen of Ernst Käsemann: this is the ever-quoted 'The Beginnings of Christian Theology', the mother of 'apocalyptic' interpretation of Paul.[11] The 'nexus of ideas' rescued from oblivion at the hands of Bultmann now comes in for fuller exposition.

Six years on, Käsemann returns once more to those early prophetic forms, proceeding more systematically to take form criticism into that earliest dawning period to which it has thus far failed in its promise to

10. The precise terms and formulations will shift somewhat, but many of the concerns to be subsequently developed are present here.

11. Käsemann, *New Testament Questions*, pp. 82-107. On the so-called 'renaissance' of 'apocalyptic', dated from the turn to this theme by Käsemann in biblical studies (1960, in this essay) and W. Pannenberg in theology (1959), see K. Koch, *Rediscovery*, pp. 13-15; cf. E.F. Tupper, 'Revival', pp. 279-80.

take us, namely, 'the beginnings of Christian theology'. In the process, the method pioneered by Bultmann is turned quite against its maker.[12] Käsemann's form-critical probing penetrates once more to the earliest post-Easter communities, in which sharp confessional controversies had already arisen, driven by the forces exerted by 'enthusiasm', the Spirit-filled celebration of the presence of redemption in the present Lordship of Christ, and 'apocalyptic', the expectation of the imminently returning Lord. These disputes, between a strict Jewish Christianity destined for oblivion and the 'Hellenists' gathered around Stephen and the Seven, whose mission prepared the way for and merged into Paul's, revolve around questions of fulfilment and expectation, continuity and discontinuity, questions which turn on the question of the Law and the Gentile mission. Each side was equally determined by 'enthusiasm' and 'apocalyptic' but unable to agree on the place of a Gentile mission in the scheme of things (whether it should be passively awaited or actively pursued), each bringing the other under the sanction of divine eschatological law (pp. 83-92). Already in the earliest community, 'enthusiasm' and 'apocalyptic' combine under the force of prophecy, 'the vehicle of enthusiasm in Jewish Christianity after Easter, as it was to be in later Gentile Christianity', with the possession of the Spirit being interpreted eschatologically as 'the pledge of the imminent parousia' (p. 92). This phenomenon of early Christian prophecy is visible in the prophetic forms, most purely in the 'sentences of holy law': 'Nowhere is there a clearer expression of the viewpoint which reckons with the imminent invasion of the Parousia, professing to know the criteria with which the universal Judge operates and deriving this knowledge from its own inspiration by the Spirit' (pp. 92-93).

Christian prophets, rooted in 'apocalyptic' and Old Testament prophecy, create, by drawing on the 'apocalyptic' motif of the correspondence of Beginning and End, an interpretative standpoint whereby, 'seen from the perspective of the End, the Beginning is mirrored in the Old Testament history. By the use of late Jewish tradition, the Old Testament itself receives an apocalyptic interpretation' (p. 96). Käsemann remarks as an aside:

> We are encountering at this point the earliest Christian understanding of history, on which all its successors have been dependent. It is the conception of the parallel, even if antithetically ordered, course of salvation history and the history of disaster; a course which finds its judgment and its

12. The challenge to Bultmann is, as is most often the case, kept implicit.

objective in the Parousia of the Son of Man, Jesus. The mythical character of such a view of history cannot well be contested. But it is certainly too facile simply to try to replace it on this account by the modern insight into the historical nature of existence; this viewpoint, taken in isolation, dissolves historical connection into a series of more or less unrelated situations, reduces God's future to man's futurity, sees the present primarily in the light of the demand it makes upon ourselves and, finally, interprets the past as a background to a mock-up of the decision which we have to face (p. 96).

Shades of Cullmann (like whom Käsemann is already beginning to sound when opposing Bultmann, like whom in turn he sounds when opposing Cullmann) and Dodd emerge, more so in the consequent assertion of the eschatological, salvation-historical narrative of Gospel and kerygma wrought by early Christian prophets in their reinterpretation of scripture and tradition (pp. 96-98). 'The Gospel history, like the prophetic proclamation, is a fruit of the apocalyptic of the period after Easter', and the pronouncement of holy law reveals that 'parenesis in the post-Easter community was founded primarily on apocalyptic' (p. 98).

'Apocalyptic' words found on the lips of Jesus are regarded by Käsemann as being the voice of these Christian prophets, who, using such 'apocalyptic' motifs as 'the restoration of Israel', 'the transvaluation of all values', and 'the coming Son of Man', remould or produce afresh (by the living voice of Christ in the Spirit) sayings of Jesus (pp. 98-103, 88). Albert Schweitzer has indeed well forced the question of 'apocalyptic', but he and his school 'got in their own way by trying to turn the whole question into a problem of research into the life of the historical Jesus and to explain the very early history of dogma in terms of the delay of the Parousia. On both occasions, they landed up in a cul-de-sac' (p. 101).

> Jesus admittedly made the apocalyptically determined message of John his point of departure; his own preaching, however, did not bear a fundamentally apocalyptic stamp but proclaimed the immediacy of the God who was near at hand. I am convinced that no one who took this step can have been prepared to wait for the coming Son of Man, the restoration of the Twelve Tribes in the Messianic Kingdom and the dawning of the Parousia (which was tied up with this) in order to experience the near presence of God. To combine the two would be, for me, to cease to make any kind of sense (pp. 101-102).

Only in the crucible of the presence of the Lord in the Spirit ('enthusiasm'), eschatologically determined by the coming Lord ('apocalyptic'), does an eschatological dialectic emerge. 'The beginnings of Christian theology', then, lie less with 'the earthly Jesus and the *ipsissima verba*' than with the situation, activity, and message of these anonymous prophets, and the motive of the development of the resulting eschatological tension is not the self-consciousness and preaching of Jesus, still less (this early on) the 'delay of the parousia', but the experience of the present and coming Lord (p. 103).[13] Thus: 'Apocalyptic was the mother of all Christian theology...' (p. 102).

To move, then, from these shadowy prophetic figures to Paul and John, the determination of their proclamation is the same, their way having been thus prepared.

> The whole history of primitive Christianity from its beginning to its issue in early Catholicism is one long struggle to formulate adequately the indissoluble and yet always precarious connection between the Spirit on the one hand and the Gospel and Christology on the other. According as this attempt succeeds or fails, the community remains Christian or lapses into Judaism and heathenism...(p. 104, emphasis added).

'Enthusiasm' brings elements of realization, but dangers as well. 'The great theologians of the New Testament...warded off the dangers of enthusiastic congregational piety from the theological inheritance handed down to them. To do so, they needed only to pick up elements present in their own tradition' (p. 104). The tradition of Jewish 'apocalyptic' was called upon in this regard.

> The heart of primitive Christian apocalyptic...is the accession to the throne of heaven by God and by his Christ as the eschatological Son of Man—an event which can also be characterized as proof of the righteousness of God...But exactly the same thing seems to me to be happening in the Pauline doctrine of God's righteousness and our justification—which I therefore derive, so far as the history of religion is concerned, from apocalyptic (p. 105).

'God's justice done on and to our earth' is no longer a remote expectation, but is imminent and is already being realized among those who in obedience accept the prophetic proclamation of its standards (p. 105).

The 'theology of the cross' both implied and made explicit in this eschatological tension opposes the triumphalism of any such

---

13. See *New Testament Questions*, pp. 102-103; 'The same problem which determines all New Testament theology is being raised—namely, that of the relation of the proclamation about Jesus to the message of Jesus...' (p. 103).

'enthusiasm' as that which Paul confronts at Corinth, by which God's future is eclipsed in the glory of the attainment of the present moment of the Church. Thus, despite the delusion the expectation of an imminent end proved to be, Käsemann suggests, tellingly, that '*primitive Christian apocalyptic may be seen as the archetype of what is always happening in the history of the Church*', and Käsemann is led, then, to ask whether theology can get by without the central theme of 'apocalyptic' and the critical perspective it provides: 'This central motive was in fact the hope of the manifestation of the Son of Man on his way to his enthronement; and we have to ask ourselves whether Christian theology can ever survive in any legitimate form without this theme, which sprang from the Easter experience and determined the Easter faith' (p. 107, emphasis added).

The exposition of Paul's 'nexus of ideas' continues with another influential and controversial essay, '"The Righteousness of God" in Paul'.[14] The opening words declare:

> The Epistle to the Romans subsumes the whole of the preaching and theology of Paul under the one head—the self-revealing righteousness of God. In so doing, it undoubtedly gives to the unique Pauline message a nucleus and a name which bring its own peculiar nature into the sharpest possible relief against the background of the rest of the New Testament. Conversely, the central problem of Pauline theology is concentrated in this theme...(p. 168).

The centre of Paul's theology, and the central problem for one who would understand Paul today, is thus the topic of concern.

Does the 'righteousness of God' speak in the first place of God's own righteousness, which proceeds from him, or of the righteousness of human beings (albeit bestowed by God), acceptable in his eyes—the Giver or the gift (an interpretative crux reflecting the ambiguity of the genitive construction δικαιοσύνη θεοῦ: subjective or objective genitive?)? 'It is beyond dispute that the general tenor of the Pauline utterances on the subject, like that of the Reformation tradition which determines our attitude, tells in favour of the objective genitive...The fundamental either/or of righteousness by or through faith and righteousness by works is only comprehensible from this perspective...' (p. 169) But might there not have been some particular local reason why Paul saw need, insofar as explicit argument is concerned, to emphasize this aspect rather than the other? The other is present for Käsemann in some of the

14. Käsemann, *New Testament Questions*, pp. 168-82.

more striking and animated contexts in which the expression occurs, where righteousness appears as 'Power', expressive of 'God's own activity and nature' (p. 169).[15] 'Have we here simply an expression of the Apostle's inconsistency, in which case the causes of this inconsistency have still to be brought out into the open? Or does the tension displayed here reveal the existence of a fundamental issue, the right understanding of which is a necessary preliminary to making a positive or negative judgment about any more comprehensive interpretation' (pp. 169-70)?

With the 'gift' aspect itself, long-standing problems remain. The eschatological tension between 'already' and 'not yet' marks the gift of righteousness: 'salvation and the things which salvation brings appears sometimes as already present by faith and baptism, sometimes as only to be realized at the End through the Parousia', a 'dialectic of having and not quite having...projected on to the very condition of being a Christian' (p. 170). The gift is grasped, but requires constantly to be grasped, and remains ultimately to be grasped. 'The gift itself has thus the character of power. The meaning of this in concrete terms is quite clear. Paul knows no gift of God which does not convey both the obligation and the capacity to serve' (p. 170).

Current attempts to resolve this tension, 'like the one which former generations attempted to make between the ethical and juridical and the mystical and sacramental approaches, only [reveal] the logical embarrassment into which the apostle here precipitates his modern readers' (p. 170). Justification is both a gift and a state, a forensic act and a state of transformed existence, united in God's righteousness. Käsemann, then, through a consideration of 'righteousness' in Paul, reopens the long-standing crux of the conceptual tension in Paul's thought, which, according to Schweitzer's presentation, separates out into two strands, two doctrines of redemption, justification by faith and eschatological participation. Clearly Käsemann is making a bid to reunite what has been treated as a fundamental dichotomy and as evidence of conceptual confusion and logical inconsistency in Paul's thought, and without surrendering the centrality of justification. Käsemann highlights

> the tensions associated with the Pauline doctrine of justification and with the theological dialectic which it reveals. This dialectic may rightly be explained in terms of the apostle's war on two fronts—against legalism on

15. Käsemann mentions here Rom. 1.17; 3.5, 25-26; 10.3ff.; 1 Cor. 1.30; 2 Cor. 5.21.

the one hand and enthusiasm on the other—and of his not infrequent stratagem of combating the one with the terminology and the motivation of the other. *But our particular problem is to identify the unitary centre from which he managed to combine present and future eschatology,* 'declare righteous' and 'make righteous', gift and service, freedom and obedience, forensic, sacramental and ethical approaches (pp. 171-72, emphasis added).

Only then is the question of the continued relevance of Paul's dialectic addressable, in answer of which partial solutions which absolutize preferred aspects, meanwhile destroying Paul's dialectic in either direction (that is, Schweitzer and Bultmann), only increase the obscurity.

Tracing the theological and history of religions ancestry of the expression 'righteousness of God' in the Old Testament and Judaism, Käsemann regards Paul as working from a concept of God's righteousness as his 'saving activity', a relational category operating in the context of covenant and community and signifying faithfulness.[16] When the need is felt to contrast sharply faith and works, the emphasis rightly falls on the 'gift' aspect of justification; but any attempt to make this juridical conception primary 'is bound to centre on the character of the righteousness as gift and, in practice, on anthropology. But the formulation which Paul has taken over speaks primarily of God's saving activity, which is present in his gift as a precipitate without being completely dissolved into it' (p. 172). Paul understands the 'gift' against the background of God's righteousness as 'power':

the gift…is never at any time separable from its Giver. It partakes of the character of power, in so far as God himself enters the arena and remains in the arena with it. Thus personal address, obligation and service are indissolubly bound up with the gift. When God enters the arena, our experience is, that he maintains his lordship even in his giving; indeed, it is his gifts which are the very means by which he subordinates us to his lordship and makes us responsible beings (p. 174).

The gift/power polarity and its connection with the divine righteousness is the key to the dialectical expressions variously surfacing in Paul, clarifying the conceptual and eschatological tension in Paul's thought and his salvation history. 'To understand the righteousness of God exclusively in terms of gift is to ask for trouble: the inevitable result is that the Pauline anthropology is sucked under by the pull of an individualistic outlook'

16. Käsemann, *New Testament Questions*, pp. 172-74; Käsemann mentions Deut. 33.21, *T. Dan* 6.10, and 1QS 11.12 as evidence for this conception.

(p. 176).[17] Existence is determined by the Lord served; the new creation effected in baptism is a change of lordship. This is an eschatological decision between 'the kingdom of Christ and the kingdom of Satan', a call issued in proclamation and renewed in temptation (p. 176). ('Legalism' and 'enthusiasm', then, are avoided.) 'What distinguishes the Pauline theology from both ['Christian enthusiasts' and 'Jewish apocalyptists'] is...*the unprecedented radicalization and universalization of the promise in the doctrine of the justification of the ungodly'* (p. 178, emphasis added). Paul's conception of the righteousness of God revealed apart from law expresses this radical universalization, that of the gracious justification of the ungodly, denying all claim and privilege before God, whether based on works or ancestry.

> The eschatological salvation thus begins with the revelation of the Godhead of God and the necessity of man's becoming human. In the new creation, there is a reference back to creation *ex nihilo* and a reference forward to the resurrection of the dead. The καινὴ διαθήκη is no longer just the Sinai covenant renewed and extended; and πίστις is its sign, not νόμος... [T]he righteousness of God is precisely what, as the power of the justification of the ungodly, it must be—God's victory amid the opposition of the world. By it, all human self-righteousness and insubordination come to destruction, while that which does not exist is called into being and the dead are made alive. Christ is the new Adam, because, as the bearer of human destiny, he brings in the world of obedience. *All that we have been saying amounts to this:* δικαιοσύνη θεοῦ *is for Paul God's sovereignty over the world revealing itself eschatologically in Jesus.* And...we may also say that it is the rightful power with which God makes his cause to triumph in the world which has fallen away from him and which yet, as creation, is his inviolable possession (p. 180, emphasis added).[18]

The 'righteousness of God' in Paul is not primarily an individual or exclusively an anthropological concern, these misunderstandings being the inevitable result of giving priority to the 'gift'. Corporate and cosmic conceptions situate and subordinate these concerns.

> It is precisely the apostle's doctrine of justification which shows that God's action in Christ, as in the creation of the world, prevails and that the

17. Here Bultmann is directly challenged, with reference to his *History and Eschatology*.

18. God keeps his covenant faithfulness in the new covenant and new Israel, the new people of God. Käsemann states, however, that Paul is not much interested in covenant theology and the 'holy remnant', and that, for Paul, Christ is 'definitely not...the second Moses' (Käsemann, *New Testament Questions*, pp. 177-78).

Pauline dialectic of present and future eschatology encroaches on Christian existence as it is actually lived out; but this doctrine is not essentially concerned with anthropology. *Consciously, and under a sense of apocalyptic pressure, Paul conceived his task to be the universalization of the Church's mission.* Any interpretation which loses sight of this fails to give historicity its due and therefore minimizes the theological problems with which Paul faces us. *The apostle's present eschatology cannot be taken out of its context of future eschatology,* any more than the gift of justification can be isolated from the context in which the righteousness of God is spoken of as a power which brings salvation to pass. *Even when he became a Christian, Paul remained an apocalyptist* (p. 181, emphasis added).[19]

(The Bultmannian trilemma concerning the acting of God in Christ, human existence, and faith is radically transformed in Käsemann's hands).

Among the early critical responses to Käsemann's polemical programme are those by Gerhard Ebeling and Ernst Fuchs, who raise a set of historical and theological questions and objections to Käsemann's account of 'the beginnings of Christian theology'.[20] Noting their common interest in both historical and theological issues, Ebeling insists that the 'dogmatician...cannot restrict himself to discussing the theological implications of particular results of the historian's work, but must also enter into a discussion of this historical work itself, however much he is then at a disadvantage as a non-specialist'.[21] Agreeing, then, that 'apocalyptic' ('near expectation') and 'enthusiasm' ('prophetic workings of the Spirit') are basic motifs beneath early Christian theology and existence, Ebeling raises a number of counter-questions.[22] How are the terms 'apocalyptic' and 'enthusiasm', so provocative and emotive

19. Käsemann states (*New Testament Questions*, p. 181 n. 9) that he is developing the perspective given in his 'The Beginnings of Christian Theology' against the responses to that essay by Fuchs and Ebeling (on whom see immediately below).

20. G. Ebeling, 'Der Grund christlicher Theologie', *ZTK* 58 (1961), pp. 227-44, ET 'The Ground of Christian Theology', *JTC* 6 (1969), pp. 47-68; E. Fuchs, 'Über die Aufgabe einer christlichen Theologie', *ZTK* 58 (1961), pp. 245-67, ET 'On the Task of Christian Theology', *JTC* 6 (1969), pp. 69-98. We insert Ebeling and Fuchs here, into the middle of Käsemann's survey, since they respond to 'Beginnings' and provoke Käsemann's extended discussion in 'Primitive Christian Apocalyptic', treated below.

21. Ebeling, 'Ground', p. 48. Thus stated, the historically disadvantaged Ebeling proceeds to raise a number of pertinent methodological questions (not precisely in the way we would wish, necessarily, but one cannot be too choosy, as such questioning comes around so seldom).

22. Ebeling, 'Ground', pp. 49-51; see pp. 51-68 for these questions.

within the Reformation tradition, being used? What are the limitations of 'apocalyptic' as an influence on early Christianity? What is the relation of this theological construct 'apocalyptic' to the apocalypses of Judaism and Christianity? To what extent is that which Käsemann labels 'apocalyptic' found in 'late Judaism' and to what extent is it a new creation of Christianity? How does faith in Jesus modify 'apocalyptic'? Is not the combination of 'apocalyptic' and 'enthusiasm' which Käsemann posits unique, as is the occurrence of the resurrection in the case of Jesus ('certainly an idea which owes something to apocalyptic, yet one which breaks the bounds of what is normally meant by apocalyptic, and which gives a new frame of reference to the apocalyptic ideas nevertheless retained')?[23] Ebeling further queries the unequal treatment of 'apocalyptic' and 'enthusiasm', whereby a critical stance is taken toward the latter but not the former (there are 'enthusiasm*s*', but not 'apocalyptic*s*'), such that, though the two are said to combine, only 'apocalyptic' is 'the mother of Christian theology', guaranteeing the right kind and repulsing the wrong kind of 'enthusiasm'. 'Enthusiasm', it seems, is dangerous, and somehow does not pose a question to dogmatics in the same way 'apocalyptic' does, since Käsemann makes 'apocalyptic Christology' identical with the early Christian message.[24] One must, says Ebeling, 'refrain from the pursuit of apocalyptic in the traditional style of late Judaism and in place of this put a response in apocalyptic terms to Jesus' preaching of the nearness of God, whereby we do not by any means merely interpret Jesus in the light of apocalyptic, but also and above all interpret apocalyptic in the light of Jesus'.[25]

Fuchs remains closer to Bultmann. If Käsemann is right, 'what would be left here to "proclaim"'?[26] Jesus' own emphasis is on the present, on the proclamation. 'My question to Käsemann can be summed up by saying that I should like to know what a Jewish-Christian apocalyptic of the kind reconstructed by Käsemann should still have to do with

23. Ebeling, 'Ground', p. 55; see further pp. 55-56.

24. For Käsemann's challenge to systematic theology on the basis of 'apocalyptic' (which takes the form of an implicit accusation of embarrassment and failure of nerve in the face of a repulsive eschatology, a charge implicitly reversed here by Ebeling in the case of 'enthusiasm'), see *New Testament Questions*, pp. 102, 107.

25. Ebeling, 'Ground', p. 58.

26. E. Fuchs, 'Über die Aufgabe einer christlichen Theologie', *ZTK* 58 (1961), pp. 245-67 (ET 'On the Task of Christian Theology', *JTC* 6 [1969], pp. 69-98 [p. 72]).

proclamation and faith'.[27] Proclamation, which concerns existence, and its dialectic of the 'two times', humanity's and God's, are central. Neither 'enthusiasm' nor the near expectation and delay of the parousia are proclamation or theology, but merely 'psychological data, as is also the Easter experience'.[28] 'What was it, then, that really kept the history of primitive Christianity going? I have said it already: a dilemma which we find everywhere and certainly already in Jesus himself, namely, the perplexity as to how the new understanding of God (the two times) is to come to grips with the traditional self-understanding, that is, with life under the law.'[29] Bultmann is alive, well, and thriving, thank you very much (so speak Bultmann's legitimate children).

Käsemann answers Ebeling and Fuchs 'by setting out, necessarily in sketchy fashion, the origin, significance, phases and vicissitudes of apocalyptic from after Easter up to, and including Paul'.[30] This means tracing 'apocalyptic' once more from Jesus up to Paul.

While acknowledging that Jesus begins his own ministry within the orbit of the 'apocalyptic' preaching of John the Baptist, with its 'burning expectation of the End', it is clear to Käsemann that Jesus makes a clean break with this beginning. Jesus reverses the deep 'apocalyptic' pessimism of the wrath-mongering and world-renouncing preaching of the Baptist, preaching instead the grace of God and the love of one's brother (of, even, strangers and enemies). 'On the basis of this remarkable "eschatology", which views all life as lived "before God", it is easy to understand how Jesus, so far as we can see, did not baptize, built up no community as a holy remnant and as the nucleus of the messianic people of God and recognized no sharpening of the Torah other than the demand for obedience and love' (p. 114). The usual categories of 'a present or a future eschatology' are 'useless when applied to the message of Jesus...It is my conviction', says Käsemann, 'that it is just the historian who is obliged to speak of a unique secret in Jesus...[E]very attempt to evaluate him according to the criteria of the comparative study of religions ends up in a blind alley' (p. 112).[31]

27. Fuchs, 'Task', p. 81.
28. Fuchs, 'Task', p. 84.
29. Fuchs, 'Task', p. 84.
30. Käsemann, 'On the Subject of Primitive Christian Apocalyptic', in *New Testament Questions*, pp. 108-37 (p. 111).
31. Käsemann continues: 'I put this forward as a remarkable historical phenomenon, not as an axiom from which we might perhaps deduce the absolute nature of Christianity' (*New Testament Questions*, pp. 112-13).

Contrasting sharply with the manner in which Jesus stands apart from his religious environment is the Jewish Christian community after Easter, which must interpret its 'enthusiastic' experience of the risen and present Lord in terms ready to hand. Central to early expectation is the return of Jesus as the heavenly Son of Man, evincing the 'apocalyptic' perspective from which Jesus' resurrection was interpreted. 'We bar our own access to the primitive Easter kerygma if we ignore its apocalyptic context' (p. 112). But this constitutes a break with the preaching of Jesus. This context of eschatological and Christological development, along with the ecclesiological categories of the 'holy remnant', the 'people of God', the 'New Covenant community', forms a salvation-historical complex which situates later anthropological developments. 'Christian theology is thus in its origins very far from being anthropology' (p. 117).

An individualistic emphasis on existence, the Law, and faith is an inadequate means of entry into this earliest theological development. The Law was at issue not as such but in the light of the controversial gentile mission. It was vital for the early community's claim to be the messianic people of God and for their mission to the 'lost sheep of the house of Israel' that the Law be both upheld and that the exclusivism of so much of contemporary Judaism, enshrined in its rigour concerning the Law, be avoided. 'In a strangely unaffected and unconsidered fashion the community followed the tracks of its Master...' (p. 118). It is, then, a clarification of its mission that defines the theological task of the early community after Easter, a deliberation undertaken within a thoroughly eschatological orientation. 'When we define the circumstances of the community before and after Easter solely or even mainly in terms of the concept "faith", we run the risk of abstracting from the breakthrough to the eschatological (Gentile) mission so decisive for Christian history and also from the minting of a first Christian theology constructed with distinctively apocalyptic themes' (p. 120).

Fully affirming with Bultmann the break between Jesus and early Christianity, Käsemann raises the question of whether this break 'signifies complete disintegration or indicates a transformation which may be interpreted as continuity within discontinuity' (p. 120). 'It seems to me that it is precisely the historian who is in no position to reject the propriety of this claim out of hand...' (p. 120). Continuity with Jesus is preserved despite the history of religions break by grasping the universalism implicit in Jesus' proclamation. 'For, even though, because of their previous history, they [Jesus' first interpreters] are bound to give a stereotyped impression, yet their general trend is towards asserting the uniqueness of him who is bringing salvation; and it is precisely this uniqueness which, in my view, the historian cannot help but establish' (p. 122). Jesus did not initiate a Gentile mission, but neither did he bind himself to notions of the 'people of God' and the 'holy remnant'. 'He did not purport to renew the privileges of Israel, he did not, like the Pharisees and Qumran, seek to make the pious more pious still. Zealots and tax collectors gather round him. His radicalization of the Torah extends the scope of grace instead of narrowing it' (p. 123). No category, no theological formulation, no contemporary pattern of piety and expectation can capture him, as 'in the totality of his being he is an enigma, a question, a promise, demanding fulfilment and response' (p. 123).[32]

> At Easter this comes home to his disciples at a depth clearly unknown before and the only response possible to them is in terms of apocalyptic. Provided we do not attempt to father upon them modern thought-forms and conceptions, we shall even regard their apocalyptic as the appropriate response to the fact that in Jesus the ultimate promise of the world is encountered. For those disciples the ultimate in authority must be also the ultimate in time, the lordship of the Free Man could become visible only in the destruction of the power of death, their teacher and helper could only have abiding and universal significance if he were bringing in the age of freedom which the earthly people of God had been so long awaiting. Their theology and their mission are the modes in which they submit to this freedom, and make it comprehensible to themselves and accessible to others. Easter points to the kingdom of freedom in the continuity of the freedom of Jesus (p. 123).

The understandable turn to 'apocalyptic' preserved something vital, allowing Jesus to speak on the matter of the clarification of the church's mission.

The question of Paul's 'apocalyptic' is not, though, directly accessible against the background of this Jewish Christianity (as the history of religions school and Bultmann have demonstrated). The environment in which he moves is that of Hellenistic Christianity, the climate of 'Hellenistic enthusiasm'. As the gospel moves out beyond the borders of Palestine into the Hellenistic world (for Käsemann, as was true generally

---

32. The frequency with which Käsemann asserts that it is precisely the historian who must acknowledge the uniqueness of Jesus would seem to betray a certain sensitivity to the possibility that the charges he directs against others for resisting 'apocalyptic' might be turned back on him where his 'non-apocalyptic' Jesus is concerned.

for his day, the latter stops at the border of the former), how will Jewish 'apocalyptic' categories fare? Thus, another question of 'inheritance and mutation', 'continuity and discontinuity' is raised.

The leading 'theologoumenon' of Hellenistic Christianity, as Käsemann credits Bousset with demonstrating, is that of the 'exalted Kyrios' (p. 127). But the 'apocalyptic' categories of the coming Son of Man and the eschatological people of God do not vanish. Rather, and under the influence of the mystery religions, other speculations are grafted onto 'apocalyptic': in particular, a Christological and salvation-historical scheme (as the history and destiny of the redeemer mirrors that of the believer) is given anthropological significance. Corinth is the paradigm case here. 'As participants of the Cross of Christ, the baptized are at the same time participants in his Resurrection and Enthronement, liberated from the old aeon of death and the powers and translated into the new aeon of the Kingdom of Christ' (p. 125). The future resurrection is denied from the standpoint of 'a sacramental realism which sees complete redemption to have already been effected, in that by baptism a heavenly spiritual body has been conferred and the earthly body has been degraded to an insubstantial, transitory veil' (p. 126). '[W]hat had previously been seen primarily as the turn of the ages was translated into a statement about man, and what had originally been a temporal and teleological assertion was transformed into a timeless Idealism' (p. 126). The expectant stance of 'apocalyptic', awaiting a now hidden and imminently returning Son of Man, proves inadequate, and Christ's resurrection becomes his exaltation as the Kyrios who even now rules over the principalities and powers, over the entire world, a conviction powerfully confirmed in the experience of the Spirit and the success of the gentile mission. But the more a present eschatology is brought to the fore, the more pressing becomes the question of the earthly contradictions to this assertion of the new creation in Christ. Here anthropological speculation concerning the two Adams, the earthly and the heavenly seed, those of the flesh and those of the Spirit, those enslaved to the powers and those granted freedom, merges with the scheme of the two succeeding ages and the two parallel worlds. 'The inheritance of apocalyptic thus extends its influence: but it is transformed by being integrated into a metaphysical dualism, which itself then finds concretion and contemporary force in a doctrine of man. The question of the reality of the saving event can now be answered in a new way by starting from this anthropology' (p. 129). The old promise/fulfilment scheme of the 'holy remnant' and the 'messianic people of God' is likewise inadequate on Hellenistic soil, and can only be retained in a figurative sense. Exalted high above the world are the redeemed, whose community, befitting its heavenly nature, denies all ethnic, social, and sexual differences. The practical result, though, is a factious community of the 'spiritual' divided against those who have not attained their exalted status, with all the attendant woes visible in the church at Corinth.

> This is Hellenistic enthusiasm's radical interpretation of the baptismal statement that the redeemed are risen with Christ and enthroned with him in the heavenly state. Expectation of an imminent Parousia thus ceases to be meaningful because everything which apocalyptic still hopes for has already been realized. What is really important to notice, however, it that a large-scale process of transformation is going on here, in which present eschatology is linked directly with Jewish Christian apocalyptic of the time after Easter (p. 131).

This is a process by which Christianity is transformed into a mystery religion, and it is becoming clear that Bultmann is seen as doing something very similar—which brings us to Paul.

'Now for the first time we are in a position to ask about Paul's place and significance within this whole context' (p. 131).

> Bultmann's fascinating interpretation of Paul is determined by its resolute placing of the apostle's present eschatology at the controlling centre of his thought. There is no reason not to admit that this interpretation is not merely tenable, but enables vital elements of Pauline theology to be unforgettably impressed on the mind. But we shall then have to regard the apostle as a representative—an extremely important one, no doubt—of the Hellenistic Church, just as radical historical criticism since Baur has actually done; the most impressive version of this view is undoubtedly Bousset's. In this case, Paul's particular contribution may be seen as his systematic development of anthropology. It certainly cannot be present eschatology, because this had already been developed by Hellenistic Christianity before his day. Seen in this light, what is the significance of the relics of apocalyptic theology which are to be found everywhere in the Pauline epistles? Indeed, is it permissible to use the phrase 'relics', unless we shut our eyes to the fact that Paul's apostolic self-consciousness is only comprehensible on the basis of his apocalyptic, and that the same is true of the method and the goal of his mission (p. 131)?

Paul does indeed combine present and future eschatology; but he is actually waging an 'anti-enthusiastic battle...under the sign of apocalyptic' (p. 132). Paul will not allow that the resurrection life is lived now, only that the 'new obedience' is the anticipation of this life. 'He does, admittedly, associate sharing in the Cross with sharing in the Resurrection: but in so doing, he builds in a remarkable caveat in the shape of an eschatological reservation. Participation in the Resurrection is spoken of not in the perfect tense, but in the future' (p. 132). 'This is evidently not merely a matter of using different language. I Cor. 15 shows that what is at stake is a fundamentally different theological conception which enables Paul to remain true at this point to the apocalyptic tradition' (p. 133). Paul here binds the anthropological hope of the general resurrection to the resurrection of Christ and to the lordship of Christ, the Second Adam, a lordship which is itself limited and is preparatory of the lordship of God.

> Christ is God's representative over against a world which is not yet fully subject to God, although its eschatological subordination is in train since Easter and its end is in sight. *No perspective could be more apocalyptic.* With the greatest clarity it emerges here that Paul is absolutely unable and unwilling to speak of any end to history which has already come to pass, but, he does, however, discern that the day of the End-time has already broken. This is the case since the Resurrection of Christ, because since then the subjection of the cosmic powers has been taking place. *The present eschatology of the enthusiasts is therefore picked up but apocalyptically anchored and delimited as it is not with them.* For Paul, it is not an alternative to, but a component of, a future eschatology—to express the position in terms of slogans (p. 133, emphasis added).

Paul's 'apocalyptic' perspective on the exaltation and reign of Christ (as distinct from the conception of the mysteries) is brought to bear on the eschatological anomalies to which 'enthusiasm' addressed itself. 'There remains only the end of the lordship of death upon earth, which is identical with the end of history' (p. 134). 'In the Church the powers, except death—note the eschatological reservation which is made even here— have lost the lordship to Christ, whereas they still reign in the world which surrounds the Church' (p. 134). Here Paul's anthropology comes into play. The Church manifests its distinction from a world outwardly the same in its obedience, following in the train of the obedient Adam, who effects the new creation, restoring the state from which Adam fell. This obedience is in the body, which, as 'that piece of world which we ourselves are', signifies the reign of Christ in the world. 'In the bodily obedience of the Christian, carried out as the service of God in the world of everyday, the lordship of Christ finds visible expression and only when this visible expression takes personal shape in us does the whole thing become credible as Gospel message' (p. 135).

> Because Christ must reign, he cannot leave his own in the grip of death. Conversely, his own are already engaged today in delivering over to Christ by their bodily obedience the piece of world which they themselves are; and in so doing they bear witness to his lordship as that of the Cosmocrator and thus anticipate the ultimate future of the reality of the Resurrection and of the untrammelled reign of Christ. *The apocalyptic question 'To whom does the sovereignty of the world belong?' stands behind the Resurrection theology of the apostle, as behind his parenesis which centres round the call to obedience in the body. Apocalyptic even underlies the particular shape of Pauline anthropology.* For the technical terms 'spirit' and 'flesh' do not signify, any more than the term 'body' does, the individuation of the individual human being, but primarily that reality which, as the power either of the heavenly or the earthly, determines him from outside, takes possession of him and thereby decides into which of the two dualistically opposed spheres he is to be integrated. Man for Paul is never just on his own. He is always a specific piece of world and therefore becomes what in the last resort he is by determination from outside, i.e. by the power which takes possession of him and the lordship to which he surrenders himself. His life is from the beginning a stake in the confrontation between God and the principalities of this world. In other words, it mirrors the cosmic contention for the lordship of the world and is its concretion. *As such, man's life can only be understood apocalyptically* (pp. 135-36, emphasis added).

Finally, then, Paul's eschatological dialectic of Christian existence is transparent: it 'is nothing else but the projection into the human condition of the Christian of the relationship of the lordship of Christ to the subjection of all cosmic principalities' (p. 136). Paul's 'eschatological reserve' and 'apocalyptic' oppose the present eschatology of the enthusiasts, renouncing their triumphant celebration of the attainment of the heavenly freedom, as Church and world together yet cry out in temptation and travail for this perfection. Paul—unlike Bultmann—draws on Jewish 'apocalyptic' (de-nationalized, as befits a Hellenistic environment) as against an assimilation of Christ into the mysteries.

> Present eschatology by itself, and not comprehended within a future eschatology—that would be for the Christian pure glorying in the flesh, such as enthusiasm has certainly sufficiently demonstrated in every epoch. It would be illusion and not reality. *It is precisely the apocalyptic of the apostle which renders to reality its due and resists pious illusion.* The Christian Church possesses the reality of sonship only in the freedom of

those under temptation—the freedom which points forward to the resurrection of the dead as the truth and the completion of the reign of Christ (pp. 136-37, emphasis added).

That, concludes Käsemann, should answer the question as to what there remains to preach.

Completing the historical sweep of Käsemann's survey of the fortunes of early 'apocalyptic', taking the story now beyond Paul, is 'Paul and Early Catholicism'.[33] A good characterization of life in the sway of Schweitzer's 'positive criticism' is given:

> Ever since the eschatological understanding of the New Testament replaced the idealistic interpretation, we can and must determine the various phases of earliest Christian history by means of the original imminent expectation of the parousia, its modifications and its final extinction. Early catholicism means that transition from earliest Christianity to the so-called ancient Church, which is completed with the disappearance of the imminent expectation (pp. 236-37).

Käsemann, in apparent provocation of Protestant self-understanding, suggests the lines of connection of the 'apocalyptic' Paul with the later salvation history of the Church whereby he prepared their way—though clearly Protestantism is not so much challenged as chastised for not being Protestant enough. 'Early catholicism' domesticates and even radically subverts the apostle's own quite different salvation history, a point hardly mitigated by Käsemann's kind allowance that the Church followed the only path open to it in the fight against 'enthusiasm', Paul's 'apocalyptic' perspective having come to seem untenable. The image of Paul constructed in 'early catholicism', that of 'the founder of the worldwide Church and its first order', beguiles us to the present day, bemoans Käsemann (p. 249). Käsemann concludes his historical survey of 'apocalyptic', which he has developed since the manifesto with which we began, in a tirade which surprises us only if we have not been listening:

> Alongside this image of Paul, to which the ecclesiastical future belonged, there is, however, the real Paul as well. This Paul remains confined in seven letters and for the most part unintelligible to posterity, not only to the ancient Church and the Middle Ages. However, whenever he is rediscovered—which happens almost exclusively in times of crisis—there issues from him explosive power which destroys as much as it opens up something new. His historical existence and activity is then repeated. The

33. Käsemann, *New Testament Questions*, pp. 236-51.

gospel of the unknown God who justifies the ungodly and none but them, and who deals with us only in this way, then comes into conflict with the Christian religion which is concerned about the piety of the pious. Then the one Lord, with the demand of this exclusive lordship, shatters those authorities which claim to be his earthly deputies. The Church becomes the creation of the word, instead of being the mother of the faithful and possessor of the truth. Worship in the secularity of the world replaces the Christian cult. Faith in him who is always and exclusively the one who awakens the dead replaces the superstitious belief in history and salvation history as sources of revelation. The universal priesthood of all believers rises up against the sacramentally guaranteed office, which claims authority on the strength of tradition. The freedom of the Christian man and of the Church of Jesus breaks through the ecclesiastical ethic and uniformity. Mission pushes aside pious self-admiration and self-assertion.

It is never long, to be sure, until orthodoxy and enthusiasm again master this Paul and banish him once more to his letters. However, the Church continues to preserve his letters in her canon and thereby latently preserves her own permanent crisis. She cannot get away from the one who for the most part only disturbs her. For he remains even for her the apostle of the heathen; the pious still hardly know what to make of him. For that very reason his central message is the voice of a preacher in the wilderness, even in Protestant Christianity, which today stands much nearer early catholicism than it supposes or is willing to believe (pp. 249-50).[34]

(Have we, in Käsemann, yet another 'new Paul'?)

Although every twist and turn of Käsemann's historical reconstruction may not be exactly clear, it is evident that for Käsemann 'apocalyptic' stands at the centre of the earliest attempt to grapple with the theological task, a task bound up with a clarification of the church's mission. What has also surfaced clearly enough is that for Käsemann this early struggle is paradigmatic for the theological task of all times, and that 'apocalyptic' somehow serves the achievement and preservation of a properly Protestant stance. As Käsemann remarked when turning to 'the beginnings of Christian theology', the historian (as he tellingly frames it) 'cannot be persuaded that beginnings do not determine what is to follow, and contain, in however veiled and strange a form, the law of the future' (p. 82). Jesus embodied the pure 'Protestant principle' without the aid of 'apocalyptic'. Such was his genius. But never mind. His earliest followers, led by the charisma-endowed Christian prophets, drew

---

34. Käsemann ends with a note (*New Testament Questions*, p. 250 n. 6) dismissing Catholic ecumenical protest over such treatment of 'early catholicism' in the New Testament.

on 'apocalyptic' to preserve this tension. Paul did likewise. We stand in their debt. This much, at least, is going on in the above, in further consideration of which we take up the question: What does 'apocalyptic' mean for Käsemann? What does it signify, to what ends is it reclaimed, what does he do with it? The particular concern here is with the polemical and ideological contours of Käsemann's 'apocalyptic' interpretation of Paul (drawing now especially on Käsemann's *Perspectives on Paul*), as well as, returning to Käsemann's manifesto, his explicit hermeneutical theorizing.

## Polemics and Politics

As has been seen above, Käsemann began with Bultmann and Paul's anthropology, and it is no surprise to see him weave together many of his interpretative concerns in a sustained treatment of this theme.[35] Here a major polemical strand of Käsemann's interpretation is visible. Against Bultmann's emphasis on the continuity and identity of an individual self, Käsemann sees in Paul's anthropology discontinuity in a corporate self defined by its spheres of influence, a discontinuity both in terms of the self within the course of its own life and in terms of the breaks in the course of salvation history.[36] For Paul a human being is radically embodied and radically bound up in structures of solidarity—under the lordship of sin, flesh, law, the 'powers', or the lordship of Christ—not free and free-floating; and this has not only anthropological, but also sacramental, ecclesiological, Christological, soteriological, cosmological, and eschatological significance.[37] 'Apocalyptic' plays a central role here:

> Only someone who does not know or share the nightmares of contemporary man can fail to sympathize with those of Paul, or can maintain—as if we were still the last custodians of the ethical idealism of a liberal world—that Paul was entirely lacking in interest in apocalyptic schemes, because he was not conscious of any plan in history and only preserved a rudimentary hope in the resurrection of believers. But according to 1 Cor. 15.25ff. the apostle's hope was directed towards the time when Christ would rule and place all his enemies under his feet, when God would be all in all. In this context our own resurrection means no more and no less than participation in a world set free by the *basileia*. What is apocalyptic here is

35. Käsemann, *Perspectives*, pp. 1-31. Page numbers in the text throughout this section refer to essays in this volume.
36. See Käsemann, *Perspectives*, pp. 8-18.
37. See Käsemann, *Perspectives*, pp. 18-31.

not merely the historical outline which is inevitably involved, with its divisions into separate epochs—Adam, Abraham, Moses, Christ and the kingdom of freedom. The idea that (according to Rom. 1.20ff.; 5.12ff.; 7.13ff.) Adam's fate is repeated and confirmed in every individual is also an apocalyptic one. Just as each person is both himself and his world, so he is also himself and Adam on the path which he follows. The view of Rom. 8.19ff. is also apocalyptic in its assertion that the whole creation waits with groaning for the glorious liberty of the sons of God and that the church in its worship even declares itself at one with creation in this expectation. The apostle's self-understanding is apocalyptic when (according to Rom. 11.11ff.) he sees his task to be to convert the Gentiles, as a step towards inciting unbelieving Israel to conversion—his mission thus being a preparation for the parousia. Apocalyptic, finally, is the disquieting question which not only moves the apostle but apparently faces every Christian, a question bound up with his task and his existence: who owns the earth (pp. 24-25)?

The political horizons of Käsemann's 'apocalyptic' approach are becoming visible. 'By abandoning the question of the meaning of history or, rather, by narrowing it down to the question of the meaning of the historical nature of existence, Bultmann was inevitably bound to maintain that Pauline theology takes its bearings from the individual'. (p. 10) What is worse, Bultmann's anthropological approach takes as its standard of measure '"modern" man', and, worse still, this figure 'belongs to the nineteenth century rather than to the second half of the twentieth' (pp. 10-11). '[M]an is . . . being interpreted as a constitutively spiritual being...' (p. 14). 'Apocalyptic' serves for Käsemann an ethical end in pointing toward what we now understand (so Käsemann) as the human being as a social, political, historical entity.[38] Paul's 'apocalyptic' perspective as Käsemann summarizes it is 'rudimentary', and it is no part, says Käsemann, of 'the demand to demythologize—a demand which I would by no means reject', to remove it, a desire for such removal stemming, where it exists, from our own 'resignation' to rest

> content with a private self-understanding, which turns the Christian practically speaking into a non-political being and confines his responsibility to personal human relationships. The apostle was more exacting than his interpreters today, in so far as these content themselves with a Christian humanism in which Christology possesses at most an awakening and a controlling function (p. 25).

38. See Käsemann, *Perspectives*, pp. 11, 13-14, 23, 25, 30.

For Paul, Christian existence is shaped by the cross and is freed for a mission of social, ethical, political responsibility toward the world (pp. 29-30). 'Contemporary theology is still having to pay for the fact that it is still a victim of the heritage or curse of idealism to a greater degree than it cares to admit. It could have learned as much from Marxism as it did from Kierkegaard and would then have been unable to go on assigning the absolutely decisive role to the individual' (p. 11). If this is a demythologizing of 'apocalyptic', it is demythologizing with a difference.[39]

Another major polemical strand of Käsemann's interpretative programme concerns 'salvation history', around a consideration of which theme, again, many of his interpretative concerns revolve.[40] It has been seen that Käsemann, in opposing Bultmann, can speak in a voice almost indistinguishable from Cullmann—salvation history, that is, is taken up as a weapon against Bultmann's existentialist approach.

> As far as I am concerned, the dispute over the question whether Paul develops a concept of salvation history or not is not a problem of Pauline theology; it is a specimen of the entanglement of all exegesis in systematic prejudices which we can diminish but never entirely rid ourselves of. Where existence and situation determine, and must determine, every theological statement, perspectives based on salvation history are bound to be passionately rejected. Yet this is to do violence to the texts (p. 65).

'Apocalyptic' once more plays a central role: 'Theology cannot begin and end with the individual where world mission appears as the Christian task pure and simple, and where this task is seen against an apocalyptic background and is described in apocalyptic terms—i.e., when it is derived from the trial-situation presented by the conflict between creator and his creatures' (p. 65).

---

39. 'We must certainly demythologize if we are to translate the message of early Christianity into our own time. But it would be a fatal mistake if we attempted to make this the pivot of theology. This could only lead to a new dispute about pure doctrine and to another kind of dogmatism. The mythical form of the biblical *kerygma* is a barrier on the road to faith. Its real enemy is and remains superstition, which may express itself in a hundred different kinds of practice and theory, but ultimately manifests itself in neglected, corrupted discipleship which fails to press forward into fresh worlds' (Käsemann, *Perspectives*, p. 27).

40. 'On the Saving Significance of the Death of Jesus in Paul' and 'Justification and Salvation History in the Epistle to the Romans', in Käsemann, *Perspectives*, pp. 32-59; 60-78.

The eschatological is neither supra-history nor the inner aspect of a historicity; it is power which changes the old world into a new one and which becomes incarnate in the earthly sphere. For it is corporeality which is the sphere of revelation—inevitably so, since this is the nature of the world and everyday life. Only a complete misunderstanding can make a spiritualist out of Paul, though strangely enough such attempts have repeatedly been made. For him, salvation history has a spatial and temporal dimension, frontiers dividing off the cosmic spheres of power and a cohesion which leads from creation to Christ and the parousia by way of the choosing of Israel and the promise (p. 68).

'It cannot be seriously disputed that salvation history forms the horizon of Pauline theology' (p. 66).

When it comes down to determining the place and weight of salvation history, Bultmann becomes an ally against Cullmann. For salvation history (as is it often conceived) compromises proclamation, faith, and the doctrine of justification. 'The current talk about the facts of redemption which, we are told, can be objectively established...conceals a deadly danger: for it is precisely talk like this which allows us to lose sight of the only place where we are not merely told about salvation but can find it. The cross helps no one who does not hear the word of the cross and ground his faith on that' (p. 50). 'To say that salvation is to be encountered in these facts is a matter of revelation and faith. Assurance of salvation only comes through preaching. The person who wants to build on historical facts as such is bound to fall into uncertainty of salvation, and historical criticism confirms that this is the case' (p. 50). 'The person who sees has no need to hear, and the person who can no longer hear will inevitably want to see. According to Paul, whether one wants to hear or to see is what divides faith from superstition' (p. 51). Paul's theology 'cannot be anything but a theology of the cross, just as, and just because, it cannot be separated from the message of justification, and counters all enthusiasm with a critical and realistic anthropology' (p. 46). On this last note, it becomes clear that Käsemann's emphasis on proclamation, faith, and justification differs also from that of Bultmann, despite what they share, for while both agree on their centrality and on the impropriety of founding faith on some visible historical process, Bultmann makes all three vulnerable to a critique from the side of salvation history by casting them in an individualistic frame (so Käsemann). From a certain point of view, Bultmann and Cullmann alike come under the critique of Paul's theology of the cross:

> Whatever the reason for the talk about the facts of redemption, and
> whatever right the spiritualists may have on their side when they surrender
> the earth as a field of decision between belief and unbelief, this talk almost
> inevitably leads to the loss of a theology of the Word...The theology of
> the cross and the theology of the Word belong together and are won or
> thrown away together (p. 51).

The salvation-historical school must consider how its emphasis on
the 'facts of redemption', though conceived as 'a defence against
existentialism', is perhaps being 'pursued, consciously or unconsciously,
in the interests of an enthusiastic anthropology and ecclesiology' (p. 56).
'The opposing camps could be much closer to one another in their
approach and intention than their slogans would suggest. The criterion is
not to be found in the alternatives of Christology or anthropology and
ecclesiology, but in the alternative between a true and a false Christology
which then projects itself into anthropology and ecclesiology' (p. 56).[41]
Käsemann, that is, can come down on neither side, and must go his own
way.

Käsemann's own preferred way orients itself neither toward anthropology nor toward salvation history, but toward that centre which may
be alternately captured in speaking of a theology of the cross/the
justification of the ungodly, the cosmic lordship of Christ/the righteousness of God, a centre which as a whole may be styled (among others
things) 'apocalyptic'. 'Apocalyptic' is again decisive for a critical perspective on salvation history and for locating it with respect to
justification. For Paul, salvation history is not 'a continuous evolutionary
process' but rather has a 'down side' covered over by a pious,
triumphalistic 'enthusiasm': it expresses

> the contrast of the two realms of Adam and Christ. Pauline theology
> unfolds this contrast extensively as the struggle between death and life, sin
> and salvation, law and gospel. The basis is the apocalyptic scheme of the
> two successive aeons which is transferred to the present. Apparently Paul
> viewed his own time as the hour of the Messiah's birth-pangs, in which
> the new creation emerges from the old world through the Christian
> proclamation. Spirits, powers and dominions part eschatologically at the
> crossroads of the gospel. We thus arrive at the dialectic of 'once' and
> 'now', which is absorbed into anthropology in the form of 'already saved'
> and 'still tempted'. In the antithesis of spirit and flesh this dialectic
> determines the cosmos until the parousia of Christ. Christians are drawn

---

41. Ecclesiology is, of course, bound up with anthropology and salvation history
(and 'apocalyptic') for Käsemann; see further, *Perspectives*, pp. 102-21.

into this conflict all their lives. Every day they have through obedience to authenticate their baptismal origin anew. The churches, too, are exposed in the same way to the attacks of nomism and enthusiasm, which threaten the lordship of Christ. The church lives under the sign of the cross, that is to say, given over to death inwardly and outwardly, waiting longingly with the whole of creation for the liberty of the children of God and manifesting the imitation of Jesus through the bearing of his cross (p. 67).

Granted, again, that salvation history is undeniably there, and is not to be passed over at that, how does it sit in relation to justification? Only where the latter is individualistically narrowed may salvation history contain it (in which regard, in fact, Käsemann has himself called on salvation history against just such a narrowing). '*The doctrine of justification*' is '*the key to salvation history, just as, conversely, salvation history forms the historical depth and cosmic breadth of the event of justification*' (p. 75, emphasis added).

Paul's doctrine of justification is about God's *basileia*. The apostle generally expresses it in anthropological terms because he is concerned that it should determine our everyday lives…The Christology inherent in the doctrine of justification corresponds to the existence led in the everyday life of the world. Justification is the stigmatization of our worldly existence through the crucified Christ. Through us and in us he simultaneously reaches out toward the world to which we belong. Paul's doctrine of justification means that under the sign of Christ, God becomes Cosmocrator, not merely the Lord of the believing individual or the god of a cult; it is not by chance that the doctrine has its roots in apocalyptic (p. 75).

For Käsemann, the current emphasis on salvation history is an enemy of the theology of the cross, both because it levels out the cross by placing it in a chain of 'redemptive facts' and because its implicit theology of glory leaves the pious obscenely comfortable in Zion. Käsemann upholds the Reformation tradition with a radical Protestantism that looks askance at any blunting of its critical edge according to the needs of the pious or of the spirit of the times, whether this expresses itself in ecumenism (in which salvation history is heavily implicated) or in accommodation to the pressures of current philosophical self-understanding.

Käsemann, though, may feel in good company in his interpretative straits. For Paul, as has already been seen, to Käsemann's good fortune, fought a strikingly similar two-front battle: 'it is important to see that although the Pauline message of the cross cites the behaviour of the Jews and Greeks as examples of enmity to the crucified Jesus, it is clearly the legalistic piety of Jewish-Christian circles and the enthusiasm of the Hellenistic church which is the real object of his attack' (p. 38).[42] Paul's doctrine of justification 'undoubtedly grew up in the course of the anti-Jewish struggle and stands or falls with this antithesis' (p. 71).[43] But justification is not to be dethroned merely because of this local polemical origin. 'Our task is to ask: what does the Jewish nomism against which Paul fought really represent? And our answer must be: it represents the community of 'good' people which turns God's promises into their own privileges and God's commandments into the instruments of self-sanctification' (p. 72). Not only so, but gentile Christianity also comes under Paul's censure, as 'the Pauline doctrine of justification is a protection not only against nomism but also against enthusiasm and mysticism' (p. 73). Käsemann reflects that 'the debate shows that I apparently stand between two fronts in refusing either to subordinate the apostle's doctrine of justification to a pattern of salvation history or to allow it to turn into a mere vehicle for the self-understanding of the believer' (p. 76 n. 27). Bultmann and Cullmann (and Schweitzer figures in here somewhere as well), then, have their analogues among Paul's opponents, while Käsemann occupies, between his two fronts, the no-man's-land of the cross.

Käsemann draws theological-hermeneutical significance from all of this: scripture has been marginalized 'by a theology which is guided by the needs of the church or its traditions' or 'by the self-understanding which is prevailing at any given moment' (p. 62). What is needed is a truly Protestant hermeneutic, for no such pietism or philosophical fashionableness 'can save people from surrendering to illusion, whether this meets them in the form of a mythology or in the ideology of a world which claims to have come of age' (p. 35). Thus 'a theological hermeneutic', 'a doctrine about the understanding and right interpretation of the biblical message', must 'be established in the shadow of a theology of the cross...if we are not merely to deal with a hermeneutical selection' (p. 35).

> My generation at least (if we have profited at all from our own experience) should surely have lost its taste for the watchword of 'history as revelation', and as regards salvation history this watchword has always

42. Cf. again "The Righteousness of God' in Paul', Käsemann, *New Testament Questions*, pp. 171-72.

43. Käsemann believes himself to be in agreement with Stendahl here, whom he takes to be saying that justification is peripheral because it is polemical (Stendahl is actually shifting the whole ground of the discussion, as witness his reply, cited below).

existed, even in secularized form. Anyone who has still not burnt his
fingers enough can continue to pursue the subject. But after only thirty
years it has apparently already been largely forgotten that it was at
precisely this point that a choice had to be made in Germany between
Yahweh and Baal, and that there is no way of wrapping up the basic nature
of the choice (p. 52).

Such a distorting emphasis on salvation history turns Christianity into
another ideology: '"Facts of redemption" are offered on every religious
and political market place, with the appropriate (and often convincing)
historical interpretations thrown in' (p. 53). A similar polemical thrust
emerges in Käsemann's clash with Krister Stendahl over 'justification
and salvation history'. Käsemann relates how he and his generation
were led through Bultmann and 'on the way to a theology of proclamation' to a rediscovery of the 'Reformation doctrine of justification',
which had been obscured by the very sort of 'theology of history' now
again on the upsurge. However, this rediscovery 'immunized us deeply
against a conception of salvation history which broke in on us in
secularized and political form with the Third Reich and its ideology', an
experience which 'made a theology of history suspect for us from the
very outset, whatever the reasons may be which are urged in its
support. It determined the liberalism whose faith in progress was finally
shattered by the First World War. However erroneously and improperly,
it was capable of serving as a shield for Nazi eschatology' (p. 64).
(Käsemann does not quite wish here to associate Bultmann with the
Third Reich as he does 'salvation history'; nevertheless, it is through, not
from, Bultmann that the equipment for resisting such ideology is
acquired, for, as Käsemann elsewhere charges, Bultmann, though properly centring himself on a proclamation of the cross and on justification
by faith, has so construed these as to surrender history as the realm of
decision. There is, then, an implicit indictment of Bultmann for not
making it his concern to provide the wherewithal to face such decisions,
irrespective of Bultmann's own personal stance in this matter. There is
an irony in all of this, for Käsemann does not seem to reflect on how his
radical Protestantism, carrying as it does a cargo of potential German
nationalism and of *actual* anti-Catholicism and anti-Judaism, pulls toward
the right, subverting his more leftist political reflexes. This irony is not
lost on Stendahl, who finds Käsemann's rather startling charge of
complicity easily turned back on its maker.[44])

44. See Stendahl's reply to Käsemann in *Paul Among Jews and Gentiles*

Another, albeit related, polemical strand concerns the more mundane world of academic Pauline studies. Here we encounter the opposition between 'mysticism' and 'justification', the two supposedly opposed strands of Paul's thought that Käsemann would bring back together. Schweitzer and Bultmann have both, each in his own way, restored Paul's thought to a striking unity, but at a cost, with Schweitzer demoting justification and Bultmann 'apocalyptic'. Käsemann's designs for offering a coherent account of Paul's thought are even grander, and he will succumb to neither of these temptations toward partial and one-sided solutions.[45] Käsemann's 'apocalyptic' approach carries within itself a critique of the 'enthusiasm' implicit in both 'mysticism' and in an individualistic, philosophical redemption, and it supplies the corporate and cosmic setting of justification in the theme of the 'righteousness of God'. (Käsemann is less than forthright here, as Schweitzer situates 'justification by faith' within a more encompassing framework, that of 'participatory eschatology'; that is, individual redemption is set within cosmic and corporate redemption. Käsemann's own procedure is not far from this, as he too sets the more individualistic aspect of 'justification by faith' within the 'apocalyptic', salvation-historical frame of the 'righteousness of God'. Käsemann has simply found a way to stretch the term 'justification'/'righteousness' to fit the whole. This leaves Bultmann's more faithful pupils mildly incredulous, to say the least, that Käsemann has saved 'justification by faith' at all.[46]) This polemic in Pauline interpretation concerns a particular history of religions point:

(Philadelphia: Fortress Press, 1976), 129-32, esp. p. 131, and note pp. 132-33 on Bornkamm.

45. To speak of Käsemann's grand designs on a synthetic account of Paul might appear to be mistaken in light of his failure or refusal to write a theology of Paul, presenting instead occasional exegetical and polemical pieces and a commentary on Romans (which itself eschews an introduction and excursuses). But one should ask when reading these whether a theology of Paul does not hover behind them. One might also wonder whether Käsemann's apparent desire to avoid such synthesis so as not to skew his exegesis (see the 'Preface' to his *Commentary on Romans*) is not both a misguided and at any rate unheeded aim. (Less charitably, we might note that an unarticulated synthesis is harder to call to account.)

46. As expressions of this suspicion, see Conzelmann, 'Current Problems', p. 180 and n. 17, and G. Bornkamm, *Paul* (trans. D.M.G. Stalker; New York: Harper & Row, 1971), p. 147. Käsemann believes his 'The Faith of Abraham in Romans 4', *Perspectives*, pp. 79-101, answers this objection (see p. 78 n. 28).

Käsemann emphasizes Jewish 'apocalyptic' as a corrective over against the emphasis on the Hellenistic mysteries and the *Kyrios* cult as a background to Paul (as opposed to, say, the church at Corinth), an emphasis characteristic of the 'history of religions school' and, following it, of Bultmann. But he must also correct the perception of 'apocalyptic' to the degree that it is perceived as crowding out 'justification'. Käsemann implicates this history of religions controversy directly into the theological battle he has waged under the sign of a theology of the cross (where the opposition is cast more as being between justification and salvation history), for, he charges, the church always tries to soften the blow of such a theology: 'In Pauline interpretation the problem is still alive. Attempts to comprehend him mystically or sacramentally, or from the standpoint of the church, or from the angle of salvation history, all demonstrate this. The history of Pauline interpretation is the history of the apostle's ecclesiastical domestication' (pp. 46-47).[47]

## Criticism Historical and Theological

It is necessary to return to the exchange with Ebeling and Fuchs in order to consider more fully Käsemann's hermeneutics. For it is polemical contexts such as these which elicit the most direct hermeneutical reflection from Käsemann. Käsemann contrasts (in what appears to be a spirit of strained condescension) their concerns with his own, but allows that their responses

> obliged me to rethink, expand and develop my essentially purely historical analysis, 'The Beginnings of Christian Theology'…The difference in our formulations of the subject show that our exchanges extend over different levels of discourse. That is also quite justifiable because the systematic question cannot and should not be separated from the historical…I nevertheless begin by continuing the historical analysis…The theological relevance of the historical, always acknowledged by the Christian Church, is not abrogated by any thesis, however arbitrary in its exaggerated one-sidedness, however problematic in its formulation. This theological relevance may primarily consist in our seeing ourselves confronted by questions which we have to answer anew. But for me it is important that questions were put to us before we began to ask and that these questions ought to guide our own…Not everyone can do everything; amid the

---

47. Käsemann, 'Justification and Salvation History', of course, likewise implicates Pauline studies directly into this theological battle (see *Perspectives*, pp. 60-65).

present flood of 'interpretation', some have to dedicate themselves to administering the literary estate of the historians with the object of preventing the interpreters from settling down too comfortably.[48]

There are doubtless many ways of distinguishing Käsemann from Ebeling and Fuchs. But is history versus theology one of them? Ebeling in particular not only raises historical questions which Käsemann passes over, but also hints at unacknowledged theological motives in Käsemann's historical analysis. One question to which Käsemann does briefly respond is that of the definition of 'apocalyptic':

> Ebeling…rightly requires me to define the word 'apocalyptic' in precise terms. Since eschatology and the doctrine of history became almost identical in Germany, we have been embarrassed by no longer having any specific term for the particular kind of eschatology which attempts to talk about ultimate history. It is not in dispute that 'apocalyptic' is ambiguous. But of what term is that not true? It emerges from the context that almost throughout I speak of primitive Christian apocalyptic to denote the expectation of an imminent Parousia…Because, in my view, primitive Christian apocalyptic in this sense was released on the Church by the experience of the Spirit in the time after Easter, preserved as a living phenomenon by those endowed with the Spirit, nourished theologically from the tradition of Jewish apocalyptic, and finally accompanied by enthusiastic hopes and manifestations, I see in it the first phase of advancing post-Easter enthusiasm (p. 109 n. 1).[49]

'The history of the theology of the last two generations shows that the rediscovery of primitive Christian apocalyptic in its significance for the New Testament, for which we are indebted especially to Kabisch, Johannes Weiss and Albert Schweitzer, provided discoverers and contemporaries alike with such a shock as we are hardly able to imagine' (p. 109 n. 2). Ever since its 'rediscovery', 'apocalyptic' has been 'more or less industriously eliminated or pushed away to the outer fringe of our awareness' (p. 110 n. 2). 'This state of affairs arouses the suspicion that history and interpretation have been secretly exchanging their proper roles; to be more specific, interpretation is no longer the servant of the history which has to be illumined, but is making the latter into a quarry for its own arbitrarily constructed buildings for homeless

---

48. *New Testament Questions*, pp. 108-109 n. *. In the present text we return to *New Testament Questions*, with page numbers in the text referring to this volume.

49. This early sort of enthusiasm results in the dialectic of present and future redemption; later, Hellenistic enthusiasm destroys this dialectic in favour of pure presence.

contemporaries' (p. 110 n. 2). On the one hand, Käsemann agrees that the 'objectivity' of natural science is foreign to the effort to understand past *or* present history. But on the other hand...

> I believe the confusion of understanding and decision to be no less ominous. The supposed compulsion always to take up a position immediately, instead of first listening and waiting for what is being given or taken away by the 'other', is mostly the death of understanding, the stifling of the real question, the missed opportunity to learn and, learning, to grow...The principal virtue of the historian and the beginning of all meaningful hermeneutics so far as I am concerned is the cultivation of the listening faculty, which is prepared to take seriously what is historically alien and does not think that violence is the basic form of engagement (p. 110 n. 2).
>
> There are historical matters of fact which, though we may shrink from them in the name of a modern dogmatic theology, can only be ignored at our peril, when they ought to be driving us to critical reappraisal...It is not only in New Testament theology that this question, which was put to us afresh two generations ago, is being reinterpreted before it has been seriously heard (pp. 110-11).

'One does not conquer apocalyptic and escape scot-free' (p. 115 n. 8).

By way of considering further Käsemann's hermeneutics, we return to his manifesto, 'New Testament Questions of Today'. For, as we noted at the outset, entry into the hermeneutical debate of its day forms part of the agenda it both projects and commences.

The very opening lines bewail the demise of the 'faculty of detachment, which is the basic presupposition of all science' (p. 1). One 'mark of our epoch' is that 'the historical critical method has in principle become common property', and yet 'historico-critical radicalism is becoming increasingly isolated and confined' (pp. 2-3). If this decline is 'analyzed without deference, except (I hope) to the facts', says Käsemann, the spirit of ecumenism may be in large part responsible for the quenching of radical criticism, as this spirit is an expression of that 'theological pietism' which marks a conservative, reactionary return to a bourgeois 'biblicism', 'positivism', and 'historicism', permitting 'the use of an historical critical method applied with varying degrees of gentleness' while giving 'plenty of scope to all styles of ecclesiastical involvement', a 'penetration of Pietism into the field of academic theology' which gives cause for grave concern, as 'a pietistic theology propagated and furthered under ecumenical auspices' cannot be regarded 'otherwise than as a menace' (pp. 3-5). Risk is the way of all true science.

[T]he impression is given that personal piety can be used as a labour-saving device in the work of systematic thinking. The churches may in general have no objection to such a development. They would be delivered by it from a seat of permanent disturbance and be confirmed in their existing continuity. Whether such a development would be a healthy one for them is another matter. For besides all this the churches—at any rate the churches of Europe—certainly stand in the twentieth century in danger of becoming a publicly recognized nature reserve set apart in the midst of the technical, social and political world (p. 6).

Reflecting on 'the gulf between contemporary systematic theology and New Testament exegesis' given expression in the debate between Barth and Bultmann, Käsemann remarks:

The systematic theologian cannot forgo exegesis and historical analyses. Conversely, the exegete may imagine that he is not a systematic theologian and that there is no necessity for him to become one; indeed, it is one of the most remarkable effects of historicism that a number of exegetes with thoroughly misplaced modesty actually suppose that they merely do the historical donkey work for the systematic theologian. But systematic theology as the unconscious background of the historical scholar is a most dangerous exercise ground for narrow-mindedness and presumption, just as on the other side disrespect for historical critical method in systematic theology gives free course to speculations of the most diverse kinds. Wherever one thinks it can do without the other we find that in reality two forms of systematic theology and exegesis are failing to establish contact; and the result at times is that the representative of the one discipline formulates his judgments in the other field more or less by rules of thumb or else out of his own wishful thinking (pp. 6-7).

This is by no means a desirable or even tolerable state of affairs, but rather, as a 'temporary theological expression of schizophrenia', it is a 'sickness which we are bound...to overcome with all the energy at our disposal' (p. 7).

[E]ach trade has its own theory of method, determined by suitability for the purpose, and anyone who utters on this point from outside usually succeeds in proving only that he knows nothing of the trade. Scripture is essentially a document of the past before it is anything else and to this extent is subject to historical criticism as the universally tried and tested way into documents of the past. That it is God's Word is a pronouncement of church proclamation which may not as such be mistaken for a methodological principle...

[I]t is precisely today that we have seriously to ask ourselves the reason why completely arbitrary historical reconstruction which does violence to the text is attaining such grotesque proportions. A deep uncertainty has set in as to the conditions under which historical judgments are possible and by which they are limited, in what sense historical work can lay claim to the nature of a science, i.e. accountability. His freedom from limitation by ecclesiastical tradition has undeniably furnished the individuality of the historian with a degree of free play in which any excess is possible and the rules of the business are not merely disregarded but become problematical. The passion for reality, that peculiar driving force of the historian, is only too often replaced by whimsy, the constant refuge of the dilettante. The indirect claim of truth from within reality increasingly loses the power by which it limits the individual and obligates to the whole. The tyranny of intuition succeeds the tutelage of tradition: and this is undoubtedly to fall out of the frying-pan into the fire (pp. 7-8).

'Historical processes...must not be reduced to the interplay of individualities. The history of primitive Christendom is not exclusively, indeed not even primarily, the history of the great theologians and of the self-understanding and understanding of existence attained by them, however attractively it is reflected and delimited therein' (pp. 8-9).

The ideological dynamics of Käsemann's hermeneutical reflections here are intriguing. Just as Bultmann's approach to Paul (toward which Käsemann is proceeding) is not addressable in isolation from Bultmann's hermeneutics, so, too, for Käsemann. It is perhaps not merely down to Käsemann's obvious antipathy for a pietistic salvation-historical approach (Käsemann adds here to his already bulging bag of polemical fronts the church-political fight against Pietism, the real-life counterpart to his constant theological attack on the 'pious') that he engages in this harangue as a preface to his own confrontation with Bultmann, which will occupy him for some years. Given the often remarkable closeness, both theologically and hermeneutically, of Käsemann's critique of Bultmann to that levelled by Cullmann and salvation history, might it be surmised that Käsemann feels compelled, in prospect of his own very conservative-seeming turn against Bultmann, to blast 'Pietism', showing where he himself stands? As for Käsemann's presentation of his dialogue (to put the best face on it) with Bultmann—who plays the role of Socrates to Käsemann's theological and intellectual birth, rather than, as we might have thought, that of Laius to Käsemann's Oedipus—he is painfully careful to acknowledge the greatness of Bultmann's contribution, and to present his own very different path as emerging from Bultmann's, so that the latter is in some sense credited for it. Käsemann even makes a point of bringing up the heresy charges against Bultmann so that he can dismiss them as 'manifestly ridiculous', distancing himself from such charges (even though Käsemann himself has in store for Bultmann charges equally severe, differing only in the cosmetic dropping of the term 'heresy') (p. 11). Käsemann is clearly worried over the sort of hermeneutical free rein that allows Pietism to have its way with Scripture, but neither does he wish to support a positivistic historicism (a version of which salvation history itself espouses), despite his scientistic rhetoric against this new conservatism. He does not wish to see theology and history remain estranged. But he cannot be satisfied with Bultmann's means of reconciling them.

To return to his argument, then, Käsemann has insisted that the history of primitive Christianity is not exclusively, not even primarily, about individuals and existence. What, then, *is* it about? Here we come closer to seeing just what it is that Käsemann is doing. For at this point he suddenly brings up the issue of the canon. It is imperative that the canon be respected in all its diversity—not, as it turns out, out of some sense of championing a hard-won truth, but because, it seems, the canon plays out before our eyes the fortunes of the Gospel amidst its various responses and challenges—that is, it plays out, the Protestant Reformation:

> For in this same canon there is the steadfast affirmation and the manifold refraction of that history in which the comfort of tempted hearts by the Gospel became and sustains reality: a reality which is at the same time always being denied anew and, even within the ranks of the witnesses themselves, misunderstood and yet ever anew of itself creating acknowledgment for itself. The witness to this reality hides within itself in exemplary fashion the whole range of possibilities open in coming to terms with this reality. It is anything but uniform. Jacob and Esau go their separate ways within it. The Gospel does not appear on the scene without arousing the reaction both of legalism and of enthusiasm. *But it is precisely in this way that the canon remains for us the witness of the history which is given and assigned to us*…(p. 9, emphasis added).

It follows from this that a critical hermeneutics is required: 'indeed, the criticism here must be a radical criticism, arising out of the demands of the Gospel itself, a content-orientated criticism casting its shadow over historical criticism' (p. 9). 'Historical criticism' performs a vital service in turning up the problem of diversity; but 'theological criticism' is required to discern the meaning of this diversity.

> The tension between Gospel and Scripture is the indispensable presupposition of all theological interpretation and the inner meaning of those problems of Scripture of which historical criticism takes account.

Whatever motive may have caused the taking over of historical criticism into the exegetical sphere, any retreat from this criticism in the present must necessarily make the problems of Scripture more obscure, reduce the diverse utterances of Scripture to a single level, remove the tension of Gospel and Scripture and endanger the proper historical character of revelation. Radical historical criticism is the logical consequence (not drawn before the modern era) in the methodological field of that theological criticism which is constitutive for Scriptural interpretation. In its attainment of independence this connection has been forgotten, the servant function has become the final objective of exegesis, and alien ideals have usurped the place of legitimate origins. The validity of this process must be questioned. For, so far as its proper task and scope is concerned, the theological clarification of historical criticism has so far been only inadequately undertaken, although this criticism is very widely treated as indispensable in practice and acknowledged as valid in principle. But this is just the point where lies the origin of the crucial tensions between exegesis and systematic theology. It cannot be left to the individual to experiment in this field in any way he likes; and it is inconceivable that in the realm of a *theologia crucis* at least some far reaching understanding should not be arrived at, impossible as this admittedly seems to be in the case of a theology of salvation history (pp. 9-10).

Finally, Käsemann raises the matter of the history of religions setting of the New Testament and Christian origins (pp. 17-22). Here again, the diversity of this religious history is strenuously insisted upon, once again especially against a salvation-historical approach. 'The one biblical theology, growing from a single root and maintaining itself in unbroken continuity, is wish-fulfilment and fantasy' (p. 18). Asserting 'the possibility present on Hellenistic soil from the beginning of understanding Christianity as an analogue of the redemption religions of the mystery cults', Käsemann regards Jewish 'apocalyptic' as providing 'a critical posture towards the enthusiasm of the religious life of the community' over against the 'ethical dualism' and 'enthusiasm' of this Hellenistic piety. (Käsemann means to make a history of religions point here, no matter how theological it sounds [pp. 19-20].)

If the New Testament really represented only an ethical dualism clothed in the garments of a world-view, *Christianity would become a Judaism which believed that the Messiah had already come. The Law would then necessarily triumph over the Gospel*. The questions which concern us today in the field of the comparative study of religions have a depth which is not usually seen for what it is. *The decision for Law and Gospel is already implicit in the attitude we take to these questions* (pp. 20-21, emphasis added).

Equally grave consequences flow from the triumph of 'early catholicism', and our perception of it, despite its laudable anti-enthusiastic mission: 'We can only make a just estimate' of 'early catholicism' from the standpoint of 'the antithesis between *theologia crucis* and *theologia gloriae* and, in so doing, raise the central problem of all Christian proclamation' (p. 22). Once again, the history of religions, Christian origins, and early church history play out before our eyes the Reformation, and diversity is protected not 'for its own sake' but so that we might all see clearly the true victor (then and now).[50]

Käsemann takes these reflections further in his 'Thoughts on the Present Controversy about Scriptural Interpretation'.[51] This 'present controversy' is apparently being pitched by a rather vocal party to the conflict as being a new 'Church Struggle' over Scripture, waged by the faithful against an unbelieving radical criticism. But Käsemann recalls attention to *the* 'Church Struggle' in claiming that, on the contrary, his own sort of criticism serves the church.

> Herein lies the continuity with what we were doing from 1933 to 1945. If you will allow me a personal word: for fifteen years I was simply the pastor of my congregation, nor did I want to be anything else. When I look back on that time, I cannot escape the conclusion that the Church Struggle scarcely led us a single step forward out of our defensive posture into the freedom of an attacking position. I cannot acknowledge as an authentic partner in dialogue anyone who does not feel deep sorrow and concern when he thinks about this. It was this anxiety which led me to take up theological work again, this time in the form of historical criticism (p. 276).

50. To see how Käsemann presents this perspective to an ecumenical assembly, see 'Unity and Multiplicity in the New Testament Doctrine of the Church', in *New Testament Questions*, pp. 252-59, which weaves together many (most, even) of the various themes we have touched on from Käsemann. Here the critical perspective of Käsemann's *theologia crucis* is gently but uncompromisingly reaffirmed and, once again, diversity is acknowledged along with the confident assurance that the cross discerns the spirits. (Contrast this with, as Käsemann himself might say, the altogether too 'nice' a picture rendered by J.D.G. Dunn in his appeal to Käsemann's assertion that the canon is the basis of multiplicity [*Unity and Diversity in the New Testament* (London: SCM/Philadelphia: Trinity, 2nd edn, 1990), p. 376], which gives an irenic, ecumenical, and pluralist sense to Käsemann's quite different point. Dunn refers to Käsemann's 'The Canon of the New Testament and the Unity of the Church', (*Essays*, pp. 95-107), but see especially pp. 103-107 as to why Käsemann cannot be read in this way, for to stop here is just what he opposes.)

51. Käsemann, *New Testament Questions*, pp. 260-85.

Käsemann puts the 'present controversy' in his own quite different terms: a distant Bible is being illicitly brought near by arbitrary pious interpretation. In such a struggle, criticism is not the enemy, but the only hope. In spelling out in his own terms the contours of this controversy, Käsemann reveals the intertwinement of what might be called the 'apocalyptic principle' with the 'Protestant principle', as worked out with reference both to hermeneutics and mission.

The real culprit in this controversy is that middle-class Pietism whose own inexorable decline sets it looking for a 'scapegoat' and whose uncritical 'biblicism' is a renunciation of 'the true Reformation succession' (pp. 266, 268):

> The Bible is a document which embraces a thousand-year-long history and was concluded eighteen hundred years ago. How can the individual Christian overcome the historical distance which separates him from such a document? How can he comprehend the historical contexts of every page and every passage in his Bible, how can he master its contradictions? In this situation is the Scripture not bound to be regarded as one single enormous book of random texts and the Holy Spirit as the means of historical knowledge and the power which enables historical gaps to be bridged? But is this a true description of the function of Bible and Holy Spirit according to the confessional documents of the Reformation (p. 269)?

Käsemann is dubious that an appeal to the illumination of the Spirit is a way out here—witness 'the sects' (p. 269).

> It would certainly be a rewarding exercise to devote one visitation entirely to eliciting the theological context of the Sunday sermons and the weekday Bible studies and fellowship meetings. We should establish the existence of a more than Babylonian confusion of voices but at the same time we should arrive at a common point of departure and a common denominator for these voices: wherever the canon in its totality is accepted as the Word of God and biblicism reigns, the personal piety of the individual will turn the scale. But is the devout man the key to the interpretation of Scripture? If this were really the position, at least there would be no need to mount a campaign against historical criticism. The truth is, that we should then be faced not by what is felt to be an arbitrary and unbelieving assault on God's gift of salvation, but by an arbitrariness confined to the pious (p. 269).

'For the most part, the only possible alternative to the scientific method is violence done by the devout' (p. 269). But what is the alternative to a bourgeois, individualistic, pietistic interpretation?

Käsemann wishes, he says, 'to show that a theology determined by historical criticism, which is the kind of theology I represent, is not necessarily bound to lack responsibility over against the community' (p. 261). For when the community comes to stand over the Word, it stands in need of radical critique, and can hardly legitimately protest—this is the principle of the Reformation. And the 'faith' of such a community is in truth superstition.

> In evangelical thought we know no sacred times, places, persons, institutions to which the Word could be inseparably bound and on the basis of which it could be handed on and authenticated. On the contrary, with Abraham, with the people of the wilderness, with the prophets and apocalyptists of the old Covenant, with Jesus and his disciples we live in a continual condition of exodus, for ever being called from traditional ties and established camps out onto the road of promise (p. 262).

The 'characteristic Reformation approach to the understanding of Scripture' is a critical one (p. 264).

> Anyone who is still prepared to learn from the Reformation must recognize that knowledge of the Gospel can never be gained and maintained otherwise than critically...Thus Paul summons his hearers...to exercise a critical judgment on prophecy or, as we should say, preaching[;] he calls the power of discrimination between spirits a gift of grace, and he himself exercised this gift by waging a life-long battle against legalism and enthusiasm as the two great adversaries of the Gospel. To sum up: the Gospel begets the critical faculty and creates the critical community, whereas the absence of criticism is the sign of spiritual impoverishment and deprivation...To be critical means: to have criteria. When we enquire about the correct criteria for Scriptural interpretation, we face what in technical language is called the problem of hermeneutics. When today ecclesiastical circles become disturbed because they believe the authority of Scripture to be threatened, this is only taking up over a wider field and at a different level the controversy about the hermeneutical problem which has already been going on for a long time in academic theology (pp. 264-65).

A return to the critical insights of the Reformation is urgently required. 'What does this mean when we apply it to the question of scriptural interpretation' (p. 267)? 'Let me formulate it in such a way as to start out form the decisive point: the Reformation did in fact recognize the Gospel as an energy of criticism over against the world of the religious man—that is, the piety of the devout—and drew conclusions from this in regard to the canon also', interpreting the Old Testament by these lights (p. 267). The Lutheran Law/Gospel distinction rests on solid foundations: 'In dealing with the problem of interpretation, I am bound to argue as an exegete who is keeping his eye on the primary fundamental consideration of hermeneutics in the New Testament itself: the Pauline distinction of *pneuma* and *gramma*' (p. 270). This is not an idealistic 'internal/external' distinction.

> On the basis of the antithesis [between 'letter' and 'spirit'] we may make this formulation: *gramma* is 'Scripture' isolated from the Spirit. The Jews value just that blind obedience which does not ask questions but follows the ordinance for God's sake, even when the human being in question no longer has any understanding of the will which is manifesting itself in the ordinance. Against this, the New Testament conceives of open-eyed obedience as the attitude of the child who knows the father's heart and will and can therefore act out of love. Thus *pneuma* is for Paul...the energy of the eschatological new covenant (2 Cor. 3); it alone can produce the circumcision of the heart (Rom. 2.29) and it alone lies at the root of Christian obedience. Summing up, we can say that *pneuma* is for Paul the divine power which conveys the righteousness of faith and therefore stands in opposition to the law of the old Mosaic covenant (p. 270).[52]

Pietistic interpretation is—in what one suspects is among Käsemann's severest insults—'Jewish hermeneutics', and is to hermeneutics what legalism is to soteriology. The 'justification of the ungodly' is the critical principle which corresponds to the 'spirit' as against the 'letter':

> Paul does not leave the reader of the Bible to his own devices, but says to him that Scripture demands to be interpreted in the light of a specific presupposition and of a specific goal. *Pneuma* and *gramma* are the two mutually exclusive possible ways both of Christian life in general and of the understanding of Scripture in particular. The Scripture becomes *gramma* when it fails to be illuminated by the power which creates the righteousness of faith and is understood instead, as the Law was understood by the Jews, to be a call to a piety of merit and achievement. The Bible is therefore for Paul in no way, in itself and apart from its use,

---

52. Käsemann notes here that Paul's 'letter and spirit' distinction demands a lecture to itself, which he actually provides in 'The Spirit and the Letter', *Perspectives*, pp. 138-66: Paul, 'for the first time in Christian history, developed an approach to a theological hermeneutic' (p. 138). See also Käsemann's *Commentary on Romans*, pp. 74-77 (on Rom. 2.29) and pp. 284-88 (on Rom. 10.5-13): 'We stand here at the commencement of a theologically reflected Christian hermeneutics' (p. 287; these pages from Käsemann's commentary are regarded by Wright as 'a good passage to study closely if one wishes to make a start in understanding the writer and his thought' ['New Tübingen School?', p. 12], forming 'as clear a summary of what Käsemann is trying to say as one is likely to come across in his writings' [Wright, Review, pp. 61-62]).

> Gospel. But it can become Gospel, when, and in so far as, it is rightly
> interpreted. This happens when we listen to it obediently in its capacity as
> the proclamation of the righteousness which is by faith and which is the
> criterion for discriminating among the spirits (p. 271).

The results of this powerful critical principle are far-reaching: *'Thus the
door is barred to every form of arbitrary interpretation which enthusiasm can beget. It is not permissible to read into Scripture what we
should like to be there'* (p. 271, emphasis added). 'Nothing is "Spirit"
which does not set us within the righteousness of faith, i.e. the
justification of the ungodly' (p. 271).

> The Gospel does not establish a new religion for those who want to be
> pious, but salvation for the ungodly; and Christians are not pious people
> resting safely on grace but ungodly people standing under grace. No one
> who has not learnt this lesson has any claim to make judgments in the
> name of faith and the Christian community about Scripture and the right
> interpretation of it (p. 272).

How does radical historical criticism relate to this Reformation critical
principle? Historical criticism reveals the distance and diversity of the
Bible, on which in turn this principle goes to work: 'the Bible does not
speak directly to our present situation as if the two thousand years in
between did not exist', but rather it 'is essentially an historical
document'; 'the road trodden by [early] Christianity leads from Jesus to
early catholicism', and 'the canon as such [that is, as uncriticized] is the
foundation not of the unity but of the diversity of the Christian churches.
Every man can find something in it to square with his own dogmatic
theology' (pp. 273-75). 'In the matter of the controversy about the
Bible, let the community be clearly aware of the context in which it has
been set. That there are pseudonymous writings in the Bible, more non-
apostolic than apostolic, even early catholic dogma, and that therefore
there is and must be historical criticism of the Bible...' (p. 277). 'For the
Law is not the Gospel, Moses is not Jesus, James is not Paul, II Peter is
not the first beatitude, and the Bible is no substitute for God' (p. 277).

Mission relates to hermeneutics as practice does to theory: 'The
question of interpretation of Scripture...must be authenticated by
standing up to the test of practice. And the critical principle is the same'
(p. 278). 'It is disturbing to see how little our congregations have any
concern for international politics' (p. 278). 'The problem of our mission
does not only come alive when we look at what is world-wide or far off.
It arises also out of our own everyday life' (p. 279).

This, then, is the point on which all the things I have been talking about converge: the problem of the relationship of Gospel, canon and interpretation, of theology and congregational piety. If the Bible has anything to say to the realities of our own time, if the interpretation of Scripture must by critical necessity be orientated around one central point and if the Christian congregation is willing and able to do some real theological thinking about this, then what is at issue—not just theoretically but practically—is this: Jesus did not come primarily and solely to the religious. The central message of the Bible is that God deals always, indeed exclusively, with the godless, because before him no man is pious and just (p. 282).

And what does this mean, not just theoretically but practically?

The piety of a congregation which may be prepared to convert the godless but is neither willing nor able to live with them is perhaps showing a greater contempt for its Lord than a theology which pursues its academic discipline according to its own logic and in so doing maintains contact with its environment in space and time. On the other hand, a theology whose vocation and operation is confined to the ghetto is only of interest to a fat, complacent community, incapable of penitence. If anyone doesn't like this, he will have to lump it. This is a simple problem of drawing the correct conclusion (p. 283).

Some years later, but in a similar—only even more highly charged—mood, Käsemann declares:

In actuality, technology and armament serve the retention of possessions, the amassing of capital, and the exploitation of nature and dependent peoples...Everyone who calls the least his own lives from the sweat, hunger, torture, and murder of those who must defend themselves in revolutionary fashion if their children are to grow up with human dignity. In this world-wide class struggle, Christianity can only side with the revolutionaries, because it sides with humanity. If it does not, then it must belong to the exploiters. It must do so out of love as well as for the sake of reason and a sense for reality.[53]

Jesus brought freedom and died at the hands of the pious.

They were unable to tolerate the free man. But it is as *the* free man that he is the promise of the earth. Nobody has said this better than Paul who sees the world waiting for the revelation of the glorious freedom of the children

---

53. Cited from Harrisville, 'Crux Sola', p. 258, from a late collection of more popular pieces by Käsemann entitled, tellingly, *Kirchliche Konflikte* (1982), I, pp. 30-31.

of God and goes on soon afterwards to interpret the sighing of the Spirit in our worship as the cry of the children of God for their perfected freedom' (p. 284).[54]

'No perspective could be more apocalyptic'.

I could go on. But this is enough at least to confuse us thoroughly, and the point has been reached where it is possible (and urgently necessary) to organize and systematize what has been covered of Käsemann's 'apocalyptic interpretation'. 'Apocalyptic', according to Käsemann's various discussions of it, is the more or less familiar cluster of eschatological themes and motifs. His incidental remarks bear this out. This conventionality is reflected in such exclamations as (to paraphrase) 'What could be more apocalyptic?' True, Käsemann makes an individual addition, particularly in his direct association of 'apocalyptic' with a theology of the cross, the justification of the ungodly, the ascendancy of the Cosmocrator, and the triumph of the righteousness of God, which Käsemann accomplishes by a history of religions association of 'justification'/'righteousness' with 'apocalyptic'. But here again (as Qumran is the primary source for Käsemann's 'apocalyptic' colouring of 'righteousness'), 'apocalyptic' means simply 'eschatological', indicating a particular *type* of eschatology (imminence, transcendence, the 'two ages'), so that even here convention is observed.[55] Käsemann has simply discovered new ways of putting an ever-obliging interpretative category to even greater use. As for his history of religions means to this end, further attention to this matter is left to his students and followers.[56]

54. See Käsemann's fuller development of this final Pauline note, based on Romans 8, in 'The Cry for Liberty in the Worship of the Church', *Perspectives*, pp. 122-37 (an 'apocalyptic' theme, p. 135); see also Käsemann's *Commentary on Romans* on the same chapter. Incidentally, Käsemann's *Romans* could be put to much more extensive illustrative use than I have chosen, preferring instead his occasional pieces. But see on 1.16-17, 3.21-26, 5.12-21, 8, 9-11. Way, *Lordship*, makes rich use of the commentary (on which itself see pp. 120-21).

55. See *New Testament Questions*, pp. 172-74, 177-79; cf. Käsemann, *Romans*, pp. 29-30.

56. See especially in this regard Peter Stuhlmacher, *Gerechtigkeit Gottes bei Paulus* (FRLANT, 87; Göttingen: Vandenhoeck & Ruprecht, 1965), pp. 145-75, and K. Kertelge, *»Rechtfertigung« bei Paulus* (Neutestamentliche Abhandlungen [NS], 3; Münster: Verlag Aschendorff, 1967), pp. 24-45. What is of interest here is not the corroboration or otherwise of Käsemann's 'apocalyptic' interpretation of 'righteousness', but rather the simple observation that 'apocalyptic' is being used,

Käsemann sets the terms for a protracted Bultmann versus Käsemann debate focused on the issues of 'apocalyptic' and 'the righteousness of God',[57] and he provokes a general renewed interest in the matter of 'apocalyptic'.[58] It is in assessing his use of the notion that it is

entirely conventionally, in the sense of (a particular type of) eschatology, and 'apocalyptic' is found in late Old Testament texts, apocrypha, pseudepigrapha, and Qumran literature.

57. Bultmann's replies to Käsemann, in characteristic style, are concise reaffirmations of his own approach. See his 'ΔΙΚΑΙΟΣΥΝΗ ΘΕΟΥ', *JBL* 83 (1964) 12-16: 'I cannot rightly hold Käsemann's interpretation, and rather I think that, for Paul, the ruling significance of δικ. θεοῦ is that of the gift which God gives to believers, and that the genitive is a genitive of the author' (p. 12); and 'Ist die Apokalyptik die Mutter der christlichen Theologie? Eine Auseinandersetzung mit Ernst Käsemann', in W. Eltester (ed.), *Apophoreta: Festschrift für Ernst Haenchen* (BZNW, 30; Berlin: Töpelmann, 1964), pp. 64-69: as to the claim that 'apocalyptic' is 'the mother of New Testament theology', Bultmann says 'I could agree, if instead of "apocalyptic" I called it "eschatology"' (p. 64)—'eschatology', that is, in Bultmann's sense ('apocalyptic' being futuristic eschatology and imminent expectation). On this whole debate, an insider's crystallization of the salient points is provided by H. Conzelmann, 'Current Problems, pp. 171-86; see the survey offered by H. Hübner, 'Paulusforschung seit 1945. Ein kritischer Literaturbericht', *ANRW* II.25.4 (1987), pp. 2649-840, esp. pp. 2694-709 (on 'justification') and 2749-808 (on 'apocalyptic'). As for the debate over 'justification'/'righteousness', the ground has been covered many times before, and the bibliography will not be repeated here; see Way, *Lordship*, pp. 177-236; a recent monograph on the theme is M.A. Seifrid, *Justification by Faith: The Origin and Development of a Central Pauline Theme* (NovTSup, 68; Leiden: E.J. Brill, 1992). On 'apocalyptic', see the following note.

58. Discussions from the period include (in addition to the Ebeling and Fuchs essays already noted): B. Vawter, '"And He Shall Come Again with Glory": Paul and Christian Apocalyptic', in *Studiorum Paulinorium Congressus Internationalis Catholicus 1961* I (Rome: Pontifical Biblical Institute, 1963), pp. 143-50; D.B. Bronson, 'Paul and Apocalyptic Judaism', *JBL* 83 (1964), pp. 287-92; P. Stuhlmacher, 'Erwägungen zum Problem von Gegenwart und Zukunft in der paulinischen Eschatologie', *ZTK* 64 (1967), pp. 423-50; H.W. Boers, 'Apocalyptic Eschatology in 1 Corinthians 15: An Essay in Contemporary Interpretation', *Int* 21 (1967), pp. 50-65; J. Becker, 'Erwägungen zur apokalyptischen Tradition in der paulinischen Theologie', *EvT* 30 (1970), pp. 593-609; W.G. Rollins, 'The New Testament and Apocalyptic', *NTS* 17 (1970-71), pp. 454-76; E. Lohse, 'Apokalyptik und Christologie', *ZNW* 62 (1971), pp. 48-67; G. Klein, 'Apokalyptische Naherwartung bei Paulus', in H.D. Betz and L. Schottroff (eds.), *Neues Testament und christliche Existenz: Festschrift für Herbert Braun* (Tübingen: Mohr [Paul Siebeck], 1973), pp. 241-62; E. Schüssler Fiorenza, 'Apocalyptic and Gnosis in the Book of Revelation and Paul', *JBL* 92 (1973), pp. 565-81; J. Baumgarten, *Paulus*

possible to come nearer to understanding him.

Some points are now familiar, others stand out as Käsemann's distinctive contribution. 'Apocalyptic' is once more decisive for restoring Paul's thought to a unity (after an 'enthusiastic' criticism has had its hand), or, from another point of view, 'apocalyptic' is decisive for Paul in allowing him to approach his theological task from a coherent centre. Relatedly, Paul's 'dialectic of Christian existence' is transparent against an 'apocalyptic' background. The interpretative questions here concern realization versus expectation and justification versus 'mysticism' or salvation history. An 'apocalyptic' interpretation situates and controls anthropology and restores and qualifies salvation history. It opposes individualism from a corporate and cosmic perspective. It anchors present eschatology in the future. Put differently, from its perspective Christology takes primacy over anthropology and ecclesiology. (Questions of law and parenesis, of new creation, 'new obedience', and resurrection, of charisma, office, and order, of Spirit and freedom, come in here.) 'Apocalyptic' is bound up with a theology of the cross, which opposes a theology of glory/'enthusiasm', and with the justification of the ungodly, which opposes legalism and exclusivism. It is implicated in clarification of mission and universalism. It is somehow, then, an expression of the 'Protestant principle', it is bound up with the lordship of Christ and the righteousness of God. It has hermeneutical and ethical/political dimensions. 'Apocalyptic', like historical criticism and radical politics, gets sucked into the Protestant universe. 'Apocalyptic' is a theological shorthand for virtually every aspect of Käsemann's self-understanding.

If other interpreters have shown themselves to be rather frugal in

---

*und die Apokalyptik: Die Auslegung apokalyptischer Überlieferungen in den echten Paulusbriefen* (WMANT, 44; Neukirchen–Vluyn: Neukirchener Verlag, 1975); H.-H. Schade, *Apokalyptische Christologie bei Paulus: Studien zum Zusammenhang von Christologie und Eschatologie in den Paulusbriefen* (GTA, 18; Göttingen: Vandenhoeck & Ruprecht, 1981); J.M. Court, 'Paul and the Apocalyptic Pattern', in Hooker and Wilson (eds.), *Paul and Paulinism*, pp. 57-66; I.H. Marshall, 'Is Apocalyptic the Mother of Christian Theology?', in G.F. Hawthorne and O. Betz (eds.), *Tradition and Interpretation in the New Testament: Essays in Honor of E. Earle Ellis* (Grand Rapids: Eerdmans, 1987), pp. 33-42. 'Apocalyptic' is a matter of eschatology, and the discussion seeks throughout to access the balance of the pull of the opposite forces of present and future ('apocalyptic') eschatology. (This observation is not meant of itself to be a criticism of the debate or a dismissal of its importance or of the interest of the various interpretative points raised; rather, the agreed general perception as to what 'apocalyptic' is about is the present concern).

squeezing every drop of utility out of 'apocalyptic', Käsemann proves downright miserly. He outdoes them all. This impression is aided by the various discursive layers across which 'apocalyptic' is being successively or alternately (or simultaneously) applied. There is the history of religions dynamic between Jewish 'legalism' and Hellenistic 'enthusiasm', with 'apocalyptic' caught in the middle, and the related Christian origins movement between a legalistic nationalism and a triumphalistic 'enthusiasm', again with 'apocalyptic' in the middle, warding off both, giving way ultimately to 'early catholicism'. Also related is the biblical-theological movement whereby the gospel of the justification of the ungodly is met by 'legalism' and 'enthusiasm', aided against both by 'apocalyptic', and sold out to 'early catholicism' in the latter's decline. On the level of hermeneutical theorizing, 'apocalyptic' becomes the principle of the 'Spirit', of 'new age hermeneutics', as against the 'letter' of 'pious' interpretation; and at the level of church mission (also, or primarily, the ethical and political level), the 'apocalyptic' principle of trial, tribulation, and travail, of exodus, pilgrimage, and protest confronts, again, a mission taken up with the piety of the pious. It is the same dynamic at each level, in a form suited to that particular discourse, and the role of 'apocalyptic' is analogous throughout. (Käsemann is a systematist in all but name.) Something like demythologization is tacitly occurring in varying senses and degrees in order to put 'apocalyptic' to these several uses (though Käsemann is not concerned to make 'demythologization' his focus).[59] These levels are by no means always kept separate, and cutting across them all is the history/theology question—that is, we are often unsure as to which level we are on and whether 'history' or 'theology' would best capture what we are witnessing. (Consider the ambiguity of such interpretative questions as the 'continuity versus discontinuity' of early Christianity with Jesus, with Judaism, and so forth: is this Christian origins or biblical theology? However, this ambiguity is by no means peculiar to Käsemann.)

I am taking Käsemann as paradigmatic for the use of 'apocalyptic' as an interpretative category. This may seem odd, as Käsemann is an ecstatic witness on anyone's view. But he serves by exaggeration to highlight certain fundamental features of 'apocalyptic interpretation' which I regard as generic and endemic (hence the sustained attention to his interpretative programme).

---

59. For an interesting discussion of demythologizing and Käsemann, see Riches, *Review*, pp. 569-74.

One very basic sense in which Käsemann is paradigmatic for 'apocalyptic interpretation' is in his very use of 'apocalyptic' as a theological shorthand. My claim is that, typically, use of this interpretative category differs only in degree, not in kind, from what we see in Käsemann. Just as Paul has that power over his interpreters whereby he moulds and makes them in his own image (that is a charitable way of putting what might appear better put the other way round), so 'apocalyptic' seems able to draw an interpreter's needs and desires onto and into itself. The next question is likely to be, simply, Why? Why would Käsemann, why would *anyone*, call what so plainly has all the marks of theology, history? Is there not some clearer and more direct way of reaching the concerns in question? The problem, I suspect, lies with the critical ethos (as I go on below to spell out further). Theological questions, if they are to be aired at all, must find some covert means of taking on historical form. 'Apocalyptic', like a set of Russian dolls, is a 'historical' shell concealing ever deepening layers of theological concern. This single, magical word is capable of conjuring up singlehandedly the most fearsome host of associations. The result is a biblical criticism which does 'history' by playing with theological picture-cards.[60]

Related to this first sense in which Käsemann is paradigmatic is a second, which has to do—to put it bluntly—with Käsemann's subversion of his hermeneutical practice by his hermeneutical theory (and vice versa).[61] Again, the hermeneutical point is not unrelated to the point

60. That Käsemann could do a great deal with a few key terms and phrases should by now be evident; indeed, he seems to have made something of a career out of operating in such impressionistic, theological shorthand terms. Käsemann was able to move from an early emphasis on gnosticism and Hellenism and on Paul's participatory themes to a later emphasis on Jewish 'apocalyptic' and on the theme of justification (see Way, *Lordship*, pp. 16-18, 29-36, 119-31, 277-79). While maintaining a largely consistent and continuous perspective on Paul's theology, revealing just how plastic such constructions are in his hands—in other words, Käsemann could stretch the terms of the polar opposite extremes in interpreting Paul (as according to his own presentation) to fit the same conception of Paul's thought.

61. So polemical is Käsemann that he easily sets his reader (or *this* reader, at least) to looking for points of tension or self-subversion, which, at any rate, with repeated reading, seem to leap out at one: thus the piety of the *im*pious reaches outrageous proportions, and one senses a certain settling in to a perpetual state of exodus. Or we might say that, so sharp is the theological tension and so fine the theological balance of what Käsemann is always driving at—so fragile the conditions of perpetual protest, recurrent reform—that, by nature, the moment it is grasped it is in danger of becoming that which it despises (as when, say, one becomes proud of one's humility).

about the use of 'apocalyptic'. In other words, Käsemann's subversion
of history by theology, when read against his stated ideals and achievements, already involves the reader in hermeneutics. For 'apocalyptic',
according to Käsemann's own self-presentation, is rescued from the
oblivion brought on by theological embarrassment by an act of historical
daring. This is becoming a tiresomely familiar refrain, except that, with
Käsemann, it is becoming less and less believable. The immediate setting
of his subversion—unsurprisingly for Käsemann, and, I should say,
characteristically for many—is polemics. Foremost here is the polemic
against Pietism and the pious (who raise Käsemann's ire like no others).
Against their manner of forcing their way with scripture, stooping even
to capitalize on the uncertainties that fashionably obtain as to the status
of historical interpretation, Käsemann re-asserts the 'passion for reality,
that peculiar driving force of the historian' and of 'the indirect claim of
truth from within reality' which 'increasingly loses the power by which
it limits the individual and obligates to the whole'—all this despite
Käsemann's denunciation of a positivistic historicism. But what lurks
beneath that simple appeal to historical 'reality'? (Might this not be in
part what lies behind Barth's query to Käsemann, cited at the head of
the present chapter?) But polemics drive him thus. Faith and tradition
are not 'labour-saving devices', nor may an affirmation of scripture as
God's word 'be mistaken for a methodological principle'. 'Scripture is
essentially a document of the past before it is anything else', and the
Holy Spirit is not 'the means to historical knowledge' and 'the power
which enables historical gaps to be bridged'. This Käsemann asserts
against pietism. But when Käsemann is found to be employing a theological-critical principle derived from the Gospel and appealing to the
Lutheran and Pauline conception whereby this critical principle is a
revealed one—is the divine power of the Spirit—so that the interpreter
is not 'left to his own devices' but rather 'Scripture demands to be
interpreted' after the principle of the justification of the ungodly, and
when Käsemann presupposes that the Bible 'has something to say to the
realities of our time' and speaks of 'the central message of the Bible'
and of a theological criticism 'casting its shadow over historical
criticism', what is to prevent us from regarding Käsemann as operating
throughout from a posture of faith and within an interpretative tradition
(call these 'labour-saving devices' or 'methodological principles' or
whatever)? As for scripture being for Käsemann first of all a document
of the past, a brute artefact, an object before a subject, this is at best true

only in that he wishes to assert that scripture's own voice is released only through the proper objectifying procedures, theologically and historically. For according to Käsemann's tradition—whose roots reach back to Luther and the Reformation (and to, as he would wish us to add, Paul) and whose motivations nearer to hand are those of Barth's biblical theology and Bultmann's wedding of historical and theological criticism—scripture has a prior claim on its hearer, and that is a point of faith which cannot be wished away or methodically reduced. Käsemann's historical criticism, coming so long after Luther, can hardly set out to discover, but only goes forth in confirmation of the theological principles Käsemann shares with the latter.

The caprice of arbitrary individual interpretation, which sanctions the illegitimacy of 'the pious' and 'the sects', exercises Käsemann no end. He determines to be different. So what is bigger than the individual but smaller than tradition? Criticism and science, of course. Käsemann is subject, in his hermeneutical theorizing and polemicizing, to a double constraint, which stands behind his self-subversion. His Protestant heritage (the un-tradition tradition), asserting that the Word of Scripture must be seen to stand over Church and tradition (which is to say, interpretation—or, at least, critical interpretation—transcends history), strongly resists and opposes a hermeneutics of tradition. One can hear, still ringing in Käsemann's ears, the Roman Catholic charge that Protestantism is itself a sect born of arbitrary individual interpretation, and Käsemann's rant against the 'pious' does double-duty against Catholic interpretation (triple-duty, actually, counting 'Jewish' interpretation). But it is not only the Reformation that constrains Käsemann. He is captive to an image of Science which it is only just barely a caricature to characterize as 'if it serves your ends, it is not science' (where the emphasis falls on 'your'). Science is a discipline of pure facts, criticism an inquiry purged of self-will. The Enlightenment opposition of reason and will, science and commitment, argument and rhetoric, fact and value is operative here. This, of course, is what lies behind that critical hagiography which delights in telling how 'apocalyptic' has been forever resisted out of fear and trembling but then shrinks back (by some lack of courage?) from recounting how it is affirmed out of need and desire on some level or other. Such an edifying tale can only owe what effect it has to rhetoric, for it would seem plain enough, once the emotive formation has been seen through, that, to turn to Käsemann's version of the story, if pietism's criticism is to be discounted because it confirms pietism and serves pietism's ends, then Käsemann's *own* criticism (not to speak of anyone else's) will now stand in a rather exposed position, raising the question as to why the same rule does not apply. In other words, the tacit formulation 'science versus commitment' does not serve him well, for, when it is crystallized in such lines as 'historical criticism will insist that it is the texts themselves that are decisive, not an image of Paul which we find desirable',[62] one might almost suspect a joke.

What sets Käsemann apart is that *he* is *critical*. He is very uncritical of criticism, however. He calls upon it in the customary way, with familiar results: '*You* interpret in an arbitrary, biased, prejudiced way, while *I* am critical, and the critical principle which saves me from your arbitrariness is *the Bible's own*'. This is not the full picture though. For, of course, for Käsemann there is both theological and historical criticism. Theological criticism undercuts pietism theologically, whereas historical criticism does so methodologically, overcoming arbitrariness by an objective method. The theological-critical principle of Law/Gospel or letter/Spirit is scripture's own, the historical-critical method is reality's own. The latter secures the former. The interpretative question is constantly being thrown back onto the interpreter in ways that Käsemann does not acknowledge. What does it mean to say that 'the texts themselves' are decisive? That 'Scripture demands' to be interpreted by a theology of the cross? That such is the 'central message of the Bible'? Käsemann speaks of 'historically determined theology', but what we want to know about is 'theologically determined history'—of the sort that seems habitually to accompany talk of 'apocalyptic' in spite of itself—a subject Käsemann is understandably not eager to take up. Käsemann does not seem to reflect much on the connection he has assumed between radical Lutheran criticism and radical historical criticism. How is it that the latter inexorably serves the former? It is not, we may assume, simply fortuitous for Käsemann. On the matter of theological criticism, we might expect Käsemann to affirm something like interpretation from within faith and tradition. Instead, even here we find that Käsemann, like Paul, has 'listened obediently' to Scripture, grasped its true voice, and become its prophet, its mouthpiece. As for historical criticism, getting *that* story straight is apparently a completely unproblematic matter (as long as one proceeds scientifically). Historical criticism cannot help helping theological criticism. For both put us in

---

62. Cited at the head of this chapter.

touch with reality. This is why it hardly occurs to Käsemann that the connection he has assumed might be problematic—it just will not be, for anyone with eyes to see.

To champion science and criticism is all well and good, until one reflects on the implications of their possibly being, not self-operative and self-authenticating (autonomous, that is, and standing above history), but tools, or weapons, in the hands of human beings, with all that this entails. It is here that our 'problems', if such they are, begin. Has Käsemann banished arbitrariness? Or have his acts of self-dispossession only driven self-will underground to multiply beyond his view, then to return with a vengeance, with the result that the latter state is worse than the first? Is criticism not always leading somewhere? Is it not always relevant to inquire of criticism as to where it is leading, and is not the reply 'to the truth' always only to beg all the important questions? (This is, ultimately, to fail to take seriously the hermeneutical questions, a resurfacing of hermeneutical antitheoreticism.) Käsemann's minute and relentless search for the fragile early environment in which the delicate flower of the Gospel could thrive in perpetual Reformation, his close scrutiny of 'the beginnings' with an eye for every detail by which *we* might be instructed, is a two-edged sword which stands in service of his simultaneous challenge to and radicalization of Protestantism. To find, then, that Käsemann's criticism is leading somewhere is not of itself to discount it. But then, hermeneutically, that is just the point.

Hermeneutically, we must decide whether Käsemann represents merely a failure of execution, leaving the objectivist ideals intact (in which case the lesson would be that we must work even harder than we might have thought to obtain the coveted objectivity, given that the best and the brightest have fallen woefully short), or whether the interpretative act has been fundamentally misdescribed according to such ideals and stands, then, in need of being fundamentally rethought and reconceptualized (and we might as well go ahead and say that we are trying to plant the seed of doubt which asks whether the motivation for such objectivist ideals—the ideal of interpretative *fixity*—is not always bound up with polemics and power-play, with ideology and control). Here we begin to raise the question as to whether the story which criticism tells about itself, filtering out of its account all that concerns ideology as being irrelevant, is not itself fully ideological.

At any rate, Käsemann's subversion of his critical and interpretative practice by his theory and polemics, arising from both theological and methodological (and cultural and ideological) motivations, and the ironic pride invested in 'apocalyptic' as the crowning achievement of his objectivist scientific method, can be taken as paradigmatic for 'apocalyptic interpretation'. It is difficult to picture a more engaged critic than Käsemann. Yet, in an uncanny and frustrating turn, he distances his criticism from any hint of the taint of such engagement. Käsemann, like the others, develops a broad interpretative perspective through which to read Paul and 'apocalyptic'; but once more objectivism intrudes. Käsemann's voice, breaking into the many polemical struggles which he takes up, is not *Käsemann's* voice, speaking from within his community and tradition, but is rather the voice of science, of method, of reality, a disembodied voice (a notion from which Käsemann's anthropology might have protected him) he has heard and obeyed and simply passed along. Only a heavy ideological mortgage, of the sort I have tried to suggest, could stand behind Käsemann's calling his 'apocalyptic' interpretation 'history of religions'.[63]

Our dealings with the various interpreters may be viewed as following a dialectical flow. The dialectic has begun even before we commence, as we approach Schweitzer over against his status as an icon in the temple of biblical criticism. As we have come to understand him, so the perception of those prior expectations shifts and Schweitzer's place in a larger story emerges. A grasp of Schweitzer then becomes the vital pre-possession for our turn to Dodd, Bultmann, and Cullmann (who must also all be read to a degree against their reputations), who, in turn, in their biblical-theological and hermeneutical theory and practice, cast light back on Schweitzer, further revealing and clarifying where he, too, is bound up in this hermeneutical dialogue. All four prepare the way for our approach to Käsemann (who, again, has his reputation), and Käsemann, in his very strenuousness, casts light forward *and* backward, highlighting features of the interpretative dialogue, both in terms of the use of 'apocalyptic' and in terms of the accompanying hermeneutical self-understanding.[64] Thus, all talk of an 'apocalyptic renaissance' aside,

63. Although Way writes with a stated interest in Käsemann's hermeneutics (see *Lordship*, pp. 15-19), his study, for all its admirable thoroughness, is on this point curiously bland considering the one of whom it treats. If I represent something of the other extreme in attending to the polemical and ideological contours of Käsemann's interpretation of Paul, this is fitting on balance.

64. One facet of the discussion of 'apocalyptic' which Käsemann allows to emerge particularly clearly is its political side. For our earlier interpreters, however,

it is clear, turning to Käsemann from Schweitzer, Dodd, Bultmann, and Cullmann, that Käsemann belongs to the very story we have been following, the story of historical and hermeneutical consciousness, of faith and criticism, Reformation and modern. The search for a non-arbitrary objectivist critical principle goes on, this time vouchsafed methodologically in a radical historical criticism which dovetails nicely with a radical Lutheran theological criticism. 'Apocalyptic', the consummate double agent, moves effortlessly between the two, passing unobserved.

Of course, Käsemann has made no such grand claims for his 'apocalyptic' interpretation as to dub it a 'renaissance'. This is left to his admirers. But he *has* written his own publicity releases in framing his approach as a heroic historical overcoming of theological cowardice. Criticism, ever jealous of its own public face, picks up these heroic and celebratory tones, and at any rate does not rush in to correct the picture.[65] (In raising the hope, as I did above at the close of the last

especially where liberalism/*Kulturprotestantismus* hovers in the background, the matter has never been very far from political. And the strategy is always available to a radical political stance to say that, even where the dialogue has not been overtly political but only 'academic', this itself is a political legitimation of the status quo.

65. K. Koch, *Rediscovery*, raises the question of 'apocalyptic' in the context of a reassertion of the rights of history in theology (against a perceived climate of opinion which regards history as a spent force). For Koch, the matter of 'apocalyptic' witnesses to the fact that much more *history* needs to be done, that a 'deeper historical consciousness' is needed (p. 11; see pp. 9-12). Käsemann, along with Pannenberg, has a special place in the discussion as having given rise to the 'renaissance' of 'apocalyptic'—though Koch raises the question of 'whether it is really historical apocalyptic which is looming up so suddenly at the centre of theological thinking', or whether perhaps 'certain contemporary ideas are being projected back and fathered upon the apocalyptic writers' (p. 15; see pp. 13-17). Still, Käsemann is applauded (pp. 75-85), though Koch raises a mild question mark about Käsemann's laxity concerning the history of religions and the primary texts (p. 78). But Koch is protective of Käsemann, it seems, out of a barely contained enthusiasm over the latter's upsetting of the Bultmann school, which greets Käsemann with 'a storm of protest. The onlooker is bound to suppose that here it is the significance of the New Testament words for the present that are decisive, rather than historical observations. Anyone who finds a futurist eschatology impossible today does not want to find one in the New Testament either, at least not exclusively. Anyone who is prevented by their historical sense from thinking in terms of salvation history finds it difficult to allow the New Testament writers to think in these terms either' (pp. 83-84; see also pp. 124-26). Thus Käsemann is not implicated in the illicit mixing up of history and theology that Koch decries. The long-standing modern search for the absoluteness of Christianity stands, for Koch, unacknowledged at the centre of the debate over

chapter, that a turn to this 'renaissance' would finally break through to fundamental questioning, I have maliciously misled the reader, but with a ruse not mine, but criticism's own.) The theological dimensions of Käsemann's appropriation of 'apocalyptic' have become too many and too grand to ignore. Käsemann's combination of large claims for and small misgivings over 'apocalyptic' throws up the first belated question marks among his respondents.[66] (Only in this sense, then, with

'apocalyptic' in biblical criticism, a search typically foisted onto the historical texts contrary to the historical facts, which are forced 'into a dogmatic bed of Procrustes' (p. 128; see pp. 126-27). Koch concludes not with a dismissal of this search, but with a redirection of it which takes its cue from none other than these 'renaissance' scholars of 'apocalyptic', Käsemann and Pannenberg, whereby, Koch believes, an objective and non-arbitrary means of address for the historical and theological questions may be obtained (pp. 127-31). (Tupper, 'Revival', is similarly celebratory of the 'renaissance'.)

66. See especially H.D. Betz, 'On the Problem of the Religio-Historical Understanding of Apocalypticism', *JTC* 6 (1969), pp. 134-56 ('Zum Problem des religionsgeschichtlichen Verständnisses der Apokalyptik', *ZTK* 63 [1966], pp. 391-409); *idem*, 'The Concept of Apocalyptic in the Theology of the Pannenberg Group', *JTC* 6 (1969), pp. 192-207 ('Das Verständnis der Apokalyptik in der Theologie der Pannenberg-Gruppe', *ZTK* 65 [1968], pp. 257-70); *JTC* 6, ed. R.W. Funk, entitled *Apocalypticism*, includes Käsemann's 'Beginnings' and 'Primitive Christian Apocalyptic', as well as responses by Ebeling and Fuchs and the two essays by Betz mentioned above; see also in this volume R.W. Funk, 'Apocalyptic as an Historical and Theological Problem in Current New Testament Scholarship': 'In what respects are the historical and theological aspects of the problem of apocalyptic intertwined in current New Testament scholarship? What firm historical bases have been established from which to face the theological issue realistically, and what conceptual hostages are likely to be given to any examination of the historical problem' [p. 175]. He concludes [p. 191]: 'For the historian is free to disillusion only when he himself is free from the tyranny of what everybody takes as self-evident'.) Betz's response to the renewed attention lavished on 'apocalyptic' by Käsemann and Pannenberg is to note the calls for clarification made by Ebeling and G. von Rad ('Problem', pp. 134-35), and he cites (p. 135) a couple of apposite remarks of the latter (from the 4th Ger. edn of his *Theologie des Alten Testaments*, 1965, pp. 330, 315): 'This, however, seems to be clear: our concept of apocalypticism urgently needs a critical revision, since its sweeping use as a definition of a literary as well as a theological phenomenon has become a problem'. 'Whoever uses the term apocalypticism ought to be aware of the fact that we have not yet succeeded in defining it in a satisfactory way'. Betz by no means makes a complete departure from familiar views here, but his questioning of the coherence and propriety of 'apocalyptic' as typically understood and of its treatment as an inner-Jewish, inter-biblical phenomenon points to basic problem areas (see pp. 134-39, 154-56). Betz's history of religions attempt to locate 'apocalyptic' in the

Käsemann—not unlike Schweitzer on the hermeneutical point—as an unwitting catalyst, is it possible to speak of his marking an interpretative breakthrough.) In general terms, this questioning may be regarded as beginning to cast doubt on the coherence and propriety of much talk of 'apocalyptic' (either in defence or rejection of it) and the biblical-theological frame of much of the discussion (this is said in prospect of the discussion in the next chapter).

Butterfield has it that 'The study of the past with one eye, so to speak, upon the present is the source of all sins and sophistries in history'.[67] If this is so, our interpreters are grievous sinners one and all. How long are they to be left languishing in purgatory (to which, it is true, they have condemned themselves, as they tend to agree with Butterfield's reckoning), and how many more will be consigned to their place (will we soon be joining them?), before we redeem our sinners by simply reversing the judgment of Butterfield? Then a climate might be created where it is no insult (or at least not necessarily one) to call an interpreter

wider Greco-Roman world as part of Hellenistic syncretism points to the encyclo-paedic interests of the apocalyptic literature in the lore in which it trades—this amounts to an implicit judgment on the arbitrary narrowing of the interests witnessed in the literature for revealed knowledge to matters of revealed eschatology. In his critique of the 'Pannenberg group', Betz highlights the diversity of the apocalyptic material and its connections with Jewish mysticism ('Pannenberg Group', p. 200). 'In his desire to gain knowledge the apocalypticist, apart from history, turns to the entire field of the ancient study of natural phenomena, especially to astronomy, astrology, demonology, psychology, botany, and pharmacy' (p. 201). A simplistic characterization of Jesus or Paul as 'apocalyptic', concludes Betz, is inadequate. Rollins ('The New Testament and Apocalyptic') follows Betz in questioning the coherence of unqualified appeals to 'apocalyptic', as the latter is a more diverse phenomenon than such would allow and is in need of social-historical clarification (Rollins's account of which still comes off sounding rather theological; see pp. 458-64). Baumgarten (*Paulus*, pp. 9-16) takes the point of Betz (pp. 14-15) and others about the literary and historical problems associated with the location of some 'essence' of 'apocalyptic', and so he frames his interest in early Christian 'apocalyptic' as 'futuristic eschatology' as a 'working hypothesis' (p. 16). What concerns Baumgarten is the Bultmann/Käsemann debate of 'Kosmologie oder Anthropologie' (pp. 1-7), and Baumgarten wishes to follow Bultmann in seeing in Paul a certain 'demythologization', or 'deapocalypticization', or 'decosmologization' of 'apocalyptic' in the direction of a 'present' eschatology while taking Käsemann's anti-individualistic point (pp. 227-43).

67. H. Butterfield, cited from A. Marwick, *The Nature of History* (London: Macmillan, 3rd edn, 1989), 'Appendix: Some Aphorisms', p. 387.

a 'new Paul'—to say, that is, that Paul mirrors that interpreter's deepest theological interests, reflecting back an image indistinguishable from the interpreter's own. It will not be an insult to say that, if 'science' is what it says it is, our interpreters are about something else. For Käsemann, quite against the canons of some purist 'science', is highly enthusiastic (though the pun is atrocious) about his 'apocalyptic' Paul. What is to prevent us from saying that his very greatness lies just in that whereby, in the name of commitment, he offends most greatly against 'science'? Is not such 'science' the 'letter' as against Käsemann's true 'spirit'? Would we even still be talking about Käsemann if he 'lived up to' the dry 'science' of his own ideal?

Even if we are having none of this, we may at least say that, after Käsemann, no one will be able to speak of 'apocalyptic' unreflectively (a truth that must rank right up there with the sun coming up tomorrow and the roundishness of the earth).

Chapter 4

## 'APOCALYPTIC' INTERPRETATION AND INTERPRETING
## 'APOCALYPTIC': A CRITIQUE

[O]nly a consistent apocalyptic interpretation of Paul's thought is able to demonstrate its fundamental coherence...Apocalyptic is not a peripheral curiosity for Paul but the central climate and focus of his thought, as it was for most early Christian thinkers...The apocalyptic world view is the fundamental carrier of Paul's thought. (J.C. Beker, *Paul The Apostle*, pp. 143, 144, 181.)

The reader has been misled again. Several years on from Käsemann, and with all the manner of one suggesting something new, it is confidently declared that Paul is an 'apocalyptic' thinker—and that no other means of regarding him will preserve his reputation as a 'thinker' at all. 'My emphasis on Paul's christological apocalyptic', asserts J. Christiaan Beker, 'involves a radical shift in traditional conceptions of Paul's theology'.[1] Others—prominently Käsemann—have brought 'apocalyptic' back before our attention. 'It is my intent', says Beker, 'to press this new appreciation of apocalyptic for a fresh understanding of Paul, because only a consistent apocalyptic interpretation of Paul's thought is able to demonstrate its fundamental coherence'.[2]

Beker's reader may reasonably expect that a concept given such weight will be given similar space for explanation. But when the point is reached in Beker's exposition at which a definition must be given, one is referred to the work of Philipp Vielhauer and (particularly) Klaus Koch, summarized as follows: 'apocalyptic revolves around three basic ideas: (1) historical dualism; (2) universal cosmic expectation; and (3) the imminent end of the world'.[3] (The sceptic may perhaps be forgiven for

1. Beker, *Triumph of God*, pp. xii-xiii.
2. Beker, *Paul*, p. 143.
3. Beker, *Paul*, p. 136. Beker expresses here a preference for Koch's continuous, salvation-historical conception of 'apocalyptic' against Vielhauer's more radically dualistic one.

suspecting that it is easier to interpret Paul in the light of Vielhauer and Koch than in the light—or darkness—of the apocalypses.) Within a couple of years, as a point of clarification, Beker adds a fourth 'basic idea', or, as he now says, a fourth 'apocalyptic motif' or 'basic component of Jewish apocalyptic', namely 'vindication' (a motif readily recognized for its Käsemannian provenance).[4] Later still, Beker notes that

> the three apocalyptic motifs of Paul's gospel are actually anchored in the even-more-central motif of the faithfulness of God. This motif undergirds the whole range of biblical thought, from the Old Testament narrative theologians and prophets via the apocalyptic writers to the New Testament authors, especially Paul.[5]

Still later, this fourth motif becomes 'the faithfulness and vindication of God', and Beker's motifs, though not intended 'to describe the general character of apocalyptic', reflect 'the central question of apocalyptic': 'Why is faithfulness to the God of the covenant and to the Torah rewarded with persecution and suffering? Apocalyptic is an attempt to overcome the discrepancy between the harsh realities of everyday life and the promises of God.'[6] His earlier reliance on Vielhauer and Koch, whose three 'essential elements' 'represent necessary heuristic models', 'neglected perhaps the most important aspect of biblical apocalyptic: the faithfulness and trustworthiness of God. This feature not only encompasses all the others but modifies them as well.'[7]

More to the point, Beker is called on to explain his use of the term 'apocalyptic' rather than simply 'eschatology' for what is clearly for Beker an eschatological construct:

---

4.    Beker, *Gospel*, pp. 14-15, 30-53; this idea is already present in Beker's earlier treatment, as he continues on from his original listing of his three 'basic ideas': 'apocalyptic is born out of a deep existential concern and is in many respects a theology of martyrdom. The apocalyptist has a profound awareness of the discrepancy between what is and what should be, and of the tragic tension between faithfulness to the Torah and its apparent futility. Therefore, he lives a hope that seems contradicted by the realities of his world but that is fed by his faith in the faithfulness of the God of Israel and his ultimate self-vindication. Will God keep his promises to his people and reward their faithfulness to the covenant? Will he, notwithstanding present persecution, establish his people in victory over their enemies and thus vindicate his glory in the glorious destiny of his people' (Beker, *Paul*, p. 136)?

5.    Beker, *Paul*, pp. xv-xvi.

6.    Beker, *Triumph of God*, pp. 20-21.

7.    Beker, *Triumph of God*, p. 64.

> My reasons for using 'apocalyptic' are twofold: first of all, the term 'apocalyptic' guards against the multivalent and often chaotic use of the concept of 'eschatology' in modern times. Eschatology refers to 'last things', but in modern use 'last things' often refer not to things that come at the end of a series but to things that are final and ultimate. In other words, the use of the term apocalyptic clarifies the future-temporal character of Paul's gospel.
>
> Secondly, apocalyptic denotes an end-time occurrence that is both cosmic-universal and definitive. Paul expects the future to be an apocalyptic closure-event in time and space embracing the whole of God's created order. Thus the term 'apocalyptic' refers more clearly than the general term 'eschatology' to the specificity and extent of the end-time occurrence.[8]

For Beker, 'apocalyptic' represents a fixed point of eschatological thought, a particular type of eschatology—futuristic, cosmic, and final—to which Paul is heir and which he may adapt in view of the Christ-event, and Beker can place his interpretation, which he regards as in the tradition of Schweitzer and Käsemann, alongside what he perceives to be its chief rivals: C.H. Dodd's 'realized eschatology', Rudolf Bultmann's 'existentialist interpretation', and Oscar Cullmann's 'salvation history'.[9] Clearly, Beker assumes transparency and lack of controversy as to what 'apocalyptic' is all about, and he feels no need to place the concept on a firmer literary-historical basis.

Beker is not alone here, for the same assumption has prevailed all through that strand of modern interpretation of Paul to which Beker's synthesis is the latest major addition: everyone knows what 'apocalyptic' is (it only remains to determine what to make of it). Indeed, bidding well to be considered this century's most valuable bequest to biblical criticism

---

8.     Beker, *Gospel*, p. 14; see also *Paul*, p. xiv: 'Questions about my use of the term "apocalyptic" could have been muted if I had frankly emphasized the polemical thrust of my usage, as directed to the systematic theologians of our time. I thought that "apocalyptic" did not allow the degree of multivalence and chaos that in recent theology adheres to "eschatology"—a concept that denotes everything from existential finality and transcendent reality to "life after death". I used "apocalyptic" not only because it is true to Paul's theology but also because its future-temporal, cosmic-universal, and dualistic components constitute a challenge for the church and its theology in our time. In other words, I intended to highlight the *offensive* character of the term, especially because both biblical and theological scholarship perpetuate the anti-apocalyptic ethos of the theological tradition' (from the 'Preface to the First Paperback Edition').

9.     Beker, *Gospel*, pp. 61-77.

is the interpretative concept of 'apocalyptic'. Introductions, monographs, collections, colloquia, conference groups, articles galore, and casual references innumerable testify to the interpretative energies expended. (Rumours persist of 'Apocalyptic: The Musical'.)

Yet such institutional supremacy *might* foster unreflective usage, of the sort that, sooner or later, forces questions otherwise begged—nagging little questions like: 'Just what *is* apocalyptic?' (or even 'Apocalyptic *what*'?). No doubt everyone who needs the term has an understanding quite suited to his or her purpose. But that purpose seems seldom to have much to do directly with the apocalypses of early Judaism and Christianity, so little in fact that one entering these through the doorway of this ostensibly self-evident approach may find himself or herself quickly exiting by the same way, perhaps never to return.

### The Tacit Consensus

I have spoken above, with varying degrees of cynicism, of an 'apocalyptic renaissance'. But there is in truth just such a renewed interest in (or 'new appreciation' of as Beker says) 'apocalyptic', which owes much to Käsemann, among others. A figure who both precedes and partakes in this 'renaissance' is H.H. Rowley, whose handbook on 'apocalyptic', appearing first in 1944 and in its third revised edition in 1963, marks a convenient beginning point to the period of interest here.[10] I have thus

10. H.H. Rowley, *The Relevance of Apocalyptic: A Study of Jewish and Christian Apocalypses from Daniel to Revelation* (Greenwood: Attic Press, 3rd edn, 1980 [1963]). Rowley may be held to mark the beginning of the period of present interest for several reasons: his work is very much a synthesis of previous research (note his extensive bibliographies), particularly of the British tradition since R.H. Charles; his handbook has had considerable and lasting influence, and coincides and merges with the 'renaissance' of 'apocalyptic'; and his first edition appeared on the eve of the Dead Sea discoveries. The period up to this is treated in J.M. Schmidt, *Die jüdische Apokalyptik. Die Geschichte ihrer Erforschung von den Anfängen bis zu den Textfunden von Qumran* (Neukirchen–Vluyn: Neukirchener Verlag, 2nd edn, 1976). For further history and critique of scholarship, see Koch, *Rediscovery*; Koch and J.M. Schmidt (eds.), *Apokalyptik*; J. Barr, 'Jewish Apocalyptic in Recent Scholarly Study', *BJRL* 58 (1975), pp. 9-35; P.D. Hanson, 'Prolegomena to the Study of Jewish Apocalyptic', in F.M. Cross, W.E. Lemke, and P.D. Miller, Jr (eds.), *Magnalia Dei: The Mighty Acts of God* (Garden City: Doubleday, 1976), pp. 389-401; *idem*, 'Apocalyptic Literature', in D.A. Knight and G.M. Tucker (eds.), *The Hebrew Bible and its Modern Interpreters* (Chico: Scholars, 1985), pp. 465-88; J. Coppens, 'L'apocalyptique: Son dossier, ses critères, ses éléments constitutifs, sa

far remained close to Paul (well, close to talk of Paul, anyway, along with talk of how to talk of Paul, or hermeneutics). But as much as I have grumbled under my breath about inattention to fundamental interpretative issues where 'apocalyptic' is concerned, it seems fitting to take a step back and look at interpretation of 'apocalyptic' generally, to see how things stand there. That is, if what we have seen of 'apocalyptic' interpretation of Paul should conspire to direct us back to the prior question 'What is apocalyptic?', then the raft of literature of this 'apocalyptic renaissance' might, it is hoped, help sort things out.[11]

portée néotestamentaire', *ETL* 53 (1976), pp. 1-23; M. Delcor, 'Bilan des études sur l'apocalyptique', in L. Monloubou (ed.), *Apocalypses et Théologie de l'Éspérance* (Paris: Cerf, 1977), pp. 27-42; E.W. Nicholson, 'Apocalyptic', in G.W. Anderson (ed.), *Tradition and Interpretation* (Oxford: Oxford University Press, 1979), pp. 189-213; J.C. VanderKam, 'Recent Studies in "Apocalyptic"', *WW* 4 (1984), pp. 70-77; J.G. Gammie, 'Recent Books and Emerging Issues in the Study of Apocalyptic', *Quarterly Review* 5 (1985), pp. 96-108; J.J. Collins, 'Apocalyptic Literature', in R.A. Kraft and G.W.E. Nickelsburg (eds.), *Early Judaism and Its Modern Interpreters* (Philadelphia: Fortress/Atlanta: Scholars Press, 1986), pp. 345-70; R.J. Bauckham, 'The Apocalypses in the New Pseudepigrapha', *JSNT* 26 (1986), pp. 97-117.

11. Handbooks on 'apocalyptic' which have appeared since the third edition of Rowley include D.S. Russell, *The Method and Message of Jewish Apocalyptic: 200 BC-AD 100* (Philadelphia: Westminster Press, 1964); J. Schreiner, *Alttestamentlich-jüdische Apokalyptik. Eine Einführung* (Munich: Kösel, 1969); L. Morris, *Apocalyptic* (London: Inter-Varsity Press, 1973); W. Schmithals, *The Apocalyptic Movement: Introduction and Interpretation* (trans. J.E. Steely; Nashville: Abingdon Press, 1975); P.S. Minear, *New Testament Apocalyptic* (Nashville: Abingdon Press, 1981); C. Rowland, *The Open Heaven: A Study of Apocalyptic in Judaism and Early Christianity* (London: SPCK, 1982); J.J. Collins, *The Apocalyptic Imagination: An Introduction to the Jewish Matrix of Christianity* (New York: Crossroad, 1984); P.D. Hanson, *Old Testament Apocalyptic* (Nashville: Abingdon Press, 1987). See also I. Gruenwald, 'Jewish Apocalyptic Literature', *ANRW* II.19.1 (1979), pp. 89-118; P.D. Hanson, A.K. Grayson, J.J. Collins and A. Yarbro Collins (eds.), 'Apocalypses and Apocalypticism', in Freedman (ed.), *Anchor Bible Dictionary*, I.279-92; M.G. Reddish (ed.), *Apocalyptic Literature: A Reader* (Nashville: Abingdon, 1990); much of the other literature on 'apocalyptic' cited in the present chapter is also introductory in nature. Appearing between Rowley's first and last editions are J. Bloch, *On the Apocalyptic in Judaism* (Philadelphia: Dropsie, 1952) and S.B. Frost, *Old Testament Apocalyptic: Its Origin and Growth* (London: Epworth, 1952). The 'renaissance' led to the major International Colloquium on Apocalypticism in Uppsala, 1979, the proceedings of which have been published as D. Hellholm (ed.), *Apocalypticism in the Mediterranean World and the Near East*

*Might*, that is, if study of the phenomenon in its own right does not suffer from such tendencies as are apparent in the attempt to apply the concept to Paul.

If it is possible—and we may by now be confident that it is—to identify an approach to 'apocalyptic' as the 'usual' one, the standard, the consensus implicit in all the throwing about of the term 'apocalyptic' (among students of New Testament literature and Christian origins in particular), a good starting point might be had in the endlessly quoted words of Rowley: 'Speaking generally, the prophets foretold the future that should arise out of the present, while the apocalyptists foretold the future that should break into the present.'[12] Embedded in this striking statement is a particular understanding of the origins of 'apocalyptic' as 'the child of prophecy' and of its essence, setting, and function as being about the future, about protest born of crisis and about 'keeping alive the flame of hope in dark and difficult days', as seen pre-eminently in Daniel, the 'first great apocalyptic work'.[13] The emphasis is on 'apocalyptic eschatology', with its pessimism[14] and imminent expectation; also implicitly captured here are the central place generally given the so-called 'two-age doctrine' and the conception of the genesis of 'apocalyptic eschatology' as emerging from a point at which, due to various pressures, something 'snaps'. Moving ahead several years in time (though little enough in method) to a recent introduction to apocalyptic studies, one reads:

> Apocalyptic is a literature that is drawn and torn by contending forces. Within the crosscurrents and eddies of this material there comes to expression an ominous sense of final ending. The present order having plunged hopelessly into degenerateness and anomie, the structures once

(Tübingen: Mohr [Paul Siebeck], 1983), a work which witnesses to the snowballing international literature on 'apocalyptic'. Noting recent trends since Uppsala is J.J. Collins and J.H. Charlesworth (eds.), *Mysteries and Revelations: Apocalyptic Studies Since the Uppsala Colloquium* (JSPSup, 9; Sheffield: Sheffield Academic Press, 1991). The select number of titles cited in the present chapter offers some indication of the growing interest and research. For further bibliography from 1960, see J.H. Charlesworth, *The Pseudepigrapha and Modern Research with a Supplement* (Chico: Scholars Press, 1981), pp. 46-52, 253-59 and the 'Supplementary Bibliography (1979-1988)', in Hellholm (ed.), *Apocalypticism* (2nd edn, 1989), pp. 795-825.

12. Rowley, *Relevance*, p. 38.
13. Rowley, *Relevance*, pp. 15, 53, 43.
14. However, Rowley dislikes the term—see Rowley, *Relevance*, pp. 38-39, 178.

capable of sustaining life are at the point of rupture. Situated at this dread threshold, the apocalypticist looks in several directions in the effort to explain the prevailing doom. A backward glance, often in the form of a resumé of history, discerns patterns and trajectories which explain why it is that things have reached this nadir. Careful scrutiny of the present in turn focuses on signs of an imminent turning, a final collapse, and reduction to a state of chaos reminiscent of primordial formlessness. Finally, since the final cataclysm is interpreted as a catharsis, the seer peers into the future to describe a new order which will supplant the old, a supernatural order of unprecedented glory and blessing for those favored by the One directing this cosmic drama.[15]

Motivated by misuse and neglect of the apocalyptic texts, Rowley stresses (as his title suggests), particularly in the case of the canonical apocalypses Daniel and Revelation, the 'great spiritual principles' which are addressed 'to every age'.[16] These include a strong affirmation of God's control of history as he directs it toward its goal and end, an acute sense of the problem of evil in the world, a living hope in the glorious future kingdom of God established by his power, a keen loyalty to God's purpose and will, and a vital future hope and perspective on final judgement. In discerning this abiding relevance, it is wise 'to avoid pressing the details, and to cherish only the great principles that underlie them', all this 'in the light of Christ's teaching as a whole'.[17] Showing somewhat less restraint, but speaking in a manner not uncommon in terms of relating study of 'apocalyptic' to present day concerns, are these sentiments taken once again from the recent introductory survey, describing how, after years of woeful neglect from enlightened modern minds, the twentieth century saw 'apocalyptic' come into its own:

Then, in a flash, the world mood changed. The optimism of a strident civilization succumbed to grave self-doubts in a world engulfed by war. This led to the rediscovery of an ancient literature which described the world as torn by opposing forces, forces larger than human in stature and battling for supremacy. Apocalypticism once again seemed relevant, and passed quickly from eclipse into the light of renewed scholarly scrutiny...

The shocking images of that specific kind of mythology we call apocalyptic arrest the attention of increasing numbers of thoughtful moderns because they recognize that the apocalyptic themes of history's decline,

---

15. P.D. Hanson (ed.), *Visionaries and Their Apocalypses* (Philadelphia: Fortress Press/London: SPCK, 1983), p. 1.

16. Rowley, *Relevance*, pp. ix-x, 13-15, 166-93.

17. Rowley, *Relevance*, pp. 166-93 (191, 193).

imminent doom, and a new order beyond the cataclysm are far more descriptive of the world they live in—or should we say, of the world they are leaving and the world they yearn to enter—than the facile assurances of their civil leaders that the future is bright if efforts at technological development, materialistic production, and accumulation are merely redoubled. There is in the *Zeitgeist* today a widespread 'sense of an ending'. Apocalypse is no further away than one error, human or electronic, in an underground nuclear command center. And apocalyptic literature, though to modern taste mythical and crude, portrays the conflict between life and death forces which once again seems to give accurate portrayal of life as it really is...The ancient Jewish apocalyptic writings grew out of the courage to stare into the abyss on the edge of which an entire civilization tottered, and a willingness to describe what the fantasy of faith enabled the human eye to glimpse beyond tragedy. Our fantasy will not be identical with that of the ancient apocalypticist; what our eye beholds of the past decline, present crisis, and future hope will not repro-duce the vision of the Jewish seer; but it is possible that the inspired fantasy and the daring vision encountered there may purge, enlarge, and enhance both our perspective and our concept of what is possible...

A modern world slipping into a deeper pessimism regarding the future has turned to the literature of an ancient era similarly plagued by pessimism *vis-à-vis* human possibilities. Since the facile promises of the prophets of weal have run aground, there arises the hope that the hard look at reality found in apocalyptic may afford a glimpse beyond the tragedy which weighs so heavily upon the consciousness of thoughtful moderns...

Cultures before our own have experienced the dread sense of ending which many persons are experiencing today, and out of those troubled times in the past there emerged those compositions we call apocalyptic, written by some of the wisest and most thoughtful savants of antiquity. It is not at all absurd to expect that from their insights we, too, may derive important perspectives on our own dilemma...[18]

This is not an attempt to rehearse the failures of an earlier generation or to make Rowley its scapegoat—besides, Rowley has perhaps proved more careful than his heirs at many points in which they have followed him. Yet tendencies present in Rowley run their full course in subsequent discussion, tendencies such as reading the apocalypses with Christian origins and biblical-theological agendas, over-emphasis on eschatology,

---

18.  Hanson (ed.), *Visionaries*, pp. 2, 3-4, 8, 14. Cf. also, pp. 166-93; D.S. Russell, *Apocalyptic: Ancient and Modern* (London: SCM Press, 1978); Reddish (ed.), *Apocalyptic Literature*, pp. 36-37. Much is said of one's approach to 'apocalyptic' in one's attempts at contemporary relevance, as witness what Hanson does here for his 'thoughtful moderns'.

especially understood as being in the line of biblical prophecy and en route to New Testament eschatology, almost exclusive interest in canonical 'apocalyptic', and a yearning for contemporary relevance.[19] There are now, quite clearly, standard lines of characterization of 'apocalyptic', of extending such characterizations to early Christianity, and even of speaking an apocalyptic word of grace to the present generation. But what does all this have to do with the apocalypses?

Those works on 'apocalyptic' which have established themselves as standards—such as those of H.H. Rowley,[20] D.S. Russell,[21] and Paul D.

---

19.   These tendencies are clear in Rowley's treatment of the texts: the canonical works are given much more space, and are in fact given a summary exposition, while the non-canonical texts are of interest for the parallels they offer of various features of 'apocalyptic eschatology'. It is clear that what is in view is the correct interpretation of the canonical texts; the other examples of apocalyptic literature are source material for comparative theological developments or for obscure features or motifs. 'Apocalyptic' is treated as 'thought', as theology, of interest for elucidating the thought of Jesus and Paul (see Rowley, *Relevance*, pp. 54, 129-38, 148-49, 160-65). The discussion is framed between Daniel, the great fount of 'apocalyptic', and Revelation, the great climax—note particularly Rowley's words at the close of his survey of texts (pp. 148-49). Also telling is the treatment of pseudonymity, which grew by a natural and rational process in the case of Daniel but was slavishly copied by lesser imitators who misunderstood their superior exemplar, a pattern finally broken in the 'Little Apocalypse' and Revelation (see pp. 39-42, 130-31, 138-39); furthermore, these clumsy imitators, 'always unable to distinguish between the accidents and the elements of what they copied', misunderstood the natural fiction of the sealing of the Book of Daniel, and so 'apocalyptic became esoteric' (p. 42). The relevance which is the particular burden of Rowley's treatment is the particular domain of the canonical 'apocalyptic'. Rowley's work is throughout a work of biblical theology. He is to be thanked for helping rescue these texts from the obscurity of scholarly lack of interest and fringe fanatical interest; but, this done, scholarship must proceed beyond this apologetic intent.

20.   Rowley's *Relevance*, 1944, 1947, and 1963 (3rd edn), reprinted as recently as the 1980 Attic Press edition cited here, was the standard English-language handbook for many years, and Koch could, as late as 1970, refer to Rowley's work in German translation (*Apokalyptik, ihre Form und Bedeutung zur biblischen Zeit*, 1965) as 'the latest comprehensive account available in German' and as the first to appear in some time (*Rediscovery*, pp. 38-39; admittedly not an ideal state of affairs for Koch).

21.   D.S. Russell, *Method and Message*; *idem*, *Between the Testaments* (London: SCM Press, 2nd edn, 1963), largely a summary and condensation of the former; *idem*, *The Jews from Alexander to Herod* (Oxford: Oxford University Press, 1967), pp. 132-54, 219-49; *idem*, *Apocalyptic: Ancient and Modern*; and, most recently, *idem*, *Divine Disclosure: An Introduction to Jewish Apocalyptic* (London: SCM

Hanson[22]—easily create dubious expectations in the unsuspecting reader of the apocalypses. The difficulty is intensified when one is concerned, not with apocalypses (directly), but with other texts or figures interpreted 'apocalyptically'. There is no true consensus view of 'apocalyptic' in the literature—the state of the question is one of continual disarray. For whatever reasons, scholars outside apocalyptic studies proper who attempt to interpret early Christian figures, literature, and movements in the light of 'apocalyptic' tend to operate with an implicit consensus view, a view which shows little awareness of or sensitivity to the diversity of opinion over 'apocalyptic' and the diverse methodological issues inherent in the task. The following attempts to highlight something of both these sets of diversities.

Press, 1992). Russell stands in acknowledged close continuity with Rowley. Once again, biblical theology is the genre of the treatment, an exercise in bridge-building 'between the testaments' (cf. Russell, *Method and Message*, p. 9). The canonical texts frame the discussion, and 'apocalyptic' is theology, eschatology. Origins and genesis are viewed similarly, and the material treated is focused through the lens of what is important for Christian biblical interpretation. Russell's *Method and Message* is a mine of information on what is of interest to it, and Russell anticipates some important recent developments, as in his awareness of the possible Mesopotamian 'wisdom' traditions of the figures of Enoch and Daniel and in his openness to the presence of religious experience, as opposed to purely literary convention, in the 'inspiration' of the apocalyptic writers. (See Russell, *Method and Message*, pp. 109-18, 158-73. On such more recently, and the difference in perspective this may make, cf. M.E. Stone in Hanson [ed.], *Visionaries*, pp. 85-100.) However, Russell's treatment remains conventional.

22. P.D. Hanson, 'Jewish Apocalyptic Against its Near Eastern Environment', *RB* 78 (1971), pp. 31-58; *idem*, 'Old Testament Apocalyptic Reexamined', *Int* 25 (1971), pp. 454-79, repr. in Hanson (ed.), *Visionaries*, pp. 37-60; *idem*, *The Dawn of Apocalyptic* (Philadelphia: Fortress Press, 2nd edn, 1979 [1975]), which includes the 'Appendix: An Overview of Early Jewish and Christian Apocalypticism', pp. 427-44; *idem*, 'Apocalypse: Genre' and 'Apocalypticism', in *IDBSup*, pp. 27-34; *idem*, *Old Testament Apocalyptic*; and, most recently, Hanson's sub-articles 'The Genre' and 'Introductory Overview' in 'Apocalypses and Apocalypticism', in Freedman (ed.), *Anchor Bible Dictionary*, I.279-82. On the influence of Rowley and Russell, see J. Barr, 'Jewish Apocalyptic', pp. 11-14; J.J. Collins, 'Apocalyptic Literature', pp. 348-49; Hanson is at present a highly influential heir of the method of (among others) Rowley and Russell. The influence of two German surveys, translated into English and widely read, may be noted: P. Vielhauer, 'Introduction to Apocalypses and Related Subjects', in E. Hennecke and W. Schneemelcher (eds.), *New Testament Apocrypha* (ET ed. R.M. Wilson; Philadelphia: Westminster, 1965), II, pp. 581-607, and Koch, *Rediscovery*.

## Interpreting 'Apocalyptic'

Above is expressed something of the need for self-consciousness and clarity concerning matters of methodology in speaking of 'apocalyptic'. My aim here is primarily to engage in a methodological critique. It is agreed that approaching the question of 'apocalyptic' via Pauline studies is not the most direct or obvious route, bringing as it might a rather foreign, and potentially distorting, set of questions. Furthermore, chasing down these questions may prove finally to be of little use to the student of Paul, a necessity laid upon him or her not by Paul himself (so to speak) but by current convention, because it is said that 'Paul is an apocalyptic theologian'. So there are risks at both ends. With this in mind, the focus on Paul properly affects the discussion by adding the dimension of a concrete interest beyond the apocalypses themselves, as the present concern is really with that most problematic abstraction, 'apocalyptic', not primarily the apocalypses. And so the methodological focus has two poles, one (to a degree) the issues inherent in the task of understanding the apocalypses, the other the further issues inherent in speaking of 'apocalyptic' or 'apocalypticism' beyond those specific texts. As for my concern with the matter of definition, recent years have seen a level of such concern which at times borders on the obsessive and to which I should not care to add.[23] I do not attempt my own definition, then, but offer something far short of—something quite other than—a full treatment of or fresh synthesis on 'apocalyptic'. I am inquiring instead after just what we are doing in our efforts to define and employ some notion of 'apocalyptic', especially as the term is applied to the New Testament. This brings me to the matter of the absence from my discussion of 'apocalyptic' of any detailed treatment of apocalyptic literature. The sort of observations I make are more of the order of simply sorting out just what it is that we are talking about, what is

---

23. Most of the literature on 'apocalyptic' cited in the present chapter (especially the more recent literature) touches on definition. For further evidence of this growing self-consciousness in talk of 'apocalyptic': M. Barker, 'Slippery Words III. Apocalyptic', *ExpTim* 89 (1978), pp. 324-29; J. Carmignac, 'Qu'est-ce que l'apocalyptique? Son emploi à Qumrân', *Revue de Qumrân* 10 (1979), pp. 3-33; R. Schröder, 'Was ist Apokalyptik?', *Theologische Versuche* 10 (1979), pp. 45-52; T.F. Glasson, 'What is Apocalyptic?', *NTS* 27 (1980), pp. 98-105; G. Rochais, 'Qu'est-ce que l'apocalyptique?', *ScEs* 36 (1984), pp. 273-86; R.L. Webb, ' "Apocalyptic": Observations on a Slippery Term', *JNES* 49 (1990), pp. 115-26.

implied about the apocalypses in talk of 'apocalyptic', what the latter would seem to suggest or assume or have us believe about the literature. Where this does involve me in direct reflection on the apocalypses, this will for my purposes be of the most simple and general kind (as should become clearer as we proceed), practically reducing to the bare observation of the irreducible diversity of this literature; the question will then be how something called 'apocalyptic' ever arose to begin with. How indeed.

## Matters of Definition

Basic to a discussion of definition is the matter of what is being defined, that is, the range and nature of data a definition must cover or take into account. In the case of 'apocalyptic', that range includes at least the literary features, and their particular combination, of the apocalypses (and the prior question of recognizing such a genre), the scope and combination of interests of these texts and the thought-world they imply, their historical and social setting and function, and the religious experience to which they bear witness.

The vast range of issues in defining 'apocalyptic' has always been there, with only more or less self-conscious awareness of this range on the part of interpreters. Attempts of earlier generations to define 'apocalyptic' often have a sort of 'shopping list' appearance, lumping together items of various order—literature, history, sociology...theology. More recently, interpreters have questioned the adequacy of such list-style definitions.[24] So, ostensibly in an attempt to manage the broad range of material under consideration, it has become common to distinguish broadly between 'literary type' and 'historical movement', as popularized by Klaus Koch.[25] This agreed basic distinction between the

24. See, e.g., Betz, 'Problem', pp. 135-36; cf. Hanson, 'Jewish Apocalyptic', p. 33, and *Dawn*, pp. 6-7, with ref. to Russell; *idem*, 'Apocalypticism', pp. 29-31; *idem*, 'Appendix', pp. 429-30. According to Russell, his 'list' 'builds up an impression of a distinct kind which conveys a particular mood of thought and belief' (Russell, *Method and Message*, p. 105). It might be noted that Hanson, criticism of Russell aside, has a very similar 'impression' of 'apocalyptic'.

25. Koch, *Rediscovery*, pp. 23, 28; Vielhauer, 'Introduction', pp. 582ff., makes a similar distinction before him, as does Betz, 'Problem', p. 135; cf. Russell's distinction between the 'method' (the literature) and the 'message' (the teaching) of 'apocalyptic' (Russell, *Method and Message*, pp. 106-107); see also Barr, 'Jewish Apocalyptic', pp. 14-15; M.E. Stone, 'Lists of Revealed Things in the Apocalyptic Literature', in F.M. Cross, W.E. Lemke and P.D. Millar, Jr (eds.), *Magnalia Dei*,

literature and the ideology, between 'apocalypse' and 'apocalyptic' or 'apocalypticism',[26] is elaborated by Paul D. Hanson in a manner which seems to have taken hold: he proposes a threefold distinction between 'apocalypse' (a literary genre), 'apocalyptic eschatology' (a religious perspective), and 'apocalypticism' (a socioreligious movement).[27] Such attempts at clarification might suggest a greater degree of critical self-awareness. But simply to make such classifications is not enough (but might just be another unhelpful sort of list-making). One must address the relation of 'apocalyptic' to the 'apocalypse': does the abstraction 'apocalyptic' express the 'essence', so to speak, of the apocalypses, or is it something found there but perhaps as much elsewhere as well; or are the two, 'apocalyptic' and the apocalypses, even necessarily related at

pp. 439-43; 'Apocalyptic Literature', pp. 383-41 (392-94); M.A. Knibb, 'Prophecy and the Emergence of the Jewish Apocalypses', in R.J. Coggins, A. Phillips, and M. Knibb (eds.), *Israel's Prophetic Tradition* (Cambridge: Cambridge University Press, 1982), pp. 157-61.

26.   At this point it might be noted that discussion of definition has often been consumed with rather simplistic argument over preferred terminology, as when A. Yarbro Collins, reviewing C. Rowland, *The Open Heaven* (*JBL* 103 [1984], pp. 465-67), is shocked that anyone could possibly continue, after the work of Stone and Hanson, to use 'apocalyptic' as a noun—'apocalypticism' is to be preferred. But surely the two mean the same thing (cf. T.F. Glasson, 'What is Apocalyptic?', p. 102: 'the only effect of the extra letters [in apocalyptic*ism*]...being to use more space and printing materials'). For that matter, Hanson continues to use the noun 'apocalyptic' (as in *The Dawn of...*), while Stone would prefer to abandon 'apocalypticism' as well as 'apocalyptic' (see Stone, 'Lists', p. 443). The real issue is not one of terminology but of the relation of 'apocalyptic' (or whatever) to the apocalypses, and so A. Yarbro Collins's charge of terminological and conceptual confusion is itself confused and misplaced. Furthermore, from the perspective of the present analysis, one could argue that the added 'ism' might have the psychological effect of further solidifying an already problematic manner of speaking. See further below.

27.   Hanson, 'Apocalypticism', pp. 29-31; cf. idem, 'Appendix', to *Dawn*, pp. 427-37; D.E. Aune, *The New Testament in its Literary Environment* (Philadelphia: Westminster Press, 1987), pp. 227, 231, adds a fourth item, 'apocalyptic imagery', '*language and conceptions* of apocalyptic eschatology found in bits and pieces in a variety of ancient literary settings' (p. 227); does the presence of 'apocalyptic imagery' count (necessarily) as 'apocalyptic', or have such language and motifs perhaps become generalized (p. 231)? The added distinction might perhaps be helpful, as it raises the question of whether or not the presence of a particular 'ism' need be inferred merely from certain themes, images, and motifs; but Aune does not criticize the propriety of the notion 'apocalyptic eschatology' from which such 'apocalyptic imagery' supposedly derives.

all? Thus Hanson distinguishes the 'apocalypse' (a favoured, though not the exclusive or even dominant, medium of 'apocalyptic' writers) from 'apocalyptic eschatology' and 'apocalypticism', and his stated concern is with the latter two, not with giving an account of the apocalypses.[28] But some relationship is assumed, as the apocalypse is at least one literary repository of his apocalypticists, and Hanson illustrates his 'apocalyptic eschatology' and 'apocalypticism' from the apocalypses; and so he clearly *thinks* he is saying something about the apocalypses. Michael E. Stone objects that such definitions of apocalypticism as Hanson's, which are largely eschatological constructions, do not apply to the apocalypses, as 'many works which belong to the genre "apocalypse" contain much that is not covered or rendered comprehensible' by such definitions, while 'many works not formally apocalypses are imbued with this apocalypticism'.[29] 'An illusion persists, because of the terminological confusion, that by defining apocalypticism something has been said about the apocalypses.'[30] 'Indeed the "truly apocalyptic" apocalypses are the exception rather than the rule.'[31] (At this point, reference may be made to the detailed interpretative work of Christopher Rowland, which is founded on a similar observation.[32])

What, then, is the relationship between such 'apocalypticism' and the apocalypses? Stone is clearly correct to insist that neither the range of interests nor the literary forms or combination of ideas of the apocalypses are covered by 'apocalypticism' as so defined.[33] This point is confirmed by the various devices of such interpretations to make the two fit: Vielhauer recognizes the presence of revelation of secrets other than the eschatological, but then denies the importance of all but the latter;[34] Koch limits himself to a rather stacked primary corpus of apoca-

---

28. Hanson, 'Apocalypticism'; Hanson, 'Appendix' to *Dawn*.

29. Stone, 'Apocalyptic Literature', pp. 392-94 (p. 393).

30. Stone, 'Apocalyptic Literature', p. 394.

31. Stone, 'Lists', p. 443.

32. See Rowland, *The Open Heaven*, pp. 9-72, and *passim*; see also *idem*, *Christian Origins* (Minneapolis: Augsburg, 1985), pp. 56-64; *idem*, Review of *The Apocalyptic Imagination* by J.J. Collins, and *Jewish Writings of the Second Period*, ed. by M.E. Stone, in *JTS* 37 (1986), pp. 484-90; *idem*, 'The Intertestamental Literature', in P. Avis (ed.), *The Study and Use of the Bible* (Basingstoke: Marshall Pickering/Grand Rapids: Eerdmans, 1988), pp. 159-60, 184-90, 200-14; 'Apocalyptic', in Coggins and Houlden (eds.), *Dictionary of Biblical Interpretation*, pp. 34-36.

33. Stone, 'Apocalyptic Literature', p. 394.

34. Vielhauer, 'Introduction', p. 589.

lypses (though even his list overreaches his definition) written in Hebrew
or Aramaic or of 'the Hebrew or Aramaic spirit' (read 'heightened
eschatological interest');[35] and Hanson smuggles back in at the level of
exposition what he has ruled out at the level of definition (that is, the
correlation of apocalypse and 'apocalypticism').[36] Stone seems content
to allow study of 'apocalypse' and 'apocalyptic (eschatology)' to go
each its own way.[37] But it is likely that an 'apocalyptic' which might
have little or nothing to do with the apocalypses will be no more satisfactory than a correlation done with mirrors or sleight of hand.
Paradoxically, the truism that 'apocalyptic' should first and foremost
address the apocalypses is something of a novelty.

At this point, an assertion may be made. The matter with which we
are dealing is clearly, at its most basic, twofold. First, there are the
apocalypses. Then, there is the abstraction 'apocalyptic'. A further
assertion may be made. The abstraction 'apocalyptic' (or whatever else it
may fittingly be called) must, if terminology is to signify anything other
than confusion, be made on the basis of the apocalypses. 'Apocalyptic',
then, will be in some sense what the apocalypses are 'about', and to
speak of 'apocalyptic' *beyond* the apocalypses, as in Paul, is an implicit
comparison with the literature and a suggestion that somehow Paul is
'about' the same thing. Hanson's threefold distinction 'apocalypse',
'apocalyptic eschatology', and 'apocalypticism' ambiguously juxtaposes
a literary, a theological, and a sociohistorical category. If our terminology suggests a relationship to the apocalypses which either is not
intended or cannot be maintained, the terminology, rather than clarity or
historical integrity, should be sacrificed. The only other alternative would
seem to be to accept the usual terminology and interpretative practice
and resign ourselves to the fact that the literature and the abstraction, all
reasonable expectation aside, are not to be taken together and have in
fact gone their own way. This is a position of expediency (or counsel of
despair) adopted by Stone, but for now rejected here because of its own
potential for confusion. Thus some sort of literary definition of
'apocalyptic' is required, a definition, that is, subject to the control of a
recognized body of literature, in this case, if we are to call our abstraction 'apocalyptic' (leaving aside for the moment the question of whether

35.   Koch, *Rediscovery*, p. 23.
36.   Hanson, 'Apocalypticism'; idem, 'Appendix' to *Dawn*.
37.   Stone, 'Apocalyptic Literature', pp. 392, 394; it seems, though, that Stone is
merely trying to be realistic.

making *any* such abstraction is a worthy or legitimate undertaking), the apocalypses.

## Excursus:
### *The Instructive Case Of Paul D. Hanson*

In the introductory survey already cited at length above, Paul D. Hanson comments on Klaus Koch's broad distinction between 'apocalypse' and 'apocalyptic': 'This distinction and the attempt at precise definitions are important contributions towards establishing a more reliable foundation under the study of apocalyptic than has been characteristic of the past'.[38] Commenting further on the present state of research: 'some conclusions which have emerged from recent writings seem to provide a solid basis for further research, whereas other questions seem poised to elicit spirited debate. Within the former category can be placed the distinction between discrete levels within the study of apocalyptic as essential to clarity and precision. In this connection the threefold division proposed by the present author in 1976 seems to have gained wide currency...'[39] Hanson's efforts at a definition of 'apocalyptic' have indeed been well rewarded in terms of the influence they have had, and so his approach is worth considering in some detail as a case study in interpreting 'apocalyptic'. His fullest account of the subject is his *The Dawn of Apocalyptic*, a study (as the title suggests) of origins. The introductory chapter of this large study includes general reflection on the problem of definition. But to get the original form of this reflection it is necessary to look back to the 1971 essay 'Jewish Apocalyptic Against its Near Eastern Environment', which, along with another essay from the same year, 'Old Testament Apocalyptic Reexamined', presents aspects of Hanson's 1969 Harvard dissertation, 'Studies in the Origins of Jewish Apocalyptic'. (*Dawn*, then, is the final outcome of years of study of 'the origins of apocalyptic'.[40]) Hanson opens with an account of the approach which he opposes: the attempt, that is, to derive 'apocalyptic' from 'foreign' sources and to deny it any essential connection with 'prophecy'. The problem here largely lies with the method of definition.

> Our point is this: the origins of apocalyptic cannot be explained by a method which juxtaposes seventh and second century compositions and then proceeds to account for the features of the latter by reference to its immediate environment. The apocalyptic literature of the second century and after is the result of a long development reaching back to pre-Exilic times, and beyond, and not the new baby of second century foreign parents. Not only the sources of origin, but the intrinsic nature of late apocalyptic compositions can be understood only by tracing the centuries-long development through which the apocalyptic literature developed from prophetic and other even more archaic native roots.

Not only does the other approach ignore this development, but it tends to offer as a definition 'long lists of random features gleaned from various apocalyptic works'.

---

38.   Hanson, *Visionaries*, p. 8.
39.   Hanson, *Visionaries*, p. 12, and see p. 8.
40.   See 'Jewish Apocalyptic', p. 33 n. 6.

Such lists are confusing, says Hanson, as they are unable to reveal 'the essential nature of apocalyptic' or to enable us 'to identify a composition as apocalyptic'. Hanson's own 'contextual-typological' method reveals the aforementioned vital historical development of 'apocalyptic' (such a recovery of origins, it is clearly assumed, settles the question of the 'essence' of 'apocalyptic').

> The conclusion emerging from the application of this method is that Jewish apocalyptic literature emerged in an unbroken, inner-Israelite development out of pre-Exilic and Exilic prophecy...Influences from Persian dualism and Hellenism were late, coming only after the essential character of apocalyptic was fully developed, and were thus limited to peripheral embellishments. Also entering the apocalyptic stream as a secondary—though important—element is the wisdom tradition.

The pre-Exilic 'prophets' develop into the post-Exilic 'visionaries', and 'apocalyptic is the mode assumed by prophetic eschatology once it had been transferred to a new and radically altered setting in the post-Exilic community'. 'Our definition of apocalyptic seeks to avoid the two ill-fated means of definition usually adopted', that is, the list-style approach and 'that which attempts to define it as a literary *Gattung*'. It is chiefly the added sociohistorical dimension that Hanson regards as setting his approach apart. Coming to his own definition, then, Hanson contrasts 'apocalyptic' with 'prophetic eschatology', which latter deals in 'terms of plain history, real politics and human instrumentality' (recall Rowley's maxim):

> Apocalyptic we define as the disclosure (usually esoteric in nature) to the elect of the prophetic vision of Yahweh's sovereignty (including his future dealings with his people, the inner secrets of the cosmos, etc.) which vision the visionaries have ceased to translate into the terms of plain history, real politics and human instrumentality because of a pessimistic view of reality growing out of the bleak post-Exilic condition in which the visionary group found itself, conditions seeming unsuitable to them as a context for the envisioned restoration of Yahweh's people.[41]

(What we need to note thus far is that Hanson is already making pronouncements on the proper method of definition, but of the entirely undifferentiated matter of something called 'apocalyptic', which is now literary, now theological, now sociohistorical—that is, it cuts across any such three-level distinction one might make. Also, the clear priority of 'apocalyptic eschatology' is to be noted.) At this point I turn to some interesting comments from Michael E. Stone. Stone appends to an essay exploring the large element of speculative lore present in the apocalypses (material largely passed over where 'eschatology' is thought to exhaust the interests and significance of this literature) a 'Postscript' which reflects in the light of this material on the matter of definition. Stone highlights the confusion which accompanies talk of 'apocalyptic' or 'apocalypticism' and the apocalypses, which confusion 'turns on the relationship' of the latter (the literature, a more or less settled generic corpus) to the former ('a certain pattern of ideas', where the concern has been with 'the relationship obtaining between the pattern of ideas and certain aspects of early Christian and New

---

41. Citations are from Hanson, *Visionaries*, pp. 31-35; Hanson points out in a footnote (p. 35 n. 9) that it might perhaps be better to use the term 'apocalyptic eschatology' in this definition in order to sustain more clearly the parallel with 'prophetic eschatology'.

Testament thought'). 'Confusion has entered at the point at which the relationship between apocalypticism and the apocalypses has been obscured.' Although the cognate terminology suggests 'that a relationship of dependence or identity exists between the two', Stone contends 'that this is not necessarily the case and, indeed, only by maintaining a clear distinction between the two can a series of problems be solved'. 'Apocalypticism' (Stone cites Koch's characterization) is an eschatological construction irrelevant to the whole of some apocalypses and to large parts of others and featuring prominently in other types of literature—'apocalypticism', that is, is plainly doing something other than giving an account of the apocalypses. Turning to Hanson's *The Dawn of Apocalyptic* (to which Stone apparently has had pre-publication access, for the wording of Stone's citations corresponds not to the (1975) published version but to the earlier 1971 essay we have cited above—in other words, Hanson has apparently made revisions in response to Stone's critique, the significance of which will be come clearer as we proceed), Stone cites the definition of 'apocalyptic' which is cited above and remarks that the reference to 'the inner secrets of the cosmos' stands out as having no real place in Hanson's thesis. Stone has no quibble with Hanson's derivation of 'apocalyptic eschatology' from 'prophetic eschatology'. 'Yet, we must maintain that Hanson has not explained the origins of the apocalypses and of many of the features that characterize them. He has provided a contribution of capital importance to the study of "apocalypticism" or "apocalyptic eschatology".' Stone asserts that 'the part of the apocalypses called "speculative" in our paper, is clearly an embarrassment to Hanson'. Stone points out that Hanson's references to 'inner secrets of the cosmos', to material arising from 'Persian dualism and Hellenism', and to 'the absorption of Wisdom materials' and 'the unveiling of secrets of the universe' stand quite apart from his concern for 'apocalyptic eschatology' and thus these points just lie there undeveloped in his treatment.

> Clearly here this scholar feels that while what he has demonstrated is crucial to the development of 'apocalyptic,' it does not explain certain features of the apocalypses. Owing to the confusion of 'apocalyptic' with 'apocalypses,' he feels that he should have explained these features of the apocalypses. He thus attempts to show his consciousness of the material unaccounted for as stated above. Yet we would maintain that this is unnecessary, for Hanson's thesis bears on 'apocalypticism,' not on the apocalypses.[42]

In other words, Hanson's undifferentiated treatment of 'apocalyptic' repeatedly makes references which can only be construed as pertaining to the literature, whereas his concern is actually with 'apocalypticism' or 'apocalyptic eschatology' and clearly *not* with giving an account of the literature. When we turn to Hanson's account of definition in *Dawn* as published, his main definition is now of 'apocalyptic eschatology' rather than simply 'apocalyptic', and the reference to 'inner secrets of the cosmos' has been dropped.[43] Various other omissions, insertions, and adjustments appear to have been made. Hanson now says:

---

42.    Citations are from Stone, 'Lists', p. 439-43.
43.    Hanson, *Dawn*, p. 11; see pp. 4-12 on definition, where now (for the most part) 'apocalyptic eschatology' is set out as the chief concern. The 2nd edn (1979) adds the subtitle '*The Historical and Sociological Roots of Jewish Apocalyptic Eschatology*'.

Only an historical investigation with more modest aspirations [than those of typical accounts of 'apocalyptic'] promises to cast useful light on a confused subject. The present study focuses upon *one* strand which can be seen running at the heart of many of the so-called apocalyptic works, the strand of apocalyptic eschatology... Tracing the development from prophetic to apocalyptic eschatology will not in itself fully answer the question of the origin of every work designated 'apocalyptic'... [, as one must also deal] not only with apocalyptic eschatology but with the origin of wisdom motifs and various foreign elements as well.

But Hanson's account of 'apocalyptic eschatology' nevertheless offers, he asserts,

The most plausible theory of origin [of what?]. This theory is based on the view that apocalyptic eschatology constitutes the heart of the major apocalyptic works [which, we may note, are defined as those works characterized by 'apocalyptic eschatology'—it is really difficult to lose like this], a view supported by two observations: (1) The basic intent of those works seems to be that of describing to the faithful the vision of Yahweh's future saving act on their behalf. (2) The apocalyptic eschatology found at the heart of the late apocalyptic compositions can be found fully developed in all its essentials in works of the mid-fifth century, compositions which at the same time do not yet betray any significant influence from the wisdom tradition or foreign sources... [Hanson's 'supporting observations' sound like simply a re-assertion of his assertion]. It would thus seem that, in tracing apocalyptic eschatology back to early prophetic roots, one is laying bare the origins of the most important current flowing into the complex phenomenon which we gather [*sic*] under the designation *apocalyptic*.

As for the speculative 'wisdom' material, Hanson refers us to Stone's essay, and Hanson opines that this turn to 'wisdom' signals the falling out of favour of 'prophetic' figures: 'By associating this learned, "scientific" material with their announcements regarding God's future dealings with his community and the peoples of the world, *the visionaries were able to cloak their eschatological message in an aura of eruditeness which helped establish its authoritativeness*'.[44] Clearly, Stone's point about the problematic connection assumed between 'apocalyptic' and the apocalypses has not been taken. What Hanson has gathered from such criticism as Stone's is that what is gathered under the heading 'apocalyptic' is a complex matter moving on various levels, and that Hanson's own foremost concern is with something called 'apocalyptic eschatology'. But the interconnection of the three levels of literature, theology, and social history is still entirely unproblematic for Hanson (as is the propriety of the levels themselves). Stone says that Hanson addresses the origins of the abstraction 'apocalyptic eschatology' and not the apocalypses, and Hanson understands from this that seeking the origins of 'apocalyptic' is a more complex matter than that of tracing a single strand. He continues to claim that his account of the origins of 'apocalyptic eschatology' isolates the 'heart' of the apocalyptic literature (which, as we have noted, is that literature which is characterized by 'apocalyptic eschatology'; in this same work Zechariah 14 is described as an 'apocalypse' and is said to mark the point at which 'one enters the period of full-blown apocalyptic literature'[45]). From this point Hanson embarks on a series of efforts at producing

44. Hanson, *Dawn*, pp. 7-9, emphasis added; see also pp. 380-81, 402-13.
45. Hanson, *Dawn*, p. 369.

and refining a definition of 'apocalyptic' which seems specifically designed to demonstrate that Stone's suspicions about Hanson's confusion were well founded. These include a pair of introductory articles in the Supplementary Volume to the *Interpreter's Dictionary of the Bible* (1976), then the appendix to the second edition of *Dawn* (1979), then *Old Testament Apocalyptic* (1987) (definition is treated on pp. 25-34), and most recently another pair of introductory articles contributed to a multi-author entry in the *Anchor Bible Dictionary* (1992). I shall confine my comments here to a few general methodological observations especially on the matter of the relation of 'apocalyptic' to the apocalypses. It is clear throughout, as indeed it is clear in the treatment of definition given in *Dawn*, that what Hanson wishes to define is the broad abstraction that he calls 'the apocalyptic phenomenon', which phenomenon has three distinct aspects or levels, the literature, the world-view, and the social movement. The 'world-view' of 'apocalyptic eschatology' is expressed pre-eminently in the apocalypse, but it reaches far wider than the confines of this one genre; under the proper conditions, the world-view crystallizes into 'apocalypticism', a social movement, an 'apocalyptic community' defined by the world-view. Hanson has simply marked off the discursive levels many wish to move on under the rubric 'apocalyptic'; that what is meant by all this is unproblematic everywhere assumed, but the terminology must be cleaned up. This is now said to be the problem with the old list-style approaches to definition—they 'indiscriminately mix the three levels'.[46] So they do. But much more insidious is the confusion between the literature and the abstraction from which Stone tried to rescue Hanson. This confusion marks Hanson's work throughout. In it, the abstraction 'apocalyptic eschatology' has the clear priority and in fact in Hanson's mind has worked its way back behind the literature itself, which latter is explained, of course, as a product of the world-view and its keepers. Indeed, by the time of Stone's critique and Hanson's adjustments (some years into Hanson's interpretative project), the shape of Hanson's understanding of 'apocalyptic' is already well set, and the ambiguities run far deeper than the reach of such minor surface changes as he makes. His complaints against other approaches to definition aside, he cannot even be held to have observed successfully his own three-level distinction since making it. To illustrate some of this, a few words are given from Hanson's popular 1987 presentation of 'Old Testament apocalyptic', which latter, when he comes to define it, hovers over and shuttles between Hanson's three levels:

> Recent attempts to introduce precision into the definition and application of the term 'apocalyptic' have proven difficult. Efforts to define it primarily by recourse to literary criteria have come up against the perplexing fact that limiting the apocalyptic corpus to writings that conform to a literary genre designated 'apocalypse' excludes many writings that for other reasons seem to give expression to an apocalyptic view of reality. The attempt to define apocalyptic on the basis of its sources has also foundered. This has proved to be especially true of attempts to define apocalyptic as a development of the wisdom tradition, since this failed to account for the central role of eschatology in most apocalyptic writings [which writings, again, are defined not formally but as those evincing 'apocalyptic eschatology']. On the other hand, exclusive attention to biblical prophecy as the mother of apocalyptic, while explaining the centrality of eschatology

46.   Hanson, 'Appendix' to *Dawn*, p. 429.

[which centrality we might more easily explain as due to the fact that this feature is used to mark off the corpus], fails to explain certain speculative elements that occupy a conspicuous place in writings usually regarded as apocalyptic, among them observations relating to meteorological phenomena and astrological systems.

Hanson continues in kind by noting that approaches that focus solely on an association with ancient myth, on the social setting of 'apocalyptic movements', or on the social function of comfort in crisis, right though they are as far as they go, are insufficient to define 'apocalyptic'. Rather, all of this must be thrown into the pot to arrive in the end at Hanson's definition of 'Old Testament apocalyptic writings', held to be (simply enough) essentially those evincing 'apocalyptic eschatology', 'since reference solely to those writings that conform to the literary type of the apocalypse would be too restrictive' (indeed). We are assured, though, that among 'the most important literary contributions of the Jewish apocalyptic seers is the apocalyptic genre'.[47] Hanson is not clear as to why, having cut the tie to a generic corpus of apocalypses, we should still use the term 'apocalyptic' (and cognates). The answer seems to be on account of association with the Apocalypse of John and with the use of ἀποκάλυψις (and cognates) in the New Testament, the 'primary meaning' of which 'root' connects it, we are told, with 'apocalyptic eschatology'.[48] The question to which Hanson's continuing effort at definition is an answer is: How can we go on speaking about 'apocalyptic' in the manner to which we have grown accustomed and which we find so useful once objections begin to be raised? If we follow his three-level explication, Hanson assures us, we need not fear or worry. By contrast, to return to Stone's essay, the latter is not concerned with some abstraction of an 'apocalyptic' with which to do whatever, but rather with the generic corpus of the apocalypses, the broad limits of which, whatever questions of genre definition remain, Stone (rightly) regards as being generally agreed. What do we make of *these* texts? Having called, in the wake of Koch and Hanson, for a separation of 'apocalypse' and 'apocalyptic/ ism' (in other words, Stone is more or less willing to allow those whose concern is with the abstraction to go on and do as they will), Stone asserts:

> in view of the fact that 'apocalypticism' does not appear either to be the ideology of the apocalypses or to exhaust the contents of the apocalypses, we can pose another type of question and suggest another focus. If the point of departure is the apocalypses and then not predominantly those two which managed to get themselves considered canonical—Daniel by the Jews and the Apocalypse of John by the Christians—what is it that makes sense of these products of the human spirit? Clearly they are not transparently simple works, and one is more than justified in asking: What ideological, theological, or conceptual patterns can be discerned which provide a basis of coherence for them? What central concerns motivate their authors? Manifestly, apocalypticism is not adequate.

Stone suggests that we reorient our approach to these texts away from such a consuming interest in eschatology to take account of the speculative and experiential

---

47. Hanson, *Old Testament Apocalyptic*, pp. 25-31.
48. Hanson, 'Apocalypticism', p. 29; *idem*, 'Appendix' to *Dawn*, pp. 428-29; on this latter matter of word study, Paul is brought in, referring especially to Gal. 1.11-17.

dimensions of this literature which connect it to other Jewish and contemporary expressions of mystical and esoteric knowledge. Stone concludes:

> Finally, it may perhaps be suggested that the terms 'apocalyptic' and 'apocalypticism' be abandoned altogether. They will continue to confuse the issue as they tend to imply an identity between the way of thought they designate and the apocalypses. The writer does not deny the tremendous importance of this pattern of thought in the apocalypses, yet it is not exclusive to the apocalypses. Indeed the 'truly apocalyptic' apocalypses are the exception rather than the rule. Daniel, Revelation, and IV Ezra (which as has been demonstrated elsewhere [in this same essay] is polemically opposed to speculations) exhaust the list. Just what term should be substituted for 'apocalyptic' and 'apocalypticism' is not clear. Perhaps Hanson's 'apocalyptic eschatology' will prove serviceable [though Stone points out in a note that 'the question may be raised as to whether this pattern of thought indeed finds its best or most explicit or clearest place of expression in the apocalypses. If an examination reveals that it is at least as prominent in works other than the apocalypses, then even the formulation "apocalyptic eschatology" should perhaps be reconsidered.']...As long as we remember that by explaining 'apocalyptic eschatology' we have not explained the apocalypses, there is hope for the future of the discussion.[49]

It might be taken as a tragicomic expression of one of those rich ironies that life and biblical criticism so abundantly afford that Stone's counsel has not won the day and that, instead, Hanson has become a guide for so many. But hope springs eternal.

The chief virtue of the threefold distinction 'apocalypse', 'apocalyptic eschatology', and 'apocalypticism' is its apparent ability to mask and legitimize problematic ways of speaking (sometimes concealing what we are talking about *even from ourselves*). Thus, to return to the example of Beker, at least one reviewer would call him to account as to the aptness of his conception of 'apocalyptic' in relation to the literature:

> Despite [Beker's] insistence on the importance of Jewish apocalyptic for Paul's gospel, his treatment of apocalyptic is very brief, relying on Koch's characterization of it and presenting no discussion of apocalyptic texts. His treatment does not do justice to the large element in apocalyptic which deals with revelations about, and present experience of, the heavenly world.[50]

Beker responds to such objections by taking confident and grateful refuge in Hanson's taxonomy.

> Paul is, after all, a writer of letters and not apocalypses; he uses apocalyptic motifs, but not the literary genre of apocalypse. Paul Hanson has convincingly pointed out that the category of 'apocalyptic' contains various forms. It can refer either to a literary *genre*, to

49. Stone, 'Lists', pp. 442-43 and pp. 451-52 n. 78.

50. A.T. Lincoln, Review of *Paul*, by J.C. Beker (cited in the following note), in *Churchman* 95 (1981), pp. 353-54 (p. 353). The reviews of Beker's *Paul* which I have checked (by no means an exhaustive search) reveal hardly a quibble over his treatment of 'apocalyptic'; H.D. Betz, in a review for *JR* 61 (1981), pp. 457-59, does note that Beker 'works with a notion of apocalyptic that will impress only a few scholars in the field of the history of religions, where the subject of apocalyptic has been under intensive discussion in recent years' (p. 458).

a prominent *motif*, or to an apocalyptic *movement*. Thus we should be aware of the fact that Paul uses apocalyptic motifs, but not the literary genre, while his churches evolve into apocalyptic movements.

...I would argue that the issue of Paul's apocalyptic can only be addressed properly if the distinction between apocalyptic *genre*, apocalyptic *movements*, and apocalyptic *motifs* is upheld.

My thesis that Jewish apocalyptic determined the symbolic framework of Paul's thought does not mean that Paul used Jewish apocalyptic as a literary genre or employed Jewish apocalypses as a literary source. Similarly, I am not interested in undertaking a semantic study of the concept 'apocalyptic' in relation to Paul. Rather, I claim that Jewish apocalyptic *motifs* dominate Paul's thought.[51]

Beker's recourse to Hanson's 'apocalyptic eschatology' has the virtual effect of placing Beker's method beyond criticism, offering an acquittal of charges of methodological lapse and a licence and encouragement to continue as before, without the need or bother of accountability to actual texts, allowing him to go on, as here, begging all the questions.

Others have preferred to maintain a simpler twofold distinction between apocalypse and 'apocalyptic eschatology' in the manner of Koch.[52] But this distinction has a marked difference from the twofold distinction pressed here in the present study: it asks for a separation between two items already recognized but sometimes unfortunately confused. For most, the construct 'apocalyptic eschatology' has been the chief interest all along. This is why earlier efforts of interpreters waver as they do between the literature and the supposed phenomenon 'apocalyptic'—in pursuit of the latter they kept bumping into the literature, which is explained as a product of the world-view, so that the abstraction insinuates itself back behind the literature. More recent attention to matters of definition has tried to reduce the confusion by a proper categorization, but this same basic confusion remains unrecognized; and to question the whole matter of speaking of 'apocalyptic' seems rarely to have been contemplated.

This is the background of the present distinction, adopted for method's sake, between speaking of the literature, with all that this entails, a notion the propriety of which is agreed by all, and speaking in a more extended sense of 'apocalyptic', a problematic notion. This distinction between literature and abstraction focuses on the method and the rationale by which one moves from apocalypse to 'apocalyptic', which process speaks volumes on one's perception and use of this literature. Such may be checked against and called into question in light of the texts. Any terminological interposition which short-circuits this process is suspect.

---

51.  Beker, *Triumph of God*, pp. 34, 63-64, 19; see also *Paul* (1984 edn), p. xv.

52.  Cf. Knibb, 'Prophecy', pp. 161, 164-65; Knibb follows Stone here, and although he does not question the matter of an 'apocalyptic eschatology', he does at least balance it with a recognition of the speculative material also present in the texts. As we have seen, Stone also accepts a pragmatic distinction between the apocalypse and 'apocalyptic eschatology', though he does introduce a measure of scepticism as to the aptness of 'apocalyptic eschatology' (that is, on the matter of retaining even here some sense of an essential connection with the apocalypses).

*Genre*

Reflection on definition of 'apocalyptic' has refocused our attention back on the apocalyptic literature, despite efforts to suggest that the literature need not so detain us. An 'apocalyptic' which resists this methodological control suggests a notion perhaps retained more for its usefulness than its integrity. Thus a literary definition has been called for. For when apocalyptic literature becomes simply a feature, a manifestation, of 'apocalyptic' or 'apocalypticism', something, we may suspect, has perhaps gone wrong.

The question of genre naturally arises when one concludes that to call any work evincing 'apocalyptic eschatology' an 'apocalyptic writing' is somehow not sufficient (a conclusion still not universally drawn). Thus genre definition has recently been a major concern.[53] But this concern,

---

53. Form-critical studies were made by Vielhauer ('Introduction') and Koch (*Rediscovery*, pp. 18-35). Hanson has offered a definition of 'apocalypse' as a *genre* ('Apocalypse: Genre'; 'Appendix' in *Dawn*, p. 430). For more recent form-critical study, see J.J. Collins, 'Introduction to Apocalyptic Literature', in *Daniel* (The Forms of Old Testament Literature, 20; Grand Rapids: Eerdmans, 1984), pp. 2-24. The most sustained attempt at a genre definition to date is that of the corresponding section of the SBL Genres Project, chaired by J.J. Collins, published in *Semeia* 14 (1979), Collins (ed.), *Apocalypse: The Morphology of a Genre*; see his 'Introduction', pp. 1-20, and his treatment of 'The Jewish Apocalypses', pp. 21-59. This project is continued in *Semeia* 36 (1986), A. Yarbro Collins (ed.), *Early Christian Apocalypticism: Genre and Social Setting*; see in this volume, A. Yarbro Collins's 'Introduction', pp. 1-11; D. Hellholm, 'The Problem of Apocalyptic Genre and the Apocalypse of John', pp. 13-64; D.E. Aune, 'The Apocalypse of John and the Problem of Genre', pp. 65-96, and M. Himmelfarb, 'The Experience of the Visionary and Genre in the Ascension of Isaiah 6-11 and the Apocalypse of Paul', pp. 97-111. Several studies in Hellholm (ed.), *Apocalypticism*, relate to genre; see the general discussion of L. Hartman, 'Survey of the Problem of the Apocalyptic Genre', in Hellholm (ed.), *Apocalypticism*, pp. 329-43; note also the studies of E.P. Sanders and J.J. Collins in the same volume. See also E.J.C. Tigchelaar, 'More on Apocalyptic and Apocalypses', *JSJ* 18 (1987), pp. 137-44. J.J. Collins's more recent reflections are given in 'Genre, Ideology and Social Movements', in J.J. Collins and Charlesworth (eds.), *Mysteries*, pp. 11-32 (pp. 13-23 on genre). In the same volume D. Hellholm continues his own interpretive project in 'Methodological Reflections on the Problem of Definition of Generic Texts', pp. 135-63. Hellholm's 'syntagmatic' approach seeks to supplement and even contain the 'paradigmatic' approach of Collins and others; but, in the nature of the case, those who acknowledge the importance of Hellholm's efforts are forced to take the wait-and-see attitude of Collins (J.J. Collins and Charlesworth [eds.], *Mysteries*, p. 14) until Hellholm's grammar of the apocalypse is completed. These several special studies are in addition to the various introductions already noted,

ostensibly purely a matter of literary theory and criticism, has not been innocent of the wider happenings in the interpretation of 'apocalyptic'.

Theoretical questions about the notion of 'genre' itself are by no means as settled and unproblematic as might at times appear. What is a genre? How can it be defined and delimited? And, once recognized, just what, if anything, can be inferred about authors and readers with respect to the use of a genre as such? Should we conceive genre more broadly as a class of phenomenologically similar texts (here the broad grouping of related ancient revelatory literature) or more narrowly as a family of historically, genetically related texts (a family of Jewish, Christian, and Gnostic texts)? A somewhat overlapping differentiation is that between a genre distinction which we impose 'from above', as it were, that is, from our point of view (whether or not the distinction would be recognized by the subjects in question), and a genre distinction self-consciously made and employed and understood 'from below', that is, by these subjects. This leads us to ask whether talk of genres necessarily discloses anything about those whom we study or whether it merely serves to tidy up scholarship.[54] At any rate, genres bend to the will of interpreters, and eschatology as key is more artificial the more narrowly conceived the genre (where it will appear that the genre has been cut to fit 'apocalyptic eschatology') and more inadequate the more broadly conceived the genre (where much more will be seen to be going on than just 'apocalyptic eschatology').

By now we should not be surprised to discover the prominence of the notion of eschatology in most attempts to define a genre 'apocalypse'. Matters of form, content, setting, and function stand in uneasy relation, with, it would seem, disproportionate emphasis placed on *eschatological*

---

many of which also include discussion of matters relevant to genre.

54. The general antiquity of a consciousness of an apocalyptic genre (let alone of a phenomenon 'apocalyptic') is worth considering. At what point *could* people of our period have begun to put things together for themselves in the manner that we have done for them? A vexing practical question we come up against here and elsewhere concerns the matter of dating various documents (or more nebulous 'theological traditions') and of deciding on their relative 'Jewish' or 'Christian' character: How much is our determination that it is possible to use some text or 'tradition' as a 'background' to the New Testament determined by our determination to do so? On this latter question, see R.A. Kraft, 'The Multiform Jewish Heritage of Early Christianity', in J. Neusner (ed.), *Christianity, Judaism and Other Greco-Roman Cults: Studies for Morton Smith at Sixty* (Leiden: E.J. Brill, 1975), III, pp. 174-99.

content.[55] Discussion of genre often feels uncannily like little more than familiar theological talk of 'apocalyptic' in literary dress. Relatedly, comparative studies, whether with biblical literature, other types of contemporary Jewish revelatory literature, or the revelatory literature of the broader contemporary environment, have tended to be made simply on the basis of comparable eschatology.[56] The clear predilection throughout (despite the occasional protest) for 'apocalyptic eschatology' points to the inherent circularity of defining the genre 'apocalypse', an enterprise usually, it seems, undertaken with a view toward marking off a corpus from which a definition of 'apocalyptic' is to arise, which latter definition, inevitably already in mind to some degree and for which definite plans are likely to be already in view, exercises its own influence on the question of genre. Thus one may even at times sense a certain haste to push through the literary-theoretical and literary-critical preliminary and get down to the real business of 'apocalyptic'—as though somehow there should correspond to the genre such a discrete phenomenon.

Attention to this literature in all its aspects is a broader matter than merely defining a genre. The matter of the phenomenology of ancient revelatory experience and practice thus arises one way or another when we inquire as to the proper wider contemporary setting of the apocalypses. This matter relates to the question of the 'authenticity of revelatory experiences narrated in apocalypses', which David E. Aune seems correct in characterizing as 'an insoluble problem'.[57] The relation

55. This is clear in the J.J. Collins (ed.), *Apocalypse*, definition (for which see Collins's 'Introduction', p. 9), which makes prominent reference to eschatology, and in the continuation in A. Yarbro Collins (ed.), *Early Christian Apocalypticism*, where, although Aune (pp. 67, 87) and Himmelfarb (pp. 97-98, 106-109) challenge the preoccupation of the Genres Project definition with 'apocalyptic eschatology', A. Yarbro Collins, unable to countenance the removal of 'eschatology', further secures it by making it doubly present in the addition made to the original definition (pp. 5-6). J.J. Collins has recently reaffirmed this insistence on eschatology ('Genre, Ideology and Social Movements', J.J. Collins and Charlesworth (eds.), *Mysteries*, pp. 15-17).

56. Cf. the J.J. Collins (ed.), *Apocalypse*, discussion: see, for example, Collins's discussion of antecedents and related works for the early Jewish apocalypses (pp. 29-30, 44-49), A. Yarbro Collins's discussion of related texts for the early Christian apocalypses (pp. 96-103), and J.J. Collins's chapter on 'Persian Apocalypses' (pp. 207-17)—all these comparative matters are conceived primarily on the basis of 'apocalyptic eschatology'. C. Rowland has been a prominent voice in favour of making the spirituality or religious experience implied primary.

57. Aune, 'Problem of Genre', p. 83.

between the ancient revelatory literature and ancient revelatory practice and experience is not uncomplicated. An apocalypse, with its visions and heavenly ascents, might be one thing, the implied revelatory experience another. Is the 'revelation' of the apocalypses a fictional mock-up for ideology and propaganda (a sectarian 'science of the end'[58]), or is there a real interest in 'higher wisdom through revelation', reflecting actual visionary experience of 'the open heaven'?[59] According to Aune, 'regardless of the stereotypical literary formulations, structures and imagery, the context in which such texts must be understood is that of the *phenomenology of revelatory experience*'.[60] John J. Collins marks a basic generic sub-classification between texts with otherworldly journeys and those without (the 'historical' type), and he makes the suggestive observation that typical generalizations about 'apocalyptic' are made with the 'historical non-otherworldly' type in view, which type he says makes up only about one third of the early Jewish works.[61] Not surprisingly, then, those who make the visions and otherworldly journeys a particular point of focus have begun to take the genre as a whole in another direction, placing the apocalypses in an entirely different frame of reference—that of the broader phenomenon of this world of revelations.[62]

*Origins, Social Setting, and other Matters Bearing on Definition*
Questions of origins have loomed large in study of 'apocalyptic'.[63] The preoccupation with eschatology continues, as discussion of origins has

58. Cf. Hanson's opinion that the visionaries 'cloak their eschatological message in an aura of eruditeness'.

59. The phrase 'higher wisdom through revelation' is from Martin Hengel's account of the history of religions milieu of the apocalypses, M. Hengel, *Judaism and Hellenism*, I, pp. 210-18; the phrase is taken up by C. Rowland in *The Open Heaven*.

60. Aune, 'Problem of Genre', p. 82; see pp. 81-84; idem, *The New Testament in its Literary Environment*, pp. 231-38; and see D.E. Aune's full study, *Prophecy in Early Christianity and the Ancient Mediterranean World* (Grand Rapids: Eerdmans, 1983).

61. See J.J. Collins (ed.), *Apocalypse*, pp. 13-14.

62. Relevant here are Rowland, Stone, and Gruenwald, among others.

63. See Vielhauer, 'Introduction', pp. 594-98; Nicholson, 'Apocalyptic'; J.J. Collins, 'Jewish Apocalyptic Against its Hellenistic Near Eastern Environment', *BASOR* 220 (1975), pp. 27-36; idem, 'Cosmos and Salvation: Jewish Wisdom and Apocalyptic in the Hellenistic Age', *HR* 17 (1977), pp. 121-42; idem, *Apocalyptic Imagination*, pp. 19-28; idem, 'The Place of Apocalypticism in the Religion of

tended to be consumed with ideas, with theology and with the theological roots of apocalyptic thought, especially in biblical literature and chiefly prophecy. This general interest in origins is never really sure whether it is talking about the origins of the literature or the abstraction (mostly the latter, of course), and we are very often unsure as to whether it is history or theology that we are being given. The confusion is absolutely typical of talk of 'apocalyptic'—indeed, study of origins was until recently the more or less undifferentiated matter of defining 'apocalyptic', where the latter stands for the literature, the thought, and who knows what else.[64] With the vogue of literary and social-scientific approaches to biblical criticism, study of genre and of social setting have taken over much of origins' trade (though their claim to have addressed the former ambiguities one might well doubt, as often enough both seem to translate old conversations into new languages). If we begin (as so many seem to do) with something like Rowley's notion of 'prophetic' and 'apocalyptic eschatology', the fact that we *can* reconstruct a process by which the latter arose from the former—a scenario complete with 'apocalyptists' (or 'apocalypticists') living in 'apocalyptic communities' with their distinctive corpora of 'apocalyptic literature' expressive of their collective ideology of 'apocalyptic eschatology' or 'apocalypticism' —ought to impress us a good deal less than it apparently does. Much of such interpretation, that is, although supposedly about literature or history or sociology, looks suspiciously like biblical theology, and as

Israel', in P.D. Miller, Jr., P.D. Hanson and S.D. McBride (eds.), *Ancient Israelite Wisdom: Essays in Honor of Frank Moore Cross* (Philadelphia: Fortress Press, 1987), pp. 539-58; *idem*, Appendix to 'Genre, Ideology and Social Movements', pp. 25-32 (discussing recent research by J.C. VanderKam and H.S. Kvanvig on the Mesopotamian backgrounds of 'apocalyptic'); R.J. Bauckham, 'The Rise of Apocalyptic', *Themelios* 3 (1978), pp. 10-23; W.G. Lambert, *The Background of Jewish Apocalyptic* (The Ethel M. Wood Lecture, 1977; London: Athlone, 1978); G.I. Davies, 'Apocalyptic and Historiography', *JSOT* 5 (1978), pp. 15-28; Knibb, 'Prophecy'; J.C. VanderKam, 'The Prophetic–Sapiential Origins of Apocalyptic Thought', in J.D. Martin and P.R. Davies (eds.), *A Word in Season: Essays in Honour of William McKane* (JSOTSup, 42; Sheffield: JSOT Press, 1986), pp. 163-76; *idem*, Hanson (ed.), *Visionaries*, pp. 85-100; *idem*, 'Apocalyptic Literature', pp. 384-92; Rowland, *The Open Heaven*, pp. 193-267; *idem*, *Christian Origins*, pp. 63-64; *idem*, 'The Intertestamental Literature', pp. 202-203; various of the introductions already noted also address origins, and see the further works cited below under 'social setting'.

64.   See again on Hanson, above.

illuminating as this may be, the apocalypses remain largely unexplained and 'apocalyptic' continues to float about restlessly in its state of disembodied existence.

I observed divergent approaches to 'apocalyptic' emerging within discussion of genre. A similar process occurs in the case of origins, and along the same lines. Rowland observes that the two chief competing views of origins, stressing 'biblical prophecy' and 'mantic wisdom', correspond to two diverging interpretations of 'apocalyptic', focusing on 'apocalyptic eschatology' and 'revelation of heavenly mysteries', respectively.[65] The latter approach may in fact constitute a complete reorientation of the question.

The shift to the inquiry into social setting[66] (as I must repeat once more) preserves and passes on the usual confusion as to whether it is the sociology of the literature or the assumed abstraction that is in view. Thus, and despite the many directions that might be taken, such inquiry has tended simply to turn earlier theological talk of crisis, persecution, alienation, despair, and dawning transcendent hope into talk of 'apocalyptic communities'. These are understood more or less along the lines marked out by study of 'millenarianism', usually following something like Hanson's threefold terminology and likewise failing to clarify the relation of all this to the apocalypses, though it is clear that, for many, so to treat of 'apocalyptic' is to take care of the apocalypses at the same time.[67] Once again, there is a certain captivity to scenarios which reconstruct a 'social setting' for the shift from 'prophetic' to 'apocalyptic eschatology'.[68] Furthermore, if we set out in search

65. Rowland, 'The Intertestamental Literature', pp. 202-203.

66. On 'social setting', see: R.R. Wilson, 'From Prophecy to Apocalyptic: Reflections on the Shape of Israelite Religion', *Semeia* 21 (1981), pp. 79-95; G.W.E. Nickelsburg, 'Social Aspects of Palestinian Jewish Apocalyptic', in Hellholm (ed.), *Apocalypticism*, pp. 641-50; L.L. Grabbe, 'The Social Setting of Early Jewish Apocalypticism', *JSP* 4 (1989), pp. 27-47; P.R. Davies, 'The Social World of Apocalyptic Writings', in R.E. Clements (ed.), *The World of Ancient Israel* (Cambridge: Cambridge University Press, 1989), pp. 251-71. See also Rowland, *The Open Heaven*, pp. 193-247.

67. Grabbe proposes that 'apocalypticism is a complex phenomenon with both literary and social aspects which should not be confused' and that 'there is no necessary connection between apocalypses and apocalyptic communities' ('Social Setting', pp. 28-30). This is simply a variation on Hanson and does not make for clarity.

68. The work of Hanson on origins and social setting is exemplary of this tendency; for critical comments see Rowland, 'The Intertestamental Literature',

of such, our 'success' should not surprise us.

There is something distinctly odd about such approaches, even if it is difficult to put our finger on it. From talk of apocalypses one moves to 'apocalyptic' as a set of ideas or doctrines presumably characteristic of them, from which we then get 'apocalyptic communities', understood as groups characterized and defined by 'apocalyptic' ideology—'thus, the validity of the term "apocalyptic" in a social sense depends on an ideological sense which in turn depends on its (proper) literary sense'.[69] What is the relationship between history, society, and literature?

> In the case of apocalyptic writings, the dominance of traditional literary-historical methods, allied to the equally traditional theological-dogmatic approach, has led to the construction of a social entity called the 'apocalyptic community'. Certainly, apocalypses have social contexts, but the existence of a literary genre does not imply a correspondingly discrete social 'genre'. The anatomy of literature and the anatomy of society are not equivalent, and one cannot infer one from the other.[70]

(While it is not beyond the realm of possibility for literature, ideology, and society to line up neatly and conveniently as suggested by typical notions of 'apocalyptic', it all appears somewhat simplistic, not to say suspicious.)

Corresponding to the diverging approaches noted with respect to genre and origins, recent inquiry into the social setting of the apocalypses asks what produced this literary combination at this time in history, and why, and emphasis here on the diverse mystical and speculative revelatory experience and lore deposited in the apocalypses suggests for some an alternative setting in the contemporary intellectual culture of scribalism in the tradition of manticism.[71]

We might also pose basic questions of definition in terms of contents, history, and essence (of the literature, we mean in each case).

pp. 184-87; Davies, 'Social World', pp. 255-58; and Knibb, 'Prophecy', pp. 169-76.

69. Davies, 'Social World', p. 252.

70. Davies, 'Social World'. This essay by Davies suggests several methodological points similar to some I have arrived at independently, owing in part, perhaps, to common influences. The opening section of this essay (pp. 251-55) I would offer as a model of sanity in treating this matter of 'apocalyptic'; see also P.R. Davies 'Qumran and Apocalyptic or *obscurum per obscurius*', *JNES* 49 (1990), pp. 127-34, especially pp. 128-30.

71. See P.R. Davies, 'Social World', pp. 260-70; cf. J.Z. Smith, 'Wisdom and Apocalyptic', in Hanson (ed.), *Visionaries*, pp. 101-20; the approach of Rowland, again, is relevant here.

Consideration of the contents of the apocalypses for many does not extend beyond a concern for eschatology, considered to be *the* defining interest of the literature and the supposed phenomenon. 'Apocalyptic', by such lights, is a distinct type of eschatology. But Stone recognizes alongside this eschatological content the 'speculative', 'the revelation of heavenly or similar secrets', which 'may include matters of cosmography and uranography, angelology and meteorology, calendar and cosmogony, and more'.[72] Rowland regards the apocalypses as being concerned with the broad range of speculative human interest in matters beyond the reach of human reason accessible only through direct revelation from God. These he sums up under the rubrics 'what is above, what is beneath, what was beforetime, and what will be hereafter'.[73] Eschatology thus takes its place, however prominent, alongside many other interests and beneath this general speculative or mystical interest. The cluster of ideas usually taken as characterizing 'apocalyptic' seems hardly to have been designed to fit the literature and must then have been cut to fit some other need, culling a few choice texts and from the vast array of apocalyptic material, leaving the bulk largely untouched, with the resulting composite seemingly bearing at best an atmospheric relation to any particular text. The biblical book of Revelation might come closest to providing a home for the orphaned phenomenon, which is hardly a triumph in the light of the degree to which this book has influenced the agenda of description.[74]

Consideration of the history of the literature raises the question of whether there is actually here a unitary phenomenon capable of or suitable for a singular treatment at all. I have observed at various points above two contending approaches to the literature, with one seeing a fairly singular and stable history of the texts as carriers of the ideology of 'apocalyptic eschatology', while the other places the apocalypses within a long tradition of mystical and speculative piety. Both attempt to unite the diversity which threatens to pull the literature in a number of directions under some 'essence'—in the first case that of the concept of 'apocalyptic eschatology', in the second case something along the lines

72. Stone, 'Apocalyptic Literature', pp. 383-84. Stone continues: 'A third, less prominent subject appears in a number of cases, a pietistic, moral preaching'.

73. See Rowland, *The Open Heaven*, p. 75; the four categories are taken from a mishnaic expression of reserve toward such speculation; see pp. 75-189 for extensive coverage of the diverse contents of the apocalypses.

74. Cf. Rowland, 'The Intertestamental Literature', pp. 205-206.

of Rowland's effort to construe the diverse material as united under a common concern for 'direct access to heavenly secrets', for 'higher wisdom through revelation'. For my own purposes I might ask why the literature should conform completely to either view, which is not at all to regard both approaches as of equal legitimacy (my sympathy for the latter approach should be clear) or to suggest that the literature could be neatly parcelled up between them, but rather simply to note that there is no controlling the use to which the genre might have been put, a matter which is past finding out.

Turning, then, to the matter of 'essence', there is no design here to extract anything of the sort (indeed, the last point begins to put the whole matter of an 'essence' to the literature on shaky ground). Rather, the customary approach is set over against alternatives variously suggested by recent challenges to the received wisdom, in the form of dichotomizations, oversimply put to set differences of perspective in sharpest focus. Is 'apocalyptic' a matter of eschatology or of vision of 'the open heaven'? Is it theology and ideology or speculation and religious experience? Is it a purely literary phenomenon or does actual visionary experience underlie its vision form? Is it prophecy or wisdom/ manticism? Pseudo-esoteric or esoteric? Inner-Jewish or Hellenistic? The 'consensus' view silently if not unconsciously assumes its position on such questions as these: the apocalypse is primarily a literary repository of 'apocalyptic', that is, the ideology of the persecuted, marginalized, disenfranchised, and oppressed, voicing its protest against such tyranny and injustice and strengthening the elect with its hope-filled picture of imminent divine intervention and judgement, reversal, and glory in the line of, though shaped by different circumstances than, biblical prophecy.

Circularities and confusions multiply. In particular, the highly self-preservative predilection for 'apocalyptic eschatology' and the near-ubiquitous confusion between the literature and such an abstraction have been much in evidence. Suspicions of Christian origins and biblical-theological agendas have been raised. The myriad times 'apocalyptic' falls lightly from the lips of New Testament scholars provokes scant suspicion of the many facets of defining this favoured term. Attention to such has a way of making hopes of simple, uncontroversial, and transparent talk of 'apocalyptic' recede into an apocalyptic mist.

### From Apocalypse to 'Apocalyptic': 'Apocalyptic Interpretation'

I return to the words of Rowley, quoted at the outset: 'the prophets foretold the future that should arise out of the present, while the apocalyptists foretold the future that should break into the present'.[75] For D.S. Russell, the movement 'between the testaments' may be characterized as a movement from prophetic to apocalyptic eschatology, a period of 'tension...between this-worldly, national and political elements on the one hand, and other-worldly, universal and transcendent elements on the other'.[76] With the ascendancy of apocalyptic eschatology:

> No longer...is the future hope simply nationalistic in the sense that it is circumscribed by the boundaries of any one nation of people; it is universalistic in the sense that God's salvation extends to the righteous and his judgments fall upon the wicked. No longer is the nation as such the only object of God's redemption...there emerges a future hope for the individual who will share in the coming kingdom by means of resurrection. No longer are God's enemies confined to men of flesh and blood; they are the demonic powers of darkness who have entrenched themselves in God's vast universe and in the heart of man. No longer are God's battles fought with sword and spear; they now assume cosmic proportions and involve the whole universe. Thus apocalyptic eschatology becomes more and more transcendent, with stress from first to last on the supernatural and the supra-mundane. Deliverance will come, not from men, but from God himself who will bring in his kingdom and usher in the age to come. This will mark the fulfillment and triumph of God's eternal purpose which has been from the beginning and will continue to the very end.[77]

The same ageing conception is given a new lease on life with a fresh coat of sociohistorical respectability in the hands of Hanson:

> Apocalyptic eschatology we define as a religious perspective which focuses on the disclosure (usually esoteric in nature) to the elect of the cosmic vision of Yahweh's sovereignty—especially as it relates to his acting to deliver his faithful—which disclosure the visionaries have largely

---

75. Rowley, *Relevance*, p. 38.

76. Russell, *Between the Testaments*, p. 121; cf. *idem*, *Jews*, pp. 139-44, where the discussion of 'apocalyptic eschatology' is part of a general section on the development of religious ideas of the period; the same is true of his *Between the Testaments*, in which, after a discussion of the history, institutions, sects, and literature of the period, the relevant (to whom or what?) religious development may be subsumed under a discussion of 'the apocalyptists' (pp. 93-162).

77. Russell, *Method and Message*, pp. 264-71 (pp. 268-69).

ceased [in direct contrast to the prophets] to translate into the terms of plain history, real politics, and human instrumentality due to a pessimistic view of reality growing out of the bleak post-exilic conditions within which those associated with the visionaries found themselves. Those conditions seemed unsuitable to them as a context for the envisioned restoration of Yahweh's people.[78]

Both Rowley and Russell before him have noticed the 'proto-apocalyptic' of the prophets; but for them such needed the infusion of religious ideas from Persia and the crisis of the Maccabean uprising to flower.[79] Hanson is eager to show that the crisis needed for the birth of 'apocalyptic eschatology' occurred much earlier, within the post-exilic community, while the source of the cosmic, transcendent perspective was the rediscovered and reappropriated indigenous ancient mythology. Thus 'Jewish apocalyptic literature emerged in an unbroken, inner-Israelite development out of pre-Exilic and Exilic prophecy...Influences from Persian dualism and Hellenism were late, coming only after the essential character of apocalyptic was fully developed, and were thus limited to peripheral embellishments'.[80] In this way, 'apocalyptic eschatology' is as securely attached to the Old Testament as Rowley and Russell have shown it to be to the New. Finally, a couple more examples (which could be greatly multiplied) of this tradition of interpretation may be noted, taken first from James H. Charlesworth, then from Helmut Koester:

> The Pseudepigrapha, generally speaking, give considerable prominence to apocalyptic thought, ideas, and symbols...[The] apocalypses bifurcate time into two ages: the first age is grinding wearily to a halt mired in tribulation; the future age is about to dawn bringing with it judgment and punishment for the wicked and a return to the blissful peace of Eden or transference to Paradise for the righteous.
>
> Two reasons for the resurging importance of the Pseudepigrapha...are the dating of some fifty documents, or portions of them, to the extremely fecund period that separates the 'Old' from the 'New' Testaments; and the recognition that the central thought of these documents, apocalyptic, is at once central to intertestamental Judaism and nascent Christianity. The new perception of the Pseudepigrapha should be linked with the growing

78. Hanson, *Dawn*, pp. 11-12.
79. Rowley, *Relevance*, pp. 24-26, 43; Russell, *Method and Message*, pp. 88-92, 19, 16.
80. Hanson, 'Jewish Apocalyptic', pp. 33-34.

appreciation for the significance of apocalyptic thought not only by historians but also by systematic theologians.[81]

The apocalyptic movement became the most important theological movement in Judaism during the Hellenistic period, and it was also to play a decisive role in the formation of Christianity. It was apocalypticism that mediated the essential inheritance of Israel and its prophetic tradition to Jesus and his followers, although in a characteristic transformation. Thus, apocalypticism is the real bridge between the Old and New Testaments; but it also decisively influenced the later development of Judaism.[82]

Even overlooking the question of the validity or otherwise of this reconstruction of the theological development of the period, we can say that the weight of the hand of such schemes on the apocalypses and on talk of 'apocalyptic' has been heavy indeed. Here one begins to see clearly what is meant by speaking of the method of and rationale behind moving beyond the apocalypses to apply the notion 'apocalyptic', as this 'between the testaments' scheme of interpretation is just such a movement: the method is via the concept 'apocalyptic eschatology', and the rationale is a Christian origins one (or, again, a biblical-theological one—the two are often so hard to distinguish, and especially so here). Such interpretations do not perceive themselves as side-stepping or steam-rolling the apocalypses, because the concept 'apocalyptic eschatology' has the priority and, as it were, the right-of-way, as it came first, and is itself responsible for the apocalypses, as well as other literature, such as, of course, much of the New Testament. To take this grand scheme of 'apocalyptic eschatology', itself apparently assembled from hopelessly scattered snippets according to the pattern presumed to be provided by some strands of New Testament thought, and to read it back fully formed into the apocalypses and other texts, only to read it back again for the 'light' it sheds on the New Testament, is both a Leviathan of a vicious circle (a sort of schizophrenic 'scripture interprets scripture') and, to borrow an appropriately ominous sounding term, an

---

81. J.H. Charlesworth, 'A History of Pseudepigrapha Research: The Re-emerging Importance of the Pseudepigrapha', *ANRW* II.19.1 (1979), pp. 75-77. Remarkably similar sentiments to this 'new' perception are expressed in Russell, *Between the Testaments*, p. 93.

82. H. Koester, *Introduction to the New Testament, Volume One: History, Culture, and Religion of the Hellenistic Age* (Philadelphia: Fortress/Berlin and New York: Walter de Gruyter, 1982), p. 230 (for all that, 'apocalypticism' gets four pages of coverage, as compared to about twice that for 'gnosticism' and about ten times that for Hellenistic syncretism and the 'mysteries').

'illegitimate totality transfer' of, well, apocalyptic proportions.

On this last note we cross over into suspicion of the scheme itself, quite apart from its hold on the apocalypses. But instead of reflecting on this situation, our attention is diverted by a sort of salvation-by-proper-terminology gospel. Thus Charlesworth elsewhere reassures us: 'So much progress has been made in the study of apocalyptic thought, the apocalypses, and apocalypticism that a scholar's competence is revealed immediately by his or her use of these three terms'.[83] Charlesworth proceeds to give his acknowledged Hansonesque terminology a fuller description: '"apocalypse" refers to literary phenomena', including not only apocalypses but 'apocalyptic writings' such as the Testaments of the Twelve Patriarchs (that is, writings characterized by 'apocalyptic eschatology'); the apocalypses are 'produced by apocalypticism', which encompasses both the thought behind the texts and 'the sociological phenomena lying behind and producing such documents', which are usually set in 'the collapse of meaningful social structures' and are 'characterized by a lament over the failure of solutions or salvations to come out of normal historical developments'. Finally, 'apocalyptic thought' is the usual 'apocalyptic eschatology', and we are told that 'Professor J. Christiaan Beker has astutely argued that the heart of Paul's theology is shaped by Jewish apocalyptic thought'.[84] Competence indeed.

What is one to make of this notion of an 'apocalyptic eschatology'? To assess fully the propriety of the notion would require considerable attention both to the Jewish eschatology of the period as a whole and to the relative place and nature of eschatology in the apocalypses. That is, to speak of 'apocalyptic eschatology' would seem to be to make large claims about contemporary Jewish thought and expectation as well as, of course, about the relation of the apocalyptic literature to such. 'Apocalyptic eschatology' suggests a more or less fixed point of eschatological thought in the contemporary period of development. It is presupposed, as Christopher Rowland suggests,

> that it is possible to extract from the literature of Judaism a body of 'apocalyptic' material and to find in it a unified eschatological picture which varies only in relatively insignificant details. Implicit also in this view is the belief that this eschatology differs from other types which could be found in Jewish literature of this period. Most attempts to define

83. J.H. Charlesworth, *Jesus Within Judaism* (New York: Doubleday, 1988), p. 34.

84. Charlesworth, *Jesus Within Judaism*, pp. 34-42 (pp. 34-35).

apocalyptic do in fact indicate that there are certain key elements which typify the apocalyptic eschatology: the doctrine of the two ages, a pessimistic attitude towards the present, supernatural intervention as the basis for redemption, and an urgent expectation of the dawn of a new age.[85]

'When one investigates the eschatology of the apocalypses, it all too quickly becomes clear that what are often regarded as typical features of apocalyptic are by no means common'.[86] Rowland argues that there is neither a singular nor a distinctive eschatology in the apocalypses but rather a variety of eschatologies corresponding to the variety of expectations of the period, further denying that the customary few instances cited of that otherworldly expectation held to typify 'apocalyptic' are characteristic of this body of literature or of contemporary expectation generally, which remains largely this-worldly in its hopes. (Rowland suggests the term 'transcendent eschatology' instead of the confusing 'apocalyptic eschatology' where it is appropriate to speak of such at all.)[87]

> In the apocalypses and in other Jewish literature we have a variety of eschatological beliefs existing alongside each other. As a result it is impossible to separate out a strand of eschatological expectations which is coherent enough to be distinguished as an apocalyptic sectarian ideology. [Consideration of] early rabbinic eschatology suggests that 'apocalyptic' eschatological elements had a fairly wide currency within Judaism and formed part of the common stock of ideas which many groups would have utilized. It is difficult to speak, therefore, of an apocalyptic eschatology existing alongside a nationalistic eschatology, the two being alternative expressions of the future hope in Judaism...
>
> All the indications are that the apocalypses share with other examples of Jewish literature similar eschatological beliefs. No doubt distinctive ideas emerge in the apocalypses but the eschatological elements hardly occur on anything like a large enough scale for us to speak of an apocalyptic eschatology over against other eschatological systems. This applies particularly to transcendent or other-worldly eschatology...The character of the eschatological beliefs is too varied, and the detail in the various apocalypses insufficient, to make a clear-cut definition of apocalyptic eschatology anything but a hazardous task.[88]

85. Rowland, *The Open Heaven*, p. 28.
86. Rowland, *Christian Origins*, p. 57.
87. Rowland, *The Open Heaven*, pp. 23-48; 'The Intertestamental Literature', pp. 200-206; Review of *The Apocalyptic Imagination*, by Collins and *Jewish Writings*, ed. Stone, pp. 486-90; *Christian Origins*, pp. 56-64.
88. Rowland, *The Open Heaven*, pp. 36-37, 48.

Not only does talk of 'apocalyptic eschatology' tend to carry questionable assumptions about trajectories of 'between-the-testaments' development and about the inexorable drift of eschatological hopes of the times, but taken as the key to the apocalypses and as the means of drawing connections beyond them to, say, Paul, it also suggests the prominence and primacy of eschatology in the apocalypses. While none would deny the frequency and importance of eschatological speculations in the apocalypses, Rowland joins many others in noting that there is much more to these texts than eschatology, making this an inadequate entrance to the apocalypses, with their more encyclopaedic interests. 'Apocalyptic eschatology' not only tends to obscure this diversity—it does not even get the apocalyptic eschatology (that is, that eschatology which is found in the apocalypses) right.

> There is great variety not only in the contents of the apocalypses, but also in their eschatology. Consequently the contents are not easily reduced to terse summaries which encapsulate apocalyptic eschatology in a sentence or two. What is more, the emphasis on the future breaking into the present as a hallmark of apocalyptic, while not entirely absent in the apocalyptic literature, hardly summarizes the varying features of the eschatological secrets. It must, therefore, be questioned whether a particular type of eschatology can so easily be used as the characteristic feature of the hope for the future in the apocalypses.[89]

If the eschatology of the apocalypses is so widespread, so varied, and so typical of the times, and if so-called 'apocalyptic eschatology' is so little expressive of the breadth of the apocalypses and so scarcely representative of these texts *or* of this period, just what good is the concept 'apocalyptic eschatology'? Does our loyalty to it extend to allowing it to skew our perception of the literature and the age as a whole?

> Nowhere has the construction of heuristic categories so influenced the reading of texts than in the case of the apocalyptic literature. In the older writing on the subject the contrast between apocalyptic and prophecy, and, in the more recent writing, the threefold division of apocalypse, apocalyptic, and apocalyptic eschatology have provided conceptual frameworks which have been the parameters within which the discussion of texts and ideas have been carried on. It is a mark of the persistence of ideologies within any sphere of human existence that, however great the distortions they lead to and however bad the match is between ideas and reality, the heuristic categories continue to demand allegiance and repudiate attempts to dismantle them. But surely it is in the study of apocalyptic particularly

89. Rowland, *The Open Heaven*, p. 29.

where probing the reality behind the appearance is so essential that we should demand a greater match between heuristic constructs and the reality of the texts?[90]

Rowland's has been among the clearest voices urging the need to hold our discourse about 'apocalyptic' accountable to the apocalypses. And the literature, he persuasively argues, does not lend itself to the grand theorizing that passes under its name.[91]

90.    Rowland, Review of *The Apocalyptic Imagination*, by Collins and *Jewish Writings*, ed. Stone, p. 488.

91.    Having raised the problem of the hegemony of heuristic categories, we might briefly relate the point to two principal reference works: the two volumes of J.H. Charlesworth (ed.), *The Old Testament Pseudepigrapha* (2 vols.; London: Darton, Longman & Todd, 1983, 1985), and the revised handbook of E. Schürer, *The History of the Jewish People in the Age of Jesus Christ (175 BC—AD 135)* (ed. Geza Vermes *et al.*; Edinburgh: T. & T. Clark, 1973-87). In the case of the former, by what 'heuristic categories' is the selection made resulting in one of the two volumes being devoted to 'Apocalyptic Literature and Testaments', one section of which collecting 'Apocalyptic Literature and Related Works' and the other 'Testaments' (often with 'Apocalyptic' Sections)? How did it come about that, for example, *Ascension of Isaiah*, 'unambiguously [an] apocalypse' according to R. Bauckham, is not numbered with these but found in the other volume (Bauckham, 'The Apocalypses in the New Pseudepigrapha', p. 97; the same is said of *Ladder of Jacob*. 'Presumably they are included in vol. 2 because they are regarded as legendary expansions of the Old Testament, but they are no more so than *1 Enoch* or the *Apocalypses of Abraham*, both of which include narrative material as well as apocalyptic visions' [p. 115 n. 3])? Incidentally (but perhaps not coincidentally), this work, whose eschatological content is slight, offers a virtual definition of the revised perspective on 'apocalyptic' promoted by Rowland and others: in setting the scene for Isaiah's heavenly ascent, the company of king, prophets, and people gathered around to hear Isaiah suddenly hear 'a door opened' and 'the voice of the Spirit', 'and they ascribed glory to the One who had thus graciously given a door in an alien world' (6.6-10, *Old Testament Pseudepigrapha* II, pp. 164-65). The point is that even the most neutral-seeming of works, a collection of primary texts in translation, inscribes a certain perspective. Turning briefly to the 'Revised Schürer', though it is a 'work of reference' self-consciously aiming 'to provide...a critical and objective presentation of all the available evidence' (I.vi), 'heuristic categories' are similarly (and unavoidably) in operation (as a revised work, many of its features are admittedly inherited). In the introduction to 'Prophetic-Apocalyptic Pseudepigrapha' (Schürer, *History*, III.1.240-44), after noting some literary characteristics, the term 'apocalyptic' is introduced as according to conventional use (Schürer, *History*, III.1.242), with an explanatory footnote: 'The concept has been the subject of much argument. In the strict sense it designates all that pertains to the literary genre of apocalyptic. Taken more broadly [it is hoped that, by now, this very move will provoke scrutiny],

Rowland's own positive approach places the eschatological interests of the apocalypses, which vary according to the interests of those responsible for them, within the context of the interest in 'the open heaven', a quest for direct access to heavenly secrets, including, where these are matters of concern (as they often are in the period under discussion), the mysteries of the future and the problem of failed hopes. Rowland sets this quest within a wider contemporary search for heavenly access and a narrower Jewish, Christian, and later mystical tradition of visionary piety, which takes its departure from obscurities in the scriptural texts concerning, for example, primordial times, the heavenly world, and the hereafter, and seeks answers, in contrast to more conventional exegetical means, from the very source. Thus, 'apocalyptic' is a religious perspective abstracted from the apocalypses and related material, located synchronically and diachronically in terms of socioreligious history. If applied to Paul, attention shifts from the 'apocalyptic eschatology' of 1 Corinthians 15 to the rapture to paradise in 2 Corinthians 12.[92] With Rowland's

however, apocalyptic can apply to a mode of thought, a religious tendency, regularly expressed in apocalypses, but capable also of being included in other types of literature...There is good reason for distinguishing further "apocalyptic" from "messianic" because the former kind of eschatology is conceivable with or without a christological figure...Rowland differentiates correctly between apocalyptic and eschatology, characterizing the former as revelation of heavenly mysteries, the latter as concern for the future age. But it is clearly undeniable that the flowering of apocalyptic occurred during an age of eschatological enthusiasm' (Schürer, *History*, III.1.242 n. 3). This latter is the rationale for departing from the 'strict sense' and taking 'apocalyptic' 'more broadly' as a distinctive eschatological perspective. Elsewhere, in a work largely devoted to history and literature, two major sections stand out as addressing topically the thought, the theology, of the day, 'Life and the Law' (Schürer, *History*, II, pp. 464-87) and 'Messianism' (Schürer, *History*, II, pp. 488-554), corresponding more or less to the common division between prophetic/rabbinic thought and 'apocalyptic'. The latter section offers 'a systematic outline of messianism', drawing on all contemporary literature, but 'presented according to the pattern emerging from the Apocalypses of Baruch and Ezra since it is in these two late compositions that eschatological expectation is most fully developed' (Schürer, *History*, II, p. 514). 'Messianism' here is the functional equivalent of 'apocalyptic', and to take the pattern for such from these two apocalypses as offering the 'most fully developed' portrait would appear to assume a certain trajectory of development. Again, the point is the degree to which the most 'neutral' of reference works lead our thinking. This is not at all to question the value of these two indispensable works, but to caution their users to reflective use, to use them and not be used by them.

92. See Rowland, *The Open Heaven*, pp. 374-86.

interpretation and related approaches, as has been suggested at various points above, a considerable shift has occurred in the understanding of the literature, which is now seen to be bound up essentially not with eschatology but with secret knowledge and with revelatory experience.[93]

The present study asks us to keep distinct, for clarity's sake, the processes by which we attempt to understand the texts, the apocalypses, in their formal distinctiveness, their ideological dimensions, both original and conventional, their settings in time and space, and their position against the background of the revelatory literature and practice of their day, and the processes by which we draw connections beyond the apocalypses by some abstraction of an apocalyptic 'essence'. 'Apocalyptic eschatology' has not proved viable as such an 'essence'. Talk of transcendent eschatology, of millenarian movements, and of theological developments 'between the testaments' may do as it likes, but such must relinquish its distorting claim and hold over the apocalypses. By focusing attention back on the literature, more defensible connections for these texts may be explored in the world of revelatory experience and practice. But it should now be asked why, even in such a case, the concept 'apocalyptic' is invoked. Thus this critique, which has made much use of Rowland's interpretation against typical notions, is not building up to a blanket endorsement of Rowland's (or anyone else's) way of speaking of 'apocalyptic'. His approach is indeed much more methodologically self-conscious, and it is built on a much sounder reading of the apocalypses.

93. For interpretation related to that direction in which Rowland's synthesis takes the literature, cf. the following (by no means amounting to a singular approach): Stone, 'Lists' (see esp. pp. 442-43); *idem*, 'Apocalyptic Literature'; *idem*, 'Apocalyptic—Vision or Hallucination?', *Milla wa-Milla* 14 (1974), pp. 47-56; and see the collection, M.E. Stone, *Selected Studies in Pseudepigrapha and Apocrypha. With Special Reference to the Armenian Tradition* (SVTP, 9; Leiden: Brill, 1991); I. Gruenwald, *Apocalyptic and Merkavah Mysticism* (AGJU, 14; Leiden: Brill, 1979); *idem*, 'Jewish Apocalypticism to the Rabbinic Period', in M. Eliade, *et al.* (ed.), *The Encyclopedia of Religion* (New York: Macmillan, 1987), I, pp. 337-42; and see the studies now collected in I. Gruenwald, *From Apocalypticism to Gnosticism: Studies in Apocalypticism, Merkavah Mysticism and Gnosticism* (BEATAJ, 14; Frankfurt am Main: Peter Lang, 1988); M. Himmelfarb, 'The Experience of the Visionary'; *idem*, *Tours of Hell: An Apocalyptic Form in Jewish and Christian Literature* (Philadelphia: Fortress Press, 1983); *idem*, 'From Prophecy to Apocalypse: The *Book of the Watchers* and Tours of Heaven', in A. Green (ed.), *Jewish Spirituality from the Bible Through the Middle Ages* (London: SCM Press, 1989), pp. 145-65; R. Bauckham, 'Early Jewish Visions of Hell', *JTS* 41 (1990), pp. 355-85 (see also Bauckham, 'The Apocalypses in the New Pseudepigrapha', pp. 112-14).

It should spell the end of former unreflective talk of 'apocalyptic' and of an 'apocalyptic eschatology'. One seeking a guide to this literature will turn to Rowland, not to typical eschatological accounts of 'apocalyptic'. But Rowland's own 'apocalyptic', though in far better stead with respect to the apocalypses, is itself a much wider phenomenon (as he well knows), and retaining by the terminology a sense of an 'essential' connection to a literary genre might be to perpetuate one of the confusions of the approach he opposes.[94]

In light of what has been said, the whole matter of abstracting some apocalyptic 'essence' should be subjected to critical scrutiny (and here I direct my criticism much more at typical notions, and not at Rowland). This is not the most natural thing to do with texts. Arguably, doing unnatural things with texts is the stock-in-trade of historical-critical reconstruction. But more justification than this is probably needed. A hurried move from the literature to some 'essence' is a flight from the texts as *texts*. Although, apparently, 'apocalyptic' is real enough for many, for most the apocalyptic literature would still seem to qualify as the most tangible entity we have, possessing by this right some prior claim as itself having something to say on the matter of 'apocalyptic'. If we wish to study this literature (and it is important to be clear about *why* we might wish to), then our work is cut out for us. Who produced these texts and why, and why and by and for whom were they preserved, and why do we now care? But to pause briefly over the literature on the way to something else, to move without further ado, or worse without even realizing it, from the literature to the abstraction 'apocalyptic' (or 'apocalyptic eschatology' or 'apocalypticism') is simply not adequate for anything.

What is to be our response to the barrage of observations made about the multi-layered problematic of this matter of 'apocalyptic'? The general level of questioning in the field has already filtered down to New Testament critics sufficiently that now recourse to Hanson's threefold typology has become common. It is clear from the above that I do not regard this shift as sufficient.[95] Rather, the essential connection of such

---

94. Perhaps the pressure Rowland has no doubt felt to replace that which he so thoroughly dismantles with some positive alternative has caused him here to go back on his own better insight.

95. In *The Open Heaven* (pp. 354-55), Rowland offers as an example of the typical approach to 'apocalyptic' and the New Testament J.D.G. Dunn's treatment in his *Unity and Diversity in the New Testament*: Dunn's approach, heavily dependent

talk of 'apocalyptic-' with the apocalyptic literature should be broken for good and all. May we, then, simply make another terminological shift and speak now of, say, 'transcendent eschatology'? Clearly, this is not enough. For I have been struggling to get across that much more than a matter of terminology is at issue here. Not just the terminology, but the

on Vielhauer, is all to do with eschatology, assumed to be what 'apocalyptic' is all to do with. While it may not seem fair to make an example of Dunn a second time on the same point, his revisions in light of Rowland's criticism are highly instructive, exemplifying the sort of response I would regard as inadequate. In the new introductory foreword to the second edition of this work, Dunn remarks that '*Chapter XIII*, "Apocalyptic Christianity", was one chapter with which I became dissatisfied quite soon after publication' (p. xxvii; see also p. xvii). Dunn acknowledges Rowland's treatment, but then says that, in making the revisions for this new edition, it was concluded 'that the issue largely boiled down to one of definition. The catch-all use of "apocalyptic" should be abandoned, and the confusion and overlap between "apocalyptic" and "eschatology" resolved by making clear that the main focus of the chapter was on "apocalyptic eschatology"—that is, not merely concerned with (the events of) the end (eschatology), but with that concern as characteristically expressed in apocalyptic literature. However, the characterisations of apocalypse and apocalyptic eschatology [formerly given] remain valid as characterisations, so all that was required was a rewriting of p. 310 to clarify the question of definition [where Dunn does so by duly adopting Hanson's threefold definition], and a consistent implementation of these definitions throughout the rest of the chapter' (pp. xxviii-xxix). In order to continue after Rowland's devastating critique to speak of 'apocalyptic eschatology', Dunn appeals to J.J. Collins, *The Apocalyptic Imagination* (p. xxxvi, n. 35), and indeed speaks of 'apocalyptic eschatology' and of an eschatological world view, 'apocalypticism', inhering in the genre. Collins stands virtually alone in insisting (admirably and in the strongest terms) on the accountability of such notions to the apocalypses and yet still managing to hold them (see J.J. Collins, *Apocalyptic Imagination*, p. 2; *idem*, 'Genre, Ideology and Social Movements', pp. 12-13). He complains that 'scholars such as Rowland and Barton [on whom see below], who see only the variety of contents [of the literature], miss the forest for the tress' (J.J. Collins, 'Genre, Ideology and Social Movements', p. 16; see also p. 15). But Collins has also accepted much of the watering down of 'apocalyptic eschatology', so that the eschatological world view held to be common to the apocalypses is 'fairly abstract and general' and includes not just 'public' but also 'personal eschatology', and to speak of this world view beyond the texts, as in Paul, is to speak 'in an extended sense' (J.J. Collins, 'Genre, Ideology and Social Movements', p. 16; *idem*, *Apocalyptic Imagination*, p. 9). But just because we can pull together all that Collins does under the term 'eschatology' (so that he can still say that there is an 'apocalyptic eschatology') says nothing (necessarily) of the period, and the other artificiality of a world-view inhering in a genre is not reflected upon.

whole conceptuality has been called into question, and on at least two scores. First, the otherworldly nature of typical expectation of the period has been questioned. I am in no position to rule on the matter, but full consideration of this point seems required. No matter what our 'apocalyptic eschatology' is called, if much is being made of what is an oddity for the period, this should be made clear.[96] Second, questions have been allowed to arise about the whole tendency to mark off the thought of the period in the way that is typically done by such schemes. What is being done when we talk about 'apocalyptic eschatology' (or, again, whatever we choose to call this 'thing') is usually that one neat stream of thought is being marked off from another, 'prophetic' or 'rabbinic eschatology', for the obvious reason that we are trying to depict the steady rise of early Christianity and Judaism. But there is no use pretending that we know more than we do. The neat picture often drawn simply looks suspicious. Knowing the beginning, so to speak (the Hebrew Bible/Old Testament), and knowing the outcome (early Christianity and rabbinic Judaism), we can certainly connect the points neatly enough. But why not rather say that the period and the literature seem to suggest an amorphous pool of eschatological speculation from which emerging Christianity (including Paul) and Judaism draw in novel and not wholly predictable ways, and not innocently of each other? But this would leave us much less to run with. Finally, I shall suggest one more problem with 'apocalyptic' that indicates that we have to do here with much more than a terminological problem remedied by a simple terminological shift. This is the whole tendency that has grown up around speaking of, say, 'wisdom', 'prophecy', or 'apocalyptic' where what is meant appears to be something like a theological essence of a set of biblical texts which has come to to be called by that name. This way of operating inevitably blinds us to the diversity of that material we pretend to have covered in so speaking, and furthermore, since the actual reality of, say, the prophet or the sage in the broad historical period of concern is clearly something quite distinct from this textual-theological 'essence', the whole procedure is clearly arbitrary and artificial, and can only have a biblical-theological rationale.[97] By such

---

96.  E.P. Sanders's treatment of Jewish eschatology in his _Judaism: Practice and Belief 63 BCE—66 CE_ (London: SCM/Philadelphia: Trinity, 1992), pp. 279-303, seconds Rowland's assertion of its this-worldly nature; he also highlights the diversity of expectations, with shared themes taken up in a variety of ways.

97.  I do not intend here to make pronouncements on all 'biblical theology'; my

means 'apocalyptic' comes to move on a level of abstraction miles above the historical period and its literature. The wide spread of this manner of operating in biblical criticism should give us long pause. The hope that a turn from Pauline studies to general interpretation of 'apocalyptic' in its own right would of itself clear things up has proved ill founded, for if anything matters are often worse here.

As a point of clarification, it is necessary to refer back to my original distinction between literature and abstraction and my invitation to those who would speak of 'apocalyptic' to work from the apocalypses and offer a 'literary definition'. It may seem that I have been a bit underhanded in calling on critics to do what I would ultimately claim to be suspect, that is, to treat 'apocalyptic' as though it were essentially bound to the apocalyptic literature. After all, have not scholars lately been insisting that 'apocalyptic eschatology' is *not* co-extensive with the literature? But again, my original call was issued both because the terminology naturally suggests a connection and because in the minds of the users there clearly *is* some kind of connection between 'apocalyptic' and the apocalypses. The discipline of thinking things through in the manner that I have tried to suggest is meant to bring us to the point where we relinquish the idea of having some 'second term'—'apocalyptic', 'apocalyptic eschatology', 'apocalypticism', or whatever—floating about beyond the literature and seeming to make some historical connection with it.[98] All the 'apocalyp-' terms will then simply refer us to the literature.[99] If we want to draw some connection to, say, Paul, we will do that in terms properly chosen for that particular purpose. Once more, we need to ask what scholars have been doing. 'Apocalyptic eschatology' in recent discussion has fluctuated oddly between being claimed to be free of the apocalyptic literature and yet still being claimed to be tied to

objection is rather to the covert sort that presses the literature and history into service they would seem incapable of rendering.

98.    Now I may address more fully the plainly inadequate notion so common in North American discussion, namely, that by no longer using 'apocalyptic' as a noun but rather as an adjective and using instead 'apocalypticism' as the noun we have sorted out the confusion and the problematic of 'apocalyptic' (a point often bolstered with the observation that 'apocalyptic' is a hybrid from the German *'Apokalyptik'*, which should come across into English as an 'ism'). The question, so to speak, is: What are we doing with a 'noun' in the first place?

99.    It will be seen in the end that I have arrived at something like Stone's suspicion of all 'second terms', though I feel he has let typical approaches off too lightly; thus, again, Rowland has been used to critique and dissolve typical views.

the literature somehow. Why? It seems that the connection must be cut to preserve the concept from attempts to make it accountable to the literature, while the connection must be retained in some sense lest it be thought that 'apocalyptic eschatology' is unaccountable and therefore artificial. But one thing is certain. When 'apocalyptic Paul' is being discussed, it should sound as if something historical is being discussed. Again, apart from the matter of the problematic connection with the apocalyptic literature, even if the terminology is changed, there remains the possibility that we are here reaching back, whatever the term, to an elaborately built up and carefully sustained illusion. Perhaps I have been extreme. Perhaps much that I have questioned—and I do seem to have set myself against a great deal—could be rebuilt on a more secure basis, so that biblical criticism will simply have to revise its methods more than its message. But I must beg indulgence for a certain scepticism.

Finally, I shall offer a couple of positive examples of how the apocalyptic literature might be handled other than as in the 'between the testaments' tradition I have questioned, offering support along the way for some of my methodological points. E.P. Sanders's treatment in his major study *Judaism: Practice and Belief 63 BCE—66 CE* is instructive.[100] In introducing his account of early Judaism, Sanders anticipates the concern (and, no doubt, the disappointment) which might greet the absence of a section devoted to 'apocalyptic'/'apocalypticism'. The apocalypses 'offer descriptions of the other world, the afterlife, God's action in the future, and other "hidden" topics', and, although few apocalypses may fall in Sanders's narrow period of interest, these concerns, he remarks, were certainly current (pp. 7, 8).[101] When Sanders wishes to discuss Jewish hopes for the future, he does so, sensibly enough, in a chapter entitled 'Hopes for the Future', where the apocalypses join other texts in contributing to a reconstruction (and where Sanders, like Rowland, portrays common hopes in this-worldly terms [pp. 279-303]). (The other, even more speculative and esoteric concerns

---

100. Rowland himself has set the literature within a broad sketch of early Judaism in his *Christian Origins* (see pp. 46-64 and pp. 87-108), a treatment in many respects similar to that by Sanders.

101. Rowland is cited here, by Sanders, in connection with this understanding of 'apocalyptic' (p. 495 n. 6). See also Sanders's *Paul*, pp. 543, 554, where his earlier incidental remarks betray more typical notions of 'apocalyptic'; here too, though, he doubts that 'apocalyptic expectation and speculation…is constitutive of a distinct type of religion' (p. 424), as eschatology is common property.

of the apocalyptic literature receive brief mention or none at all—understandable in a work devoted to common theology and focusing on everyday practice [pp. 8-10].) Why no separate treatment of 'apocalypticism'?

> One [reason] is that I do not regard apocalyptic*ism* as an ideology that competed with other ideologies, or as a movement that included only people who were not in other movements...Our ideas about Judaism are often shaped by the way people of previous centuries (both ancient and modern) preserved, organized and published Jewish literature (p. 8).

But the various corpora do not somehow demarcate discrete groups without overlap, nor does one necessarily express all one's interests in a singular genre, but rather one may, on pragmatic grounds, categorize them—Sanders offers the telling example of Isaac Newton (that paragon of enlightened reason), who wrote scientific treatises *and* apocalyptic speculations (pp. 8-9).[102]

> I think that the description of first-century Judaism according to the categories of surviving literature (apocalyptic, rabbinic, philosophical, mystical and the like) is an error. It makes a lot of sense to study one body of literature at a time, but it is unreasonable to think that a convenient way of arranging our own time reflects the social organization of living and breathing people in the first century. A collection of literary remains represents one of the special interests of an individual or a group; but we should not suppose that each collection corresponds to an isolated group of people who had no other ideas and who would have denounced other literary collections as belonging to a different 'Judaism', or would have found them incomprehensible...Thus in dealing with religious practice, I think I am also dealing with 'apocalyptists'...(p. 9).

(Sanders's comments, though perhaps more immediately directed toward his concern for a portrayal of 'common Judaism', are also germane to our point about 'textual-theological essences' like 'apocalyptic', 'wisdom', or 'prophecy'.)

Another important work deserving of more attention by New Testament critics is John Barton's *Oracles of God: Perceptions of Ancient Prophecy in Israel after the Exile*.[103] This work has the virtual effect of placing the entire literature of the period in a different light, by a proposal of the sort 'Suppose we looked at things *this* way?' (pp. 1-11) The genres which in the light of critical analysis appear to be virtually an

---

102. On Newton, cf. Alan Richardson, *Bible*, p. 41.
103. J. Barton, *Oracles of God: Perceptions of Ancient Prophecy in Israel after the Exile* (London: Darton, Longman and Todd, 1986).

automatic feature of an intelligent reading of the biblical and extra-biblical literature were simply not functional in the period (pp. 141-49). Nor were the historical-critical strictures as to what a 'prophet' is and does. (This is not to say that awareness of genre and history is in itself useless or inappropriate, only that, if 'perceptions of prophecy' are what we are after, our own way of marking things off may be unhelpful, irrelevant, or even misleading.) What is a 'prophet'? A 'prophet' is one who enjoys a special relationship to God, by virtue of which access is had to privileged information not otherwise available, and a 'Prophet' is simply a book, *any* book, by such a one (pp. 96-140). In a lengthy and persuasive discussion of the questions of canon relative to this matter (pp. 13-95), Barton argues that, for our period, over against the Torah, which is first-order Scripture for all, stands 'the Prophets', which includes everything else. This is a large, formless, open pool of 'prophetic writings', and, at a time when questions of canon are anachronistic, these writings form together a second-order Scripture (where 'Scripture' is 'old books written by prophets' and authoritative on that account). This is not, of course, to say that all these writings stand on equal footing with each other for all the parties concerned. Barton rather thinks that the (ultimately) canonical works were recognized everywhere, only there were a number of other works recognized by some, some books here, others there. In a culture that values old books and that sees itself in an inferior light as against the ancients, and where, although (what is understood as) 'prophetic activity' continues, it is felt to be of a different class than that of the ancients, books (which we now put in various categories) continued to be written as contributions to that broad 'genre' of 'Prophets' vying for the attention of readers, as it were. Such books are fathered on the prophetic past.

The books of the Prophets are 'oracles of God', and as such it makes no sense for the times to inquire as to what sort of truth they convey and to whom (as modern generic and historical analysis might ask)— they convey every kind of truth there is, and to us. Again, a prophet is privy to extraordinary information, knowledge of the proper conduct of life, of the imminent decisive outworking of expectations, of God's plan in history, of God's nature and the heavenly world. One reads the Prophets accordingly, that is, in accordance with one's own interests and one's perceptions of what it is that a prophet does, what one turns to the Prophets for. Barton isolates four 'modes of reading the Prophets': 'prophecy as ethical instruction', 'prophetic foreknowledge of the present day', 'prophecy and the divine plan for history', and 'the prophet as theologian and mystic'.[104] These are four majors keys in which one might have read, four reading strategies that determine what one gets out of a prophetic book. This is relevant not just to the consumption of literature, but to its production as well. For prophets are still at work, even if they might refer to themselves in other terms (whether they are forced to do so, or they see themselves so). More books are written in imitation of those already valued, and according to the perceptions and current conventions through which the earlier literature is seen. The Torah, by the prophet Moses, is definitive for all and suitable for all. The Prophets are books of revelations to Moses' successors (or predecessors), the prophets, some of which books range into esoteric areas only hinted at in the Torah, material suitable only for the wise (by which process the second-order writings subtly assume a place above the Torah). But the starting point is there in Moses and the former prophets.

Barton's way of relativizing our own distinctions—canonical and critical (historical, generic)—from the point of view of the period certainly opens fresh perspectives on those who wrote and those who read the writings among which are numbered the apocalypses. His 'modes' suggest reading-interests to which these various writings were subject, interests which cut across any such distinctions. Those who wrote the apocalypses and related works were those who read the Scriptures for the sort of esoteric knowledge they valued, and they wrote as imitators of the Scriptures (as seen through their eyes). By this genre and others (all of which seek to imitate the Scriptures) the authority of the past attaches to these 'new' works (some of which perhaps, in the minds of their authors, establish by the religious experience they imply an actual connection with the ancient seer invoked as author [pp. 211-12]). That is to say, these various genres offer means, fictitious or 'real', of moving back into the past. Old books of revealed knowledge carried a weight of authority among those credulous of such—just about everyone, that is.

Along the way, the matter of 'apocalyptic' arises (as well it would in such a consideration of the literature and the period). Concerning such developmental schemes as the 'transition from prophecy to apocalyptic' through which the material is often read, it is obvious that, on this view,

---

104. This occupies Barton through the bulk of the work; see Barton, *Oracles*, chaps. 4-8.

such a process could not have been recognized as such, for ancient prophecy was understood in the light of contemporary notions of prophecy.[105] Also, essential connections between genres and ideologies and social groups (such as those implied in the 'theocracy versus eschatology' scenarios of Hanson and others against which Barton argues at length[106]) make no sense on Barton's view, where the development and use of genres is a rather simple, pragmatic, unreflective and inherently uncontrollable, matter. Such categories as 'eschatology', 'apocalyptic', and 'theocracy', when used in this connection, raise, says Barton, 'certain questions which appear to me to be really non-questions, while making it very difficult to find words to draw other, more important distinctions...Shorthand terms have, I believe, seriously hindered the study of our period and its literature'. (p. 234) Further, Barton questions the interpretative move so rapidly made whereby often similar sounding language is taken as 'metaphorical' in the prophets and as 'literal' in the apocalypses so that a clear shift to a cosmic and otherworldly perspective is observed (pp. 203-208). The suggestion of a 'gradual lengthening of perspective' from prophecy to 'apocalyptic' is really 'no more than a trick of the light', 'a function of attributing to ancient figures predictions which people believed to apply to their own time' (p. 200).[107]

> In effect this means that the 'transition from prophecy to apocalyptic' is the title of a process that never occurred. Rowland has striven to show that prophecy did not 'turn into' apocalyptic because the two 'movements' have a different subject-matter: prophecy is concerned with the future (not in a crystal-gazing way, but as the consequence of present action), whereas apocalyptic is literature that concerns itself with the disclosure of secrets. So far as it goes, this is quite compatible with my own argument, but I should want to go further. What happened was that prophecy, which (in the sense just defined) continued to exist even when the word was no longer used to describe the activity of contemporaries, came to be seen as essentially the disclosure of secrets. Sometimes these secrets were seen as concerning the future, and then the prophets of old were conceived of in exactly the same way as the seers on whom apocalypses were being fathered. But prophets in the true sense continued to speak to people about the likely consequences of present conduct, and to assure them (either as a promise or as a threat) that God was about to act in vindication of his

---

105. See Barton, *Oracles*, pp. 198-200; see also the following note, and *passim*.

106. Barton, *Oracles*, pp. 111-14, 122, 125-27, 167-68, 176-77, 193, 198-202, 202-210, 230-34, 264-65, 266-67.

107. Barton, *Oracles*, p. 200.

purposes. Sometimes these prophets did this by writing apocalypses (of the kind where the secrets revealed to the seer concern 'what will be hereafter' [the fourth of Rowland's four rubrics]). They used the convention that these secrets had been shown to a prophetic figure long ago, because that is what they thought 'prophetic' inspiration had been like: their own kind of vocation (which Amos or Isaiah would as a matter of fact have recognized instantly as prophetic, being concerned with contemporary problems and God's imminent solution to them) they did not describe in those terms. Indeed, we do not know how they did describe themselves, since they hide completely behind the persona of the seer who is the subject of the apocalypse; but a reasonable guess would be that they described themselves in language drawn from the old wisdom tradition: 'wise', 'teachers', 'learned'. Phenomenologically, however, they were prophets. What had changed was the vehicle through which it was deemed appropriate to express a prophetic message, that is, a message about what God is about to do in view of the parlous condition his people find themselves in.

It will be seen...that this has the effect of abolishing the noun 'apocalyptic'. As the name of a literary genre, 'apocalypse' is indispensable. But Rowland seems to me already to have shown that the attempt to find any unifying theme among all the apocalypses that are extant is doomed to failure. Apocalypses were certainly all written to describe the disclosure of secrets, but what the secrets had as their subject matter varies widely. We could of course use the adjective 'apocalyptic' to mean 'concerned with the disclosure of secrets' and it would then make sense to say that there is 'apocalyptic literature' which is not in the apocalypse form. But if we are serious about including under that heading all the works that were so considered in the period when apocalypses were being written, we shall have to include the whole of the prophetic literature, and perhaps the whole of the Old Testament, Apocrypha, and Pseudepigrapha, for we have seen that all this material was widely regarded as 'apocalyptic' in that sense. The adjective is therefore defensible but, if strictly used, not very useful. In our period it would make no sense, for example, to speak of an apocalyptic *movement*. But the *noun* 'apocalyptic' seems on this showing as devoid of content as it is lacking in any ancient pedigree. 'Apocalyptists' (or even, if you insist, 'apocalypticists') will be those who wrote apocalypses, but nothing will thereby be implied about what we expect to find in their books in terms of content...We could use 'apocalyptist' to mean 'one who believes that God revealed secrets to prophets in antiquity'—but that would mean just about everyone in the world of the New Testament. On the whole it seems better to abandon all the terms except 'apocalypse' (pp. 200-202).[108]

108. Concerning (under 'mode 4') interest in the heavenly realm and angelic beings, Rowland is implicitly criticized: 'One may state the relationship between apocalypses and an interest in the denizens of the other world as follows: many but

Barton's phenomenology of 'prophecy' and its literature in the period and his suggestive identification of interpretative 'modes' applied to scripture and operative in contemporary literary activity offer perspectives worth pursuing further. As well as contributing from another angle toward our questioning of the 'textual-theological essences' whereby dubious theological developments are created, further exposing as artificial some typical means of approach to the literature, Barton's account of the logic of 'oracles of God', which extends Rowland's account of the logic of 'the open heaven', makes much about the literature seem more natural.

If New Testament scholars need reassuring that nobody is trying to take their apocalyptic literature away from them, they may note that it is still there, to be mined for parallels to this or that feature of the eschatology of this or that figure or work. But the grander designs of 'apocalyptic eschatology' and 'apocalypticism', it is hoped, will soon be put to rest. The many, many historical and theological things that we seem to wish to accomplish under the banner of these terms could surely be done (assuming they are worth doing) more clearly and more competently in other terms better thought through. Genuine clarification of our terminology, of our concepts (the oft cited but seldom researched 'two-age doctrine' would be a good start), and of our method (that is, the literary history that is a mainstay of the discipline), as well as hermeneutical clarification, seem urgent. It is to escape the vagaries of the term 'eschatology' that many have sought recourse to 'apocalyptic'. But the latter is no more safe from the whim of interpreters than the former. *Both*, in fact, as well as carrying along a heavy theological cargo, seem also to carry questionable historical notions, both order things a bit too neatly and a bit more to our purposes than we might have reason to believe they could or should (though the term 'eschatology' seems difficult to avoid in covering twentieth-century history of interpretation,

not all apocalypses are interested in angels and in the events that take place in heaven; many but not all of the works with this interest are apocalypses. As soon as one tries to use the term "apocalyptic" the fact that the two categories of literature overlap but are not coterminous becomes a problem—the more so if one has a prior commitment to the idea that "apocalyptic" is essentially about "eschatology"...Heavenly journeys and cosmic geography appear as an interest both within and outside apocalypses, and may or may not be linked with eschatological questions. There is no reason to think that writers in our period would have felt there to be any oddity in any possible combinations of these features: "prophecy" could include all or any of them' (Barton, *Oracles*, p. 254).

and we do not *necessarily* mean here to shackle it with all the strictures we have raised against 'apocalyptic'). This leaves us asking whether both terms do not tend in practice to reduce to the whim of interpreters.

## Paul and 'Apocalyptic', Beker and Beyond

The 'apocalyptic' Paul was last seen where I left him, with Käsemann and, in his wake, in the midst of questions beginning to arise. I have followed through in my own way that spirit of questioning, and now it remains to take the story roughly up to the present—as I have begun to do above with Beker—in a better position, it is hoped, to evaluate this more recent interpretation of Paul and 'apocalyptic', where the matter of the definition of 'apocalyptic' is just beginning to haunt discussion.

In the preface to his major work on Paul, Beker epitomizes his programme clearly and succinctly:

> This study attempts to move toward an understanding of 'the whole Paul' by focusing on two fundamental questions. What is the coherent theme of Paul's thought and what is the texture of his hermeneutic?
>
> I posit the triumph of God as the coherent theme of Paul's gospel; that is, the hope in the dawning victory of God and in the imminent redemption of the created order, which he has inaugurated in Christ. Moreover, I claim that Paul's hermeneutic translates the apocalyptic theme of the gospel into the contingent particularities of the human situation. Paul's ability to correlate the consistent theme of the gospel and its contingent relevance constitutes his unique achievement in the history of early Christian thought.[109]

Beker's leading interest both in method in reconstructing Paul's thought (or, viewed from Paul's side, in establishing the 'coherent centre' from which he operated) and in the role played by 'apocalyptic' in providing that centre is evident.

Beker wishes to show, against a climate he perceives as hostile to such a conclusion, that Paul is a coherent, consistent thinker—for his own

---

109. Beker, *Paul*, p. ix; on Beker's programme, in addition to his other two books on Paul, already cited, see J.C. Beker, 'Paul's Theology: Consistent or Inconsistent?', *NTS* 34 (1988), pp. 364-77; 'Paul the Theologian: Major Motifs in Pauline Theology', *Int* 43 (1989), pp. 352-65, repr. in Beker, *Triumph of God*, pp. 117-35 (cited here); 'Recasting Pauline Theology: The Coherence–Contingency Scheme as Interpretive Model', in J.M. Bassler (ed.), *Pauline Theology, Volume One*, pp. 15-24. On Beker, reference should also be made back to my coverage of his discussion of definition earlier in this chapter.

time *and* for us today—and 'apocalyptic' lets Beker do that. He also wishes, in addressing the matter of the coherent centre of Paul's thought, to correct what he regards as the dismal and confused state of the question in Pauline studies, avoiding choosing as a centre some vague generality (like 'salvation') or some arbitrarily chosen contingent symbol (like 'justification by faith') or some contentless 'kerygma', further avoiding having Paul work from some dogmatic core casuistically applied—and the contingency/coherence scheme lets Beker do all that. Juggling all the directives of this scheme—which wants to see Paul *and* Paul's interpreter working in a certain way—will inevitably involve Beker, in the effort to articulate Paul's 'apocalyptic centre', in some verbal gymnastics.

> ...Paul's coherent center must be viewed as a symbolic structure in which a primordial experience (Paul's call) is brought into language in a particular way. The symbolic structure comprises the language in which Paul expresses the Christ-event. That language is, for Paul, the apocalyptic language of Judaism, in which he lived and thought...It is in this sense that I speak about the coherent center of Paul's gospel as a symbolic structure: it is a Christian apocalyptic structure of thought—derived from a constitutive primordial experience and delineating the Christ-event in its meaning for the apocalyptic consummation of history, that is, in its meaning for the triumph of God.[110]

Paul's 'apocalyptic' is the 'deep structure', the various contingent expressions of his 'apocalyptic' the 'surface structure', of his thought. 'My claim...is that the *character* of Paul's contingent hermeneutic is shaped by his apocalyptic core in that in nearly all cases the contingent interpretation of the gospel points—whether implicitly or explicitly—to the imminent cosmic triumph of God'.[111] This last phrase encapsulates Beker's 'apocalyptic motifs' nicely.

Again, it proves very difficult for Beker to articulate Paul's 'apocalyptic' without falling foul of his own contingency/coherence scheme. Beker must even distance himself from the crystallization 'the triumph of God' (a phrase for which he shows some fondness, as it occurs in the titles of all three of Beker's books on Paul) as an expression of the 'essence' of Paul's 'apocalyptic' and thus of Paul's thought. For, the objection arises, is this not an arbitrarily chosen contingent symbol? Thus Beker steps up the quasi-linguistic analogy he earlier employed:

110. Beker, *Paul*, pp. 15-16.
111. Beker, *Paul*, p. 19.

I suggest that Jewish apocalyptic is the substratum and master symbolism of Paul's thought because it constituted the linguistic world of Paul the Pharisee and therefore formed the indispensable filter, context, and grammar by which he appropriated and interpreted the Christ-event, the ἀποκάλυψις Ἰησοῦ Χριστοῦ (Gal. 1.12; see also 1.16; 2.2).[112]

'Coherence cannot be restricted to one particular "contingent" symbol—for instance, to the eschatological triumph of God, as I proposed in my book [*Paul the Apostle*]—because it implies a network of symbolic relations and does not refer to one specific idea or *Mitte*'.[113] Still, the formulation 'the triumph of God' is too good to give up entirely: 'the coherence of the gospel involves a series of affirmations which are stamped by apocalyptic thought and which in turn cannot be divorced from their ultimate point of reference, namely, the imminent apocalyptic triumph of God'.[114] At any rate, there is at least enough coherence to Beker's contingent expressions of what he means by 'apocalyptic' to say without equivocation that it all comes down to futuristic eschatology.

Indeed, as we saw earlier, 'apocalyptic' signifies for Beker futurity as against the interpretative effort to make present or 'realized' eschatology decisive for Paul, cosmic breadth as against an individualistic narrowing of his thought, and closure/finality as against any attempt to construe the gospel story as complete without that which 'apocalyptic' holds as still in prospect. Here we see Beker taking up familiar uses of 'apocalyptic'. Again, as we noted earlier, 'apocalyptic' is for Beker a tradition to which Paul is heir and which he adapts and modifies in light of the Christ event and his call and conversion, which are fitted into Paul's 'apocalyptic'. 'No doubt Paul was an apocalyptist during his Pharisaic career'—an assertion in support of which it is apparently sufficient for Beker to cite the zeal of Paul's former life.[115] Paul's modifications of 'apocalyptic' consist chiefly for Beker in the absence of those 'fantastic' and 'escapist' elements of 'apocalyptic' which most often give offence and in the softening of the traditional dualism of 'apocalyptic' in a more biblical-theological, salvation-historical direction.[116]

---

112. Beker, 'Recasting Pauline Theology', p. 17.
113. Beker, 'Recasting Pauline Theology', p. 18.
114. Beker, 'Recasting Pauline Theology', p. 18.
115. Beker, *Paul*, pp. 143-44 (p. 143).
116. Beker, *Paul*, pp. 145-46. It is well-nigh universal to associate 'apocalyptic' with 'escapist fantasy' (eschatological timetables, otherworldliness, and so forth) and

If I were to relate Beker to our former interpreters, I might say he is something like a Käsemann who has softened considerably toward Cullmann. More pointedly, Beker insists, in a manner recalling Cullmann, on a literal and realistic interpretation of 'apocalyptic', and on its abiding relevance—voiced along with repeated disavowals of 'biblicism' and 'fundamentalism'—as any other interpretation is a departure from the gospel.[117] Beker also takes up Cullmann's line, *contra* Bultmann, that the precise eschatological character of 'apocalyptic' (imminent, cosmic-universal expectation) constitutes a 'stumbling block' of Paul's gospel for many moderns, which partly explains for Beker the interpretative effort to reduce or transform 'apocalyptic'.[118] On the narrower matter of Beker's application of 'apocalyptic' to Paul, we are everywhere on familiar ground, and the details will not concern us here—'apocalyptic' bears on such matters as the eschatological tension in Paul's thought and the resulting dialectic of Christian existence (and thus it easily becomes a totalizing interpretative centre).[119] If Beker gives anywhere a distinctive

then to distance Jesus and Paul from such to the degree that it is allowed they are influenced by 'apocalyptic'—*all* the interpreters discussed above do this, though I have not made a point of it. And Beker complains of the theological resistance to 'apocalyptic' over just such associations, while showing that he too makes the same associations and that he is driven by the same reflexes against such when he assures us that *Paul's* 'apocalyptic' is not like that, but concerns rather the theologically indispensable matter of the 'coming triumph of God'.

117. This concern is ubiquitous, but see, e.g., Beker, *Paul*, pp. xix, 16-19, 138-81, 351-67; *Gospel*, pp. 61-121.

118. Beker, *Paul*, p. 141. On the matter of Beker's relation to Käsemann, he is much more dependent on the latter than he might suggest, for, just as Käsemann drove a somewhat artificial wedge between himself and Schweitzer on the matter of 'justification' when in fact Käsemann was carrying out a similar interpretative project of containing 'justification' within an 'apocalyptic righteousness', stretching the term δικαιοσύνη so that it could still function as the operative centre, Beker does the same in reverse to Käsemann, repeatedly occupying a methodological high ground over Käsemann. Beker asserts that Käsemann takes as Paul's 'coherent centre' one of Paul's 'contingent symbols' when in fact what Käsemann means by 'righteousness/ justification' is often indistinguishable from Beker's own centre (see Beker, *Paul*, pp. 14, 17; *Triumph of God*, p. 62; 'Paul the Theologian', pp. 130-31; Beker says in the preface to *Triumph of God*, p. xiii, that he was 'stimulated by the studies of A. Schweitzer and E. Käsemann').

119. This is not, of course, to pass judgment on the originality or importance of Beker's interpretation and its details; only our interest here is with what, generally, 'apocalyptic' is taken to mean in Beker's programme.

slant to 'apocalyptic', it is in his direct association of 'apocalyptic' with one of his own leading concerns, namely, 'the integral connection between apocalyptic and *theocentrism*'.[120] Following on from this, 'apocalyptic' for Beker stands in service of a renewed 'biblical theology'.[121] Beker, in fact, makes everywhere a particular point of the continued relevance of 'apocalyptic'.[122] One more signpost to the familiar ground we are on: by now we should probably be disappointed if Beker did not join the chorus and gravely inform us that 'apocalyptic' has been resolutely resisted throughout the history of Pauline interpretation, ancient and modern, out of theological embarrassment, a disinclination which Beker will keep in check.[123]

Many find Beker's conception of 'apocalyptic' (often along with Käsemann's) suited enough to their purposes.[124] Others, though sharing

120. Beker, *Triumph of God*, p. xiii, emphasis added; see also *Paul*, pp. 356-58, 362-67.

121. Beker, *Paul*, p. xiv; *idem, Triumph of God*, pp. xiii-iv. Cf. Beker's earlier 'Reflections on Biblical Theology', *Int* 24 (1970), pp. 303-20, where, interestingly, the 'apocalyptic world view' is a bygone thing and an obstacle to a revitalizing of a biblical religion focused on experience of the historical Jesus (pp. 311-20). (Incidentally, Beker offers throughout this essay a critique of playing with empty theological concepts which we would think could well be turned against 'apocalyptic' [see esp. pp. 304-306].)

122. See, e.g., Beker, *Gospel*, pp. 79-121; this biblical-theological concern is especially apparent in Beker's *Suffering and Hope: The Biblical Vision and the Human Predicament* (Philadelphia: Fortress Press, 1987), where the deep personal resonances of Beker's work are especially apparent.

123. See, e.g., Beker, *Paul*, pp. 18-19, 138-43, 351-67; *Gospel*, pp. 61-77. This stance is set alongside that reassurance that 'apocalyptic' is not as bad as we have been led to believe.

124. See, e.g., M.A. Getty, 'An Apocalyptic Perspective on Rom 10.4', *HBT* 4/5 (1982-83), pp. 79-131; P.J. Achtemeier, 'An Apocalyptic Shift in Early Christian Tradition: Reflections on Some Canonical Evidence', *CBQ* 45 (1983), pp. 231-48; K.P. Donfried, 'Paul and Judaism: 1 Thessalonians 2.13 as a Test Case', *Int* 38 (1984), pp. 242-53; H.C. Kee, 'Pauline Eschatology: Relationships with Apocalyptic and Stoic Thought', in E. Gräßer and O. Merk (eds.), *Glaube und Eschatologie: Festschrift für Werner Georg Kümmel zum 80. Geburtstag* (Tübingen: Mohr [Paul Siebeck], 1985), pp. 135-58. Seifrid, *Justification by Faith*, follows Käsemann and Beker in setting 'justification' within the salvation-historical, eschatological frame of 'apocalyptic'—see pp. xi, 1-6, 55-62, 264-70.) We would also include here E.E. Johnson, *The Function of Apocalyptic and Wisdom Traditions in Romans 9-11* (SBLDS, 109; Atlanta: Scholars, 1989), a 1987 Princeton Theological Seminary PhD thesis advised by Beker. See pp. 1-73, esp. pp. 61-70. 'Apocalyptic' is understood,

on the whole Beker's understanding of 'apocalyptic', would amend his claims for its significance in Paul or otherwise add slight nuances.[125] Others would, to varying degrees, register more thoroughgoing objections where the matter of 'apocalyptic' itself is concerned, adjusting the portrait of Paul accordingly.

'"[A]pocalyptic" may be the most misused word in the scholar's vocabulary because it resists definition'—so asserts Leander E. Keck.[126] 'To begin with, "apocalyptic" is an adjective which should be used to characterize the thought and imagery, of those texts regarded as apocalypses. However, it is commonly used as a surrogate for

as with Beker, as essentially a matter of eschatology, and Hanson's distinctions are observed (pp. 19-21, 61 n. 15, 67 n. 37). Johnson well remarks of definitions of 'apocalyptic' that 'each one seems to be tailored by its author to his own understanding of Paul' (p. 21), but the point is lost on her own treatment. Along with all the problems that are inherent in speaking of 'apocalyptic', they are joined here by 'wisdom', as Johnson wishes to argue that, rather than being mutually exclusive, there is a 'confluence' of the two categories (though I might argue for a simpler solution, asking how much of a 'confluence' it would take to provoke an outright distrust of our categories). What Johnson wishes to address is a certain theological tension in Romans 9-11 (immanence versus transcendence, etc.), and of course Paul was not the first to take up such things, but Johnson wants some way of talking about coherent prior traditions Paul can be seen to be working from, and 'apocalyptic' and 'wisdom', called on in this regard, do not serve her thorough exegetical study well.

125. V.P. Branick, 'Apocalyptic Paul?', asserts: 'An apocalyptic worldview shapes much of Paul's thinking and provides an important context in which that thinking is comprehensible' (p. 664). He accepts Beker's definition of 'apocalyptic', as 'any further argument here would consist of semantic haggling' (p. 665). Branick's concern is with the already/not yet tension in Paul's thought, with Paul's anticipatory and participatory themes, and he suggests that Paul's elements of realization mark him as a transitional figure pointing the way, in his partial and even inconsistent formulations, to future developments in this direction. See also R.H. Fuller, 'Jesus, Paul and Apocalyptic', *ATR* 71 (1989), pp. 134-42; H. Moore, 'Paul and Apocalyptic', *Irish Biblical Studies* 9 (1987), pp. 35-46 (and cf. his 'The Problem of Apocalyptic as Evidenced in Recent Discussion', *Irish Biblical Studies* 8 [1986], pp. 76-91, and 'New Testament Apocalyptic in Twentieth Century Discussion', *Irish Biblical Studies* 11 [1989], pp. 197-206); D.M. Scholer, '"The God of Peace Will Shortly Crush Satan Under Your Feet" (Romans 16.20a): The Function of Apocalyptic Eschatology in Paul', *Ex Auditu* 6 (1990), pp. 53-61; David E. Aune, 'Apocalypticism', in G.F. Hawthorne and R.P. Martin, *et al.* (eds.), *Dictionary of Paul and His Letters* (Downers Grove: Inter-Varsity Press, 1993), pp. 25-35.

126. L.E. Keck, 'Paul and Apocalyptic Theology', *Int* 38 (1984), pp. 229-41 (p. 230).

"apocalypticism"' (p. 230).[127] Even used adjectivally, the diversity and confusion of the materials make for ambiguities.

> Furthermore, the theological content of 'apocalyptic' (and of apoca-lypticism) remains hard to define because the content of apocalypses varies so greatly on the one hand and because ideas found in apocalypses are found in quite different texts as well... One should be cautious in labelling an idea 'apocalyptic' simply because it is found, or even emphasized, in apocalypses (pp. 230-31).

Since, says Keck, we cannot show that Paul was directly influenced by apocalypses, one must inquire into Paul's possible reception and (inevitable) modification of 'apocalyptic theology' as passed on in Christian tradition, an issue of persistent controversy.[128] Keck claims that 'as an historical problem "Paul and apocalyptic theology" is insoluble. It is more fruitful to compare the theology of the Pauline letters with apocalyptic theology, and to explore the logic of their similarities and differences, without thereby positing genetic relationships between them' (p. 233). What, then, is 'apocalyptic theology'? 'Apocalyptic theology'

> locates the constitutive questions with which apocalypses wrestle. In short, 'apocalyptic' is an adjective which characterizes *a type of theology*, not merely a type of eschatology. The Old Testament-Jewish tradition developed three types of theology: (a) one based on the bond between God and people (the theology of the saving acts of God, Covenant and law, nation and land), (b) one based on insight into human experience irrespec-tive of any bond between God and people (the wisdom theology before it was absorbed by covenant/law theology), and (c) one based on the religious pilgrimage of the individual (Philo). Apocalyptic theology belongs to the first type (p. 233).

Keck proceeds to sketch his 'apocalyptic theology' in terms that are pure H.H. Rowley. 'The driving question of apocalyptic theology is the theodicy issue' (p. 233). The answer cannot emerge from the past and present 'but come[s] as God's alternative to it': thus 'the theme of two aeons was fundamental', and 'the heart of apocalyptic theology is the doctrine of a radically discontinuous future, made necessary by the

---

127. This latter term is introduced as though transparent; apparently Keck follows (somewhat loosely) Hanson's terminology.

128. See Keck, 'Paul and Apocalyptic Theology', pp. 231-33; the precise distinc-tion being made between 'apocalyptic' and 'apocalyptic theology' is unclear, though the latter appears to be another means of moving beyond apocalyptic texts to speak of a more generalized phenomenon; see further below.

undeniable scope of evil and made possible by the unquestionable sovereignty of a righteous God' (p. 234). Keck notes Wayne Meeks's three 'dualities' (see below) and adds a fourth of his own, the 'epistemological', concerning 'revelation [of] otherworldly knowledge, privileged information, whatever the actual content' (p. 234 and n. 17). Keck proceeds to show how Paul differs from, follows, and modifies such 'apocalyptic theology', closing with a response to Beker:

> Suffice it to say that Paul's theology (not the same as his gospel) is apocalyptic not because it includes 'vindication, universalism, dualism and imminence' [Beker's 'motifs']—some of these categories apply also to other theologies—but because it shares with apocalyptic theology the perspective of discontinuity...At the same time, God's freedom from the world makes possible a relation to it which is grounded solely in God's integrity. In this regard, Paul's interpretation of the Christ-event is thoroughly apocalyptic, however many other theologies contributed to his Christology at certain points. In working out this perspective as he wrote to Christian house churches, however, Paul did not produce apocalyptic theology, but his own creative grasp of the consequences of the Christ-event, a grasp which transformed Christian tradition and experience no less than it did apocalyptic—or any other—theology (p. 241).

Looking over what Keck has given us, and despite the expectations he might have raised of taking some new tack, we can say that whatever potentially liberating insights are present here come to naught in what is essentially an 'i'-dotting and 't'-crossing exercise on entirely typical notions of 'apocalyptic'—how has anything been clarified, how have we been taken a single step forward?

Appearing about the same time as, and independently of, Beker is Wayne A. Meeks's study of 'Social Functions of Apocalyptic Language in Pauline Christianity'.[129] Meeks asserts that a more promising approach to the vexed question of Paul and 'apocalyptic' may be had in a social-scientific inquiry into the 'function' of 'apocalyptic language' in Paul. Yet, it may be noted, traditional ways of speaking of 'apocalyptic' seem to translate directly and literally into talk of 'millenarian movements' (pp. 687-89). The meaning of 'apocalyptic' is not a matter of controversy. 'The problems involved in defining "apocalyptic" are notorious', admits Meeks, 'but I believe we could agree that the

129. In Hellholm (ed.), *Apocalypticism*, pp. 687-705. See also W.A. Meeks, *The First Urban Christians: The Social World of the Apostle Paul* (New Haven: Yale, 1983), pp. 171-80.

following characteristics would appear in any literature we would call "apocalyptic", though they need not be regarded as definitive', which characteristics he summarizes as follows: 'the apocalyptic universe is characterized by three corresponding dualities: (a) the cosmic duality heaven/earth, (b) the temporal duality this age/the age to come, and (c) a social duality: the sons of light/the sons of darkness, the righteous/the unrighteous, the elect/the world' (p. 689). How, precisely, Meeks's 'more promising' approach clarifies any of the confusion which he would claim to reduce is unclear—were he to specify in practical terms the results of his functionalist interpretation, would they not fall somewhere in the interpretative spectrum marked out from Schweitzer-to-Käsemann?—as he somehow manages to change the subject while allowing it to remain the same.

But Meeks has his followers against Beker. In a recent monograph, David W. Kuck briefly surveys 'approaches to Paul's use of apocalyptic eschatology' from Kabisch and Schweitzer to the present, and complains of Beker that he has a 'vague and limited understanding of "apocalyptic"' and that he 'fails to see how future motifs function in different ways in different contexts'.[130] Kuck prefers the approach of Meeks, who 'opts for using a sociological perspective to better understand the function of eschatological beliefs in specific settings, namely, the Pauline congregations' (p. 15). A major concern is again Paul's eschatological dialectic, 'the relation of present Christian existence to the future hope', to which is added the dimension of an inquiry into 'social function' (p. 16). In outlining his method, Kuck briefly addresses the matter of what he means by 'apocalyptic', or rather (following Hanson) 'apocalyptic eschatology' (pp. 31-33). He may leave aside, he claims, all the difficult literary and social-historical questions because his focus is on 'apocalyptic eschatology': 'This "apocalyptic eschatology" is a relatively neutral descriptive term' (p. 31). 'My starting point, then, is the analysis of apocalyptic eschatology, which already assumes that the basic characteristic of such language is its future orientation' (p. 32). Other interests may be found in the apocalypses, notes Kuck, and he mentions Meeks's three 'dualities', the cosmic, temporal, and social, along with Keck's fourth, the epistemological; but *temporal* dualism is basic to all, says Kuck (pp. 32-33). 'The cosmic duality of heaven and earth has been the

---

130. D.W. Kuck, *Judgment and Community Conflict: Paul's Use of Apocalyptic Judgment Language in 1 Corinthians 3:5-4:5* (*NovTSup*, 66; Leiden: Brill, 1992), pp. 7-16 (p. 11).

subject of some recent studies which demonstrate the importance of this duality in apocalyptic thinking, but in Paul, at least, such spatial dualism seems to be complementary and subordinate to the duality of present and future. In any case, spatial dualism plays a minor role in 1 Corinthians' (pp. 32-33).[131] 'So I am justified in setting aside all the other definitional problems and stating simply that I will be concerned in this study with Paul's statements about the supra-historical future action of God, i.e., with his apocalyptic eschatology' (p. 33).[132]

Another distinctive angle of critique of Beker is taken by J. Louis Martyn. In a rather glowing review of Beker's *Paul the Apostle*, Martyn questions Beker's progressive, salvation-historical conception of 'apocalyptic', which 'plays down the disjunctive dualism of the ages', and he asks concerning Galatians: 'Is the apocalyptic theme of the gospel suppressed [as Beker claims] in that letter in which Paul says with unmistakable emphasis that the truth of the gospel is a matter of apocalypse (Gal. 1.12, 16; 2.2, 5, 14)'?[133] Martyn later returns to the matter in a treatment of 'Apocalyptic Antinomies in Paul's Letter to the Galatians'.[134] His point of departure is a general agreement with Käsemann and Beker that 'Paul's theology is thoroughly apocalyptic' (p. 411). But what of Galatians, wonders Martyn, passed over by these two where 'apocalyptic' is concerned? 'Could Galatians perhaps be allowed to play its own role in showing us precisely what the nature of Paul's apocalyptic was' (p. 412)? Martyn has Paul in Galatians working against a background of a 'very nearly ubiquitous' ancient tendency to see reality divided into cosmic 'pairs of opposites'; for Paul, the old pairings are dissolved with the cosmic turning of the ages, while a fundamental new pair has emerged, that of 'flesh and Spirit', locked in fierce combat (pp. 412-16). But what of this is 'apocalyptic'? Of course, this has to do with eschatology and the two ages, and that is enough for most. But in addition Martyn asserts that 'when we probe more deeply into the nature of this pair, we find ourselves dealing with motifs clearly

131. As such 'recent studies' Kuck mentions Rowland's *The Open Heaven* and A.T. Lincoln's *Paradise Now and Not Yet* (cited below).

132. Kuck well exemplifies the methodological lapse endemic to Hanson's terminology and the tendency to turn 'apocalyptic' to whatever purposes chance to be at hand.

133. J.L. Martyn, Review of *Paul* by J.C. Beker, *WW* 2 (1982), pp. 194-98 (p. 196).

134. J.L. Martyn, 'Apocalyptic Antimomies in Paul's Letter to the Galatians', *NTS* 31 (1985), pp. 410-24.

apocalyptic' (p. 416). Such as? Well, there is 'the connection of this pair of opposites with the dawn of God's New Creation, an expression at home in apocalyptic texts' (p. 417). Then there is the fact that this New Creation concerns 'God's sending both of his Son and the Spirit of his Son' (p. 417). Furthermore:

> The advent of the Son and of his Spirit is also the coming of Faith, an event that Paul explicitly calls an apocalypse (note the parallel expressions 'to come' and 'to be apocalypsed' in 3.23). Indeed it is precisely *the Paul of Galatians* who says with emphasis that the cosmos in which he previously lived met its end in God's apocalypse of Jesus Christ (1.12, 16; 6.14). It is this same Paul who identifies that apocalypse as the birth of his gospel-mission (1.16), and who speaks of the battles he has to wage for the truth of the gospel as events to be understood under the banner of apocalypse (2.2, 5, 14). It is also clear that Paul brings this apocalyptic frame of reference to his remarks about the Spirit and the Flesh. There was a 'before', and there is now an 'after'; and it is at the point at which the 'after' meets the 'before' that the Spirit and the Flesh have become a pair of opposites. We will do well, therefore, to refer to the Spirit and the Flesh not as an archaic pair of opposites inhering in the cosmos from creation, but rather as an *apocalyptic antinomy* characteristic of the dawn of God's New Creation (p. 417).

Also specifically 'apocalyptic' is the theme of warfare: 'the Spirit and the Flesh constitute an apocalyptic antinomy in the sense that they are two opposed orbs of power, actively at war with one another *since* the apocalyptic advent of Christ and of his Spirit. The space in which human beings now live is a newly invaded space, and that means that its structures cannot remain unchanged' (p. 417).[135] This antinomy marks Christian existence in opposing Law and Christ/Spirit. 'For the true war of liberation has been initiated not at Sinai, but rather in the apocalypse of the crucified one and in the coming of his Spirit' (p. 418).

> All of the preceding motifs come together in the question that Paul causes to be the crucial issue of the entire letter: What time is it? One hardly needs to point out that the matter of discerning the time lies at the very heart of apocalyptic; and as the preceding motifs show, in none of his letters does Paul address that issue in terms more clearly apocalyptic than in Galatians. What time is it? It is the time after the apocalypse of the faith of Christ, the time therefore of rectification by that faith, the time of the presence of the Spirit, and thus the time of the war of liberation commenced by the Spirit (p. 418).

135. This emphasis on 'warfare' sets this 'apocalyptic antinomy' apart from 'wisdom' conceptions of 'the two ways'.

Martyn concludes by echoing Käsemann: 'no perspective could be more apocalyptic' (p. 420). Paul's 'apocalyptic', then, is shown (so Martyn) to have, like 'apocalyptic' generally, a strong epistemological side, involving at the point of the turn of the ages—the point of the cross—a 'new manner of perception' of the present moment and the imminent future transformation focused through the cross, which event for Paul is 'fully as apocalyptic as is his hope for Jesus' parousia'. In fact, 'through the whole of Galatians the focus of Paul's apocalyptic lies not on Christ's parousia, but rather on his death' (pp. 420-21).[136] 'Thus the subject of his letter to the Galatians is precisely an apocalypse, the apocalypse of Jesus Christ, and specifically the apocalypse of his cross.' (p. 421) As a whole, 'apocalyptic' is, yet once more, the familiar eschatological construction, focused especially on the 'turn of the ages'. Martyn succeeds, though, in giving to Paul's 'apocalyptic' a greater emphasis on realization and on a theology of the cross. Why it is that Martyn's desire to nuance and to emend in certain respects Beker's perception of Paul should be framed as a correction of the perception of 'apocalyptic' and thus of some supposed something that lies behind Paul is not clear—it seems almost as if this matter of 'apocalyptic' is something we are stuck with, and whatever we want to do with Paul, we had better work it so that we can call it 'apocalyptic'. As though dissatisfied with the degree of tenuousness already achieved in talk of 'apocalyptic', Martyn manages to add his own idiosyncratic touch in apparently wishing to pour all of what we mean by 'apocalyptic' into the occurrence in Paul of ἀποκάλυψις (and ἀποκαλύπτω), which, we might otherwise have thought, is a simple enough term, like our own 'revelation'.[137]

136. See also, Martyn, 'Apocalyptic Antinomies', p. 424 n. 28 (Martyn refers here to Keck's 'epistemological duality'), and Martyn's earlier 'Epistemology at the Turn of the Ages: 2 Corinthians 5.16', in W.R. Farmer, C.F.D. Moule, R.R. Niebuhr (eds.), *Christian History and Interpretation: Studies Presented to John Knox* (Cambridge: Cambridge University Press, 1967), pp. 269-87.

137. On the matter of the terminology and the absence of any essential connection in our period with what we now wish to call 'apocalyptic', see M. Smith, 'On the History of ΑΠΟΚΑΛΥΠΤΩ and ΑΠΟΚΑΛΥΨΙΣ', in Hellholm (ed.), *Apocalypticism*, pp. 9-19 (pp. 15-17 on Paul's usage); on a similar bit of lexical theologizing to that of Martyn, Smith remarks that 'a revelation does not become "apocalyptic" (in the modern sense) whenever it is described by a common verb meaning "uncover"' (p. 10), and he concludes that those works of our period 'commonly listed as evidence of "the apocalyptic movement" owe their apocalyptic titles either to patristic references, or to late manuscripts, or to modern scholars—and

Testifying to the fruitfulness of Martyn's contribution to the question of 'apocalyptic' is the recent appearance of a festschrift in his honour entitled *Apocalyptic and the New Testament*.[138] The lead essay by Richard E. Sturm, drawing on a thesis written under Martyn's direction, concerns 'Defining the Word "Apocalyptic": A Problem in Biblical Criticism' (a title apparently going for understatement).[139] Sturm acknowledges that the controversy here is such that some would abandon the term altogether, but he insists that 'such a desperate conclusion is unnecessary', and that 'the very fact that the word continues to be used shows that there must be a need for it' (p. 17). Sturm turns to the history of research for clarification. 'One particular question we shall have in mind is whether or not we can identify the apostle Paul's thought as "apocalyptic"', and Sturm apparently hopes very much that we can (p. 18). He identifies two tendencies of research: to regard 'apocalyptic' primarily as a 'literary genre' or as a 'theological concept'. (Sturm is after, as is Martyn, the theological construct 'revelation' as definitive for 'apocalyptic' [pp. 18-37].) Approaching 'apocalyptic primarily as a literary genre' just will not do (the abstraction 'apocalyptic' has clear priority for Sturm), necessary though genre study is, because on such an approach 'the ideas of apocalyptic are important but *secondary*, as general features characteristic of the literature', and, even where 'a link between apocalyptic and revelation is posited, what "revelation" really means remains unclear'. Finally, this approach leaves us to ask: 'must persons who did not write apocalypses, like Jesus or Paul, be neglected or ignored? Would their omission mean that it is improper to refer to their ideas and images as "apocalyptic"?' (p. 25). Much to be preferred, then, is the approach which takes 'apocalyptic' as a 'theological concept', where it becomes clear that, although it is 'literary in form', it is 'theological in content'. More specifically, 'apocalyptic eschatology' is hereby shown to be primary (Hanson's 'helpful'

none of these sources is reliable' (p. 19). Incidentally, Hanson does a similar thing to Martyn with the Greek terms, as noted in the excursus above, and Beker, too, seems to have picked up the habit, apparently from Martyn (cf. Beker, *Paul*, pp. xviii-xix [the 1984 preface, responding to Martyn]; *idem*, *Triumph of God*, pp. 19, 65-66).

138. J. Marcus and M.L. Soards (eds.), *Apocalyptic and the New Testament: Essays in Honor of J. Louis Martyn* (JSNTSup, 24; Sheffield: Sheffield Adademic Press, 1989); see pp. 37-42, 147-48, 191 for summary discussion of Martyn's approach to Paul and 'apocalyptic'.

139. Marcus and Soards (eds.), *Apocalyptic*, pp. 17-48; Sturm's unpublished thesis is cited on p. 42 n. *.

terminology is followed [p. 25]) and the connection of 'apocalyptic' with revelation occasionally emerges.[140]

> There is strength in the way this research generally attempts to weigh theo-
> logically the significance of apocalyptic concepts. These concepts include
> (1) the idea of two Aeons, (2) the embattled sovereignty of God over time
> and cosmos, (3) the revelation of an imminent eschaton. Indeed, clarity
> about the content of apocalyptic seems to be achieved in the way some
> researchers describe apocalyptic as an eschatological frame of mind in
> which history and God's rule are perceived and finally understood...
> Finally, the theological concept research not only includes the thought of
> Jesus and Paul, in it their theological expressions of apocalyptic become
> central (pp. 36-37).

However, the 'essence', of 'apocalyptic' remains unclear. 'One of the most promising points...is the *intersection of apocalyptic and revelation*' (p. 37). 'Do we have, in this almost unnoticed line of research, a clue for resolving some of the confusion in the way the word "apocalyptic" functions' (p. 38)? This question sets up Sturm's appropriation of Martyn's perspective (pp. 38-42). Sturm has in mind particularly Martyn's use of

> the word 'apocalypse' not in its common literary sense, but as a literal
> translation of Paul's theological use of the noun and verb *apokalyptô/
> apokalypsis*. The word in Galatians is used most significantly, to *reveal* the
> coming of Christ, the Spirit, and faith, as well as the true course of cosmic
> history, the ground of his own apostleship, and the battle commands for
> obeying the gospel...(pp. 40-41).

'For Paul, Martyn perceptively concludes, the gospel itself is an "apocalypse". That is, not in some ahistorical ecstatic vision, but in "the word of the cross" (1 Cor. 1.18), apocalyptic and revelation intersect. In Paul's gospel the power and purpose of God are ultimately disclosed' (p. 41). Of course, concludes Sturm, etymology is not decisive for the definition of words. 'Nevertheless, it is unfortunate when a word is used haphazardly in contradictory ways, and Martyn's discoveries regarding Paul's epistemological understanding of the gospel link apocalyptic and

140. See R.E. Sturm, 'Defining the Word "Apocalyptic"', in Marcus and Soards (eds.), *Apocalyptic*, pp. 17-48 (pp. 25-37); Hanson is treated on p. 35; Sturm repeats Martyn's complaint about Beker's definition of 'apocalyptic' (pp. 35-36); Sturm likes Rowland's association of 'apocalyptic' with 'revelation', but not his attempt to tie the concept to the literature (pp. 36, 38); the 'Pannenberg group' is especially credited with perceiving the connection with 'revelation' (pp. 31-32, 38).

revelation in a way that may provide the theological focus that would allow us at least to define *Paul's* apocalyptic comprehensively and in depth' (pp. 41-42).[141] This last line speaks volumes for 'apocalyptic interpretation of Paul'. The determination to speak undeterred about Paul's 'apocalyptic'—indeed, throughout this essay it is of itself a methodological point in favour of a perspective if it allows us to call Jesus and Paul 'apocalyptic'—is obvious. The assertion that, whatever problems may attach to the effort generally, Martyn hands us at least a means of clarifying *Paul's* 'apocalyptic' patently begs all the questions, forgetting, in the confidence that, after all, we really *do* know what we mean when we talk about 'apocalyptic' (and in the haste to do just that), that *it* is just the issue. No doubt Martyn and Sturm have made some insightful exegetical observations. But why call it all 'apocalyptic'? Of course, if this is what they are bound to do, we cannot stop them—but we may reserve the right to question the assumption they both seem to make and to assert rather that to use the label 'apocalyptic' in this way provides nothing like a historical explanation of anything, but speaks only of a penchant for the term itself.

In the same collection of essays on 'apocalyptic' presented to Martyn is an essay by Martinus C. de Boer on 'Paul and Jewish Apocalyptic Eschatology',[142] itself also a presentation of some aspects of a thesis directed by Martyn, and published as *The Defeat of Death: Apocalyptic Eschatology in 1 Corinthians 15 and Romans 5*.[143] 'Apocalyptic eschatology' (following Hanson's terminology) is the focus of interest.[144] This 'apocalyptic eschatology' amounts, at its most basic, to the eschatological dualism of the 'two-ages', and it is, as such, not tied to any

---

141. The title of Sturm's 1984 thesis, noted earlier, is 'An Exegetical Study of the Apostle Paul's Use of the Words *apokalyptô/apokalysis*: The Gospel as God's Apocalypse', and Martyn, in his 'Apocalyptic Antinomies', refers the reader to this study in remarking that 'Paul employs at crucial points the noun ἀποκάλυψις and the verb ἀποκαλύπτω. It is strange that in the investigation of apocalyptic patterns in Paul's thought relatively little attention has been given to the Apostle's use of these vocables...' (p. 424 n. 26). Stranger still, from my own point of view, is the use made of this point by Martyn and Sturm.

142. Marcus and Soards (eds.), *Apocalyptic*, pp. 169-90.

143. M.C. de Boer, *The Defeat of Death: Apocalyptic Eschatology in 1 Corinthians 15 and Romans 5* (JSNTSup, 22; Sheffield: Sheffield Academic Press, 1988).

144. M.C. de Boer, 'Paul and Jewish Apocalyptic Eschatology', p. 173; *Defeat of Death*, p. 21.

particular literary genre (such as the apocalypses), but rather any literature evincing this 'two-age' eschatology is 'apocalyptic literature' (a
very wide grouping indeed, taking in, of course, Paul).[145] Nor is
'apocalyptic eschatology' a unitary phenomenon, for, pointing to such
interpretative questions as the 'anthropology versus cosmology' debate
over 'apocalyptic' (Bultmann and Käsemann) and the conception of the
'two ages' of 'apocalyptic eschatology' as being two conflicting spheres
of power or two succeeding ages (Käsemann and Beker—de Boer
repeats Martyn's criticism of Beker), de Boer asks whether there might
not be two types of 'apocalyptic eschatology', so that each side might
be able to some degree to appeal to 'apocalyptic' and be justified
in speaking in its own sense of an 'apocalyptic' Paul.[146] He goes
on, in fact, to isolate two 'tracks' of 'apocalyptic eschatology', the
'cosmological' and the 'forensic', the former focused on cosmic powers
of evil and an impending eschatological battle, the latter on wilful rejection of God and his Law and an impending eschatological judgment.
These two types may stand separate and even directly opposed or may
be found variously combined.[147] Also, de Boer takes up Martyn's
manner of speaking of 'apocalyptic eschatology' as 'revealed' eschatology, on the strength of the use of ἀποκάλυψις/ἀποκαλύπτω.[148] We
see, perhaps, something of the rationale for this way of speaking as well,
for if it is unhelpful to limit 'apocalyptic eschatology' to the apocalypses—as this would expose our definition to doubts *and* leave Paul in
the lurch—then the question sooner or later arises as to why we still talk
about 'apocalyptic' eschatology, in preservation of which term we then
choose to latch onto Paul's use of the cognate vocabulary. What de
Boer wishes to do is to undertake an exegetical study of Paul's 'already/
not yet' tension in the tradition of Käsemann and Beker, to which
tradition he makes a valuable contribution. But the notion of 'apocalyptic'
does not serve him well. In fact, he has only given us, in further pointing
to its diversity and to the finesse required to go on speaking of it, still

145. De Boer, 'Paul', p. 172-74; *Defeat of Death*, pp. 21-23, 35-42.

146. De Boer, 'Paul', *passim*; *Defeat of Death*, pp. 21-37, 83-91.

147. De Boer, *Defeat of Death*, pp. 21-37, 83-91. We leave aside the matter of the
apparent ease with which de Boer puts together two coherent 'tracks' out of
seemingly chaotic materials, though we have above raised the suspicion that such is
often tacitly done from scattered bits and pieces according to some completed picture
already in mind from the New Testament.

148. De Boer, 'Paul', p. 173-74, 184-85; *Defeat of Death*, pp. 21, 34-35, 40-42.

more reason to distrust the notion much more than he apparently does.[149]

Where there occasionally arises a suspicion that something is amiss with Paul and 'apocalyptic', recent interpretation has found it difficult to put its finger on the problem. I have offered my assistance above. It should not now be felt incumbent upon the present study, I should insist, to offer new ways of having an 'apocalyptic' Paul. I was serious in my claim not to offer a new definition. The commerce that New Testament scholars (only to speak of *them*) have had with the apocalyptic literature—with the literature generally—has often been deeply flawed. Caution is in order. I might point out, though, that, where the apocalyptic literature is understood in a speculative and experiential frame of reference, studies which relate Paul to such have already been quietly and contentedly proceeding without the 'apocalyptic' flag: here we may mention Andrew Lincoln, *Paradise Now and Not Yet*;[150] James Tabor, *Things Unutterable*;[151] and Alan Segal, *Paul the Convert*.[152] This attention to the 'spatial' and 'vertical' dimension in Paul's theory and practice makes an obvious connection with a 'vertical' approach to 'apocalyptic', though even here, of course, in light of what has been said, we would not speak of an 'apocalyptic' Paul. Much else besides could no doubt be done to relate Paul to this literature without invoking 'apocalyptic' (or any grand functional equivalent). Following Barton's attempt to provide a fresh perspective on the Second Temple literature

---

149. De Boer repeatedly makes what appears to be a mild disclaimer in saying that he is using by convention the scholarly construct 'apocalyptic eschatology' to address those affinities between Paul's eschatology and that Jewish eschatology 'also labeled "apocalyptic"' (repeated in De Boer, 'Paul', p. 173, and *Defeat of Death*, pp. 7, 19).

150. A.T. Lincoln, *Paradise Now and Not Yet: Studies in the Role of the Heavenly Dimension in Paul's Thought with Special Reference to his Eschatology* (SNTSMS, 43; Cambridge: Cambridge University Press, 1981); see also A.T. Lincoln, '"Paul the Visionary": The Setting and Significance of the Rapture to Paradise in II Corinthians XII.1-10', *NTS* 25 (1979), pp. 204-20.

151. J.D. Tabor, *Things Unutterable: Paul's Ascent to Paradise in its Greco-Roman, Judaic, and Early Christian Contexts* (Lanham: University Press of America, 1986).

152. A.F. Segal, *Paul the Convert: The Apostolate and Apostasy of Saul the Pharisee* (New Haven: Yale, 1990); Segal has contributed other relevant studies of the Jewish literature and thought, and this book, as well as the other select titles cited here, will lead to further secondary literature.

generally, I suggest that many questions of a more or less *hermeneutical* character begin to arise in relating Paul and the continuing prophetic voice (including that of vision and ascent) to developing notions of and contemporary controversies over Torah and Prophets. Having somehow come round to hermeneutics once more, I come to a close by taking up what remains to be considered of this intermittent but never distant concern.

## Chapter 5

### ONCE MORE HERMENEUTICS

> Mornings, before daylight, I slipped into corn fields and borrowed a watermelon, or a mushmellon, or a punkin, or some new corn, or things of that kind. Pap always said it warn't no harm to borrow things, if you was meaning to pay them back, sometime; but the widow said it warn't anything but a soft name for stealing, and no decent body would do it. Jim said he reckoned the widow was partly right and pap was partly right; so the best way would be for us to pick out two or three things from the list and say we wouldn't borrow them any more—then he reckoned it wouldn't be no harm to borrow the others. So we talked it over all one night, drifting along down the river, trying to make up our minds whether to drop the watermelons, or the cantalopes, or the mushmelons, or what. But towards daylight we got it all settled satisfactory, and concluded to drop crabapples and p'simmons. We warn't feeling just right, before that, but it was all comfortable now. I was glad the way it come out, too, because crabapples ain't ever good, and the p'simmons wouldn't be ripe for two or three months yet. (M. Twain, *Adventures of Huckleberry Finn.*[1])

Whatever the moral satisfaction in seeing, with the coming of daylight, the bright dawning of the resolution of the ethical dilemma Huck and Jim find thrust upon them, a petty doubt intrudes to darken the moment with the suspicion that Huck probably should not have been so (albeit pleasantly) surprised at the outcome.

Such is innocence.

But this is fiction. What has all this to do with the *real* world ('scholarship', that is, of course)? What indeed.

For what Mark Twain is doing in this brief episode—a point which has escaped the attention of all literary critics and literary historians known to me right up until now—is to present an allegory of biblical

---

1. Cited from S.L. Clemens (Mark Twain), *Adventures of Huckleberry Finn* (S. Bradley, *et al.* [eds.]; Norton Critical Edition; New York: W.W. Norton and Company, 2nd edn, 1977), p. 56 (Chapter XII).

criticism, whose flow is captured by the sublime symbol of the mighty River which carries the twilight ethicists along. (The further significations are doubtless beyond need of pointing out, once the bare suggestion has opened up the interpretive imagination—and biblical scholars will be familiar enough anyway with Huck's sentiment, so often finding themselves, at the end of the critical process, 'glad the way it come out'.)

What I am after at this juncture of my hermeneutical musings is some reflection on *our* place in the critical enterprise. Where is the missing horizon of the present, of the interpreter, the one who is both to carry out detachedly the task of criticism and to greet the results with a proper sense of gravity...and relief?

From observing at the outset that 'apocalyptic' signifies the same basic set of notions right the way through our field of interest (the 'two ages' and all that is thought to go with this), and that, in contrast, what is *done* with this 'apocalyptic' is a story of some intrigue, I have gone on to sort through the notion of 'apocalyptic' itself, to question it, interrogate it, in a way I had hoped for but not found in our interpreters of Paul. This has frankly had the effect of dissolving much of such talk. For, above and beyond all the methodological confusion engendered by 'apocalyptic' as to the expectations it creates with respect to the literature, it has in the end become a legitimate question, at least, whether such talk reaches back to anything, whether what has constantly been sought as a background to Paul is back there at all. Even assuming 'apocalyptic' interpretation of Paul has got *Paul* right (a very large assumption), by such a turn Paul could well be the first witness to the tradition from which he has arisen—which, it is safe to say, is not what anybody intends when they position Paul as an 'apocalyptic' thinker. How often have we, in attempting to determine the precise constraints on Paul's development of his 'dialectic of Christian existence' exercised by his prior system of expectations, regarded as a distinct, coherent futuristic eschatology, created insoluble or even artificial problems for ourselves, hanging large interpretative issues on wishful thinking or thin air?

In the end, I did not even offer a new sense for 'apocalyptic'. Worse still, the eschatological debates, which, as I said in the beginning, were thrust upon me, are left largely as they were, with only a caution as to reading back later coherent schemes into earlier chaotic states. It was only ever my aim to sort through the matter of 'apocalyptic', not to offer solutions to these eschatological debates in the form of suggesting how Paul's eschatology should be construed and (even more urgently for many) what it might mean for us today.

As I return in the end to some of the hermeneutical points I have left dangling here and there, I must reveal that not even here do I have answers. My only defence in this is that I see a certain belated virtue in the very raising of such questions as those over which I have laboured. I return, then, to 'the critical ethos' and its objectivist two-stage critical ideal, which have intruded insistently from time to time into my story of Paul and 'apocalyptic'. The interpreter required for such an act of self-dispossession as the logic of this ideal demands is clearly a Cartesian one, one for whom a simplified Enlightenment world of fact and value has been constructed.

It is not as though criticism has had no reminders of the problems that reside here. Prominent among such correctives would be Anthony C. Thiselton's *The Two Horizons*.[2] In contrast to such hermeneutical anti-theoreticism as is instanced in Cullmann (where interpretation is of the falling-off-a-log order of theoretical complexity), for Thiselton foremost among those areas to which criticism must apply 'philosophical description' is the hermeneutical task itself, the intent expressed in his title. The allusion here is, of course, to Gadamer, whose philosophical hermeneutics highlight 'the two horizons' such that, as Thiselton reminds us, we ought not be able to look at 'interpretation' in quite the same way again.

> For Gadamer stresses that today we can no longer talk innocently about understanding an ancient text, or a past tradition, in isolation from a responsible consideration of the philosophical problems that have emerged with the rise of historical consciousness...Gadamer...asks questions about the way in which both the interpreter and the text stand in given historical traditions (p. 5).

Even apart from 'the modern reader's *historical* conditionedness, we are still faced with the undeniable fact that if a text is to be *understood* there must occur an engagement between two sets of horizons (to use Gadamer's phrase), namely, those of the ancient text and those of the modern reader or hearer' (p. 15).

> Traditionally hermeneutics entailed the formulation of rules for the under-standing of an ancient text, especially in linguistic and historical terms. The interpreter was urged to begin with the language of the text, including its grammar, vocabulary, and style. He examined its linguistic, literary, and

2.   A.C. Thiselton, *The Two Horizons*.

historical context. In other words, traditional hermeneutics began with the recognition that a text was conditioned by a given historical context. However, hermeneutics in the more recent sense of the term begins with the recognition that historical conditioning is two-sided: *the modern inter-preter, no less than the text, stands in a given historical context and tradition* (p. 11).

A hermeneutical consciousness, then, is a further outworking of a historical consciousness. But traditional hermeneutics has not taken this lying down, for it is just this near horizon that, by method and rule, it would remove from our consciousness, that we might trouble ourselves over it no more. Indeed, were he not at pains to reassure his reader that a recognition of the present horizon does not of itself swallow the past horizon in historical and theological interpretation, Thiselton might well, considering those in need of its correction, have called his study 'The Forgotten Horizon' (the *other* of the two, all things being equal, having already fully been given its due—in fact, 'The Suppressed Horizon' might be even more to the point).

As though to remind us that critical memory is short, a decade on Heikki Räisänen calls us back to 'Gabler's enterprise' and 'Wrede's vision' thus to take us '*beyond* New Testament theology'.[3] According to Räisänen, things went off the rails with Barth and the hermeneutical shock waves he set off. A sharp Gablerian and Wredian separation between history and theology as two qualitatively distinct stages is what is required to restore order and legitimacy. The pressing need is for synthesizing accounts which mediate between the specialist findings of exegesis and, not the church, as customarily, but the world at large, all those 'reflecting on questions of world-view and values' (p. xii). Indeed, says Räisänen, in addition to historical interpretation, 'exegetes should also engage in a theological (or philosophical, or some other type of critically actualizing) interpretation of their work', though 'the chances of an exegete contributing qua exegete to the philosophical-theological quest are, in my view, far more limited' than one might have been led to expect (p. xviii). What modest role does Räisänen have in mind for the biblical scholar? Well, in all this reflection on value, someone has to be trusted to bring home the factual bacon. 'What he can do is above all to analyse the ways in which the Bible has been treated in religion, theology and society and relate his findings to what can be said about *the original meaning* of the relevant passages' (p. xviii, emphasis added).

---

3.   Räisänen, *Beyond New Testament Theology*, pp. xvi-xvii; see pp. xi-xviii.

To summarize the thesis. 'New Testament theology' may be a legitimate part of self-consciously *ecclesial* theology. By contrast, those of us who work in a broader *academic* context should abandon such an enterprise... More precisely, 'New Testament theology' ought to be replaced , in this context, with two projects: first, the 'history of early Christian thought' (or theology, if you like), evolving in the context of early Judaism; second, critical philosophical and/or theological 'reflection on the New Testament', as well as on its influence on our history and its significance for contemporary life.

My contention is not that these two tasks ought to be carried out separately, the one first and the other afterwards; that does not seem to be the way the human mind works. Nonetheless, the two tasks ought to be kept distinct (which is possible to a greater degree than some apologetic hermeneuticians claim), and it would be wise to set out the results of each at different stages in the presentation. It is not the scholar's business to make the 'two horizons', past and present, fuse together. Such an assimilation may eventually take place, but that should be left to the readers (p. xviii).[4]

(With that, one of a grudging few indications is given that Räisänen has heard of—which is not to say understood—the likes of Gadamer and Thiselton.)

Räisänen's task involves him not only in offering a programme of his own (to which I turn in more detail below) but also in tracing the history of 'New Testament theology' from Gabler to the present. In stating the interests of his review, among those things he is particularly concerned to look for are a clear separation between history and theology and an awareness of the problem of relating them, an awareness of the distance which separates us from the New Testament, and, as 'a particularly important aspect of the [latter], recognition of the centrality of futuristic eschatology in large parts of the New Testament' (p. xiv). These concerns inform the standard of evaluation to which the various works brought under review are subjected, and the details of this review need not concern us—other than to note that, judging from the account Räisänen gives, it is apparently not necessary, when one is offering a *history* of 'New Testament theology', to isolate a descriptive and an evaluative moment. A single stage will do. (We might put the same point in terms of challenging Räisänen to separate for us these moments in his agenda-laden review, to show us how he would mark off pure interpretative facts without the intervention of value. May we surmise that the

4.   No 'apologetic hermeneuticians' are cited (not even a mildly remorseful one).

question does not arise for him because, in his mind, he imposes no real agenda but rather subjects the various theologies surveyed to the standard of simple and unproblematic *reality*?)

When it comes to outlining a programme for the two stages of 'historical' and 'actualizing' interpretation, Räisänen offers many clear, practical suggestions for producing the sort of synthesis he would like to see. But as to reflection on the hermeneutical task, Räisänen falls far short, both in terms of actual space and attention given to the matter and in terms of evidencing a clear prior understanding of the demands of such reflection. We can approach his hermeneutical discussion from two separate directions, from the rhetoric of the self-presentation of his programme and from his direct hermeneutical reflection (such as there is), providing together his implicit and explicit hermeneutics.

As I have noted, Räisänen wishes to resurrect and repristinate a two-stage manner of proceeding in interpretation. The first question he raises in staking out his first stage is 'Whom does historical interpretation serve?' (pp. 93-97). Traditionally, a church audience has been in view. Räisänen prefers to address society as a whole, indeed, humanity as a whole, where the goal will be to promote peace and understanding (a goal to which Räisänen is likely to find little opposition). But Räisänen's way of framing his call is what is of interest. Before coming to that, I note that the next two questions raised concern whether the task is to be conceived as offering 'proclamation or information' and whether 'the New Testament or early Christianity' is to provide the proper object of study (pp. 97-103). It follows from Räisänen's decision to address humanity at large that proclamation (and the goal of faith) and the canon (and related notions such as 'revelation' and 'inspiration', 'orthodoxy' and 'heresy') belong to the logic of a quite different setting.

But now to Räisänen's framing of his alternative proposal for addressing 'society' rather than 'the church'.

> If one is free to choose one's course, it seems natural to take a broader view. Exegesis, as well as social sciences or medical science, can be pursued with the aim of providing people with means of coping with life—in this case, with their cultural and religious heritage.
>
> To confine oneself to serving a church is—to exaggerate only slightly—comparable to a social scientist's or a historian's confining himself to serve a certain political party (or a certain nation) with his research. It is hard to see much difference in principle between a historian committed to a party and an exegete committed to a church. In both cases a broader perspective seems desirable. A synthesis directed to the wider society, to

people interested in the findings of New Testament study independently of their relationship to a church, seems preferable to a church-orientated way of conceiving the task (p. 95).

Now Räisänen's is not the *only* way:

> It is, of course, perfectly possible to opt for a different strategy and pursue exegesis and New Testament theology in a church context. In that case many other methodological choices will—indeed must—be different, if the path chosen is followed consistently. It is not my intention to try to do away with church-theological study of the Bible. My point is simply that we may not have always realized how very different such a task is from a historical interpretation of the material (pp. 95-96).

Just, as it happens, the *best* way. The question of whether to 'preach' or to 'inform' comes down to this: 'Is the historical work ultimately designed to appeal to people in the interests of a given community (an outsider would speak of propagandistic aims), or does its goal consist in the clarification of the issues at hand' (p. 97)? The latter goal is still possible, Räisänen allows, in a church context, but only with some strenuous effort. Exegesis, then, cannot, where society is concerned and in a 'post-Christian period', operate in such a 'normative' framework: 'What exegesis can do instead is to provide sober information on the background, rise and early history of Christianity...' (p. 98). Propaganda and partisanship are to be replaced, pursuant to the goal of peace and understanding and commensurate with the attitude of 'science', by 'empathy' and 'fair play'.[5]

Räisänen is clearly operating throughout with a history versus theology dichotomy that he works out in blatant science versus commitment terms. But the problems with this are obvious. An easy point to raise is the practicality of Räisänen's scenario—the real interest, that is, of society in biblical criticism, since it is society that will have to be persuaded to pay for it. More to the point is the startling (and chilling) innocence of the role that is assumed here for the scholar in society, that of the neutral, detached specialist.[6] Are we really to believe, even if we allow that the scholar can attain to such a self-emptying (and that it makes sense so to do), that there exists such a realm of (interesting) information free of implication in society, ethics, politics, ideology,

---

5. See Räisänen, *Beyond New Testament Theology*, pp. 99-100.
6. Räisänen shows an awareness of the bare possibility of a problem here, but the lesson he draws is simply that the scholar must be careful lest, released from the church, he or she should become bound to some other master (see p. 187 nn. 9, 10).

theology for the scholar to mine? (For Räisänen, a church-theological setting is inherently biased and propagandistic, difficult to overcome from within, whereas in society, unless one *chooses* to operate according to some or other blatant ideological commitment and attachment, this is not a problem—the subtler ways in which interpretation betrays interestedness seem to escape Räisänen.) Furthermore, Räisänen clearly thinks he is offering, not just a different way, but a better one. But from where does this evaluation come? How is it that one way is to take a *theological* approach to the material, but the other is not, but is rather a *historical* approach, a project of pure inquiry? In other words, Räisänen would find himself hard put, to say the least, to argue the superiority of his decision for a different audience and correspondingly different aims in non-circular terms. The point here is not to re-assert the rights of church-theological interpretation, which surely can take care of itself, but to consider the move Räisänen is making and the scholarly self-understanding he reveals.

I turn, then, to Räisänen's brief explicit consideration of hermeneutics, where he raises the question of whether interpretation can be 'purely historical' and where he inquires as to 'the attitude of the scholar' properly conceived.

> In distinguishing between history of religion and theology, Wrede wished to leave theology completely to the dogmaticians. Historical research had no aims beyond history itself. Yet it should be clear, after the discussions in hermeneutics and the philosophy of science this century that the person of the scholar cannot be wholly bracketed out in historical work. The scholar's perception is influenced by his or her own situation and interests. An actualizing concern always exists, consciously or unconsciously. But the concerns of the reader can be kept under control within certain limits. 'It is true that complete objectivity is not attainable, but a high degree of objectivity is attainable, and a high degree of it is very much better than a low degree' (p. 106).[7]

Though for a moment Räisänen might appear to have mitigated the sort of critique that I have been suggesting, it becomes clear, that he has only softened the edges of his positivism, in the easy manner in which any contemporary positivist must and does. But the objectivist logic and rhetoric continue undiminished. For Räisänen, hermeneutics is all about subjectivity versus objectivity, and the lesson to be taken is that objectivity is harder to come by than once was thought. Thus warned, we try

---

7. The inner-citation is from J. Barr.

harder, now better equipped with an awareness of how things can go wrong. This, he feels, should cause him to clarify his 'two stages':

> The understanding of a text takes place between two foci, the pastness of the text and the presentness of the reader. In penetrating deeper into understanding, the reader learns to relate what he or she understands in an increasingly organized way between these foci (rather than simply letting the 'two horizons' fuse together). He or she learns to discern similarities and dissimilarities, points of contact and lack of them, possibilities and limits of interpretation. It is probably misleading to speak of two chronologically successive separate stages in the process of research. The scholar presumably thinks both of the past and of the present all (or most of) the time. But it is still possible to keep the horizons distinct (p. 106).[8]

How, then, does this affect Räisänen's conception of inquiry? 'Modern problems affect the choice of perspective and the way various phenomena are emphasized' (p. 108). 'But such shaping is only possible as regards the questions asked and the manner and order of presentation. The results, of course, must remain independent of the interests of any group of readers' (p. 109).[9]

As to the proper 'attitude' of the scholar, Räisänen has in mind the question of whether faith is required of the scholar or whether 'the will to take the material seriously' is sufficient—empathy does not require belief: 'This is often denied by theologians with a hermeneutical orientation, but a moment of reflection on the study of religions other than one's own should make clear that empathetic understanding is fully possible without ultimate commitment to the tradition studied' (p. 110).[10] (Räisänen, then, makes the frequently met association according to which hermeneutics renders understanding interior to a perspective and thus leaves those occupying different conceptual schemes unable to understand each other.) As to the matter of faith supposedly strengthening empathy with early Christianity: 'A scholar's own faith only helps him to

8.    Contrast Räisänen's apparent conception of a 'fusion of horizons' with Gadamer's in *Truth and Method*, pp. 306-307; cf. Thiselton, *The Two Horizons*, pp. 307-308. A comparison here will highlight both the positivism of Räisänen's conception of the two discrete 'foci' and the lapse involved in his seeming to think that the concept in Gadamer (who is not named) is a covering over of the distinction or tension between the two.

9.    Again, when Räisänen thinks of the present affecting interpretation, he seems only to think in terms of some special interest dictating results; no account seems to be taken of a more insidious interestedness (let alone a productive interestedness).

10.    Again, no 'theologians with a hermeneutical orientation' are cited.

understand certain types of expressions of religious life—those congenial to himself. What is worse, an unwary interpreter will tend to discover his own image at possible and impossible points in the sources' (p. 111). This is true enough, but a phenomenon, one would have thought, of truly ecumenical scope.[11] Such are the interests of hermeneutics in rampant subjectivity in Räisänen's mind that he feels he must once again plead the cause of objectivity and extol the virtues of justice and fair play against bias and prejudice:

> Whatever one's personal prejudice, it has to be held under control. For 'the relativity of human objectivity does not give us an excuse to excel in bias, not even when we state our bias in an introductory chapter'. An important practical criterion with which the attitude of a scholar can be tested is that of *fair play*: can he do equal justice to all parties of the process he is studying (p. 112)?

My point is not to reassert the rights of faith, which, again, can presumably take care of itself, but to note Räisänen's perception of philosophical hermeneutics.

When Räisänen turns briefly in the end to 'actualizing interpretation', that second stage toward which he, in distinction from Wrede, urges the exegete to move, he introduces a realm in which the exegete is no longer, as in the first stage, the undisputed master of the terrain. 'Clearly a biblical scholar is qualified to make statements on modern religious questions in so far as the Bible is appealed to in support of modern decisions. But that is where his competence normally reaches its limit.' (p. 140) (Somehow, the scholar still seems to hold a rather powerful position.) Räisänen closes on a grand either/or reminiscent of Schweitzer:

> Biblical scholars will soon find themselves at a crossroads. Will they remain guardians of cherished confessional traditions, anxious to provide modern man with whatever normative guidance they still manage to squeeze out of the sacred texts? Or will they follow those pioneering theologians and

---

11. Räisänen goes on here to offer the following gem: 'The fact is certainly worth pondering that the very scholar [Bultmann] who wrote so eruditely about the conditions of understanding was totally incapable of doing justice to the Jewish religion, of which he drew a gloomy caricature. By contrast, scholars who have written little on the theory of understanding have succeeded far better than the master of hermeneutics in understanding the rival tradition'. Shall we say, then, that interpretative understanding is exercised in inverse proportion to hermeneutical theorizing? Cullmann would approve, at any rate. Räisänen certainly highlights a bitter irony, but it is an irony of humanity, not hermeneutics.

others congenial to them on their novel paths, fearlessly reflecting on the
biblical material from a truly ecumenical, global point of view (p. 141)?

(If those are the choices, Räisänen should make many converts.)

In order to relate Räisänen further to our overall concern for
'apocalyptic interpretation', I take a step back and pick up a smaller
point of detail from his programme for historical (first-stage) interpretation. I have already noted that he applies to New Testament theologies
as a litmus test of critical integrity 'recognition of the centrality of
futuristic eschatology'. When the question arises as to the proper starting
point for a thematic synthesis of exegesis, for Räisänen 'the two serious
alternatives would seem to be christology and eschatology', and he opts
for the latter as being more fundamental (p. 118). Typically, says
Räisänen, New Testament theologies are hardly abreast of many recent
exegetical insights:

> This is even true of eschatology, although its centrality was discovered as
> early as the last century. Bultmann does start his presentation of Jesus
> with eschatology, but it soon turns out that this belongs to the unimportant
> husk, not to the existential core of the message...A related issue is the new
> interest in and evaluation of apocalyptic, which can no longer be seen
> merely as fanciful and absurd day-dreaming (pp. 119-20).[12]

Clearly, 'eschatology', or 'apocalyptic', barring such hermeneutical
obfuscation as Bultmann's, is presumed to be a straightforward matter.

Yet the time we have spent with the question offers little confidence
that this is so. We have rather been given every reason to expect that
the interpretative questions which have been carried along by discourse
on 'apocalyptic', questions hardly liquidated by my critique of the latter,
are highly tenacious ones. These, as I have suggested, have had to do
with language and myth, history, and eschatology, with faith, criticism,
and modernity—with the very meaning and possibility of faith. The
interpretative questions here are: Literal or figurative? Clear or obscure?
Relative or absolute?[13] And what *counts* as what, or where Paul's escha-

12. To cast Bultmann in these terms should be seen for all its question-begging
hastiness, for he does not discard eschatology, as Räisänen suggests, but reinterprets
it, or offers a 'depth-interpretation' of it.

13. These questions are used by M. Silva to characterize the history of interpretation in *Has the Church Misread the Bible? The History of Interpretation in the Light
of Current Issues* (Grand Rapids: Academie, 1987), chs. 3–5. We also get questions
like 'literally figurative' (that is, known and intended to be so) versus 'really figurative'
(whether this was realized or not). This separates Dodd and Bultmann to a degree (in

tology is thought to fall, always throws the question back onto the interpreter—and not as an isolated individual, but an interpreter with a historical and social story. This has the effect of re-opening the hermeneutical dialogue (or rather, of recognizing that this dialogue continues through the modern critical period) of the church's long history where literal and allegorical, individual and communal (Reformation and Modern versus Medieval, Protestant versus Catholic) interpretation continue to be debated—questions which have been raised at points above.

The whole debate over 'apocalyptic' is hermeneutical through and through. This is clear on a practical level in the interpretative perspectives being forged through which to approach the questions raised by Paul and 'apocalyptic'. We are encouraged to move to the theoretical level by the accompanying theoretical efforts of interpreters and the tension in which these often stand in relation to interpretative practice. The early eschatology, contemporary faith, and interpretative reason are all on the table of the dialogue, with varying patterns and degrees of give and take discernible.

Criticism itself has by now a long history of impatiently trying to shut down this dialogue by appeal to 'the plain and simple facts of the matter'. But there is little here of the plain or simple, and this sort of appeal to 'facts' is always a circular affair. It is only obvious that the question of 'eschatology' should, as a plain matter of *fact*, go a particular way according to that view, with the commitments, near and far, to which it attaches. The cogency of the objectivist hermeneutical perspective called on to vouchsafe this obviousness is itself only obvious where historical and cultural assumptions make it so. Cartesian and Enlightenment criticism has a history.

Part of that history of late is hermeneutical antitheoreticism, whether from the 'right', as with Cullmann, or from the 'left', as with Räisänen. (Positivism may serve very different interests.[14]) It is from such that

the case of Bultmann, we might also, or rather, say that he offers, not exactly a 'figurative', but a 'demystifying' interpretation). To further complicate the picture, we might note S. Fish's slant on 'the literal', which is always a space awaiting filling, so that, in this case, competing conceptions of the 'literal meaning' of eschatology are colliding (see S. Fish, *Is There a Text in This Class?*, pp. 268-92, esp. pp. 276-77).

14. To read between the lines of both somewhat, for Cullmann, no interpretive tinkering with eschatology is allowed because it is *literally* believed in; for Räisänen, no interpretive tinkering with eschatology is allowed because it is *literally dis*believed in. Cullmann desires to preserve historic Christianity; Räisänen desires not to let it off the hook.

Räisänen's hermeneutical simplicity arises, hence his colouring of hermeneutics as 'apologetic' and his construal of hermeneutics as promoting 'subjectivity'. These are misunderstandings (or rhetorical devices) that Cullmann and Räisänen share. Such a positivistic stance has never been so critically isolated, and from such a variety of directions, as I now spare a moment to indicate.

A watershed may be located in the vicinity of the 1960 appearance of Hans-Georg Gadamer's *Wahrheit und Methode*, falling alongside of which are monographs by Peter Winch and Thomas Kuhn throwing open the whole question of the philosophy of social and natural science.[15] Both these continuing debates in post-empiricist philosophy of natural and social science intersect explicitly with the ongoing theoretical and practical dialogue over philosophical hermeneutics,[16] and are joined by discussion emerging from 'post-analytic philosophy' (Richard Rorty)[17] and philo-

15. P. Winch, *The Idea of a Social Science and its Relation to Philosophy* (London: Routledge & Kegan Paul, 1958, 2nd edn, 1990); T.S. Kuhn, *The Structure of Scientific Revolutions* (Chicago: University of Chicago Press, 1962, 2nd edn 1970); see R.J. Bernstein, *Beyond Objectivism and Relativism: Science, Hermeneutics, and Praxis* (Philadelphia: University of Pennsylvania Press, 1983), pp. 20-37.

16. On the debate in the history and philosophy of natural science, see also P. Feyerabend, *Against Method* (London: Verso, 2nd edn, 1988); M. Hesse, *Revolutions and Reconstructions in the Philosophy of Science* (Brighton: Harvester, 1980); on the intersection with hermeneutics, T.S. Kuhn notes such a connection in his *The Essential Tension: Selected Studies in Scientific Tradition and Change* (Chicago: University of Chicago Press, 1977), pp. xii, xv; see also Hesse; Bernstein, *Beyond Objectivism and Relativism*, D.R. Hiley, J.F. Bohman, and R. Shusterman (eds.), *The Interpretive Turn: Philosophy, Science, Culture* (Ithaca: Cornell University Press, 1991), which includes continued dialogue with Kuhn; in social science, see B.R. Wilson (ed.), *Rationality* (Oxford: Blackwell, 1970); M. Hollis and S. Lukes (eds.), *Rationality and Relativism* (Cambridge, MA: MIT, 1982); on the intersection with hermeneutics, see F.R. Dallmayr and T. McCarthy (eds.), *Understanding and Social Inquiry* (Notre Dame: University of Notre Dame Press, 1977); P. Rabinow and W.M. Sullivan (eds.), *Interpretive Social Science: A Reader* (Berkeley: University of California Press, 1979); P. Rabinow and W.M. Sullivan (eds.), *Interpretive Social Science: A Second Look* (Berkeley: University of California Press, 1987); Q. Skinner (ed.), *The Return of Grand Theory in the Human Sciences* (Cambridge: Cambridge University Press, 1985); R.J. Bernstein, *The Restructuring of Social and Political Theory* (London: Methuen, 1979 [1976]).

17. R. Rorty, *Philosophy and the Mirror of Nature* (Princeton: Princeton University Press, 1979); see pp. 357-65 for interaction with Gadamer and hermeneutics; see also Bernstein, *Beyond Objectivism and Relativism*; H. Putnam, *Reason, Truth and History* (Cambridge: Cambridge University Press, 1981); J. Stout,

sophical anthropology (Charles Taylor),[18] and combine Continental and Anglo-American traditions, with reverberations through many theoretical/ critical disciplines: social/philosophical (Jürgen Habermas),[19] ethical/political (Alasdair MacIntyre),[20] literary/cultural (Stanley Fish).[21] A kindred

*The Flight From Authority: Religion, Morality, and the Quest for Autonomy* (Notre Dame: University of Notre Dame Press, 1981); *idem*, *Ethics After Babel: The Languages of Morals and Their Discontents* (Cambridge: James Clarke, 1990); and J. Rajchman and C. West (eds.), *Post-Analytic Philosophy* (New York: Columbia University Press, 1985); touching on all the themes of this paragraph is K. Baynes, J. Bohman, and T. McCarthy (eds.), *After Philosophy: End or Transformation?* (Cambridge, MA: MIT, 1987), which includes a general introduction to such trends as are in review here and introductions to and selections from key thinkers.

18. On Taylor, who interacts significantly with hermeneutics, see Baynes, *et al.* (eds.), *After Philosophy*, pp. 459-88.

19. For an entrance to Habermas's sprawling critical work, which falls broadly in the tradition of hermeneutics and *Ideologiekritik*, see Baynes, *et al.* (eds.), *After Philosophy*, pp. 291-315; see also pp. 245-90 on Karl-Otto Apel.

20. A. MacIntyre, *After Virtue: A Study in Moral Theory* (London: Duckworth, 2nd edn, 1985); see also Baynes, *et al.* (eds.), *After Philosophy*, pp. 385-422; A. MacIntyre, 'Epistemological Crises, Dramatic Narrative and the Philosophy of Science', *The Monist* 60 (1977), pp. 453-72; S. Hauerwas and A. MacIntyre (eds.), *Revisions: Changing Perspectives in Moral Philosophy* (Notre Dame: University of Notre Dame Press, 1983); for MacIntyre on Gadamer and hermeneutics, see 'Contexts of Interpretation', *Boston University Journal* 44 (1976), pp. 41-46; on hermeneutics in ethics and politics, see R. Hollinger (ed.), *Hermeneutics and Praxis* (Notre Dame: University of Notre Dame Press, 1985); M. Kelly (ed.), *Hermeneutics and Critical Theory in Ethics and Politics* (Cambridge, MA: MIT, 1990).

21. See S. Fish, *Is There a Text in This Class?*; *idem*, *Doing What Comes Naturally*; *idem*, *There's No Such Thing as Free Speech*; and cf. the note in the Introduction, above, on 'rhetoric of inquiry'; on hermeneutics and literary theory, see also D.C. Hoy, *The Critical Circle: Literature, History, and Philosophical Hermeneutics* (Berkeley: University of California Press, 1978); G.L. Bruns, *Inventions: Writing, Textuality, and Understanding in Literary History* (New Haven: Yale, 1982); J.C. Weinsheimer, *Philosophical Hermeneutics and Literary Theory* (New Haven: Yale, 1991); F. Lentricchia, *After the New Criticism* (Chicago: University of Chicago Press, 1980), and cf. on E.D. Hirsch, Jr's 'hermeneutics of innocence' (very apposite to typical hermeneutical theory in biblical criticism) (p. 263): 'There is, in so many words, no unmediated historical knowledge. That is reserved for God, or for theorists like Hirsch who believe that objective knowledge can be acquired in a massive act of dispossessing ourselves of the only route to knowledge that we have: the historicized self. What Hirsch's readings of Heidegger and Gadamer may ultimately indicate is the traditional Anglo-American fear and manhandling of any sort of thought which does not work from Cartesian premises.'

phenomenon is the continuing tradition of the sociology of knowledge.[22] Recent philosophy of history should also be mentioned in this connection.[23] 'Left-Nietzschean','left-Heideggerian', 'deconstructive', 'post-structuralist', 'post-modernist' trends are also relevant here.[24] 'Pragmatism'/'neopragmatism' figures significantly as well.[25] In recent years, all this cross-pollination has brought hermeneutics into its own.[26]

Cf. also various 'new historicisms', efforts to locate the critic, historically, ideologically, and so forth; see F. Jameson, *The Political Unconscious: Narrative as a Socially Symbolic Act* (London: Routledge & Kegan Paul, 1983); E. Said, *The World, the Text, and the Critic* (Cambridge, MA: Harvard University Press, 1983); H. White, *Tropics of Discourse: Essays in Cultural Criticism* (Baltimore: The Johns Hopkins University Press, 1978); *idem, The Content of the Form: Narrative Discourse and Historical Representation* (Baltimore: The Johns Hopkins University Press, 1987).

22. Sociology of knowledge has moved on since the synthesis of Berger and Luckmann widely known to biblical scholars (a version which deals a positivistic exemption to the scientific work of the scholar); for a recent introduction, see S. Richards, *Philosophy and Sociology of Science: An Introduction* (Oxford: Blackwell, 1987 2nd edn). The recent, more radical direction of the sociology of knowledge is represented particularly by the 'strong programme' of B. Barnes and D. Bloor (see their 'Relativism, Rationalism and the Sociology of Knowledge', in Hollis and Lukes [eds.], *Rationality and Relativism*, pp. 21-47); and see S.J. Hekman, *Hermeneutics and the Sociology of Knowledge* (Notre Dame: University of Notre Dame Press, 1985).

23. For a recent primer see K. Jenkins, *Re-thinking History* (London: Routledge & Kegan Paul, 1991), drawing particularly on Hayden White.

24. See Baynes, *et al.* (eds.), chs. 2, 3, and 4 on Lyotard, Foucault, and Derrida; and see R.J. Bernstein, *The New Constellation: The Ethical–Political Horizons of Modernity/Postmodernity* (Cambridge: Polity, 1991).

25. Rorty, Bernstein, Putnam, Stout, and Fish figure here. See C. West, *The American Evasion of Philosophy: A Genealogy of Pragmatism* (Madison: The University of Wisconsin Press, 1989); J.P. Murphy, *Pragmatism: From Peirce to Davidson* (Boulder: Westview Press, 1990); R.B. Goodman (ed.), *Pragmatism: A Contemporary Reader* (New York: Routledge, 1995); S. Mailloux (ed.), *Rhetoric, Sophistry, and Pragmatism* (Literature, Culture, Theory 15; Cambridge: Cambridge University Press, 1995), and the extensive literature cited there, esp. pp. 242-47.

26. Cf. J. Bleicher, *Contemporary Hermeneutics: Hermeneutics as Method, Philosophy and Critique* (London: Routledge, 1980); R.J. Howard, *Three Faces of Hermeneutics: An Introduction to Current Theories of Understanding* (Berkeley: University of California Press, 1982); G.L. Bruns, *Hermeneutics Ancient and Modern*; J. Grondin, *Introduction to Philosophical Hermeneutics* (trans. J. Weinsheimer; Yale: New Haven, 1994); and note the earlier introduction of R.E. Palmer, *Hermeneutics: Interpretation Theory in Schleiermacher, Dilthey, Heidegger, and Gadamer* (Evanston: Northwestern University Press, 1969); see also the collections of

There is nothing like a singular perspective emerging from all this. But there is a notable common anti-positivist and anti-foundationalist critique of varying severity directed against the Cartesian and Enlightenment heritage of modernity in the interests of a broad emphasis on the finitude of human reason. All these strands intersect explicitly with philosophical hermeneutics out of a certain shared holism (where parts are related to wholes) and historicism (where history in various senses contributes to or constitutes such wholes), and a wide-ranging judgment emerges, in terms of our present concern, against the Cartesian self and the fact/value, scheme/content, theory/observation divide required to give a 'two-stage' critical method its cogency.

A new 'method' does not emerge from philosophical hermeneutics, however. Rather, as suggested by Gadamer's title, understanding and inquiry are being newly thought through in opposition to a conception of a method-controlled process of objectification. Interpretation is more of being than consciousness. David E. Linge captures well this aspect of Gadamer's hermeneutics:

> [Traditional hermeneutics pays] homage to the Cartesian and Enlightenment ideal of the autonomous subject who successfully extricates himself from the immediate entanglements of history and the prejudices that come with that entanglement. What the interpreter negates, then, is his own present as a vital extension of the past.

G. Shapiro and A. Sica (eds.), *Hermeneutics: Questions and Prospects* (Amherst: University of Massachusetts Press, 1984); B.R. Wachterhauser (ed.), *Hermeneutics and Modern Philosophy* (Albany: SUNY, 1986); B.R. Wachterhauser (ed.), *Hermeneutics and Truth* (Evanston: Northwestern, 1994); Hollinger (ed.), *Hermeneutics*; Kelly (ed.), *Hermeneutics and Critical Theory*; D.R. Hiley, J.F. Bohman and R. Shusterman (eds.), *The Interpretive Turn: Philosophy, Science, Culture* (Ithaca: Cornell University Press, 1991); and see D.E. Klemm (ed.), *Hermeneutical Inquiry* (2 vols.; Atlanta: Scholars Press, 1986); K. Mueller-Vollmer (ed.), *The Hermeneutics Reader*; G.L. Ormiston and A.D. Schrift (eds.), *The Hermeneutic Tradition: From Ast to Ricoeur* (Albany: SUNY, 1990); on Gadamer, see J.C. Weinsheimer, *Gadamer's Hermeneutics: A Reading of* Truth and Method (New Haven: Yale, 1985); G. Warnke, *Gadamer: Hermeneutics, Tradition and Reason* (Stanford: Stanford University Press, 1987); H.J. Silverman (ed.), *Gadamer and Hermeneutics* (London: Routledge & Kegan Paul, 1991); and Bernstein, *Beyond Objectivism and Relativism*; Paul Ricoeur (on whom see Baynes, *et al.* [eds.], *After Philosophy*, pp. 351-80) and Jürgen Habermas also belong within the hermeneutic tradition, among other contexts, and they are addressed among the various introductory works cited above, along with selections of their work among the collections cited.

This methodological alienation of the knower from his own historicity is precisely the focus of Gadamer's criticism. Is it the case, Gadamer asks, that the knower can leave his immediate situation in the present merely by adopting an attitude? An ideal of understanding that asks us to overcome our own present is intelligible only on the assumption that our own historicity is an accidental factor. But if it is an *ontological* rather than a merely accidental and subjective condition, then the knower's own present situation is already constitutively involved in any process of understanding. Thus Gadamer takes the knower's boundness to his present horizons and the temporal gulf separating him from his object to be the productive ground of all understanding rather than negative factors and impediments to be overcome.[27]

A certain coming full circle may be seen in the turn of philosophical hermeneutics away from aspects of characteristically modern hermeneutics and toward a new perception of more ancient themes, as indicated by Gerald L. Bruns:

Formerly people thought of understanding as a matter of entering into the mind of God, becoming privy to his secrets or his will or what he knows of the future, mystically entering into his own spirit or life, hearing him speak, seeing him, quite possibly, face-to-face…Most often understanding what is said or written just means understanding how it applies to you, how it fits you, how it was meant for you…, so that taking a text in the right spirit means taking it to heart, not trying to evade it…The history of interpretation is, not surprisingly perhaps, preoccupied with the questions of prophecy and law, where there can be no such thing as interpretation at a safe distance.

After Luther, however, these various hermeneutical traditions begin to drift to the margins, to be repressed or reassimilated in various obscure ways by a figure of the reader as a solitary subject alone with a printed text, that is, a demystified or reduced text, the text as decontextualized object whose sense and force are, in a manner of speaking, enclosed in brackets or quotation marks, placed in suspension or suspended animation: distanced. Of course a legal text cannot be bracketed quite so easily as this (certainly not in the way we have learned to bracket literary texts), but even with legal texts the idea is also very strong that one can understand the text only from the outside as someone not addressed by it; which is what our idea of objectivity comes to, namely, that if a text is meant for you, if you're subject to it in some way, bound by it, you're not in a position to

27. 'Editor's Introduction', in H.-G. Gadamer, *Philosophical Hermeneutics*, p. xiv.

make sense of it, as if making sense meant making the text subject to the hypnotic power of your analytical gaze, bringing it under your conceptual control.[28]

One could say that ideas of objectivity come down to reading, interpreting, understanding as though one were someone else, or as oneself but as one who does not care about what one approaches.

In the face of the critique of the sort of objectivist hermeneutics Räisänen assumes as self-evident, a near-dismissal of contemporary hermeneutics as 'apologetic' looks, well, apologetic.[29] One is left with fewer and fewer places to turn in support of such a conservative plea for traditional hermeneutics (E.D. Hirsch, Jr, is a clear favourite of biblical critics). The *'blitzkrieg'* theory of criticism, where we are taken by storm by our own interpretative manoeuvres, quite apart from our will (or call it the 'crabapple and p'simmon' theory of criticism), can no longer be simply assumed.

Räisänen's comments on hermeneutics are instructive both in the perceptions they reveal of philosophical hermeneutics and in the weddedness to the paradigm against which hermeneutics struggles that they betray. To take hermeneutics as a bid for greater subjectivity against which one must reassert interpretative honesty and integrity is to fail to recognize that philosophical hermeneutics is an attempt (alongside many others of late) to think through the interpretative process apart from the condition of alienation inherent in the separation of subject and object. This is to fail to recognize that it only makes sense on a certain view to demand an 'objectivity' such as is typically conceived, a view now under increasing suspicion. Gadamer himself has encountered such objections often enough, and he has been forced to take pains to point

28. Bruns, *Hermeneutics Ancient and Modern*, p. 162. (Bruns treats Luther as a pivotal and symbolic figure, and not, of course, as instancing fully in himself the shift from ancient to modern; see pp. 139-58, 162-63; see also Thiselton, *New Horizons in Hermeneutics*, pp. 179-90). Bruns's account of the history of hermeneutics makes a particular theme of the relativization of the modern by a recovery of ancient insights (or, we might say, the relativization of our ascriptions of 'ancient' and 'modern').

29. One might suspect that, in terms of refusing to accept uncritically the myths and rhetoric of criticism, Barth has given better than he has got from such dismissive critics as Räisänen (see *Beyond New Testament Theology*, pp. xiv-xv, 35-37, 43, 90); see the excerpts from Barth's famous prefaces and the often rather shrill replies collected in W.G. Kümmel, *History*, pp. 363-71. (Who has the better of this debate is anything but a neutral question, of course—the objectivist will most likely simply identify with Barth's early critics, as does Räisänen here).

out that his attempt to be truer to our hermeneutical experience is not about promoting greater subjectivity or shirking scientific integrity. He has little difficulty, in fact, in turning the whole accusation around and insisting that it is a matter of scientific integrity that we acknowledge what a hermeneutical consciousness reveals of our interpretative experience. On the question of inquiry, interpretation, and understanding one must determine *what is* and not assert dogmatically *what should be*. Furthermore, it is 'objectivist' hermeneutics that remains bound up with subjectivity, where objectivity is entrusted to the interpreter's subjective efforts. Significantly, Gadamer sets his philosophical hermeneutics in the context of a protest against the hegemony of the 'scientific expert' in contemporary social and political life, trust in whose detached and disinterested ability to predict and control stifles the cultivation of responsible communal experience in practical reason, in dialogue and consensus building.[30]

I make no pretence of offering an account of such a philosophical hermeneutics as I am pointing toward here, for which lack I appeal to the limitations of time and space (though limitations of present expertise are more to the point). Others have given such accounts. Rather, my scattered and unsystematic observations move on that metacommentary level where I inquire as to what philosophical hermeneutics is itself doing, what it reacts against and aims for. Philosophical hermeneutics offers both a powerful critique of objectivism and points in positive directions worth pursuing. Nor would I claim that all that I wish to say about hermeneutics somehow follows as a matter of course from the present study. What I *do* claim is that the story of 'apocalyptic interpretation' may function as a case study which, working up from the level of interpretative *practice*, joins hands with attempts at *theorizing* hermeneutics.

If we desire to rethink understanding and inquiry—rethink criticism—

---

30. These points and others are lucidly covered in Gadamer's 'Afterword' to *Truth and Method*, pp. 551-79, where criticisms, responses, and further developments are addressed. On the other matter of taking hermeneutics to be imprisoning us within interpretative perspectives impenetrable from outside, so that we cannot talk to or understand one another, this is perhaps to confuse hermeneutics with 'incommensurability', so much discussed of late. (For a recent review of the issues, see Bernstein, *Beyond Objectivism and Relativism*, pp. 79-108). But even if there are some family resemblances here, 'incommensurability' is a formulation foreign to a hermeneutical mindset, where the pursuit of understanding is such that this sort of negative formulation could never ultimately satisfy.

in terms suggested by philosophical hermeneutics, our work is cut out, not least because the tradition against which hermeneutics works permeates us, is inscribed into our very language and thus imparted as part of our world. For indeed the Enlightenment tradition itself is not something we can simply step out of, but something we must work through to the other side (if there is another side). Something of the difficulties here have been put thus by Paul Feyerabend:

> A society that is based on a set of well-defined and restrictive rules so that being human becomes synonymous with obeying these rules, *forces the dissenter into a no-man's-land of no rules at all and thus robs him of his reason and his humanity.* It is the paradox of modern irrationalism that its proponents silently identify rationalism with order and articulate speech and thus see themselves forced to promote stammering and absurdity— many forms of 'mysticism' and 'existentialism' are impossible without a firm but unrealized commitment to some principles of the despised ideology...[31]

The 'stammering and absurdity' which may accompany a dissatisfaction with a positivistic criticism in the attempt to spell out what is wrong with such and to suggest which way to turn may be instanced in the tensions the present study creates for itself—complaint over the illicit blend of history and theology that is 'apocalyptic' and insistence on the interpretative interpenetration of the historical and theological issues. But I should prefer to see such tension as indicating both that criticism is still being taken seriously here and that it is regarded as failing on its own usual terms. Words such as 'scientific' and 'objectivity' have come to function rhetorically and emotively, and they carry along, without argument, whole epistemologies and anthropologies. Can such terms be reconceptualized? Rethinking criticism is nothing less than rethinking interpretative reason and the interpretive reasoner...and interpretative truth.

Why does it matter? The answer lies somewhere with the ethics of interpretation. To return to some comments made more in the abstract at the close of my first chapter, I questioned there, with respect to a

31. Feyerabend, *Against Method*, p. 168; he continues: 'Remove the principles, admit the possibility of many different forms of life, and such phenomena will disappear like a bad dream'. Cf. Bernstein, *Beyond Objectivism and Relativism*, p. 63 (to whom the citation is owed), on these remarks. Feyerabend, whose title suggests comparison with Gadamer, represents the same sort of ethical protest against the heavy hand of 'science' reaching into every corner of life (which is even more apparent in the revised edition cited here). Feyerabend is especially adept at exposing the ideological, quasi-religious dimensions of modern scientism.

'purely historical' method, any claim, by means of methodical, purely descriptive rigour, to lift the veil of illusion and usher us into the presence of reality without concealing normative pretensions. Such a claim to reveal the pure truth is one of the most heavy-weight weapons in the rhetorical armoury. Thus, even it we find ourselves able to go along with such an implied notion of self-dispossessive objectivity, 'detachment' is stillborn. This can only mean that the scholar makes whatever contribution he or she makes within the interpretative dialogue, and not from some 'critical' point high above it. In the same place above I went on to assert that this 'purely historical' ideal, in conceiving its goal as an 'arrival' rather than as an open-ended dialogue, tends always to shut things down prematurely, and that, even as it does so, it attempts to occupy a moral and methodological high-ground to which it has no right, tending always to subvert its own claims in ways blind to itself. For, again, criticism is caught up in a dialogue, taking positions in a debate, making choices of its own, while its whole temperament moves in the opposite direction of such dialogue. Its voice is not thought to be a human voice in a human dialogue, but a disembodied, monological divine fiat. This is the logic of such an ideal of 'criticism'. It cuts through interpretation and gives us the facts, about which each person must then decide how he or she should feel. The fundamental self-deception (or deception outright) could not be more evident. The ethical point concerns how we treat one another in dialogue, whether face to face or hiding behind our 'method'. Criticism is just more interpretation, not the terminus of all such. Philosophical hermeneutics questions the self-important self-understanding of such 'science'. The practice of understanding proceeds as it does and will, as dialogue; so it has been with Paul and 'apocalyptic'. It is our self-understanding which lies in need of correction, and this is a profoundly ethical matter.

Our experience of surveying the interpretative dialogue over 'apocalyptic' or early Christian eschatology—perhaps our experience of belonging to this dialogue—is not satisfied by a call to quit the foolishness and just admit the centrality of futuristic eschatology. Our way of inhabiting the various interpretative choices falsifies such a move. A hermeneutic attempt at a dialogical anthropology and epistemology, where we are somehow our dialogical selves and interpretative engagement is dialogical engagement, seems truer to our experience of *this* dialogue. Here the matter of an 'insider' and an 'outsider' viewpoint returns. For rather than asserting, as an objectivist logic would have us do, that only from a perspective of exterior detachment may we see clearly on this matter—a fundamentally incoherent requirement, for where *in* this dialogue (where in *any* dialogue) is there a position *outside* it—we might appeal, as against this ever circular claim to understand the other better than it understands itself, to Gadamer's maxim that *we understand differently if we understand at all.*[32]

It is all well and good to say that what Paul thought, he thought, full stop. But this gets us nowhere, foundering on the matter of our access to such 'original meaning' (itself a circular expression), thus throwing the question back on the interpreter once again. Bultmann serves particularly well as an illustration that there is much more to this whole business than that, anyway. For on his view there is another, more basic, more primary and originary story beneath that of 'the eschatological world view', namely the story of 'historicity'.

One can always and without end assert the rights of one notion as prior to and underlying another held to be a secondary and imperfect expression of the same—an allegorical move of ancient pedigree and enduring popularity—and the result is an approach, such as Bultmann's, which is unassailable in its own terms but which will always look like special pleading in other terms. The search for a non-arbitrary way to such a move continues. Thus, even assuming that we had the story of Paul's eschatology settled and agreed, that would be just the beginning, with no end in sight.

It is simply all too easy to turn an objectivist account of the critical task around on itself as being itself fully ideological. Objectivism is self-subversive to the point of incoherence. As I hinted earlier, the goal of interpretative fixity, of interpretative univocity, seems, almost by definition, an interested move in a power play. The insistence on the rights of the 'one right answer' rarely disappoints in following up that insistence with the one right answer.

Objectivism as ideological would go some way toward explaining the vehement resistance with which hermeneutics is met, resistance which is far from cool and detached and by no means above presenting the most facile of caricatures of hermeneutics—or if such misunderstandings as are often encountered of a hermeneutical account of understanding are more innocent, this still says little for 'objectivity'. It is not the case that according to a hermeneutical consciousness it is no longer possible to 'get it wrong'. But neither is it possible to devise some ahistorical set of

32. See Gadamer, *Truth and Method*, pp. 296-97.

rules to tell us when we have 'got it right'. Both matters are particular to the dialogue in question. What we should ask ourselves is under what circumstances we begin really to care about such things, really to desire such rules. Surely not in the abstract. How often does concern for such matters coincide with an insistence on having it right pressed against those who have it wrong? Hermeneutics would deprive us of this. For 'getting it right' and 'getting it wrong', again, cannot be treated ahistorically, and furthermore they cannot any longer be treated as entirely discrete, for the subtle moves and shifts experienced by all true parties to a genuine dialogue make such points moot. Proponents of objectivism and hermeneutics live in different and opposed interpretative worlds *on the question of interpretation*—working through which might well be the greatest possible test of each.

Indeed, the struggle over interpretation is itself of considerable ideological complexity. Not only does the polemics-fraught tradition of ecclesiastical-theological hermeneutical debate noted above figure here. There is also an ideological battle (by no means unrelated to the earlier and ongoing church struggles) of enormous extent and subtlety animating so much hermeneutical debate, a battle which lies at the heart of modernity. This is the fundamental opposition between 'science and religion'. The image which 'Science' has built up of itself is one of being different, of emerging triumphant over religion and superstition, tradition and authority. It is polemics such as these—ecclesiastical and cultural— that often seem to force us into self-subversive postures of defending impossible hermeneutical positions, where hermeneutical theory comes to be at wide variance with hermeneutical practice. But such scientism is demystified in the recognition of the interestedness and situatedness of all human inquiry. Ideology was given its own back door key even as religion was being shown out at the front. 'Science' becomes itself an authoritative, ideological tradition. To state the matter thus is a great blow to the ego, a great shock to the system, of 'Science'. There is much more than pride and vanity at stake here, for the modern cultural figure of the scientist as 'detached specialist' is *paid* to be so. If 'Science' raises suspicions of itself as operating as one more ideology, 'Reason' as one more cult, a modern myth of enormous power loses much of its force. These are the winds of 'post-modernity', and we need not subscribe to any 'ism' here to take the point, the point being, one might say, the irony of Enlightenment, where modernity is the very image of that which it rejects and despises, that from which it was to have saved us. It turns out, that is, to be human, a fall from great heights.

On the view which our tradition has nurtured, the field of interpretative engagement is a field of battle. The combatants there are winners, losers, or cheats, the latter being those who fix it so none can tell. It is an all or nothing affair. In this, further explanation of the stout resistance to a hermeneutical consciousness is provided, for the disappointment felt here is that of the general who, with crushing victory in his grasp, has his hand stayed by news of armistice (or, more gruesomely still, that of the hangman cheated by the governor's reprieve). The hermeneutical triumphalism that has (albeit ultimately unimpressively) accompanied the 'apocalyptic Paul' comes to grief just here. Dialogue is not of winners and losers but of mutuality. No victor, no spoils.

With my opening words on Schweitzer I mused, as an aside, as to whether the Schweitzerian 'age of eschatology' for criticism is not in fact 'the eschatological age'. That we are fond of seeing ourselves in such terms cannot be doubted (perhaps there is more that a mere punning correspondence between the 'two ages' and the 'two stages'). But it appears on reflection that such an arrival must await another arrival— that is a hermeneutical, not a theological point. For the 'God's eye view' of our interpretative longing we would require an eschatological age that yet prolongs its coming, a dominical visitor who yet delays his appearing. Here and now, such a view eludes us. Babel it is. Until we come to speak with one voice, we must learn to speak with many. Toward that end, in pursuit of a more peaceable kingdom for lion and lamb, philosophical hermeneutics is a beating of our critical swords into ploughshares, our interpretative spears into pruning hooks.

# BIBLIOGRAPHY

Achtemeier, P.J., 'An Apocalyptic Shift in Early Christian Tradition: Reflections on Some Canonical Evidence', *CBQ* 45 (1983), pp. 231-48.

Aune, D.E., *Prophecy in Early Christianity and the Ancient Mediterranean World* (Grand Rapids: Eerdmans, 1983).

—'The Apocalypse of John and the Problem of Genre', *Semeia* 36 (1986), pp. 65-96.

—*The New Testament in its Literary Environment* (Philadelphia: Westminster Press, 1987).

—'Apocalypticism', in G.F. Hawthorne and R.P. Martin, *et al.* (eds.), *Dictionary of Paul and His Letters* (Downers Grove: Inter-Varsity Press, 1993), pp. 25-35.

Barker, M., 'Slippery Words III. Apocalyptic', *ExpTim* 89 (1978), pp. 324-29.

Barnes, B., and D. Bloor, 'Relativism, Rationalism and the Sociology of Knowledge', in M. Hollis and S. Lukes (eds.), *Rationality and Relativism*, pp. 21-47.

Barr, J., 'Jewish Apocalyptic in Recent Scholarly Study', *BJRL* 58 (1975), pp. 9-35.

Barrett, C.K., 'New Testament Eschatology', *SJT* 6 (1953), pp. 136-55, 225-43.

—'Important and Influential Foreign Books: Cullmann's "Christ and Time"', *ExpTim* 65 (1954), pp. 369-72.

—'Albert Schweitzer and the New Testament', *ExpTim* 87 (1975), pp. 4-10.

Barth, K., *The Epistle to the Romans* (trans. E.C. Hoskyns; London: Oxford University Press, 1933).

Barton, J., *Oracles of God: Perceptions of Ancient Prophecy in Israel after the Exile* (London: Darton, Longman and Todd, 1986).

Bartsch, H.W. (ed.), *Kerygma and Myth: A Theological Debate* (trans. R.H. Fuller; 2 vols.; London: SPCK, 2nd edn, 1964 and 1962).

Bauckham, R.J., 'The Rise of Apocalyptic', *Themelios* 3 (1978), pp. 10-23.

—'The Apocalypses in the New Pseudepigrapha', *JSNT* 26 (1986), pp. 97-117.

—'Early Jewish Visions of Hell', *JTS* 41 (1990), pp. 355-85.

Baumgarten, J., *Paulus und die Apokalyptik: Die Auslegung apokalyptischer Überlieferungen in den echten Paulusbriefen* (WMANT, 44; Neukirchen–Vluyn: Neukirchener Verlag, 1975).

Baxter, C.A. 'Barth, K', Coggins and Houlden (eds.), *Dictionary of Biblical Interpretation*, pp. 77-79.

Baynes, K., J. Bohman and T. McCarthy (eds.), *After Philosophy: End or Transformation?* (Cambridge, MA: MIT, 1987).

Becker, J., 'Erwägungen zur apokalyptischen Tradition in der paulinischen Theologie', *EvT* 30 (1970), pp. 593-609.

Beker, J.C., 'Reflections on Biblical Theology', *Int* 24 (1970), pp. 303-20.

—*Paul the Apostle: The Triumph of God in Life and Thought* (Philadelphia: Fortress Press, 1984 [1980]).

—*Paul's Apocalyptic Gospel: The Coming Triumph of God* (Philadelphia: Fortress Press, 1982).

—*Suffering and Hope: The Biblical Vision and the Human Predicament* (Philadelphia: Fortress Press, 1987).

—*The Triumph of God: The Essence of Paul's Thought* (trans. L.T. Stuckenbruck; Minneapolis: Fortress Press, 1990 [Ger. orig. 1988]).

—'Paul's Theology: Consistent or Inconsistent?', *NTS* 34 (1988), pp. 364-77.

—'Paul the Theologian: Major Motifs in Pauline Theology', *Int* 43 (1989), pp. 352-65, repr. in Beker, *Triumph of God*, pp. 117-35.

—'Recasting Pauline Theology: The Coherence–Contingency Scheme as Interpretive Model', in J.M. Bassler (ed.), *Pauline Theology, Volume One: Thessalonians, Phillipians, Galatians, Philemon* (Minneapolis: Fortress Press, 1991), pp. 15-24.

Bernstein, R.J., *The Restructuring of Social and Political Theory* (London: Methuen, 1979 [1976]).

—*Beyond Objectivism and Relativism: Science, Hermeneutics, and Praxis* (Philadelphia: University of Pennsylvania Press, 1983).

—*The New Constellation: The Ethical–Political Horizons of Modernity/ Postmodernity* (Cambridge: Polity, 1991).

Betz, H.D., 'Zum Problem des religionsgeschichtlichen Verständnisses der Apokalyptik', *ZTK* 63 (1966), pp. 391-409. ET 'On the Problem of the Religio-Historical Understanding of Apocalypticism', *JTC* 6 (1969), pp. 134-56.

—'Das Verständnis der Apokalyptik in der Theologie der Pannenberg-Gruppe', *ZTK* 65 (1968), pp. 257-70. ET 'The Concept of Apocalyptic in the Theology of the Pannenberg Group', *JTC* 6 (1969), pp. 192-207.

—Review of Beker, *Paul*, *JR* 61 (1981), pp. 457-59.

Bleicher, J., *Contemporary Hermeneutics: Hermeneutics as Method, Philosophy and Critique* (London: Routledge & Kegan Paul, 1980).

Bloch, J. *On the Apocalyptic in Judaism* (Philadelphia: Dropsie, 1952).

Boer, M.C. de, *The Defeat of Death: Apocalyptic Eschatology in 1 Corinthians 15 and Romans 5* (JSNTSup, 22; Sheffield: Sheffield Academic Press, 1988).

—'Paul and Jewish Apocalyptic Eschatology', in Marcus and Soards (eds.), *Apocalyptic*, pp. 169-90.

Boers, H.W., 'Apocalyptic Eschatology in 1 Corinthians 15: An Essay in Contemporary Interpretation', *Int* 21 (1967), pp. 50-65.

—*What is New Testament Theology? The Rise of Criticism and the Problem of a Theology of the New Testament* (Philadelphia: Fortress Press, 1979).

Bornkamm, G., 'The Theology of Rudolf Bultmann', in Kegley (ed.), *Theology*, pp. 3-20.

—*Paul* (trans. D.M.G. Stalker; New York: Harper and Row, 1971).

Braaten, C.E., *History and Hermeneutics* (London: Lutterworth, 1968).

—'The Significance of Apocalypticism for Systematic Theology', *Int* 25 (1971), pp. 480-99.

Branick, V.P., 'Apocalyptic Paul?', *CBQ* 47 (1985), pp. 664-75.

Bronson, D.B., 'Paul and Apocalyptic Judaism', *JBL* 83 (1964), pp. 287-92.

Bruns, G.L., *Inventions: Writing, Textuality, and Understanding in Literary History* (New Haven: Yale, 1982).

—*Hermeneutics Ancient and Modern* (New Haven: Yale, 1992).

Bultmann, R., *Jesus and the Word* (trans. L.P. Smith and E.H. Lantero; New York: Charles Scribner's Sons, 1934 [1926]).

—'Zur Geschichte der Paulus-Forschung', *TRu* 1 (1929), pp. 26-59, repr. in K.H. Rengstorf (ed.), *Das Paulusbild in der neueren deutschen Forschung* (Darmstadt: Wissenschaftliche Buchgesellschaft, 2nd edn, 1969), pp. 304-37.

—Review of Schweitzer, *Die Mystik des Apostels Paulus*, *Deutsche Literaturzeitung* 52 (1931), cols. 1153-58.

—'Neueste Paulusforschung I', and 'Neueste Paulinsforschung II', *TRu* 6 (1934), pp. 229-46, 8 (1936), pp. 1-22.

—*Theology of the New Testament* (trans. K. Grobel; 2 vols.; New York: Charles Scribner's Sons, 1951, 1955 repr. in one vol.; New York: Macmillan, n.d. [Ger. orig., 1948-53]).

—'History and Eschatology in the New Testament', *NTS* 1 (1954), pp. 5-16.

—'"The Bible Today" und die Eschatologie', in W.D. Davies and D. Daube (eds.), *The Background of the New Testament and Its Eschatology: Essays in Honour of C.H. Dodd* (Cambridge: Cambridge University Press, 1956), pp. 402-408.

—*History and Eschatology* (Edinburgh: Edinburgh University Press, 1957).

—*Primitive Christianity in its Contemporary Setting* (trans. R.H. Fuller; London: Collins, 1960).

—*Jesus Christ and Mythology* (London: SCM Press, 1960).

—*Existence and Faith: Shorter Writings of Rudolf Bultmann* (trans. and ed., S.M. Ogden; London: Hodder and Stoughton, 1961).

—'ΔΙΚΑΙΟΣΥΝΗ ΘΕΟΥ', *JBL* 83 (1964), pp. 12-16.

—'Ist die Apokalyptik die Mutter der christlichen Theologie? Eine Auseinandersetzung mit Ernst Käsemann', in W. Eltester (ed.), *Apophoreta: Festschrift für Ernst Haenchen* (BZNW, 30; Berlin: Töpelmann, 1964), pp. 64-69.

—*Faith and Understanding* (trans. L.P. Smith, edited with an introduction by R.W. Funk; Philadelphia: Fortress Press, 1987 [1969]).

—*New Testament and Mythology and Other Basic Writings* (trans. and ed., S.M. Ogden; London: SCM Press, 1985).

Busch, E., *Karl Barth: His Life from Letters and Autobiographical Texts* (trans. J. Bowden; London: SCM Press, 1976).

Caird, G.B., 'C.H. Dodd', in D.G. Peerman and M.E. Marty (eds.), *A Handbook of Christian Theologians: Enlarged Edition* (Nashville: Abingdon Press, 1984 [1965]), pp. 320-37.

—*The Language and Imagery of the Bible* (London: Duckworth, 1980).

Carmignac, J., 'Qu'est-ce que l'apocalyptique? Son emploi à Qumrân', *Revue de Qumrân* 10 (1979), pp. 3-33.

Charles, R.H., *A Critical History of the Doctrine of a Future Life in Israel, in Judaism, and in Christianity* (London: A. & C. Black, 2nd edn, 1913).

Charlesworth, J.H., 'A History of Pseudepigrapha Research: The Re-emerging Importance of the Pseudepigrapha', *ANRW* II.19.1 (1979), pp. 75-77.

—*The Pseudepigrapha and Modern Research with a Supplement* (Chico: Scholars Press, 1981).

—*Jesus Within Judaism* (New York: Doubleday, 1988).

Charlesworth, J.H. (ed.), *The Old Testament Pseudepigrapha* (2 vols.; London: Darton, Longman & Todd, 1983, 1985).

Chilton, B. (ed.), *The Kingdom of God in the Teaching of Jesus* (Philadelphia: Fortress Presss/London: SPCK, 1984).

Clemens, S.L. (Mark Twain), *Adventures of Huckleberry Finn* (S. Bradley *et al.* [eds.], Norton Critical Edition; New York: W.W. Norton and Company, 2nd edn, 1977).

Coggins, R.J. and J.L. Houlden (eds.), *Dictionary of Biblical Interpretation* (London: SCM/Philadelphia: Trinity, 1990).

Collins, J.J., 'Jewish Apocalyptic Against its Hellenistic Near Eastern Environment', *BASOR* 220 (1975), pp. 27-36.

—'Cosmos and Salvation: Jewish Wisdom and Apocalyptic in the Hellenistic Age', *HR* 17 (1977), pp. 121-42.

—*The Apocalyptic Imagination: An Introduction to the Jewish Matrix of Christianity* (New York: Crossroad, 1984).

—'Introduction to Apocalyptic Literature', in *Daniel* (The Forms of Old Testament Literature, 20; Grand Rapids: Eerdmans, 1984), pp. 2-24.

—'Apocalyptic Literature', in R.A. Kraft and G.W.E. Nickelsburg (eds.), *Early Judaism and Its Modern Interpreters* (Philadelphia: Fortress/Atlanta: Scholars Press, 1986), pp. 345-70.

—'The Place of Apocalypticism in the Religion of Israel', in P.D. Miller, Jr, P.D. Hanson, and S.D. McBride (eds.), *Ancient Israelite Wisdom: Essays in Honor of Frank Moore Cross* (Philadelphia: Fortress Press, 1987), pp. 539-58.

—'Genre, Ideology and Social Movements', in Collins and Charlesworth (eds.), *Mysteries*, pp. 11-32.

Collins, J.J (ed.), *Apocalypse: The Morphology of a Genre*, *Semeia* 14 (1979).

Collins, J.J., and J.H. Charlesworth (eds.), *Mysteries and Revelations: Apocalyptic Studies Since the Uppsala Colloquium* (JSPSup, 9; Sheffield: Sheffield Academic Press, 1991).

Conzelmann, H., 'Current Problems in Pauline Research', *Int* 22 (1968), pp. 171-86.

Coppens, J., 'L'apocalyptique: Son dossier, ses critères, ses éléments constitutifs, sa portée néotestamentaire', *ETL* 53 (1976), pp. 1-23.

Court, J.M., 'Paul and the Apocalyptic Pattern', in M.D. Hooker and S.G. Wilson (eds.), *Paul and Paulinism: Essays in Honor of C.K. Barrett* (London: SPCK, 1982), pp. 57-66

Cousar, C.B., *A Theology of the Cross: The Death of Jesus in the Pauline Letters* (Minneapolis: Fortress Press, 1990).

Cullmann, O., *Christ and Time: The Primitive Christian Conception of Time and History* (trans. F.V. Filson; London: SCM Press, 2nd edn, 1962 [3rd Ger. edn, 1962 (1946)]).

—'The Necessity and Function of Higher Criticism', in A.J.B. Higgins (ed.), *The Early Church* (London: SCM Press, 1956), pp. 3-16.

—*The Christology of the New Testament* (trans. S.C. Guthrie and C.A.M. Hall; London: SCM Press, 2nd edn, 1963 [Ger. orig. 1957]).

—*Salvation in History* (trans. S.G. Sowers, *et al.*; London: SCM Press, 1967 [Ger. edn, 1965]).

Dahl, N.A. 'Rudolf Bultmann's Theology of the New Testament', in *The Crucified Messiah and Other Essays* (Minneapolis: Augsburg, 1974), pp. 90-128.

Dallmayr, F.R., and T. McCarthy (eds.), *Understanding and Social Inquiry* (Notre Dame: University of Notre Dame Press, 1977).

Davies, G.I., 'Apocalyptic and Historiography', *JSOT* 5 (1978), pp. 15-28.

Davies, P.R., 'The Social World of Apocalyptic Writings', in R.E. Clements (ed.), *The World of Ancient Israel* (Cambridge: Cambridge University Press, 1989), pp. 251-71.

—'Qumran and Apocalyptic or *obscurum per obscurius*', *JNES* 49 (1990), pp. 127-34.

Davies, W.D., *Paul and Rabbinic Judaism: Some Rabbinic Elements in Pauline Theology* (London: SPCK, 2nd edn, 1955).

—'Paul and Judaism', in J.P. Hyatt (ed.), *The Bible in Modern Scholarship* (Nashville: Abingdon Press, 1965), pp. 178-86.

Delcor, M., 'Bilan des études sur l'apocalyptique', in L. Monloubou (ed.), *Apocalypses et Théologie de l'Éspérance* (Paris: Cerf, 1977), pp. 27-42.

Dillistone, F.W., *C.H. Dodd: Interpreter of the New Testament* (London: Hodder & Stoughton, 1977).

Dodd, C.H., *The Meaning of Paul for Today* (London: Swarthmore, 1920; London: Fontana, 2nd edn, 1958).

—*The Authority of the Bible* (London: Nisbet, 2nd edn, 1938 [1928]).

—*The Epistle of Paul to the Romans* (MNTC; London: Hodder & Stoughton, 1932).

—'The Mind of Paul: I' and 'The Mind of Paul: II', *BJRL* 1933 and 1934, repr. in C.H. Dodd, *New Testament Studies* (Manchester: Manchester University Press, 1953), pp. 67-128.

—*The Parables of the Kingdom* (London: Nisbet, 3rd edn, 1936).

—*The Apostolic Preaching and its Developments* (London: Hodder & Stoughton, 1936; reset 1944).

—*The Present Task in New Testament Studies* (Cambridge: Cambridge University Press, 1936).

—*History and the Gospel* (London: Nisbet, 1938; London: Hodder & Stoughton rev. edn, 1964).

—*The Bible Today* (Cambridge: Cambridge University Press, 1946).

—'Thirty Years of New Testament Study', *USQR* 5 (1950), pp. 5-12, repr. in *Religion in Life* 47 (1978), pp. 320-29.

—*According to the Scriptures: The Substructure of New Testament Theology* (London: Nisbet, 1952).

—*The Interpretation of the Fourth Gospel* (Cambridge: Cambridge University Press, 1953).

—*Historical Tradition in the Fourth Gospel* (Cambridge: Cambridge University Press, 1963).

Donfried, K.P., Review of *Romans*, by E. Käsemann, *RelSRev* 7 (1981), pp. 226-28.

—'Paul and Judaism: 1 Thessalonians 2.13 as a Test Case', *Int* 38 (1984), pp. 242-53.

Dorman, T.M., *The Hermeneutics of Oscar Cullmann* (New York: Edwin Mellen Press, 1991).

Duling, D.C., 'Kingdom of God, Kingdom of Heaven', in Freedman (ed.), *The Anchor Bible Dictionary*, IV.49-69.

Dunn, J.D.G., *Unity and Diversity in the New Testament* (London: SCM/Philadelphia: Trinity, 2nd edn, 1990).

Ebeling, G., 'Der Grund christlicher Theologie', *ZTK* 58 (1961), pp. 227-44. ET 'The Ground of Christian Theology', *JTC* 6 (1969), pp. 47-68.

Ehler, B., *Die Herrschaft des Gekreuzigten: Ernst Käsemanns Frage nach der Mitte der Schrift* (BZNW, 46; Berlin and New York: Walter de Gruyter, 1986).

Evans, G.R., 'Mediaeval Interpretation', Coggins and Houlden (eds.), *Dictionary of Biblical Interpretation*, pp. 438-40.

Evans, O.E., 'Dodd, C.H', Coggins and Houlden (eds.), *Dictionary of Biblical Interpretation*, pp. 179-81.

Feyerabend, P., *Against Method* (London: Verso, 2nd edn, 1988).

Fish, S., *Is There a Text in This Class? The Authority of Interpretive Communities* (Cambridge, MA: Harvard University Press, 1980).

—*Doing What Comes Naturally: Change, Rhetoric, and the Practice of Theory in Literary and Legal Studies* (Oxford: Oxford University Press, 1989).

—*There's No Such Thing as Free Speech, And It's a Good Thing, Too* (Oxford: Oxford University Press, 1994).

Ford, D.F. (ed.), *The Modern Theologians* (2 vols.; Oxford: Blackwell, 1989).

Freedman, D.N. *et al.* (eds.), *The Anchor Bible Dictionary* (New York: Doubleday, 1992).

Frei, H.W., *The Eclipse of Biblical Narrative: A Study in Eighteenth and Nineteenth Century Hermeneutics* (New Haven: Yale, 1974).

Friedrich, J., W. Pöhlman and P. Stuhlmacher (eds.), *Rechtfertigung: Festschrift für Ernst Käsemann zum 70. Geburtstag* (Tübingen: Mohr [Paul Siebeck]/Göttingen: Vandenhoeck & Ruprecht, 1976).

Frost, S.B., *Old Testament Apocalyptic: Its Origin and Growth* (London: Epworth, 1952).

Fuchs, E., 'Über die Aufgabe einer christlichen Theologie', *ZTK* 58 (1961), pp. 245-67 (ET 'On the Task of Christian Theology', *JTC* 6 [1969], pp. 69-98).

Fuller, R.H., 'Jesus, Paul and Apocalyptic', *ATR* 71 (1989), pp. 134-42.

Funk, R.W., 'Apocalyptic as an Historical and Theological Problem in Current New Testament Scholarship', *JTC* 6 (1969), pp. 175-91.

Gabler, J.P., 'On the Proper Distinction between Biblical and Dogmatic Theology and the Specific Objectives of Each', 1787. Translated by J. Sandys-Wunsch and L. Eldridge in 'J.P. Gabler and the Distinction between Biblical and Dogmatic Theology: Translation, Commentary, and Discussion of His Originality', *SJT* 33 (1980), pp. 133-58.

Gadamer, H.-G., *Truth and Method* (trans. and rev., J. Weinsheimer and D.G. Marshall; New York: Crossroad, rev. 2nd edn, 1989).

—*Philosophical Hermeneutics* (trans. and ed. D.E. Linge; Berkeley: University of California Press, 1976).

—*Reason in the Age of Science* (trans. F.G. Lawrence; Cambridge, MA: MIT, 1981).

Galloway, A.D., 'Nineteenth and Twentieth Century Theology', in P. Avis (ed.), *The History of Christian Theology, Volume One: The Science of Theology* (Basingstoke: Marshall Pickering/Grand Rapids: Eerdmans, 1986), pp. 231-352.

Gammie, J.G., 'Recent Books and Emerging Issues in the Study of Apocalyptic', *Quarterly Review* 5 (1985), pp. 96-108.

Getty, M.A., 'An Apocalyptic Perspective on Rom 10.4', *HBT* 4/5 (1982-83), pp. 79-131.

Gisel, P., *Vérité et histoire. La théologie dans la modernité. Ernst Käsemann* (Théologie historique, 41; Paris: Beauchesne, 1977).

Glasson, T.F., *The Second Advent: The Origin of the New Testament Doctrine* (London: Epworth, 3rd edn, 1963 [1945]).

—'What is Apocalyptic?', *NTS* 27 (1980), pp. 98-105.

—'Schweitzer's Influence—Blessing or Bane?', *JTS* 28 (1977), pp. 289-302.

Goodman, R.B. (ed.), *Pragmatism: A Contemporary Reader* (New York: Routledge, 1995).

Goppelt, L., *Theology of the New Testament* (2 vols.; trans. J.E. Alsup; ed. J. Roloff; Grand Rapids: Eerdmans, 1981-82).

—'Apocalypticism and Typology in Paul', repr. in *Typos: The Typological Interpretation of the Old Testament in the New* (trans. D.H. Madvig; Grand Rapids: Eerdmans, 1982).

Grabbe, L.L., 'The Social Setting of Early Jewish Apocalypticism', *JSP* 4 (1989), pp. 27-47.

Grant, R.M., with D. Tracy, *A Short History of the Interpretation of the Bible* (Philadelphia: Fortress Press, 2nd edn, 1984).

Grässer, E., *Albert Schweitzer als Theologe* (BHT, 60; Tübingen: Mohr [Paul Siebeck], 1979).

Groos, H., *Albert Schweitzer: Größe und Grenzen* (München: E. Reinhardt Verlag, 1974).

Grondin, J., *Introduction to Philosophical Hermeneutics* (trans. J. Weinsheimer; Yale: New Haven, 1994).

Gruenwald, I., 'Jewish Apocalyptic Literature', *ANRW* II.19.1 (1979), pp. 89-118.

—*Apocalyptic and Merkavah Mysticism* (AGJU, 14; Leiden: Brill, 1979).

—'Jewish Apocalypticism to the Rabbinic Period', in M. Eliade, *et al.* (eds.), *The Encyclopedia of Religion* (New York: Macmillan, 1987), I, pp. 337-42.

—*From Apocalypticism to Gnosticism: Studies in Apocalypticism, Merkavah Mysticism and Gnosticism* (BEATAJ, 14; Frankfurt am Main: Peter Lang, 1988).

Guthrie, S.C., Jr, 'Oscar Cullmann', in M.E. Marty and D.G. Peerman (eds.), *A Handbook of Christian Theologians: Enlarged Edition* (Nashville: Abingdon Press, 1984 [1965]), pp. 338-54.

Hamilton, N.Q., *The Holy Spirit and Eschatology in Paul* (Edinburgh: Oliver and Boyd, 1957).

Hanson, P.D., 'Jewish Apocalyptic Against its Near Eastern Environment', *RB* 78 (1971), pp. 31-58.

—'Old Testament Apocalyptic Reexamined', *Int* 25 (1971), pp. 454-79, repr. in Hanson (ed.), *Visionaries*, pp. 37-60.

—'Prolegomena to the Study of Jewish Apocalyptic', in F.M. Cross, W.E. Lemke, and P.D. Miller, Jr (eds.), *Magnalia Dei: The Mighty Acts of God* (Garden City: Doubleday, 1976), pp. 389-401.

—*The Dawn of Apocalyptic* (Philadelphia: Fortress Press, 2nd edn, 1979 [1975]), which includes the 'Appendix: An Overview of Early Jewish and Christian Apocalypticism', pp. 427-44.

—'Apocalypse: Genre' and 'Apocalypticism', *IDBSup*, pp. 27-34.

—'Apocalyptic Literature', in D.A. Knight and G.M. Tucker (eds.), *The Hebrew Bible and its Modern Interpreters* (Chico: Scholars, 1985), pp. 465-88.

—*Old Testament Apocalyptic* (Nashville: Abingdon Press, 1987).

Hanson, P.D., A.K. Grayson, J.J. Collins and A. Yarbro Collins (eds.), 'Apocalypses and Apocalypticism', in Freedman, *et al.* (eds.), *Anchor Bible Dictionary*, I, pp. 279-92.

Hanson, P.D (ed.), *Visionaries and Their Apocalypses* (Philadelphia: Fortress/London: SPCK, 1983).

Harrisville, R.A., 'Crux Sola Nostra Theologia: A Retrospective Review of the Work of Ernst Käsemann', *RelSRev* 11 (1985), pp. 256-58.

Hartman, L., 'Survey of the Problem of the Apocalyptic Genre', in Hellholm (ed.), *Apocalypticism*, pp. 329-43.

Harvey, V.A., *The Historian and the Believer: The Morality of Historical Knowledge and Christian Belief* (London: SCM Press, 1967).

Hasel, G.F., *New Testament Theology: Basic Issues in the Current Debate* (Grand Rapids: Eerdmans, 1978).

Hauerwas, S., and A. MacIntyre (eds.), *Revisions: Changing Perspectives in Moral Philosophy* (Notre Dame: University of Notre Dame Press, 1983).

Hekman, S.J., *Hermeneutics and the Sociology of Knowledge* (Notre Dame: University of Notre Dame Press, 1985).

Hellholm, D., 'The Problem of Apocalyptic Genre and the Apocalypse of John', *Semeia* 36 (1986), pp. 13-64.

—'Methodological Reflections on the Problem of Definition of Generic Texts', in Collins and Charlesworth (eds.), *Mysteries*, pp. 135-63.

Hellholm, D. (ed.), *Apocalypticism in the Mediterranean World and the Near East* (Tübingen: Mohr [Paul Siebeck], 1983).

Hengel, M., *Judaism and Hellenism* (trans. J. Bowden; London: SCM Press, 1974).

Hesse, M., *Revolutions and Reconstructions in the Philosophy of Science* (Brighton: Harvester, 1980).

Hiley, D.R., J.F. Bohman and R. Shusterman (eds.), *The Interpretive Turn: Philosophy, Science, Culture* (Ithaca: Cornell University Press, 1991).

Himmelfarb, M., *Tours of Hell: An Apocalyptic Form in Jewish and Christian Literature* (Philadelphia: Fortress Press, 1983).

—'From Prophecy to Apocalypse: The *Book of the Watchers* and Tours of Heaven', in A. Green (ed.), *Jewish Spirituality from the Bible Through the Middle Ages* (London: SCM Press, 1989), pp. 145-65.

—'The Experience of the Visionary and Genre in the Ascension of Isaiah 6-11 and the Apocalypse of Paul', *Semeia* 36 (1986), pp. 97-111.

Hollingdale, R.J. (ed.), *A Nietzsche Reader* (Harmondsworth: Penguin, 1977).

Hollinger, R. (ed.), *Hermeneutics and Praxis* (Notre Dame: University of Notre Dame Press, 1985).

Hollis, M., and S. Lukes (eds.), *Rationality and Relativism* (Cambridge, MA: MIT, 1982).

Howard, R.J., *Three Faces of Hermeneutics: An Introduction to Current Theories of Understanding* (Berkeley: University of California Press, 1982).

Hoy, D.C., *The Critical Circle: Literature, History, and Philosophical Hermeneutics* (Berkeley: University of California Press, 1978).

Hübner, H., 'Paulusforschung seit 1945. Ein kritischer Literaturbericht', *ANRW* II.25.4 (1987), pp. 2649-840.

Jameson, F., *The Political Unconscious: Narrative as a Socially Symbolic Act* (London: Routledge & Kegan Paul, 1983).

Jenkins, K., *Re-thinking History* (London: Routledge & Kegan Paul, 1991).

Johnson, E.E., *The Function of Apocalyptic and Wisdom Traditions in Romans 9-11* (SBLDS, 109; Atlanta: Scholars Press, 1989).

Johnson, R.A., *The Origins of Demythologizing: Philosophy and Historiography in the Theology of Rudolf Bultmann* (Leiden: E.J. Brill, 1974).

Johnson, R.A. (ed.), *Rudolf Bultmann: Interpreting Faith for the Modern Era* (London: Collins, 1987).

Jüngel, E., *Karl Barth: A Theological Legacy* (trans. G.E. Paul; Philadelphia: Westminster Press, 1986).

Kant, I., *The Critique of Pure Reason* (trans. N.K. Smith; London: Macmillan, 2nd edn, 1933).

Kaplan, J. (ed.), *The Signet Classic Book of Mark Twain's Stories* (New York: New American Library, 1985).

Käsemann, E., *Essays on New Testament Themes* (trans. W.J. Montague; London: SCM Press, 1964).

—*New Testament Questions of Today* (trans. W.J. Montague; London: SCM Press, 1969).

—*Jesus Means Freedom: A Polemical Survey of the New Testament* (trans. F. Clarke; London: SCM Press, 1969 [3rd Ger. edn, 1968]).

—*Perspectives on Paul* (trans. M. Kohl; London: SCM Press, 1971 [Ger. orig., 1969]).

—'The Problem of a New Testament Theology', *NTS* 19 (1972-73), pp. 235-45.

—*Commentary on Romans* (trans. and ed. G.W. Bromiley; Grand Rapids: Eerdmans, 1980 [4th Ger. edn, 1980]).

Keck, L.E., *Paul and His Letters* (Philadelphia: Fortress Press, 2nd edn, 1988 [1979]).

—'Käsemann on Romans', *Int* 36 (1982), pp. 413-19.

—'Paul and Apocalyptic Theology', *Int* 38 (1984), pp. 229-41.

Kee, H.C., 'Pauline Eschatology: Relationships with Apocalyptic and Stoic Thought', in E. Gräßer and O. Merk (eds.), *Glaube und Eschatologie: Festschrift für Werner Georg Kümmel zum 80. Geburtstag* (Tübingen: Mohr [Paul Siebeck], 1985, pp. 135-58).

Kegley, C.W. (ed.), *The Theology of Rudolf Bultmann* (London: SCM Press, 1966).

Kelly, M. (ed.), *Hermeneutics and Critical Theory in Ethics and Politics* (Cambridge, MA: MIT, 1990).

Kerr, F., 'The Theology of Ernst Käsemann - I' and 'The Theology of Ernst Käsemann - II', *New Blackfriars* 62 (1981), pp. 100-13, 148-57.

Kertelge, K., *'Rechtfertigung' bei Paulus* (Neutestamentliche Abhandlungen [NS], 3; Münster: Verlag Aschendorff, 1967).

Klein, G., 'Apokalyptische Naherwartung bei Paulus', in H.D. Betz and L. Schottroff (eds.), *Neues Testament und christliche Existenz: Festschrift für Herbert Braun* (Tübingen: Mohr [Paul Siebeck], 1973), pp. 241-62.

Klemm, D.E. (ed.), *Hermeneutical Inquiry* (2 vols.; Atlanta: Scholars Press, 1986).

Knibb, M.A., 'Prophecy and the Emergence of the Jewish Apocalypses', in R.J. Coggins, A. Phillips and M. Knibb (eds.), *Israel's Prophetic Tradition* (Cambridge: Cambridge University Press, 1982), pp. 157-61.

Koch, K., *The Rediscovery of Apocalyptic* (trans. M. Kohl; London: SCM Press, 1972).

Koch, K., and J.M. Schmidt (eds.), *Apokalyptik* (Darmstadt: Wissenschaftliche Buchgesellschaft, 1982).

Koester, H., 'Paul and Hellenism', in J.P. Hyatt (ed.), *The Bible in Modern Scholarship* (Nashville: Abingdon Press, 1965), pp. 187-95.

—*Introduction to the New Testament, Volume One: History, Culture, and Religion of the Hellenistic Age* (Philadelphia: Fortress/Berlin and New York: Walter de Gruyter, 1982).

Kraft, R.A., 'The Multiform Jewish Heritage of Early Christianity', in J. Neusner (ed.),

*Christianity, Judaism and Other Greco-Roman Cults: Studies for Morton Smith at Sixty* (Leiden: E.J. Brill, 1975), III, pp. 174-99.

Krentz, E., *The Historical-Critical Method* (Philadelphia: Fortress Press, 1975).

Kuck, D.W., *Judgment and Community Conflict: Paul's Use of Apocalyptic Judgment Language in 1 Corinthians 3.5-4.5* (NovTSup, 66; Leiden: Brill, 1992).

Kuhn, T.S., *The Structure of Scientific Revolutions* (Chicago: University of Chicago Press, 2nd edn, 1970).

—*The Essential Tension: Selected Studies in Scientific Tradition and Change* (Chicago: University of Chicago Press, 1977).

Kümmel, W.G., *The New Testament: The History of the Investigation of its Problems* (trans. S.M. Gilmour and H.C. Kee; London: SCM Press, 1973).

—*The Theology of the New Testament* (trans. J.E. Steely; London: SCM Press, 1974).

—'Albert Schweitzer als Paulusforscher', in Friedrich, *et al.* (eds.), *Rechtfertigung*, pp. 269-89.

—'Rudolf Bultmann als Paulusforscher', in B. Jaspert (ed.), *Rudolf Bultmanns Werk und Wirkung* (Darmstadt: Wissenschaftliche Buchgesellschaft, 1984), pp. 174-93.

Lambert, W.G., *The Background of Jewish Apocalyptic* (The Ethel M. Wood Lecture, 1977; London: Athlone, 1978).

Laws, S., 'Can Apocalyptic be Relevant?', in M. Hooker and C. Hickling (eds.), *What About the New Testament? Essays in Honour of Christopher Evans* (London: SCM Press, 1975), pp. 89-102.

Lentricchia, F., *After the New Criticism* (Chicago: University of Chicago Press, 1980).

Lewandowski, G.A., 'An Introduction to Ernst Käsemann's Theology', *Encounter* 35 (1974), pp. 222-42.

Lincoln, A.T., '"Paul the Visionary": The Setting and Significance of the Rapture to Paradise in II Corinthians XII.1-10', *NTS* 25 (1979), pp. 204-20.

—*Paradise Now and Not Yet: Studies in the Role of the Heavenly Dimension in Paul's Thought with Special Reference to his Eschatology* (SNTSMS, 43; Cambridge: Cambridge University Press, 1981).

—Review of *Paul The Apostle*, by J.C. Beker, *Churchman* 95 (1981), pp. 353-54.

Lohse, E., 'Apokalyptik und Christologie', *ZNW* 62 (1971), pp. 48-67.

Louth, A., 'Allegorical Interpretation', Coggins and Houlden (eds.), *Dictionary of Biblical Interpretation*, pp. 12-15.

MacIntyre, A., 'Contexts of Interpretation', *Boston University Journal* 44 (1976), pp. 41-46.

—'Epistemological Crises, Dramatic Narrative and the Philosophy of Science', *The Monist* 60 (1977), pp. 453-72.

—*After Virtue: A Study in Moral Theory* (London: Duckworth, 2nd edn, 1985).

Macquarrie, J., *An Existentialist Theology* (London: SCM Press, 2nd edn, 1960).

Mailloux, S. (ed.), *Rhetoric, Sophistry, and Pragmatism* (Literature, Culture, Theory, 15; Cambridge: Cambridge University Press, 1995).

Marcus, J., and M.L. Soards (eds.), *Apocalyptic and the New Testament: Essays in Honor of J. Louis Martyn* (JSNTSup, 24; Sheffield: Sheffield Adademic Press, 1989).

Marshall, I.H., 'Is Apocalyptic the Mother of Christian Theology?', in G.F. Hawthorne and O. Betz (eds.), *Tradition and Interpretation: Essays in Honor of E. Earle Ellis* (Grand Rapids: Eerdmans, 1987).

Martin, J.P., 'A Hermeneutical Gem' (Review of Cullmann, *Heils als Geschichte*), *Int* 20 (1966), pp. 340-46.

Martyn, J.L., 'Epistemology at the Turn of the Ages: 2 Corinthians 5.16', in W.R. Farmer, C.F.D. Moule, R.R. Niebuhr (eds.), *Christian History and Interpretation: Studies Presented to John Knox* (Cambridge: Cambridge University Press, 1967), pp. 269-87.

—Review of *Paul*, by J.C. Beker, *WW* 2 (1982), pp. 194-98.

—'Apocalyptic Antinomies in Paul's Letter to the Galatians', *NTS* 31 (1985), pp. 410-24.

Marwick, A., *The Nature of History* (London: Macmillan, 3rd edn, 1989).

McGrath, A.E., 'Reformation', Coggins and Houlden (eds.), *Dictionary of Biblical Interpretation*, pp. 582-85.

Meeks, W.A., 'Social Functions of Apocalyptic Language in Pauline Christianity', in Hellholm (ed.), *Apocalypticism*, pp. 687-705.

—*The First Urban Christians: The Social World of the Apostle Paul* (New Haven: Yale, 1983).

Meeks, W.A. (ed.), *The Writings of Saint Paul* (New York: Norton, 1972).

Megill, A. (ed.), *Rethinking Objectivity* (Durham: Duke University Press, 1994).

Minear, P.S., 'Rudolf Bultmann's Interpretation of New Testament Eschatology', in Kegley (ed.), *Theology*, pp. 65-82.

—*New Testament Apocalyptic* (Nashville: Abingdon Press, 1981).

Moltmann, J., *Theology of Hope* (trans. J.W. Leitch; London: SCM Press, 1967).

Moore, H., 'The Problem of Apocalyptic as Evidenced in Recent Discussion', *Irish Biblical Studies* 8 (1986), pp. 76-91.

—'Paul and Apocalyptic', *Irish Biblical Studies* 9 (1987), pp. 35-46.

—'New Testament Apocalyptic in Twentieth-Century Discussion', *Irish Biblical Studies* 11 (1989), pp. 197-206.

Morgan, R., *The Nature of New Testament Theology: The Contribution of William Wrede and Adolf Schlatter* (ed. and trans., R. Morgan; London: SCM Press, 1973).

—Review of *Romans*, by E. Käsemann, *HeyJ* 16 (1975), pp. 68-70.

—'A Straussian Question to "New Testament Theology"', *NTS* 23 (1977), pp. 243-65.

—'F. C. Baur's Lectures on New Testament Theology', *ExpTim* 88 (1977), pp. 202-206.

—'Biblical Classics II: F.C. Baur', *ExpTim* 88 (1979), pp. 4-10.

—'The Significance of "Paulinism"', in M.D. Hooker and S.G. Wilson (eds.), *Paul and Paulinism: Essays in Honour of C.K. Barrett* (London: SPCK, 1982), pp. 320-38.

—'Gabler's Bicentenary', *ExpTim* 98 (1987), pp. 164-68.

—'Rudolf Bultmann', in Ford (ed.), *Modern Theologians*, I, pp. 109-33.

—'Bultmann, R', Coggins and Houlden (eds.), *Dictionary of Biblical Interpretation*, pp. 93-95.

—'Sachkritik', Coggins and Houlden (eds.), *Dictionary of Biblical Interpretation*, pp. 604-605.

Morgan, R., with J. Barton, *Biblical Interpretation* (Oxford: Oxford University Press, 1988).

Morgan, W., *The Religion and Theology of Paul* (Edinburgh: T. & T. Clark, 1917).

Morris, L., *Apocalyptic* (London: Inter-Varsity Press, 1973).

Mueller-Vollmer, K., *The Hermeneutics Reader* (New York: Continuum, 1990).

Munck, J., *Paul and the Salvation of Mankind* (trans. F. Clarke; Richmond: John Knox Press, 1959).

Murphy, J.P., *Pragmatism: From Peirce to Davidson* (Boulder: Westview Press, 1990).

Neill, S., and T. Wright, *The Interpretation of the New Testament 1861-1986* (Oxford: Oxford University Press, 2nd edn, 1988).

Nelson, J.S., A. Megill and D.N. McCloskey, *The Rhetoric of the Human Sciences: Language and Argument in Scholarship and Public Affairs* (Madison: University of Wisconsin Press, 1987).

Nicholson, E.W., 'Apocalyptic', in G.W. Anderson (ed.), *Tradition and Interpretation* (Oxford: Oxford University Press, 1979), pp. 189-213.

Nickelsburg, G.W.E., 'Social Aspects of Palestinian Jewish Apocalyptic', in Hellholm (ed.), *Apocalypticism*, pp. 641-50.

—'Son of Man', in Freedman, *et al.* (eds.), *The Anchor Bible Dictionary*, VI, pp. 137-50.

Nineham, D.E., 'Schweitzer Revisited', in *Explorations in Theology 1* (London: SCM Press, 1977), pp. 112-33.

—'Schweitzer, A', Coggins and Houlden (eds.), *Dictionary of Biblical Interpretation*, pp. 613-16.

—'Cultural Relativism', Coggins and Houlden (eds.), *Dictionary of Biblical Interpretation*, pp. 155-59.

Ormiston, G.L., and A.D. Schrift, *The Hermeneutic Tradition: From Ast to Ricoeur* (Albany: SUNY, 1990).

Ott, H., 'Rudolf Bultmann's Philosophy of History', in Kegley (ed.), *Theology*, pp. 51-64.

Painter, J., *Theology as Hermeneutics: Rudolf Bultmann's Interpretation of the History of Jesus* (Sheffield: Almond Press, 1987).

Palmer, R.E., *Hermeneutics: Interpretation Theory in Schleiermacher, Dilthey, Heidegger, and Gadamer* (Evanston: Northwestern University Press, 1969).

Pannenberg, W., *Jesus—God and Man* (trans. L.L. Wilkens and D.A. Priebe; Philadelphia: Westminster Press, 1968).

Pannenberg, W. (ed.), *Revelation as History* (trans. D. Granskou; London: Macmillan, 1968).

Porter, F.C., *The Messages of the Apocalyptical Writings* (New York: Charles Scribner's Sons, 1905).

—'The Place of Apocalyptical Conceptions in the Thought of Paul', *JBL* 41 (1922), pp. 183-204.

—*The Mind of Christ in Paul* (New York: Charles Scribner's Sons, 1930).

Putnam, H., *Reason, Truth and History* (Cambridge: Cambridge University Press, 1981).

Rabinow, P., and W.M. Sullivan (eds.), *Interpretive Social Science: A Reader* (Berkeley: University of California Press, 1979).

—*Interpretive Social Science: A Second Look* (Berkeley: University of California Press, 1987).

Räisänen, H., *Beyond New Testament Theology: A Story and a Programme* (London: SCM/Philadelphia: Trinity, 1990).

Rajchman, J., and C. West (eds.), *Post-Analytic Philosophy* (New York: Columbia University Press, 1985).

Reddish, M.G. (ed.), *Apocalyptic Literature: A Reader* (Nashville: Abingdon Press, 1990).

Richards, S., *Philosophy and Sociology of Science: An Introduction* (Oxford: Blackwell, 2nd edn, 1987).

Richardson, A., *The Bible in the Age of Science* (London: SCM Press, 1961).

Riches, J.K., Review of Käsemann, *An die Römer*, *SJT* 29 (1976), pp. 557-74.

Ridderbos, H., *Paul: An Outline of His Theology* (trans. J.R. de Witt; Grand Rapids: Eerdmans, 1975).

Robinson, J.A.T., *Jesus and His Coming: The Emergence of a Doctrine* (London: SCM Press, 1957).

—'Theologians of Our Time XII: C.H. Dodd', *ExpTim* 75 (1963-64), pp. 100-102.

Robinson, J.M., 'Hermeneutic Since Barth', in Robinson and Cobb (eds.), *The New Hermeneutic*, pp. 1-77.

—'Introduction', in Schweitzer, *Quest*, 1968, pp. xi-xxxiii.

Robinson, J.M, and J.B. Cobb, Jr (eds.), *The New Hermeneutic* (New Frontiers in Theology, II; New York: Harper & Row, 1964).

—*Theology as History* (New Frontiers in Theology, III; New York: Harper & Row, 1967).

Rochais, G., 'Qu'est-ce que l'apocalyptique?', *ScEs* 36 (1984), pp. 273-86.

Roetzel, C.J., *The Letters of Paul: Conversations in Context* (Louisville: Westminster/ John Knox Press, 3rd. edn, 1991).

Rollins, W.G., 'The New Testament and Apocalyptic', *NTS* 17 (1970-71), pp. 454-76.

Rorty, R., *Philosophy and the Mirror of Nature* (Princeton: Princeton University Press, 1979).

Rowland, C., *The Open Heaven: A Study of Apocalyptic in Judaism and Early Christianity* (London: SPCK, 1982).

—*Christian Origins* (Minneapolis: Augsburg, 1985).

—Review of *The Apocalyptic Imagination*, by J.J. Collins and *Jewish Writings of the Second Temple Period*, ed. by M.E. Stone, *JTS* 37 (1986), pp. 484-90.

—'The Intertestamental Literature', in P. Avis (ed.), *The History of Christian Theology, Volume Two: The Study and Use of the Bible* (Basingstoke: Marshall Pickering/ Grand Rapids: Eerdmans, 1988), pp. 151-225.

—'Apocalyptic', Coggins and Houlden (eds.), *Dictionary of Biblical Interpretation*, pp. 34-36.

Rowley, H.H., *The Relevance of Apocalyptic: A Study of Jewish and Christian Apocalypses from Daniel to Revelation* (Greenwood: Attic Press, 1980 [3rd edn, 1963]).

Russell, D.S., *Between the Testaments* (London: SCM Press, 2nd edn, 1963).

—*The Method and Message of Jewish Apocalyptic: 200 BC-AD 100* (Philadelphia: Westminster Press, 1964).

—*The Jews from Alexander to Herod* (Oxford: Oxford University Press, 1967).

—*Apocalyptic: Ancient and Modern* (London: SCM Press, 1978).

—*Divine Disclosure: An Introduction to Jewish Apocalyptic* (London: SCM Press, 1992).

Said, E., *The World, the Text, and the Critic* (Cambridge, MA: Harvard University Press, 1983).

Sanders, E.P., *Paul and Palestinian Judaism* (Philadelphia: Fortress Press, 1977).

—*Judaism: Belief and Practice 63 BCE–66 CE* (London: SCM/Philadelphia: Trinity, 1992).

Sauter, G., 'Systematische Gesichtspunkte in Ernst Käsemanns Römerbrief-Kommentar', *Verkündigung und Forschung* 21 (1976), pp. 80-94.

Schade, H.-H., *Apokalyptische Christologie bei Paulus: Studien zum Zusammenhang*

354     *Unveiling the Apocalyptic Paul*

*von Christologie und Eschatologie in den Paulusbriefen* (GTA, 18; Göttingen: Vandenhoeck & Ruprecht, 1981).

Schmidt, J.M., *Die jüdische Apokalyptik. Die Geschichte ihrer Erforschung von den Anfängen bis zu den Textfunden von Qumran* (Neukirchen–Vluyn: Neukirchener Verlag, 2nd edn, 1976).

Schmithals, W., *An Introduction to the Theology of Rudolf Bultmann* (trans. J. Bowden; London: SCM Press, 1968).

—*The Apocalyptic Movement: Introduction and Interpretation* (trans. J.E. Steely; Nashville: Abingdon Press, 1975).

Schoeps, H.J., *Paul: The Theology of the Apostle in the Light of Jewish Religious History* (trans. H. Knight; London: Lutterworth, 1961).

Scholer, D.M., '"The God of Peace Will Shortly Crush Satan Under Your Feet" (Romans 16.20a): The Function of Apocalyptic Eschatology in Paul', *Ex Auditu* 6 (1990), pp. 53-61.

Schreiner, J., *Alttestamentlich-jüdische Apokalyptik. Eine Einführung* (Munich: Kösel, 1969).

Schröder, R., 'Was ist Apokalyptik?', *Theologische Versuche* 10 (1979), pp. 45-52.

Schürer, E., *The History of the Jewish People in the Age of Jesus Christ (175 BC–AD 135)* (ed. G. Vermes *et al.*; 3 vols.; Edinburgh: T. & T. Clark, 1978–87).

Schüssler Fiorenza, E., 'Apocalyptic and Gnosis in the Book of Revelation and Paul', *JBL* 92 (1973), pp. 565-81.

Schweitzer, A., *The Quest of the Historical Jesus: A Critical Study of its Progress from Reimarus to Wrede* (trans. W. Montgomery; New York: Macmillan, 1968).

—*Paul and His Interpreters: A Critical History* (trans. W. Montgomery; London: A. & C. Black, 1912).

—*The Mysticism of Paul the Apostle* (trans. W. Montgomery; London: A. & C. Black, 2nd edn, 1953).

—*My Life and Thought: An Autobiography* (trans. C.T. Campion; London: Allen & Unwin, 1933).

Scroggs, R., 'Ernst Käsemann: The Divine *agent provocateur*', *RelSRev* 11 (1985), pp. 260-63.

Seaver, G., *Albert Schweitzer: The Man and His Mind* (London: A & C Black, 6th edn, 1969).

Segal, A.F., *Paul the Convert: The Apostolate and Apostasy of Saul the Pharisee* (New Haven: Yale, 1990).

Seifrid, M.A., *Justification by Faith: The Origin and Development of a Central Pauline Theme* (NovTSup, 68; Leiden: E.J. Brill, 1992).

Shapiro, G., and A. Sica (eds.), *Hermeneutics: Questions and Prospects* (Amherst: University of Massachusetts Press, 1984).

Silva, M., *Has the Church Misread the Bible? The History of Interpretation in the Light of Current Issues* (Grand Rapids: Academie, 1987).

Silverman, H.J. (ed.), *Gadamer and Hermeneutics* (London: Routledge & Kegan Paul, 1991).

Simons, H.W. (ed.), *The Rhetorical Turn: Invention and Persuasion in the Conduct of Inquiry* (Chicago: University of Chicago Press, 1990).

Skinner, Q. (ed.), *The Return of Grand Theory in the Human Sciences* (Cambridge: Cambridge University Press, 1985).

Smith, J.Z., 'Wisdom and Apocalyptic', in Hanson (ed.), *Visionaries*, pp. 101-20.

Smith, M., 'On the History of ΑΠΟΚΑΛΥΠΤΩ and ΑΠΟΚΑΛΥΨΙΣ', in Hellholm (ed.), *Apocalypticism*, pp. 9-19.

Soards, M.L., *The Apostle Paul: An Introduction to His Writings and Teachings* (New York: Paulist, 1987).

Stauffer, E., *New Testament Theology* (trans. J. March; London: SCM Press, 1955).

Stendahl, K., 'Biblical Theology, Contemporary', *IDB*, I, pp. 418-32.

—'Method in the Study of Biblical Theology', in J.P. Hyatt (ed.), *The Bible in Modern Scholarship* (Nashville: Abingdon Press, 1965), pp. 196-209.

—*Paul Among Jews and Gentiles* (Philadelphia: Fortress Press, 1976).

Stone, M.E., 'Apocalyptic—Vision or Hallucination?', *Milla wa-Milla* 14 (1974), pp. 47-56.

—'Lists of Revealed Things in the Apocalyptic Literature', in F.M. Cross, W.E. Lemke and P.D. Miller, Jr (eds.), *Magnalia Dei: The Mighty Acts of God* (Garden City: Doubleday, 1976), pp. 414-52.

—'Apocalyptic Literature', in M.E. Stone (ed.), *Jewish Writings of the Second Temple Period* (CRINT, 2.2; Assen: Van Gorcum/Philadelphia: Fortress Press, 1984), pp. 383-441.

—*Selected Studies in Pseudepigrapha and Apocrypha. With Special Reference to the Armenian Tradition* (SVTP, 9; Leiden: E.J. Brill, 1991).

Stout, J., *The Flight From Authority: Religion, Morality, and the Quest for Autonomy* (Notre Dame: University of Notre Dame Press, 1981).

—*Ethics After Babel: The Languages of Morals and Their Discontents* (Cambridge: James Clarke, 1990).

Strecker, G., 'Perspektiven der Römerbriefauslegung', *LR* 24 (1974), pp. 285-98.

Stuhlmacher, P., *Gerechtigkeit Gottes bei Paulus* (FRLANT, 87; Göttingen: Vandenhoeck & Ruprecht, 1965).

—'Erwägungen zum Problem von Gegenwart und Zukunft in der paulinischen Eschatologie', *ZTK* 64 (1967), pp. 423-50.

Sturm, R.E., 'Defining the Word "Apocalyptic": A Problem in Biblical Criticism', in Marcus and Soards (eds.), *Apocalyptic*, pp. 17-48.

Sykes, S.W., 'Theology through History', in Ford (ed.), *Modern Theologians*, II, pp. 11-14.

Tabor, J.D., *Things Unutterable: Paul's Ascent to Paradise in Its Greco-Roman, Judaic, and Early Christian Contexts* (Lanham: University Press of America, 1986).

Taylor, V., 'Professor Oscar Cullmann's "Die Christologie des Neuen Testaments"', *ExpTim* 70 (1959), pp. 136-40.

Thiselton, A.C., 'Biblical Classics VI: Schweitzer's Interpretation of Paul', *ExpTim* 90 (1979-1980), pp. 132-37.

—*The Two Horizons: New Testament Hermeneutics and Philosophical Description with Special Reference to Heidegger, Bultmann, Gadamer, and Wittgenstein* (Grand Rapids: Eerdmans, 1980).

—*New Horizons in Hermeneutics: The Theory and Practice of Transforming Biblical Reading* (Grand Rapids: Zondervan, 1992).

Tigchelaar, E.J.C., 'More on Apocalyptic and Apocalypses', *JSJ* 18 (1987), pp. 137-44.

Toynbee, A.J., 'Christianity and Civilization', in *Civilization on Trial* (Oxford: Oxford University Press, 1948).

Tupper, E.F., 'The Revival of Apocalyptic in Biblical and Theological Studies', *RevExp* 72 (1976), pp. 279-303.

VanderKam, J.C., 'Recent Studies in "Apocalyptic"', *WW* 4 (1984), pp. 70-77.

—'The Prophetic–Sapiential Origins of Apocalyptic Thought', in J.D. Martin and P.R. Davies (eds.), *A Word in Season: Essays in Honour of William McKane* (JSOTSup, 42; Sheffield: JSOT Press, 1986), pp. 163-76.

Vawter, B., '"And He Shall Come Again with Glory": Paul and Christian Apocalyptic', in *Studiorum Paulinorium Congressus Internationalis Catholicus 1961* (Rome: Pontifical Biblical Institute, 1963), I, pp. 143-50.

Vielhauer, P., 'Introduction to Apocalypses and Related Subjects', in E. Hennecke, W. Schneemelcher (eds.), ET R.M. Wilson (ed.), *New Testament Apocrypha* (Philadelphia: Westminster Press, 1965), II, pp. 581-607.

Vos, G., *The Pauline Eschatology* (Princeton: Princeton University Press, 1930; repr. Phillipsburg, NJ: Presbyterian and Reformed, 1986).

Wachterhauser, B.R. (ed.), *Hermeneutics and Modern Philosophy* (Albany: SUNY, 1986).

—*Hermeneutics and Truth* (Evanston: Northwestern University Press, 1994).

Warnke, G., *Gadamer: Hermeneutics, Tradition and Reason* (Stanford: Stanford University Press, 1987).

Watson, F., 'Enlightenment', Coggins and Houlden (eds.), *Dictionary of Biblical Interpretation*, pp. 191-94.

Way, D.V., *The Lordship of Christ: Ernst Käsemann's Interpretation of Pauline Theology* (Oxford Theological Monographs; Oxford: Clarendon Press, 1991).

Webb, R.L., '"Apocalyptic": Observations on a Slippery Term', *JNES* 49 (1990), pp. 115-26.

Weinsheimer, J.C., *Gadamer's Hermeneutics: A Reading of* Truth and Method (New Haven: Yale, 1985).

—*Philosophical Hermeneutics and Literary Theory* (New Haven: Yale, 1991).

Werner, M., *The Formation of Christian Dogma: An Historical Study of its Problem* (trans. S.G.F. Brandon; London: A. & C. Black, 1957 [Ger. edn, 1941]).

West, C., *The American Evasion of Philosophy: A Genealogy of Pragmatism* (Madison: The University of Wisconsin Press, 1989)

Westerholm, S., *Israel's Law and the Church's Faith: Paul and His Recent Interpreters* (Grand Rapids: Eerdmans, 1988).

White, H., *Tropics of Discourse: Essays in Cultural Criticism* (Baltimore: The Johns Hopkins University Press, 1978).

—*The Content of the Form: Narrative Discourse and Historical Representation* (Baltimore: The Johns Hopkins University Press, 1987).

Wilckens, U., 'Die Bekehrung des Paulus als religionsgeschichtliches Problem', *ZTK* 56 (1959), pp. 273-93.

Willis, W. (ed.), *The Kingdom of God in 20th-Century Interpretation* (Peabody, MA: Hendrikson, 1987).

Wilson, B.R. (ed.), *Rationality* (Oxford: Blackwell, 1970).

Wilson, R.R., 'From Prophecy to Apocalyptic: Reflections on the Shape of Israelite Religion', *Semeia* 21 (1981), pp. 79-95.

Winch, P., *The Idea of a Social Science and its Relation to Philosophy* (London: Routledge & Kegan Paul, 1958, 2nd edn, 1990).

Wolfzorn, E.E., *Realized Eschatology: An Exposition of Charles H. Dodd's Thesis* (Bruges: Louvain, 1962).

Wrede, W., *Paulus* (Halle: Religionsgeschichtliche Volksbücher, 1904), repr. in K.H. Rengstorf (ed.), *Das Paulusbild in der neueren deutschen Forschung* (Darmstadt: Wissenschaftliche Buchgesellschaft, 2nd edn, 1969), pp. 1-97. ET *Paul* (trans. E. Lummis; London: Philip Green, 1907).

—'The Task and Method of "New Testament Theology"', in R. Morgan (ed.), *Nature*, pp. 68-116, 182-93.

Wright, N.T., 'A New Tübingen School? Ernst Käsemann and his Commentary on Romans', *Themelios* 7 (1982), pp. 6-16.

—Review of *Romans*, by E. Käsemann, *Churchman* 96 (1982), pp. 60-62.

—'Putting Paul Together Again: Toward a Synthesis of Pauline Theology', in J.M. Bassler (ed.), *Pauline Theology, Volume One: Thessalonians, Philippians, Galatians, Philemon* (Minneapolis: Fortress Press, 1991), pp. 183-211.

—*The Climax of the Covenant: Christ and the Law in Pauline Theology* (Edinburgh: T. & T. Clark, 1991).

—*The New Testament and the People of God* (London: SPCK, 1992).

Yarbro Collins, A., Review of Rowland, *The Open Heaven*, *JBL* 103 (1984), pp. 465-67.

Yarbro Collins, A. (ed.), *Early Christian Apocalypticism: Genre and Social Setting*, *Semeia* 36 (1986).

Yoder, J.H., *The Politics of Jesus* (Grand Rapids: Eerdmans, 1972).

Ziesler, J.A., 'New Testament Theology', in A. Richardson and J. Bowden (eds.), *A New Dictionary of Christian Theology* (London: SCM Press, 2nd edn, 1983), pp. 398-403.

## INDEX OF AUTHORS

# JOURNAL FOR THE STUDY OF THE NEW TESTAMENT
## SUPPLEMENT SERIES